GREGG SHORTHAND DICTIONARY

Diamond Jubilee Series

GREGG
SHORTHAND
DICTIONARY

John Robert Gregg

Louis A. Leslie

Charles E. Zoubek

Shorthand written by Charles Rader

GREGG Diamond Jubilee Series

Gregg Division

McGraw-Hill Book Company

New York   Chicago   Dallas   San Francisco

Toronto   London   Sydney

FOREWORD

Gregg Shorthand Dictionary, Diamond Jubilee Series, is divided into two parts:

Part One contains, in alphabetic order, the shorthand outlines for 34,055 words. These 34,055 words, however, represent a considerably larger vocabulary, as many simple derivatives of those words — those ending in *-ing* and *-s*, for example, which present no stenographic problem — have been omitted.

Part Two contains, in alphabetic order, the shorthand outlines for 1,314 entries for personal and geographical names.

It is easily possible to construct briefer outlines for many of the scientific and literary words for which full outlines are given in this dictionary. It is not advisable to do so, however, unless the writer is certain that he will use those briefer outlines with sufficient frequency to justify the effort of learning them. Otherwise, the brief, but half-remembered, outline will cause mental hesitation that will result in slower, rather than faster, writing.

Research techniques using high-speed motion pictures have proved that most shorthand writers actually write each outline at about the same speed, regardless of the speed of the dictation. That is why the writer who can take dictation at only 100 words a minute writes each outline as rapidly as it is written by another writer taking the same material at 200 words a minute. What, then, is the difference between the two writers?

The difference is that the writer who can write only 100 words a minute is wasting time thinking, pausing, hesitating. The writer who can write 200 words a minute does not need to stop to think. He writes the outlines little, if any, faster than the writer who can write only 100 words a minute; but the 200-word writer writes *continuously*.

The problem of increasing shorthand speed, therefore, is actually a problem of decreasing hesitations in writing. What causes hesitations in writing? They are caused by the struggle of the mind to remember and use the abbreviating material provided in the shorthand system.

The fewer shortcuts and exceptions the mind must remember and use, the easier it is for the writer to decrease or eliminate the hesitations that reduce speed. Therefore, any attempt by the writer to manufacture additional shortcuts is more likely to reduce his speed than to increase it, unless the new shortcuts are used in his daily work with such great frequency that they readily become automatized.

The experience of expert shorthand writers of every system is conclusive in establishing the inadvisability of attempting to gain speed by devising and learning lists of brief outlines. Longer outlines that are quickly constructed by the mind under pressure of dictation give the writer more speed; the attempt to remember and use large numbers of abbreviated outlines tends to reduce the writer's speed.

There is often room for some difference of opinion as to the most appropriate outline for a word. This dictionary offers outlines that have been discussed and considered by experts. Sometimes an apparently obvious improvement in an outline will actually create the danger of a conflict in reading. More often an outline different from that provided in this dictionary would be individually satisfactory but would not be consistent with the outlines for other members of the same word family.

Of one thing the reader may be sure — every outline in this dictionary is the result of serious thought and consideration. Where possible alternate outlines exist, each alternate has been discussed and considered. This dictionary as a whole represents the accumulated experience of all those who have worked with Gregg Shorthand since its first publication in 1888.

It is hoped that this volume will render a useful service to the shorthand writer by placing at his disposal a facile and fluent outline for any word in which he may be interested.

The Publishers

PART ONE

Part One of *Gregg Shorthand Dictionary, Diamond Jubilee Series*, contains 34,055 word entries, alphabetically arranged. This is a gross increase of 7,957 words over the previous edition. Actually, more than 8,000 new words were added, because it was found possible to drop some of the entries given in the previous edition. Many of the more than 8,000 new words were suggested by users of the *Gregg Shorthand Dictionary Simplified* or by the reading done by the authors.

Some words, like *sputnik, defector, plutonium, orbited, imperialistic, isotope,* and a number of others, were added because of their greatly expanded use in the field of "peaceful coexistence." Other words, like *stereophonic, transistor, tranquilizer, epoxy, fluoridate, video, togetherness, programed,* and *geriatrics,* were invented or came into general use in our speech since the publication of the *Gregg Shorthand Dictionary Simplified.* Some new words may be frowned upon, like *definitize, motivational, moonlighting;* but they have been included because the stenographer may have to write them from dictation.

Experience has proved that those using a shorthand dictionary often consult it for the simple words formerly omitted from shorthand dictionaries or for rare and unusual words likewise formerly omitted.

The present list, therefore, includes many of the apparently simple words formerly omitted. It includes many of the simple derivatives formerly omitted. Most readily apparent will be the addition of the many rare and unusual words that experience has proved are wanted by users of a list such as this.

Many words are included because the shorthand learner, while still in school, has occasion to use them in his schoolwork. For this reason many mathematical, mineralogical, chemical, physical, botanical, and physiological terms are included. For the same reason many literary words are included, words that are usually of no business value but that the high school or college learner uses in his schoolwork. The bulk of the vocabulary, however, consists of words generally used in business-office dictation.

It must be remembered, too, that in many types of office work the stenographer may have occasion to use these scientific or literary words. The editor's stenographer will need the literary words. The professor's secretary will need many of the mathematical or chemical or physiological words — according to the professor's field of interest.

Consistency, rather than brevity of outline, has been the guiding principle in the construction of the shorthand outlines in this *Gregg Shorthand Dictionary, Diamond Jubilee Series.* The fastest shorthand outline (within reasonable limits) is the outline that requires the least mental effort, the outline that is written consistently and analogically. The speed of a shorthand outline is not to be judged by its brevity to the eye, nor even by its facility for the hand; it is to be judged by the speed with which it may be constructed by the mind and supplied by the mind to the hand.

Many shorthand writers experience difficulty in understanding the principle that guides the shorthand author in devising shortcuts. If the preceding paragraph is true, why are there any shortcuts? Why not write out everything in full? The secret of the good shortcut is the frequency of use of the word or phrase. If a dictator says *as a matter of fact* fifty times a day, the shorthand writer should, of course, use a very brief shortcut for that phrase. Because of this extreme frequency of use, the shortcut will come as quickly to the mind as though the phrase had been written in full.

There is no value, however, in having every shorthand writer learn a shortcut for the phrase *as a matter of fact,* for some dictators may never use the phrase; and if it should occur infrequently in the dictation, the mental effort needed to recall the phrase would require far more time than would have been necessary to write it in full.

It is strongly urged, therefore, that the outline in this dictionary be accepted as the normal outline for any word unless that word occurs so frequently in the writer's dictation (at least several times a day) that learning a shortcut is thoroughly justified. A long list of seldom-used shortcuts can be a very heavy burden on the mind and will almost invariably result in decreasing one's writing speed rather than increasing it. As a famous shorthand reporter of an earlier generation once said: "The longer I write shorthand, the *longer* I write shorthand."

aaaaaaaaaaaaaaaaa
aaaaaaaaaaaaaaaaa
aaaaaaaaaaaaaaaaa
aaaaaaaaaaaaaaaaa
aaaaaaaaaaaaaaaaa
aaaaaaaaaaaaaaaaa

ab′a·cus
a·baft′
ab′a·lo′ne
a·ban′don
a·ban′doned
a·ban′don·ment
a·base′
a·based′
a·base′ment
a·bash′
a·bat′a·ble
a·bate′
a·bat′ed
a·bate′ment
ab′bess
ab′bey
ab′bot
ab·bre′vi·ate
ab·bre′vi·at′ed
ab·bre′vi·a′tion
ab′di·cate
ab′di·cat′ed

ab′di·ca′tion
ab·do′men
ab·dom′i·nal
ab·duct′
ab·duc′tion
a·bed′
ab′er·ra′tion
ab′er·ra′tion·al
a·bet′
a·bet′ted
a·bet′tor
a·bey′ance
ab·hor′
ab·horred′
ab·hor′rence
ab·hor′rent
a·bide′
a·bil′i·ty
ab′ject
ab′ju·ra′tion
ab·jure′
ab·jured′

ab·jure′ment
ab′la·tive
ab′laut
a·blaze′
a′ble
a′ble-bod′ied
ab·lu′tion
a′bly
ab′ne·ga′tion
ab·nor′mal
ab′nor·mal′i·ty
ab·nor′mi·ty
a·board′
a·bode′
a·bol′ish
a·bol′ished
ab′o·li′tion
ab′o·li′tion·ism
ab′o·li′tion·ist
a·bom′i·na·ble
a·bom′i·na·bly
a·bom′i·nate

1

a·bom′i·na′tion	ab′sence	ab·stract′ed
ab′o·rig′i·nal	ab′sent	ab·stract′ed·ly
ab′o·rig′i·ne	ab′sen·tee′	ab·strac′tion
a·bor′tive	ab′sen·tee′ism	ab·strac′tion·ist
a·bound′	ab′sent·ly	ab′stract·ly
a·bound′ing·ly	ab′sinthe	ab·struse′
a·bout′	ab′so·lute	ab·struse′ness
a·bove′	ab′so·lute·ly	ab·surd′
ab·rade′	ab′so·lute·ness	ab·surd′i·ty
ab·rad′ed	ab′so·lu′tion	ab·surd′ly
ab·ra′sion	ab′so·lut·ism	a·bun′dance
ab·ra′sive	ab′so·lut·ist	a·bun′dant
ab′re·ac′tion	ab·solve′	a·bun′dant·ly
a·breast′	ab·solved′	a·buse′
a·bridge′	ab·sorb′	a·bused′
a·bridged′	ab·sorbed′	a·bu′sive
a·bridg′ment	ab·sorb′en·cy	a·bu′sive·ly
a·broad′	ab·sorb′ent	a·bu′sive·ness
ab′ro·gate	ab·sorb′ing·ly	a·but′
ab′ro·gat′ed	ab·sorp′tion	a·but′ment
ab′ro·ga′tion	ab·sorp′tive	a·but′tal
ab′ro·ga′tive	ab·stain′	a·but′ted
ab·rupt′	ab·stained′	a·but′ter
ab·rupt′ly	ab·stain′er	a·bysm′
ab·rupt′ness	ab·ste′mi·ous	a·bys′mal
ab′scess	ab·ste′mi·ous·ly	a·byss′
ab′scessed	ab·ste′mi·ous·ness	a·ca′cia
ab·scis′sa	ab·sten′tion	ac′a·dem′ic
ab·scis′sion	ab′sti·nence	a·cad′e·mi′cian
ab·scond′	ab′sti·nent	a·cad′e·mies
ab·scond′ed	ab′sti·nent·ly	a·cad′e·my
ab·scond′er	ab′stract	A·ca′di·an

a·can'thus

ac·cede'

ac·ced'ed

ac·cel'er·an'do

ac·cel'er·ant

ac·cel'er·ate

ac·cel'er·at'ed

ac·cel'er·a'tion

ac·cel'er·a'tive

ac·cel'er·a'tor

ac·cel'er·a·to'ry

ac'cent

ac·cent'ed

ac·cen'tu·ate

ac·cen'tu·at'ed

ac·cen'tu·a'tion

ac·cept'

ac·cept'a·bil'i·ty

ac·cept'a·ble

ac·cept'ance

ac'cep·ta'tion

ac·cept'ed

ac'cess

ac·ces'si·bil'i·ty

ac·ces'si·ble

ac·ces'sion

ac·ces'so·ry

ac'ci·dence

ac'ci·dent

ac'ci·den'tal

ac'ci·den'tal·ly

ac·cip'i·trine

ac·claim'

ac·claimed'

ac'cla·ma'tion

ac·clam'a·to'ry

ac·cli'mate

ac·cli'mat·ed

ac'cli·ma'tion

ac·cli'ma·ti·za'tion

ac·cli'ma·tize

ac·cli'ma·tized

ac·cliv'i·ty

ac'co·lade'

ac·com'mo·date

ac·com'mo·dat'ed

ac·com'mo·dat'ing·ly

ac·com'mo·da'tion

ac·com'mo·da'tive

ac·com'pa·nied

ac·com'pa·ni·ment

ac·com'pa·nist

ac·com'pa·ny

ac·com'plice

ac·com'plish

ac·com'plished

ac·com'plish·ment

ac·cord'

ac·cord'ance

ac·cord'ed

ac·cord'ing·ly

ac·cor'di·on

ac·cost'

ac·cost'ed

ac·count'

ac·count'a·bil'i·ty

ac·count'a·ble

ac·count'an·cy

ac·count'ant

ac·count'ed

ac·cou'tered

ac·cou'ter·ment

ac·cred'it

ac·cred'it·ed

ac·cre'tion

ac·cru'al

ac·crue'

ac·crued'

ac·cu'mu·late

ac·cu'mu·lat'ed

ac·cu'mu·lates

ac·cu'mu·la'tion

ac·cu'mu·la'tive

ac·cu'mu·la'tor

ac'cu·ra·cy

ac'cu·rate

ac'cu·rate·ly

ac·cu·sa'tion

ac·cu'sa·tive

ac·cu'sa·to'ry

ac·cuse'

ac·cused'

ac·cus'er

ac·cus'ing·ly

ac·cus'tom

ac·cus'tomed

ace 9

a·cerb'

a·cer'bic

a·cer'bi·ty

ac'e·tate

a·ce'tic

ac'e·tone

a·cet'y·lene

ache

ached

a·chiev'a·ble

a·chieve'

a·chieved'

a·chieve'ment

ach'ro·mat'ic

ach'ro·mat'i·cal·ly

a·chro'ma·to'sis

ac'id

a·cid'i·fi·ca'tion

a·cid'i·fi'er

a·cid'i·fy

a·cid'i·ty

ac'i·do'sis

ac'id·proof'

a·cid'u·late

a·cid'u·lat'ed

a·cid'u·lous

ac·knowl'edge

ac·knowl'edged

ac·knowl'edg·ment

ac'me

ac'ne

ac'o·lyte

ac'o·nite

a'corn

a·cous'tic

a·cous'ti·cal

a·cous'ti·cal·ly

a·cous'tics

ac·quaint'

ac·quaint'ance

ac·quaint'ance·ship

ac·quaint'ed

ac'qui·esce'

ac'qui·esced'

ac'qui·es'cence

ac'qui·es'cent

ac·quire'

ac·quired'

ac·quire'ment

ac·quires'

ac'qui·si'tion

ac·quis'i·tive

ac·quis'i·tive·ness

ac·quit'

ac·quit'tal

ac·quit'ted

a'cre

a'cre·age

ac'rid

a·crid'i·ty

ac'rid·ly

ac'ri·mo'ni·ous

ac'ri·mo'ni·ous·ly

ac'ri·mo'ni·ous·ness

ac'ri·mo'ny

ac'ro·bat

ac'ro·bat'ic

ac'ro·bat'i·cal·ly

ac'ro·bat'ics

a·crop'o·lis

a·cross'

a·cros'tic

act

act'ed

ac·tin'ic

ac·tin'i·um

ac'tion

ac'tion·a·ble

ac'ti·vate

ac'ti·vat'ed

ac'ti·va'tion

ac'ti·va'tor

ac'tive

ac'tive·ly

ac·tiv'i·ties

ac·tiv'i·ty

ac'tiv·ize

ac'tor

ac'tress

ac'tu·al

ac'tu·al'i·ties

ac'tu·al'i·ty

ac'tu·al·ly

ac'tu·ar'i·al

ac'tu·ar'y

ac'tu·ate	ad·dress	ad·join'
ac'tu·at'ed	ad·dressed'	ad·joined'
a·cu'i·ty	ad'dress·ee'	ad·journ'
a·cu'men	Ad·dres'so·graph	ad·journed'
a·cute'	ad·duce'	ad·journ'ment
a·cute'ly	ad·duced'	ad·judge'
a·cute'ness	ad·duct'	ad·judged'
ad'age	ad·duc'tion	ad·ju'di·cate
a·da'gio	ad·duc'tive	ad·ju'di·cat'ed
ad'a·mant	ad·duc'tor	ad·ju'di·ca'tion
ad'a·man'tine	ad'e·noid	ad·ju'di·ca'tive
a·dapt'	ad'e·nol'o·gy	ad·ju'di·ca'tor
a·dapt'a·bil'i·ty	ad'e·no'ma	ad'junct
a·dapt'a·ble	a·dept'	ad'ju·ra'tion
a·dap·ta'tion	ad'e·qua·cy	ad·jur'a·to'ry
a·dapt'ed	ad'e·quate	ad·jure'
a·dapt'er	ad'e·quate·ly	ad·jured'
a·dap'tive	ad'e·quate·ness	ad·just'
add	ad·here'	ad·just'a·ble
add'ed	ad·hered'	ad·just'ed
ad·den'da	ad·her'ence	ad·just'er
ad·den'dum	ad·her'ent	ad·just'ment
ad'der	ad·he'sion	ad'ju·tan·cy
ad'dict	ad·he'sive	ad'ju·tant
ad·dict'ed	ad·he'sive·ness	ad·min'is·ter
ad·dic'tion	a·dieu'	ad·min'is·tered
ad·di'tion	ad'i·pose	ad·min'is·tra'tion
ad·di'tion·al	ad'i·pos'i·ty	ad·min'is·tra'tive
ad·di'tion·al·ly	ad·ja'cen·cy	ad·min'is·tra'tive·ly
ad'di·tive	ad·ja'cent	ad·min'is·tra'tor
ad'dle	ad'jec·ti'val	ad·min'is·tra'trix
ad'dled	ad'jec·tive	ad'mi·ra·ble

ad'mi·ra·bly

ad'mi·ral

ad'mi·ral·ty

ad'mi·ra'tion

ad·mire'

ad·mired'

ad·mis'si·bil'i·ty

ad·mis'si·ble

ad·mis'sion

ad·mit'

ad·mit'tance

ad·mit'ted

ad·mit'ted·ly

ad·mix'ture

ad·mon'ish

ad'mo·ni'tion

ad·mon'i·to'ry

a·do'be

ad'o·les'cence

ad'o·les'cent

a·dopt'

a·dopt'ed

a·dop'tion

a·dop'tive

a·dor'a·ble

ad'o·ra'tion

a·dore'

a·dored'

a·dor'ing·ly

a·dorn'

a·dorned'

a·dorn'ment

ad·re'nal

ad·ren'al·ine

a·drift'

a·droit'

a·droit'ly

a·droit'ness

ad·sorb'

ad·sorp'tion

ad'u·la'tion

ad'u·la·to'ry

a·dult'

a·dul'ter·ant

a·dul'ter·ate

a·dul'ter·at'ed

a·dul'ter·a'tion

a·dul'ter·er

a·dul'ter·ous

a·dul'ter·y

a·dult'hood

ad·um'brate

ad·um'brat·ed

ad'um·bra'tion

ad·vance'

ad·vanced'

ad·vance'ment

ad·van'tage

ad'van·ta'geous

ad'vent

Ad'vent·ist

ad'ven·ti'tious

ad·ven'ture

ad·ven'tur·er

ad·ven'ture·some

ad·ven'tur·ess

ad·ven'tur·ous

ad'verb

ad·ver'bi·al

ad·ver'bi·al·ly

ad'ver·sar'y

ad·ver'sa·tive

ad·verse'

ad·verse'ly

ad·ver'si·ty

ad·vert'

ad·ver·tise

ad·ver'tise·ment

ad·ver·tis'er

ad·vice'

ad·vis'a·bil'i·ty

ad·vis'a·ble

ad·vise'

ad·vised'

ad·vis'ed·ly

ad'vi·see'

ad·vise'ment

ad·vi'so·ry

ad'vo·ca·cy

ad'vo·cate

ad'vo·cat'ed

ad·vow'son

adz

ae'gis

ae·o'li·an

ae'on

a'er·ate

a'er·at'ed

a'er·a'tion

a'er·a'tor

a·e'ri·al

a'er·o·nau'ti·cal

aes·thet'ic

a·far'

af'fa·bil'i·ty

af'fa·ble

af'fa·bly

af·fair'

af·fect'

af'fec·ta'tion

af·fect'ed

af·fect'ed·ly

af·fect'ing·ly

af·fec'tion

af·fec'tion·ate

af·fec'tion·ate·ly

af'fec·tiv'i·ty

af·fi'ance

af·fi'anced

af·fi'ant

af'fi·da'vit

af·fil'i·ate

af·fil'i·at'ed

af·fil'i·a'tion

af·fin'i·ty

af·firm'

af·firm'a·ble

af'fir·ma'tion

af·firm'a·tive

af·firm'a·to'ry

af·firmed'

af·fix'

af·fixed'

af·fla'tus

af·flict'

af·flict'ed

af·flic'tion

af·flic'tive

af·flu·ence

af'flu·ent

af·ford'

af·ford'ed

af·for'est

af·for'est·a'tion

af·fray'

af·fright'

af·fright'ed

af·front'

af·front'ed

af'ghan

a·field'

a·fire'

a·flame'

a·float'

a·foot'

a·fore'said'

a·fore'thought'

a·fore'time'

a·foul'

a·fraid'

a·fresh'

aft'er

aft'er·beat'

aft'er·care'

aft'er·clap'

aft'er·deck'

aft'er·din'ner

aft'er·ef·fect'

aft'er·glow'

aft'er·growth'

aft'er·guard'

aft'er·hatch'

aft'er·hold'

aft'er·im'age

aft'er·life'

aft'er·math

aft'er·most

aft'er·noon'

aft'er·part'

aft'er·taste'

aft'er·thought'

aft'er·time'

aft'er·ward

a·gain'

a·gainst'

a·gape'

ag'ate

ag'ate·ware'

a·ga've

age

aged

age'less

a'gen·cy	ag'i·ta'tor	ai'ler·on
a·gen'da	a·gleam'	ail'ment
a·gen'dum	ag'nate	aim
a'gent	ag·nos'tic	aim'less
a·ger'a·tum	ag·nos'ti·cism	air
ag·glom'er·ate	a·gog'	air'brush'
ag·glom'er·at'ed	ag'o·nize	air'-dry'
ag·glom'er·a'tion	ag'o·nized	aired
ag·glom'er·a'tive	ag'o·niz'ing·ly	air'field'
ag·glu'ti·nate	ag'o·ny	air'foil'
ag·glu'ti·na'tion	a·grar'i·an	air'i·ly
ag·glu'ti·na'tive	a·gree'	air'lin'er
ag'gran·dize	a·gree'a·bil'i·ty	air'mail'
ag·gran'dize·ment	a·gree'a·ble	air'man
ag'gra·vate	a·gree'a·ble·ness	air'plane'
ag'gra·vat'ed	a·greed'	air'port'
ag'gra·vat'ing·ly	a·gree'ment	air'ship'
ag'gra·va'tion	ag'ri·cul'tur·al	air'sick'
ag'gre·gate	ag'ri·cul'ture	air'space'
ag'gre·ga'tion	a·gron'o·my	air'tight'
ag·gres'sion	a·ground'	air'way'
ag·gres'sive	a'gue	air'wor'thy
ag·gres'sor	a·head'	air'y
ag·grieve'	a·hoy'	aisle
ag·grieved'	a·hun'gered	a·jar'
a·ghast'	aid	a·kim'bo
ag'ile	aid'ed	a·kin'
a·gil'i·ty	ai·grette'	al'a·bas'ter
ag'i·o	ai'guil·lette'	a·lac'ri·ty
ag'i·tate	ail	al'a·mo
ag'i·tat'ed	ai·lan'thus	a·larm'
ag'i·ta'tion	ailed	a·larmed'

al·larm'ing·ly

al·larm'ist

a·las'

al'ba·core

al'ba·tross

al·bi'no

al'bum

al·bu'min

al·bu'mi·nous

al'che·mist

al'che·my

al'co·hol

al'co·hol'ic

al'co·hol·ism

al'co·hol·ize

al'cove

al'der

al'der·man

al'der·man'ic

Al'der·ney

a'le·a·to'ry

a·lem'bic

a·lem'bi·cate

Al'e·mite

a·lert'

a·lert'ly

a·lert'ness

ale'wife'

al'ex·an'drite

al·fal'fa

al'ge·bra

al'ge·bra'ic

Al·ge'ri·an

a'li·as

al'i·bi

al'i·dade

al'ien

al'ien·a·bil'i·ty

al'ien·a·ble

al'ien·ate

al'ien·at'ed

al'ien·a'tion

al'ien·ist

a·light'

a·lign'

a·lign'ment

a·like'

al'i·men'ta·ry

al'i·men·ta'tion

al'i·mo'ny

al'i·quant

al'i·quot

a·live'

a·live'ness

a·liz'a·rin

al'ka·li

al'ka·lin'i·ty

all

al·lay'

al·layed'

al'le·ga'tion

al·lege'

al·leged'

al·leg'ed·ly

al·le'giance

al'le·gor'i·cal

al'le·go·rize

al'le·go'ry

al'le·gret'to

al'le·gro

al'ler·gen

al·ler'gic

al'ler·gy

al·le'vi·ate

al·le'vi·at'ed

al·le'vi·a'tion

al'ley

al'ley·way'

al·li'ance

al·lied'

al'li·ga'tor

al·lit'er·ate

al·lit'er·a'tion

al·lit'er·a'tive

al·lit'er·a'tive·ly

al'lo·ca·ble

al'lo·cate

al'lo·cat'ed

al'lo·ca'tion

al'lo·cu'tion

al'lo·path

al'lo·path'ic

al·lop'a·thy

al·lot'

al·lot'ment

al·lot'ted

al·low'

al·low'a·ble

al·low'ance

al·lowed'

al·low'ed·ly

al·loy'

al·loy'age

al·loyed'

all'spice'

al·lude'

al·lud'ed

al·lure'

al·lured'

al·lure'ment

al·lur'ing·ly

al·lu'sion

al·lu'sive

al·lu'sive·ly

al·lu'sive·ness

al·lu'vi·al

al·lu'vi·um

al·ly'

al'ma·nac

al·might'y

al'mond

al'mon·er

al'most

alms

alms'house'

a·lo'di·um

al'oe

a·loft'

a·lo'ha

a·lone'

a·long'

a·long'side'

a·loof'

a·loof'ly

al·o'pe'ci·a

a·loud'

al·pac'a

al'pha·bet

al'pha·bet'ic

al'pha·bet'i·cal

al'pha·bet·ize

al·read'y

al'so

al'tar

al'tar·piece'

al'ter

al'ter·a·ble

al'ter·a'tion

al'ter·a'tive

al'ter·cate

al'ter·ca'tion

al'tered

al'ter·nate

al'ter·nat'ed

al'ter·na'tion

al·ter'na·tive

al'ter·na'tor

al·though'

al'ti·graph

al·tim'e·ter

al'ti·pla'no

al·tis'si·mo

al'ti·tude

al'to

al'to·geth'er

al'tru·ism

al'tru·ist

al'tru·is'tic

al'tru·is'ti·cal·ly

al'um

a·lu'mi·na

a·lu'mi·nate

a·lu'mi·nif'er·ous

a·lu'mi·no'sis

a·lu'mi·num

a·lum'na

a·lum'nae

a·lum'ni

a·lum'nus

al·ve'o·lar

al·ve'o·lus

al'ways

a·lys'sum

a·mal'gam

a·mal'gam·ate

a·mal'gam·at'ed

a·mal'gam·a'tion

a·man'u·en'sis

am'a·ranth

am'a·ran'thine

a·mass'

a·massed'

am′a·teur′

am′a·teur′ish

am′a·teur′ism

am′a·tive

am′a·tive·ness

am′a·to′ry

a·maze′

a·mazed′

a·maze′ment

a·maz′ing·ly

Am′a·zon

Am′a·zo′ni·an

am·bas′sa·dor

am·bas′sa·do′ri·al

am·bas′sa·do′ri·al·ly

am·bas′sa·dress

am′ber

am′ber·gris

am′bi·dex·ter′i·ty

am′bi·dex′trous

am′bi·dex′trous·ly

am′bi·dex′trous·ness

am′bi·ent

am′bi·gu′i·ty

am·big′u·ous

am·big′u·ous·ly

am·big′u·ous·ness

am·bi′tion

am·bi′tious

am·bi′tious·ly

am·biv′a·lence

am·biv′a·lent

am′ble

am·bro′si·a

am·bro′si·al

am·bro′si·al·ly

am′bro·type

am′bu·lance

am′bu·lant

am′bu·la·to′ry

am′bus·cade′

am′bush

a·mel′io·rate

a·mel′io·rat′ed

a·mel′io·ra′tion

a·mel′io·ra′tive

a′men′

a·me′na·bil′i·ty

a·me′na·ble

a·mend′

a·mend′ed

a·mend′ment

a·men′i·ty

A·mer′i·can

A·mer′i·can·i·za′tion

A·mer′i·can·ize

am′e·thyst

a′mi·a·bil′i·ty

a′mi·a·ble

am′i·ca·bil′i·ty

am′i·ca·ble

a·mid′ships

a·midst′

a·miss′

am′i·ty

am′me′ter

am·mo′ni·a

am·mo′ni·um

am′mu·ni′tion

am·ne′si·a

am′nes·ty

a·moe′ba

a·mong′

a·mongst′

a·mor′al

am′o·rous

am′o·rous·ly

am′o·rous·ness

a·mor′phous

a·mor′ti·za′tion

a·mor′tize

a·mor′tized

a·mount′

a·mount′ed

a·mour′

am·per′age

am′pere

am′per·sand

am·phib′i·an

am·phib′i·ous

am·phib′i·ous·ly

am′phi·the′a·ter

am′pho·ra

am′ple

am′pli·fi·ca′tion

am′pli·fied

am′pli·fi′er

am′pli·fy

am′pli·tude

am′ply

am·pul′la

am′pu·tate

am′pu·tat′ed

am′pu·ta′tion

am′pu·ta′tive

am′pu·tee′

a·muck′

am′u·let

a·muse′

a·mused′

a·muse′ment

a·mus′ing·ly

a·nab′o·lism

a·nach′ro·nism

a·nach′ro·nis′tic

a·nach′ro·nous

an′a·con′da

an′a·gram

an′a·lects

an′al·ge′si·a

an′al·ge′sic

an′a·log′i·cal

a·nal′o·gies

a·nal′o·gous

a·nal′o·gous·ly

an′a·logue

a·nal′o·gy

a·nal′y·ses

a·nal′y·sis

an′a·lyst

an′a·lyt′ic

an′a·lyt′i·cal

an′a·lyt′i·cal·ly

an′a·lyze

an′a·lyzed

an′a·lyz′er

an′am·ne′sis

an·ar′chic

an·ar′chi·cal

an′arch·ism

an′arch·ist

an′arch·y

an·as′tig·mat′ic

a·nath′e·ma·tize

an′a·tom′ic

an′a·tom′i·cal

a·nat′o·mist

a·nat′o·mize

a·nat′o·mized

a·nat′o·my

an′ces′tor

an′ces′tors

an·ces′tral

an′ces′try

an′chor

an′chor·age

an′chored

an′cho·rite

an·cho′vy

an′cient

an′cil·lar′y

and

an·dan′te

and′i′ron

an′ec·dot′age

an′ec·dote

a·ne′mi·a

an′e·mom′e·ter

an′e·mom′e·try

a·nem′o·ne

a·nent′

an′er·oid

an′es·the′si·a

an′es·the′si·ol′o·gy

an′es·the′sis

an′es·thet′ic

an′es·thet′i·za′tion

an·es′the·tize

an·es′the·tized

an′eu·rysm

a·new′

an′gel

an·gel′ic

An′ge·lus

an′ger

an′gered

an′gle

an′gled

an′gler

An′gli·can

An′glo-Sax′on

An·go′ra

an'gri·er

an'gri·est

an'gri·ly

an'gry

an'guish

an'guished

an'gu·lar

an'gu·lar'i·ty

an'gu·la'tion

an·hy'drous

an'i·line

an'i·mad·ver'sion

an'i·mal

an'i·mate

an'i·mat'ed

an'i·mat'ed·ly

an'i·ma'tion

an'i·ma'tor

an'i·mism

an'i·mist

an'i·mis'tic

an'i·mos'i·ty

an'i·mus

an'ise

an'ise·root'

an'kle

an'kle·bone'

an'klet

an'ky·lo'sis

an'nal·ist

an'nals

an·neal'

an·nealed'

an·nex'

an'nex·a'tion

an'nex·a'tion·ist

an·nexed'

an·ni'hi·late

an·ni'hi·lat'ed

an·ni'hi·la'tion

an'ni·ver'sa·ry

an'no·tate

an'no·tat'ed

an'no·ta'tion

an·nounce'

an·nounced'

an·nounce'ment

an·nounc'er

an·noy'

an·noy'ance

an·noyed'

an·noy'ing·ly

an'nu·al

an'nu·al·ly

an·nu'i·tant

an·nu'i·ty

an·nul'

an'nu·lar

an·nulled'

an·nul'ment

an·nun'ci·a'tion

an·nun'ci·a'tor

an'ode

an'o·dyne

a·noint'

a·noint'ed

a·nom'a·lies

a·nom'a·lous

a·nom'a·lous·ly

a·nom'a·ly

a·non'

an'o·nym'i·ty

a·non'y·mous

a·non'y·mous·ly

a·noph'e·les

an·oth'er

an'swer

an'swer·a·ble

an'swered

ant

ant·ac'id

an·tag'o·nism

an·tag'o·nist

an·tag'o·nis'tic

an·tag'o·nis'ti·cal·ly

an·tag'o·nize

an·tag'o·nized

ant·arc'tic

an'te

ant'eat'er

an'te·ced'ent

an'te·cham'ber

an'te·date'

an'te·dat'ed

an'te·lope

an'te·na'tal

an·ten'na

an·te'ri·or

an'te·room'

an'them

an·thol'o·gies

an·thol'o·gist

an·thol'o·gize

an·thol'o·gy

an'thra·cite

an'thrax

an'thro·poid

an'thro·po·log'i·cal

an'thro·pol'o·gy

an'ti·bod'y

an'tic

an'ti·christ'

an·tic'i·pate

an·tic'i·pat'ed

an·tic'i·pa'tion

an·tic'i·pa·to'ry

an'ti·cli'max

an'ti·cline

an'ti·dote

an'ti·gen

an'ti·knock'

an'ti·mo'ny

an·tin'o·my

an·tip'a·thies

an·tip'a·thy

an·tiph'o·nal

an·tip'o·des

an'ti·quar'i·an

an'ti·quar'y

an'ti·quat'ed

an·tique'

an·tiqued'

an·tiq'ui·ty

an'ti·sep'sis

an'ti·sep'tic

an'ti·sep'ti·cal·ly

an'ti·so'cial

an'ti·tank'

an·tith'e·ses

an·tith'e·sis

an'ti·thet'i·cal

an'ti·tox'in

an'ti·trust'

ant'ler

ant'lered

an'to·nym

an'trum

an'vil

anx·i'e·ty

anx'ious

anx'ious·ly

an'y

an'y·bod'y

an'y·one

an'y·thing

an'y·way

an'y·where

a·or'ta

a·or'tic

a·pace'

a·part'

a·part'ment

ap'a·thet'ic

ap'a·thet'i·cal·ly

ap'a·thy

a·pe'ri·ent

a·per'i·tive

ap'er·ture

a'pex

a'pex·es

a·pha'si·a

a'phid

aph'o·rism

aph'o·ris'tic

a'pi·a·rist

a'pi·ar'y

ap'i·cal

ap'i·ces

a·piece'

a·poc'a·lypse

a·poc'ry·phal

ap'o·gee

a·pol'o·get'ic

a·pol'o·get'i·cal

a·pol'o·gies

a·pol'o·gist

a·pol'o·gize

a·pol'o·gized

a·pol'o·gy

ap'o·plec'tic

ap'o·plex'y

a·pos'ta·sy

a·pos'tate

a·pos'tle

ap'os·tol'ic

ap'os·tol'i·cal

a·pos'tro·phe

a·pos'tro·phize

a·poth'e·car'y

ap'o·thegm

a·poth'e·o'sis

ap·pall'

ap·palled'

ap·pall'ing·ly

ap'pa·nage

ap'pa·ra'tus

ap'pa·ra'tus·es

ap·par'el

ap·par'eled

ap·par'ent

ap'pa·ri'tion

ap·peal'

ap·pealed'

ap·peal'ing·ly

ap·pear'

ap·pear'ance

ap·peared'

ap·peas'a·ble

ap·pease'

ap·peased'

ap·pease'ment

ap·peas'ing·ly

ap·pel'lant

ap·pel'late

ap'pel·la'tion

ap'pel·lee'

ap·pend'

ap·pend'age

ap'pen·dec'to·my

ap·pend'ed

ap·pen'di·ci'tis

ap·pen'dix

ap·pen'dix·es

ap'per·ceive'

ap'per·ceived'

ap'per·cep'tion

ap'per·cep'tive

ap'per·tain'

ap'per·tained'

ap'pe·tite

ap'pe·tiz'er

ap'pe·tiz'ing·ly

ap·plaud'

ap·plaud'ed

ap·plause'

ap'ple

ap'ple·jack'

ap'ple·nut'

ap'ple·sauce'

ap·pli'ance

ap'pli·ca·bil'i·ty

ap'pli·ca·ble

ap'pli·cant

ap'pli·ca'tion

ap'pli·ca'tor

ap·plied'

ap'pli·qué'

ap·ply'

ap·point'

ap·point'ed

ap·point'ee'

ap·poin'tive

ap·point'ment

ap·por'tion

ap·por'tioned

ap·por'tion·ment

ap'po·site

ap'po·si'tion

ap·prais'al

ap·praise'

ap·praised'

ap·prais'er

ap·prais'ing·ly

ap·pre'ci·a·ble

ap·pre'ci·a·bly

ap·pre'ci·ate

ap·pre'ci·at'ed

ap·pre'ci·a'tion

ap·pre'ci·a'tive

ap·pre'ci·a'tive·ly

ap'pre·hend'

ap'pre·hend'ed

ap'pre·hend'ing·ly

ap'pre·hen'sion

ap'pre·hen'sive

ap'pre·hen'sive·ly

ap'pre·hen'sive·ness

ap·pren'tice

ap·pren'ticed	ap'ti·tude	ar'bi·trat'ed
ap·pren'tice·ship	apt'ly	ar'bi·tra'tion
ap·prise'	apt'ness	ar'bi·tra'tive
ap·prised'	aq'ua·ma·rine'	ar'bi·tra'tor
ap·proach'	aq'ua·relle'	ar'bor
ap·proach'a·ble	a·quar'i·um	ar·bo're·al
ap·proached'	aq'ua·scu'tum	ar·bo're·ous
ap'pro·ba'tion	a·quat'ic	ar'bo·re'tum
ap'pro·ba'tive	aq'ua·tint'	ar·bu'tus
ap'pro·ba'tive·ness	aq'ue·duct	arc
ap·pro'pri·ate	a'que·ous	ar·cade'
ap·pro'pri·at'ed	aq'ui·line	ar·cad'ed
ap·pro'pri·ate·ly	Ar'ab	Ar·ca'di·a
ap·pro'pri·ate·ness	ar'a·besque'	ar·ca'num
ap·pro'pri·a'tion	A·ra'bi·an	arch
ap·prov'al	Ar'a·bic	ar'chae·ol'o·gist
ap·prove'	ar'a·bil'i·ty	ar'chae·ol'o·gy
ap·proved'	Ar'ab·ist	ar·cha'ic
ap·prov'ing·ly	ar'a·ble	arch'an'gel
ap·prox'i·mate	a·rach'nid	arch'an·gel'ic
ap·prox'i·mat'ed	a·rach'noid	arch'bish'op
ap·prox'i·mate·ly	a·rag'o·nite	arch'dea'con
ap·prox'i·ma'tion	Ar'a·ma'ic	arch'di'o·cese
ap·pur'te·nance	ar'ba·lest	arch'du'cal
ap·pur'te·nant	ar'bi·ter	arch'duch'ess
a'pri·cot	ar'bi·tra·ble	arch'duch'y
A'pril	ar'bi·trage	arch'duke'
a'pron	ar·bit'ra·ment	arch'er
ap'ro·pos'	ar'bi·trar'i·ly	arch'er·fish'
apse	ar'bi·trar'i·ness	arch'er·y
ap'sis	ar'bi·trar'y	ar'che·typ'al
apt	ar'bi·trate	ar'che·type

arch'fiend'

ar'chi·pel'a·go

ar'chi·tect

ar'chi·tec·ton'ic

ar'chi·tec'tur·al

ar'chi·tec'tur·al·ly

ar'chi·tec'ture

ar'chi·trave

ar'chives

ar'chi·vist

arch'ly

arch'ness

arch'way

arc'tic

ar'dent

ar'dent·ly

ar'dor

ar'du·ous

ar'du·ous·ly

are

a're·a

a·re'na

ar'gent

ar'gen·tif'er·ous

ar'gon

Ar'go·naut

ar'got

ar'gu·a·ble

ar'gue

ar'gued

ar'gu·ment

ar'gu·men·ta'tion

ar'gu·men'ta·tive

Ar'gy·rol

a'ri·a

ar'id

a·rid'i·ty

a·right'

a·rise'

a·ris'en

ar'is·toc'ra·cy

a·ris'to·crat

a·ris'to·crat'ic

a·rith'me·tic

ar'ith·met'i·cal

ark

arm

ar·ma'da

ar'ma·dil'lo

ar'ma·ment

ar'ma·ture

arm'chair

armed

Ar·me'ni·an

arm'ful

arm'hole'

ar'mi·stice

arm'let

ar'mor

ar'mored

ar·mo'ri·al

ar'mor·y

arm'pit'

arm'rest'

arm'scye'

ar'my

ar'ni·ca

a·ro'ma

ar'o·mat'ic

a·round'

a·rouse'

ar·peg'gio

ar·raign'

ar·raigned'

ar·raign'ment

ar·range'

ar·ranged'

ar·range'ment

ar·rang'er

ar'ras

ar·ray'

ar·rayed'

ar·rear'age

ar·rears'

ar·rest'

ar·rest'er

ar·rhyth'mic

ar·riv'al

ar·rive'

ar·rived'

ar'ro·gance

ar'ro·gant

ar'ro·gant·ly

ar'ro·gate

ar'ro·gat'ed

ar'ro·ga'tion

ar'row	ar·tif'i·cer	a·sep'tic
ar'row·head'	ar'ti·fi'cial	ash
ar'row·head'ed	ar'ti·fi'ci·al'i·ty	a·shamed'
ar'row·wood'	ar'ti·fi'cial·ly	ash'en
ar'row·y	ar·til'ler·ist	ash'es
ar·roy'o	ar·til'ler·y	ash'lar
ar'se·nal	ar'ti·san	a·shore'
ar'se·nate	art'ist	ash'pit'
ar·sen'ic	ar·tis'tic	ash'wort'
ar·sen'i·cal	art'ist·ry	ash'y
ar'se·nide	art'less	A'sian
ar'se·nite	Ar'y·an	A'si·at'ic
ar'son	as	a·side'
ar'son·ist	as'a·fet'i·da	as'i·nine
art	as·bes'tos	as'i·nin'i·ty
ar·te'ri·al	as·cend'	ask
ar'ter·y	as·cend'an·cy	a·skance'
art'ful	as·cend'ant	a·skew'
art'ful·ly	as·cend'er	a·slant'
ar·thrit'ic	as·cen'sion	a·sleep'
ar·thrit'i·cal	as·cent'	asp
ar·thri'tis	as'cer·tain'	as·par'a·gus
ar'thro·plas'ty	as'cer·tain'ment	as'pect
ar'ti·choke	as·cet'ic	as'pen
ar'ti·cle	as·cet'i·cism	as·per'i·ty
ar'ti·cled	as·ci'tes	as·perse'
ar·tic'u·late	a·scor'bic	as·persed'
ar·tic'u·lat'ed	as'cot	as·per'sion
ar·tic'u·la'tion	as·cribe'	as'phalt
ar·tic'u·la'tive	as·cribed'	as·phal'tic
ar'ti·fact	as·crip'tion	as'pho·del
ar'ti·fice	a·sep'sis	as·phyx'i·a

as·phyx'i·ate

as·phyx'i·a'tion

as'pic

as·pir'ant

as'pi·rate

as'pi·rat'ed

as'pi·ra'tion

as'pi·ra'tor

as·pire'

as·pired'

as'pi·rin

as'sa·gai

as·sail'

as·sail'ant

as·sailed'

as·sas'sin

as·sas'si·nate

as·sas'si·nat'ed

as·sas'si·na'tion

as·sault'

as·sault'ed

as·say'

as·sayed'

as·say'er

as·sem'blage

as·sem'ble

as·sem'bled

as·sem'bler

as·sem'bly

as·sent'

as·sent'ed

as·sent'ing·ly

as·sert'

as·sert'ed

as·ser'tion

as·ser'tive

as·ser'tive·ly

as·sess'

as·sess'a·ble

as·sessed'

as·sess'ment

as·ses'sor

as·ses'sor·ship

as'set

as·sev'er·ate

as·sev'er·a'tion

as'si·du'i·ty

as·sid'u·ous

as·sid'u·ous·ly

as·sign'

as·sign'a·ble

as'sig·na'tion

as·signed'

as'sign·ee'

as·sign'ment

as'sign·or'

as·sim'i·la·ble

as·sim'i·late

as·sim'i·lat'ed

as·sim'i·la'tion

as·sim'i·la'tive

as·sim'i·la·to'ry

as·sist'

as·sist'ance

as·sist'ant

as·sist'ed

as·sists'

as·size'

as·so'ci·ate

as·so'ci·at'ed

as·so'ci·a'tion

as·so'ci·a'tive

as'so·nance

as'so·nant

as·sort'

as·sort'ed

as·sort'ment

as·suage'

as·suaged'

as·sum'a·ble

as·sum'a·bly

as·sume'

as·sumed'

as·sum'ed·ly

as·sump'sit

as·sump'tion

as·sur'ance

as·sure'

as·sured'

as·sur'ed·ly

as·sur'ed·ness

as·sur'er

As·syr'i·an

as'ter

as'ter·isk

a·stern'

as·ter·oid	as·tute'ly	a·tone'
as·the'ni·a	as·tute'ness	a·toned'
as·then'ic	a·sun'der	a·tone'ment
asth'ma	a·sy'lum	a'tri·um
asth·mat'ic	a'sym·met'ric	a·tro'cious
as'tig·mat'ic	a'sym·met'ri·cal	a·tro'cious·ly
a·stig'ma·tism	a·sym'me·try	a·troc'i·ty
as·ton'ish	at	at'ro·phied
as·ton'ish·ing·ly	at'a·rax'i·a	at'ro·phy
as·ton'ish·ment	at'a·vism	at'ro·pine
as·tound'	at'a·vis'tic	at·tach'
as·tound'ed	a'the·ism	at·tached'
as·tound'ing·ly	a'the·ist	at·tach'ment
a·strad'dle	a'the·is'tic	at·tack'
as·trag'a·lus	ath'e·nae'um	at·tack'er
as'tra·khan	A·the'ni·an	at·tain'
as'tral	ath'lete	at·tain'a·ble
a·stray'	ath·let'ic	at·tain'der
a·stride'	ath·let'ics	at·tained'
as·trin'gen·cy	a·thwart'	at·tain'ment
as·trin'gent	at'mos·phere	at'tar
as'tro·labe	at'mos·pher'ic	at·tempt'
as·trol'o·ger	at'oll	at·tempt'ed
as·trol'o·gy	at'om	at·tend'
as'tro·nau'tics	at'om·at'ic	at·tend'ance
as·tron'o·mer	a·tom'ic	at·tend'ant
as'tro·nom'i·cal	at'om·is'tic	at·ten'tion
as·tron'o·my	at'om·ize	at·ten'tive
as'tro·phys'i·cal	at'om·ized	at·ten'tive·ly
as'tro·phys'i·cist	at'om·iz'er	at·ten'tive·ness
as'tro·phys'ics	a·ton'al	at·ten'u·ate
as·tute'	a'to·nal'i·ty	at·ten'u·at'ed

at·ten'u·a'tion
at·test'
at'tes·ta'tion
at·tests'
at'tic
at·tire'
at·tired'
at'ti·tude
at'ti·tu'di·nize
at·tor'ney
at·tor'neys
at·tract'
at·tract'ed
at·trac'tion
at·trac'tive
at·trac'tive·ly
at·trib'ute
at·trib'ut·ed
at'tri·bu'tion
at·trib'u·tive
at·tri'tion
at·tune'
at·tuned'
a·twit'ter
a·typ'i·cal
au'burn
auc'tion
auc'tioned
auc'tion·eer'
au·da'cious
au·da'cious·ly
au·dac'i·ty

au'di·bil'i·ty
au'di·ble
au'di·bly
au'di·ence
au'di·o
au'di·om'e·ter
au'dit
au'dit·ed
au·di'tion
au'di·tor
au'di·to'ri·um
au'di·to'ry
au'ger
aught
aug·ment'
aug'men·ta'tion
aug·ment'a·tive
aug·ment'ed
au'gur
au'gured
au'gu·ry
au·gust'
Au'gust
aunt
au'ra
au'ral
au're·ole
au'ri·cle
au·ric'u·lar
au·rif'er·ous
au·ro'ra
au·ro'ral

aus'cul·tate
aus'cul·ta'tion
aus'pice
aus'pic·es
aus·pi'cious
aus·tere'
aus·tere'ly
aus·ter'i·ty
Aus·tral'ian
Aus'tri·an
au·then'tic
au·then'ti·cate
au·then'ti·cat'ed
au·then'ti·ca'tion
au'then·tic'i·ty
au'thor
au·thor'i·tar'i·an
au·thor'i·ta'tive
au·thor'i·ta'tive·ly
au·thor'i·ty
au'thor·i·za'tion
au'thor·ize
au'thor·ized
au'thor·ship
au'to·bi'o·graph'i·cal
au'to·bi·og'ra·phy
au·toch'tho·nous
au'to·clave
au·toc'ra·cy
au'to·crat
au'to·crat'ic
au'to·crat'i·cal·ly

au'to·graph	a·ver'	a·wak'ened
au'to·in·tox'i·ca'tion	av'er·age	a·ward'
au'to·mat'ic	av'er·aged	a·ward'ed
au·tom'a·tism	a·ver'ment	a·ware'
au·tom'a·tize	a·verred'	a·ware'ness
au·tom'a·ton	a·verse'	a·wash'
au'to·mo·bile'	a·ver'sion	a·way'
au·ton'o·mize	a·vert'	awe
au·ton'o·mous	a·vert'ed	awe'some
au·ton'o·my	a'vi·ar'y	aw'ful
au'top·sies	a'vi·a'tion	aw'ful·ly
au'top·sy	a'vi·a'tor	awk'ward
au'to·sug·ges'tion	av'id	awk'ward·ly
au'tumn	a·vid'i·ty	awk'ward·ness
au·tum'nal	av'id·ly	awl
aux·il'ia·ry	av'i·ga'tion	awn'ing
a·vail'	av'o·ca'do	a·woke'
a·vail'a·bil'i·ty	av'o·ca'tion	a·wry'
a·vail'a·ble	a·void'	ax
a·vailed'	a·void'a·ble	ax'i·om
av'a·lanche	a·void'ed	ax'i·o·mat'ic
av'a·rice	a·vow'al	ax'is
av'a·ri'cious	a·vow'ed·ly	ax'le
av'a·ri'cious·ly	a·vun'cu·lar	a·za'le·a
av'a·tar'	a·wait'	az'i·muth
a·venge'	a·wait'ed	Az'tec
a·venged'	a·wake'	az'ure
av'e·nue	a·wak'en	az'u·rite

B

bab'bitt

bab'ble

ba·boon'

ba'by

Bab'y·lo'ni·an

bac'ca·lau're·ate

bac'cha·nal

bac'cha·na'li·an

bach'e·lor

bach'e·lor·hood'

ba·cil'lus

back

back'ache'

back'board'

back'bone'

back'break'er

back'drop'

back'er

back'fire'

back'gam'mon

back'ground'

back'hand'

back'hand'ed

back'lash'

back'log'

back'saw'

back'slide'

back'slid'er

back'spin'

back'stage'

back'stamp'

back'stitch'

back'stop'

back'stroke'

back'track'

back'ward

back'ward·ness

back'wash'

back'wa'ter

back'woods'

ba'con

bac·te'ri·a

bac·te'ri·al

bac·te'ri·cid'al

bac·te'ri·cide

bac·te'ri·o·log'i·cal

bac·te'ri·ol'o·gy

bac·te'ri·um

bad

badge

badg'er

bad'i·nage'

bad'lands'

bad'ly

bad'min·ton

bad'ness

baf'fle

baf'fled

bag

ba·gasse'

bag'a·telle'

bag'gage

bagged

bag'pipe'

bail

bailed

23

bail'ee'

bail'iff

bail'i·wick

bail'ment

bait

baize

bake

Ba'ke·lite

bak'er

bak'er·y

bal'ance

bal'anced

bal·bo'a

bal·brig'gan

bal'co·ny

bald

bal'da·chin

bal'der·dash

bald'ness

bal'dric

bale

baled

bale'ful

balk

ball

bal'lad

bal'last

balled

bal'le·ri'na

bal'let

bal·let'o·mane

bal·lis'tics

bal·loon'

bal·loon'ist

bal'lot

ball'play'er

ball'room'

balm

bal'sa

bal'sam

bal'sam·if'er·ous

bal'us·ter

bal'us·trade'

bam·boo'

bam·boo'zle

bam·boo'zled

ban

ba'nal

ba·nal'i·ty

ba·nan'a

band

band'age

ban·dan'na

band'box'

ban·deau'

band'ed

ban'de·role

ban'di·coot

ban'dit

band'mas'ter

ban'do·leer'

band'stand'

ban'dy

bane'ful

bang

bang'board'

banged

bang'le

ban'ish

ban'ish·ment

ban'is·ter

ban'jo

bank

bank'book'

banked

bank'er

bank'rupt

bank'rupt·cy

banned

ban'ner

banns

ban'quet

ban'quet·ed

ban'shee

ban'tam

ban'ter

ban'tered

ban'ter·ing·ly

ban'yan

ban'zai'

bap'tism

bap·tis'mal

Bap'tist

bap·tize'

bap·tized'

bap·tize'ment

bar	bar'na·cle	base'board'
barb	barn'yard'	based
bar·bar'i·an	bar'o·gram	base'less
bar·bar'ic	bar'o·graph	base'ly
bar'ba·rism	ba·rom'e·ter	base'ment
bar·bar'i·ty	bar'o·met'ric	base'ness
bar'ba·rous	bar'on	bas'er
bar'be·cue	bar'on·age	bas'est
barbed	bar'on·ess	bash'ful
bar'ber	bar'on·et	bas'ic
bar'ber'ry	bar'on·et·cy	bas'i·cal·ly
bar·bette'	ba·ro'ni·al	ba·sil'i·ca
bar'bi·can	bar'o·ny	bas'i·lisk
bard	ba·roque'	ba'sin
bare	bar'rack	ba'sis
bare'back'	bar'ra·cu'da	bask
bared	bar·rage'	bas'ket
bare'faced'	bar'ra·try	bas'ket·ball'
bare'foot'	bar'rel	bas'ket·work'
bare'head'ed	bar'ren	bas'-re·lief'
bare'ly	bar'ren·ness	bass
bare'ness	bar'ri·cade'	bas'si·net'
bar'gain	bar'ri·cad'ed	bas'so
bar'gained	bar'ri·er	bas·soon'
barge	bar'ris·ter	bass'wood'
barge'man	bar'row	bast'ed
bar'i·tone	bar'ter	bas'ti·na'do
bar'i·um	bar'tered	bas'tion
bark	bas'al	bat
bar'ley	ba·salt'	batch
bar'maid'	bas'cule	bath
barn	base	bathe

bathed	bea'dle	be·calm'
bath'er	bead'work'	be·calmed'
bath'house'	bea'gle	be·came'
ba'thos	beak	be·cause'
bath'robe'	beak'er	beck'on
bath'room'	beam	beck'oned
ba·tiste'	beamed	be·cloud'
ba'ton'	bean	be·come'
bat·tal'ion	bear	be·com'ing·ly
bat'ten	bear'a·ble	be·com'ing·ness
bat'tened	beard	bed
bat'ter	beard'ed	be·daub'
bat'tered	bear'er	bed'bug'
bat'ter·y	bear'ish	bed'cham'ber
bat'tle	bear'skin'	bed'clothes'
bat'tled	beast	bed'ded
bat'tle·ment	beast'li·ness	be·deck'
bat'tle·ship'	beast'ly	be·dev'il
bawl	beat	be·dev'iled
bawled	beat'en	bed'fel'low
bay'ber'ry	beat'er	be·diz'en
bay'o·net	be'a·tif'ic	bed'lam
bay'o·net'ed	be·at'i·fi·ca'tion	bed'post'
bay'ou	be·at'i·fy	bed'rid'den
ba·zaar'	beat'ings	bed'rock'
be	be·at'i·tude	bed'roll'
beach	beau'te·ous	bed'room'
beached	beau'ti·ful	bed'side'
beach'comb'er	beau'ti·ful·ly	bed'spread'
bea'con	beau'ti·fy	bed'spring'
bead	beau'ty	bed'stead
bead'ed	bea'ver	bed'time'

bee

beech

beef

beef'steak'

bee'line'

beer

bees'wax'

bee'tle

be·fall'

be·fell'

be·fit'

be·fog'

be·fore'

be·fore'hand'

be·friend'

be·fud'dle

be·fud'dled

beg

be·get'

beg'gar

begged

be·gin'

be·gone'

be·go'ni·a

be·got'

be·grime'

be·guile'

be·guiled'

be'gum

be·gun'

be·half'

be·have'

be·hav'ior

be·hav'ior·al

be·hav'ior·ism

be·head'

be·head'ings

be·held'

be·he'moth

be·hest'

be·hind'

be·hold'

be·hold'en

be·hold'er

be·hoove'

beige

be·jew'el

be·jew'eled

be·la'bor

be·lat'ed

be·lat'ed·ly

belch

be·lea'guer

be·lea'guered

bel'fry

Bel'gi·an

be·lie'

be·lief'

be·liev'a·ble

be·lieve'

be·lit'tle

be·lit'tled

bell

bel'la·don'na

bell'bird'

bell'boy'

bel'li·cose

bel'li·cos'i·ty

bel·lig'er·ence

bel·lig'er·en·cy

bel·lig'er·ent

bel·lig'er·ent·ly

bel'lowed

bel'lows

be·long'

be·longed'

be·long'ings

be·lov'ed

be·low'

belt

belt'ed

bel've·dere'

be·moan'

be·moaned'

be·mused'

bench

bend

bend'ed

be·neath'

ben'e·dic'tion

ben'e·fac'tion

ben'e·fac'tor

ben'e·fac'tress

ben'e·fice

be·nef'i·cent

ben'e·fi'ci·ar'y

ben'e·fit

ben'e·fit'ed

be·nev'o·lence

be·nev'o·lent

be·night'ed

be·nign'

be·nig'nan·cy

be·nig'nant

be·nig'ni·ty

bent

ben'zene

be·queath'

be·quest'

be·rate'

be·rat'ed

be·reave'

be·reaved'

be·reave'ment

ber'ry

berth

ber'yl

be·seech'

be·seeched'

be·seech'ing·ly

be·set'

be·side'

be·sides'

be·siege'

be·sieged'

be·smirch'

be·sot'ted

be·span'gle

be·speak'

Bes'se·mer

best

bes'tial

bes'ti·al'i·ty

be·stow'

be·stowed'

be·stride'

bet

be·take'

be·tide'

be·times'

be·to'ken

be·tray'

be·tray'al

be·tray'er

be·troth'

be·troth'al

bet'ter

bet'tered

bet'ter·ment

be·tween'

be·twixt'

bev'el

bev'eled

bev'er·age

bev'y

be·wail'

be·wailed'

be·ware'

be·wil'der

be·wil'dered

be·wil'der·ing·ly

be·wil'der·ment

be·witch'

be·witch'ing·ly

be·yond'

bez'el

bi·an'nu·al

bi·an'nu·al·ly

bi'as

bi'ased

bi'be·lot'

Bi'ble

Bib'li·cal

bib'li·o·graph'i·cal

bib'li·og'ra·phy

bib'u·lous

bi·cam'er·al

bi·car'bon·ate

bi·cen'te·nar'y

bi'ceps

bi·chlo'ride

bi·chro'mate

bi·cus'pid

bi'cy·cle

bid

bid'der

bide

bi·en'ni·al

bi·en'ni·um

bier

bi·fo'cal

big

big'a·mist	bill'stick'er	birch
big'a·mous	bi'me·tal'lic	bird
big'a·my	bi·met'al·lism	bird'lime'
big'ger	bi·met'al·list	bird'man'
big'gest	bi·month'ly	birth
big'horn'	bin	birth'day'
bight	bi'na·ry	birth'mark'
big'ot	bin·au'ral	birth'place'
big'ot·ed	bind	birth'right'
big'ot·ry	bind'er	bis'cuit
bi'jou	bind'er·y	bi'sect
bi·lat'er·al	bind'ing·ly	bish'op
bile	bind'ings	bish'op·ric
bilge	bind'weed'	bis'muth
bil'i·ar'y	bin'go	bi'son
bi·lin'gual	bin'na·cle	bisque
bil'ious	bin·oc'u·lar	bit
bilk	bi·no'mi·al	bite
bill	bi·og'ra·pher	bit'er
bill'board'	bi'o·graph'ic	bit'ing·ly
billed	bi'o·graph'i·cal	bit'ten
bil'let	bi'o·graph'i·cal·ly	bit'ter
bil'let·ed	bi·og'ra·phy	bit'ter·est
bill'fish'	bi'o·log'i·cal	bit'ter·ly
bill'fold'	bi'o·log'i·cal·ly	bit'tern
bill'head'	bi·ol'o·gist	bit'ter·ness
bil'liards	bi·ol'o·gy	bit'ters
bil'lings	bi'op·sy	bit'ter·weed'
bil'lion	bi·par'tite	bi·tu'men
bil'lion·aire'	bi'ped	bi·tu'mi·nous
bil'low	bi'plane'	biv'ouac
bill'post'er	bi·po'lar	bi·zarre'

black	blan'dish·ing·ly	bleed'er
black'ball'	blan'dish·ment	blem'ish
black'ber'ry	bland'ly	blench
black'bird'	bland·ness	blend
black'board'	blank	blend'ed
black'en	blanked	blend'ings
black'er	blank'er	bless
black'est	blank'est	bless'ed·ness
black'fish'	blan'ket	bless'ings
black'guard	blank'ly	blew
black'head'	blare	blight
black'ish	blared	blight'ed
black'jack'	blar'ney	blimp
black'leg'	blas·pheme'	blind
black'mail'	blas·phemed'	blind'ed
black'mail'er	blas·phem'er	blind'er
black'ness	blas'phe·mous	blind'fold'
black'smith'	blas'phe·my	blind'ly
black'strap'	blast	blind'ness
black'thorn'	blast'ed	blink
blad'der	bla'tant	blinked
blade	blaze	blink'er
blame	blazed	bliss
blamed	blaz'er	bliss'ful
blame'less	bla'zon	bliss'ful·ly
blame'less·ly	bla'zoned	blis'ter
blame'less·ness	bleach	blis'tered
blame'wor'thy	bleached	blis'ter·ing·ly
blanch	bleach'er	blis'ter·y
blanc·mange'	bleak	blithe
bland	bleat	blithe'ly
blan'dish	bleed	blithe'some

bliz'zard	blow	blunt'ness
bloat	blow'er	blur
bloat'ed	blow'fish'	blurb
block	blow'fly'	blurred
block·ade'	blow'gun'	blurt
block·ad'ed	blow'hard'	blush
block·ad'er	blow'hole'	blushed
block'head'	blown	blush'ing·ly
block'house'	blow'off'	blus'ter
blond	blow'out'	blus'tered
blood	blow'pipe'	blus'ter·ing·ly
blood'ed	blow'torch'	blus'ter·y
blood'hound'	blow'y	bo'a
blood'i·est	blub'ber	board
blood'less	bludg'eon	board'ed
blood'let'ting	bludg'eoned	board'er
blood'line'	blue	boast
blood'root'	blue'fish'	boast'ed
blood'shed'	blue'grass'	boast'er
blood'shot'	blue'nose'	boast'ful
blood·stain'	blue'stock'ing	boast'ful·ly
blood'wood'	bluff	boat
blood'y	bluffed	boat'load'
bloom	bluff'er	boat'man'
bloomed	blun'der	boat'swain'
bloom'er	blun'dered	bob'bin
blos'som	blun'der·buss	bob'cat'
blos'somed	blun'der·er	bob'o·link
blot	blun'der·ing·ly	bob'tail'
blotch	blunt	bode
blot'ter	blunt'ed	bod'ice
blouse	blunt'ly	bod'i·ly

bod'kin

bod'y

bod'y·guard'

bod'y·mak'er

bog

bo'gey

bog'gle

bog'gled

bo'gus

bog'wood'

Bo·he'mi·an

boil

boiled

boil'er

bois'ter·ous

bois'ter·ous·ly

bo'la

bold

bold'er

bold'est

bold'face'

bold'ly

bold'ness

bo·le'ro

bole'weed'

bo·liv'i·a

bo·li'via'no

boll

bo'lo

bo·lom'e·ter

bol'she·vik

bol'ster

bol'stered

bolt

bolt'ed

bolt'head'

bo'lus

bomb

bom·bard'

bom·bard'ed

bom'bard·ier'

bom·bard'ment

bom'bast

bom·bas'tic

bombed

bomb'er

bomb'proof'

bomb'shell'

bo·nan'za

bon'bon'

bond

bond'age

bond'ed

bond'hold'er

bond'man

bond'slave'

bonds'man

bone

boned

bone'fish'

bone'less

bone'set'

bon'fire'

bon'go

bo·ni'to

bon'net

bon'net·ed

bo'nus

bon'y

boo'by

boo'dle

book

book'bind'er

booked

book'ings

book'ish

book'keep'er

book'keep'ing

book'let

book'lets

book'mak'er

book'man

book'mark'

book'plate'

book'rack'

book'rest'

book'sell'er

book'shelf

book'stall'

book'stand'

book'worm'

boom

boomed

boom'er·ang

boon

boor

boor'ish

boost

boost'ed

boost'er

boot

boot'black'

boot'ed

boot'ee'

boot'er·y

booth

boot'jack'

boot'leg'

boot'leg'ger

boot'less

boot'strap'

boo'ty

booze

bo·rac'ic

bo'rate

bo'rax

Bor'deaux'

bor'der

bor'de·reau'

bor'dered

bore

bored

bo're·al

bo're·a'lis

bore'dom

bor'er

bore'some

bo'ric

bo'rine

bor'ings

born

bo'ron

bor'ough

bor'row

bor'rowed

bor'row·er

bor'row·ings

borsch

bosk'y

Bos'ni·an

bos'om

boss

bossed

boss'ism

boss'y

bo·tan'ic

bo·tan'i·cal

bot'a·nist

bot'a·nize

bot'a·nized

bot'a·ny

botch

botched

bot'fly'

both

both'er

both'ered

both'er·some

Both'ni·an

bot'tle

bot'tle·bird'

bot'tled

bot'tle·head'

bot'tle·hold'er

bot'tle·neck'

bot'tle·nose'

bot'tom

bot'tom·less

bot'tom·ry

bot'u·lism

bou'doir

bough

boughed

bought

bouil'la·baisse'

bouil'lon'

boul'der

bou'le·vard

bounce

bounced

bounc'er

bound

bound'a·ry

bound'ed

bound'en

bound'er

bound'less

boun'te·ous

boun'te·ous·ly

boun'ti·ful

boun'ty

bou·quet'

bour·geois'	boy'cott	brake'man
bour'geoi'sie'	boy'hood	bram'ble
bourse	boy'ish	bran
bout	boy'ish·ness	branch
bo'va·rysm	brace	branched
bo'vine	braced	branch'ling
bow	brace'let	brand
bow	brack'en	brand'ed
bowd'ler·ize	brack'et	bran'died
bowed	brack'et·ed	bran'dish
bowed	brack'ish	bran'dished
bow'el	brad'awl'	brand'-new'
bow'er	brag	bran'dy
bow'er·bird'	bragged	brash
bow'fin'	brag'ga·do'ci·o	brass
bow'ie	brag'gart	bras'sard
bow'knot'	Brah'man	brass'bound'
bowl	braid	brass'ie
bowled	braid'ed	brass'i·ness
bow'leg'ged	Braille	brass'y
bowl'er	brain	brat
bow'man	brained	brat'ling
bow'shot'	brain'fag'	bra·va'do
bow'sprit	brain'less	brave
bow'string'	brain'sick'	brave'ly
box	brain'work'	brav'er
box'board'	brain'y	brav'er·y
box'car'	braise	brav'est
boxed	braised	bra'vo
box'er	brake	bra·vu'ra
box'wood'	brake'age	brawl
boy	braked	brawled

brawl'er

brawn

brawn'y

bray

brayed

braze

brazed

bra'zen

bra'zened

bra'zier

bra·zil'ite

bra·zil'wood'

breach

breached

bread

bread'bas'ket

bread'board'

bread'ed

bread'fruit'

bread'root'

bread'stuff'

breadth

bread'win·ner'

break

break'a·ble

break'age

break'down'

break'er

break'fast

break'neck'

break'off'

break'out'

break'o·ver'

break'-through'

break'up'

break'wa'ter

breast

breast'band'

breast'bone'

breast'ed

breast'-fed'

breast'mark'

breast'pin'

breast'plate'

breast'weed'

breast'work'

breath

breathed

breath'less

bred

breech

breed

breed'er

breeze

breezed

breez'y

breth'ren

breve

bre·vet'

bre'vi·ar'y

bre·vier'

brev'i·ty

brew

brewed

brew'er

brew'er·y

brew'house'

bribe

bribed

brib'er·y

bric'-a-brac'

brick

brick'bat'

bricked

brick'lay'er

brick'ma'son

brick'yard'

brid'al

bride

bride'groom'

brides'maid'

bridge

bridged

bridge'head'

bridge'work'

bri'dle

bri'dled

brief

brief'er

brief'est

brief'ly

brief'ness

bri'er

brig

bri·gade'

brig'a·dier'

brig'and		bris'tle		broc'a·tel'	
brig'and·age		bris'tled		broc'co·li	
brig'an·tine		bris'tli·er		bro·chette'	
bright		bris'tli·est		bro·chure'	
bright'en		bris'tly		bro'gan	
bright'er		Bri·tan'ni·a		brogue	
bright'est		Bri·tan'nic		broil	
bright'ly		Brit'i·cism		broiled	
bright'ness		Brit'ish		broil'er	
bright'work'		Brit'ish·er		broke	
bril'liance		Brit'on		bro'ken	
bril'lian·cy		brit'tle		brok'en·ly	
bril'liant		brit'tle·ness		bro'ker	
bril'lian·tine'		broach		bro'ker·age	
bril'liant·ly		broached		bro'mate	
bril'liant·ness		broad		bro'mide	
brim		broad'ax'		bro·mid'ic	
brim'ful'		broad'bill'		bro'mine	
brimmed		broad'brim'		bron'chi·al	
brim'stone'		broad'cast'		bron·chi'tis	
brin'dled		broad'cast'er		bron'cho·scope	
brine		broad'en		bron'chus	
bring		broad'er		bron'co	
brink		broad'est		bronze	
brin'y		broad'leaf'		bronzed	
bri·oche'		broad'loom'		brooch	
bri·quette'		broad'ly		brood	
brisk		broad'side'		brood'ed	
brisk'en		broad'way'		brood'er	
bris'ket		broad'wise'		brood'ling	
brisk'ly		bro·cade'		brook	
brisk'ness		bro·cad'ed		brook'let	

broom	brush'work'	bu·col'ic
broom'weed'	brusque	bud
broom'wood'	bru'tal	bud'ded
broth	bru·tal'i·ty	bud'dy
broth'er	bru'tal·i·za'tion	budge
broth'er·hood	bru'tal·ize	budged
broth'er-in-law'	bru'tal·ized	budg'et
broth'er·li·ness	bru'tal·ly	budg'et·ar'y
broth'er·ly	brute	budg'et·ed
brougham	brut'ish	bud'wood'
brought	brut'ish·ly	bud'worm'
brow	brut'ish·ness	buff
brown	bub'ble	buf'fa·lo
brown'er	bub'bled	buff'er
brown'est	bub'bly	buff'ered
brown'ie	bu·bon'ic	buf'fet
browse	buc'cal	buf·fet'
browsed	buc'ca·neer'	buf'fet·ed
bru'in	buck	buf·foon'
bruise	buck'board'	buf·foon'er·y
bruised	bucked	bug
bruit	buck'et	bug'bear'
brum'ma·gem	buck'et·ed	bugged
brunch	buck'et·ful	bug'gy
bru·net'	buck'le	bu'gle
bru·nette'	buck'led	bu'gler
brunt	buck'ler	bu'gle·weed'
brush	buck'ram	bug'proof'
brushed	buck'saw'	bug'weed'
brush'ful	buck'shot'	build
brush'less	buck'skin'	build'ed
brush'wood'	buck'wheat'	build'er

build'ing

build'ings

built

bulb

bulb'ous

bulge

bulged

bulk

bulk'head'

bulk'i·er

bulk'i·est

bulk'y

bull

bull'doze'

bull'dozed'

bull'doz'er

bul'let

bul'le·tin

bull'fight'

bull'finch'

bull'frog'

bull'head'

bul'lion

bull'ish

bull'ock

bull'weed

bul'ly

bul'ly·rag'

bul'rush'

bul'wark

bum

bum'boat'

bump

bump'er

bump'i·er

bump'i·est

bump'kin

bump'y

bu'na

bunch

bunched

bun'dle

bun'dled

bung

bun'ga·low

bun'gle

bun'gled

bun'gler

bun'ion

bunk'er

bunk'house'

bunt

buoy

buoy'ant

buoy'ant·ly

bur'den

bur'dened

bur'den·some

bu'reau

bu·reauc'ra·cy

bu'reau·crat

bu·rette'

bur'gee

bur'geon

bur'geoned

bur'gess

bur'glar

bur'i·al

bu'rin

bur'lap

bur·lesque'

bur·lesqued'

bur'ly

burn

burned

burn'er

bur'nish

bur'nish·er

burn'out'

burnt

burr

bur'ro

bur'row

bur'rowed

bur'sar

bur·si'tis

burst

bur'y

bus

bus'es

bush

bushed

bush'el

bush'el·er

bush'ings

bus'i·ly

busi′ness

busi′ness·es

busi′ness·like′

bus′kin

bust

bus′tard

bus′tle

bus′tled

bus′y

bus′y·bod′y

but

butch′er

butch′ered

butch′er·y

but′ler

butt

but′ter

but′ter·ball′

but′ter·cup′

but′tered

but′ter·fat′

but′ter·fish′

but′ter·fly′

but′ter·nut′

but′ter·scotch′

but′ter·y

but′ton

but′toned

but′ton·hole′

but′ton·holed′

but′ton·weed′

but′ton·wood′

but′tress

but′tressed

bux′om

buy

buy′er

buzz

buz′zard

buzzed

buzz′er

by

by′gone′

by′pass′

by′path′

by′play′

by′-prod′uct

By·ron′ic

by′stand′er

by′way′

by′word′

C

cab	cac'tus·es	cai'tiff
ca·bal'	ca·dav'er	ca·jole'
cab'bage	ca·dav'er·ous	ca·joled'
cab'in	cad'die	ca·jol'er·y
cab'i·net	ca'dence	cake
ca'ble	ca·den'za	cake'walk'
ca'bled	ca·det'	cal'a·bash
ca'ble·gram	cad'mi·um	cal'a·mine
ca·boose'	Cad'mus	ca·lam'i·tous
cab'ri·o·let'	ca'dre	ca·lam'i·tous·ly
ca·ca'o	ca·du'ce·us	ca·lam'i·ty
cach'a·lot	cad'weed	cal·car'e·ous
cache	Cae·sar'e·an	cal'ci·fi·ca'tion
ca·chet'	cae·su'ra	cal'ci·fy
cach'in·na'tion	ca·fé'	cal'ci·mine
cack'le	caf'e·te'ri·a	cal'cine
cack'led	caf'fe·ine	cal·cined'
ca·coph'o·nous	cage	cal'ci·um
ca·coph'o·ny	caged	cal'cu·late
cac'ti	cairn	cal'cu·lat'ed
cac'toid	cais'son	cal'cu·la'tion
cac'tus	cais'soned	cal'cu·la'tor

40

cal'dron

cal'en·dar

cal'en·der

cal'en·dered

calf

calf'skin'

cal'i·ber

cal'i·brate

cal'i·brat'ed

cal'i·bra'tion

cal'i·co

cal'i·per

ca'liph

cal'is·then'ics

calk

calked

calk'er

call

cal'la

call'a·ble

called

cal'ler

cal·lig'ra·phy

cal·li'o·pe

cal·los'i·ty

cal'lous

cal'loused

cal'lous·ly

cal'low

cal'low·ly

cal'lus

calm

calmed

calm'er

calm'est

calm'ly

calm'ness

cal'o·mel

ca·lor'ic

cal'o·rie

cal'u·met

ca·lum'ni·ate

ca·lum'ni·at'ed

ca·lum'ni·a'tion

ca·lum'ni·a'tor

cal'um·ny

Cal'va·ry

calved

ca·lyp'so

ca'lyx

ca'ma·ra'de·rie

cam'ber

cam'bi·um

cam'bric

came

cam'el

cam'el·eer'

Cam'e·lot

Cam'em·bert'

cam'e·o

cam'er·a

cam'er·a·man'

cam'i·sole

cam'o·mile

cam'ou·flage

camp

cam·paign'

cam·pa·ni'le

camp'er

camp'fire'

cam'phor

cam'phor·ate

cam'phor·at'ed

cam'pus

can

ca·nal'

ca·nal'i·za'tion

ca·nar'y

can'can

can'cel

can'celed

can'cel·la'tion

can'cer

can'cer·ous

can'cer·weed'

can'de·la'brum

can'did

can'di·da·cy

can'di·date

can'did·ly

can'died

can'dle

can'dled

can'dle·fish'

can'dle·light'

can'dle·nut'

can'dle·stick'	can'ta·loupe	ca'per
can'dor	can·tan'ker·ous	ca'pered
can'dy	can·ta'ta	ca'per·ings
can'dy·mak'er	can·teen'	cap'il·lar'i·ty
cane	cant'er	cap'il·lar'y
cane'brake'	can'tered	cap'i·tal
ca'nine	can'ti·cle	cap'i·tal·ism
can'is·ter	can'ti·cles	cap'i·tal·ist
can'ker	can'ti·le'ver	cap'i·tal·is'tic
can'kered	can'tle	cap'i·tal·ists
can'ker·ous	can'to	cap'i·tal·i·za'tion
can'ker·weed'	can'ton	cap'i·tal·ize
can'ker·worm'	can·ton'ment	cap'i·tal·ized
canned	can'tor	cap'i·tol
can'ner	can'vas	ca·pit'u·late
can'ner·y	can'vased	ca·pit'u·lat'ed
can'ni·bal	can'vass	ca·pit'u·lates
can'ni·bal·ism	can'vassed	ca·pit'u·la'tion
can'ni·ly	can'vass·er	ca'pon
can'non	can'yon	capped
can'non·ade'	caou'tchouc	ca·price'
can'non·eer'	ca'pa·bil'i·ties	ca·pri'cious
can'ny	ca'pa·bil'i·ty	cap·size'
ca·noe'	ca'pa·ble	cap·sized'
can'on	ca'pa·bly	cap'stan
ca·non'i·cal	ca·pa'cious	cap'sule
ca·non'i·cals	ca·pac'i·tance	cap'tain
can'on·i·za'tion	ca·pac'i·tate	cap'tain·cy
can'on·ize	ca·pac'i·tat'ed	cap'tion
can'o·py	ca·pac'i·tor	cap'tious
cant	ca·pac'i·ty	cap'tious·ly
can't	cape	cap'tious·ness

cap'ti·vate

cap'ti·vat'ed

cap'ti·va'tion

cap'tive

cap·tiv'i·ty

cap'ture

cap'tured

car

ca'ra·ba'o

car'a·bi·neer'

car'a·cal

car'a·cole

ca·rafe'

car'a·mel

car'a·mel·ize

car'a·pace

car'at

car'a·van

car'a·van'sa·ry

car'a·vel

car'a·way

car'bide

car'bine

car'bo·hy'drate

car·bol'ic

car'bon

car'bon·ate

car'bon·at'ed

car·bon'ic

car·bon·if'er·ous

car'bon·ize

car'bon·ized

car'bo·run'dum

car'boy

car'bun·cle

car'bu·ret'or

car'cass

car'ci·no'ma

card

card'board'

card'ed

car'di·ac

car'di·gan

car'di·nal

car'di·nal·ate

car'di·o·gram'

car'di·o·graph'

car'di·ol'o·gy

care

cared

ca·reen'

ca·reened'

ca·reer'

care'free'

care'ful

care'ful·ly

care'less

care'less·ly

care'less·ness

ca·ress'

ca·ressed'

ca·ress'ing·ly

car'et

car'fare'

car'go

car'i·bou

car'i·ca·ture

car'i·es

car'il·lon

car'load·ings'

car·min'a·tive

car'mine

car'nage

car'nal

car'nal·ly

car·na'tion

car·nel'ian

car'ni·val

car·niv'o·rous

car'ol

car'oled

car'om

car'omed

ca·rot'id

ca·rous'al

ca·rouse'

ca·roused'

carp

car'pal

car'pen·ter

car'pet

car'pet·ed

car'riage

car'ried

car'ri·er

car'ri·on

car'rot

car'rou·sel'

car'ry

cart

cart'age

cart'ed

car'tel

car'ti·lage

car'ti·lag'i·nous

car·tog'ra·phy

car'ton

car·toon'

car·touche'

car'tridge

carve

carved

carv'er

carv'ings

car'y·at'id

ca·sa'ba

cas·cade'

cas·cad'ed

cas·car'a

case

ca'se·in

case'ment

case'work'

cash

cash'book'

cash'box'

cashed

ca·shew'

cash·ier'

cash·iered'

cash'mere

ca·si'no

cask

cas'ket

cas·sa'tion

cas·sa'va

cas'se·role

cas'si·a

cas·si'no

cas'sock

cast

cas'ta·net'

caste

cast'er

cas'ti·gate

cas'ti·gat'ed

cas'ti·ga'tion

cas'tle

cast'off'

cas'tor

cas'tra·me·ta'tion

cas'u·al

cas'u·al·ly

cas'u·al·ty

cas'u·ist

cas'u·ist·ry

ca·tab'o·lism

cat'a·clysm

cat'a·comb

cat'a·falque

cat'a·lep'sy

cat'a·lep'tic

cat'a·logue

cat'a·logued

ca·tal'pa

ca·tal'y·sis

cat'a·lyst

cat'a·lyt'ic

cat'a·lyze

cat'a·mount

cat'a·pult

cat'a·ract

ca·tarrh'

ca·tarrh'al

ca·tas'tro·phe

cat'a·stroph'ic

cat'a·stroph'i·cal·ly

cat'a·ton'ic

Ca·taw'ba

cat'bird'

cat'boat'

cat'call'

catch

catch'er

catch'weed'

catch'word'

catch'y

cat'e·che'sis

cat'e·chet'i·cal

cat'e·chism

cat'e·chize

cat'e·gor'i·cal

cat'e·go·rize	cau·sal'i·ty	cease'less
cat'e·go'ry	cau·sa'tion	cease'less·ly
cat'e·nar'y	caus'a·tive	ce'cum
ca'ter	cause	ce'dar
ca'tered	caused	ce'dar·bird'
ca'ter·er	cause'less	cede
cat'er·pil'lar	cau'se·rie'	ced'ed
cat'fish'	cause'way'	ce·dil'la
cat'gut'	caus'tic	ced'ing
ca·thar'sis	cau·ter·i·za'tion	ceil'ings
ca·thar'tic	cau'ter·ize	cel'e·brant
cat'head'	cau'ter·ized	cel'e·brate
ca·the'dral	cau'ter·y	cel'e·brat'ed
cath'e·ter	cau'tion	cel'e·bra'tion
cath'e·ter·ize	cau'tion·ar'y	ce·leb'ri·ty
cath'ode	cau'tioned	ce·ler'i·ty
cath'o·lic	cau'tious	cel'er·y
ca·thol'i·cism	cav'al·cade'	ce·les'ta
cath'o·lic'i·ty	cav'a·lier'	ce·les'tial
ca·thol'i·cize	cav'al·ry	ce·les'tial·ly
cat'kin	ca·va·ti'na	cel'i·ba·cy
cat'like'	cave	cel'i·bate
cat'nip	ca've·at	cell
cat'tail'	cav'ern	cel'lar
cat'tle	cav'ern·ous	cel'lar·er
cat'walk'	cav'i·ar	cel'lar·et'
cau'cus	cav'il	cel'list
cau'cused	cav'i·ty	cel'lo
cau'dal	ca·vort'	cel'lo·phane
caught	cay·enne'	cel'lu·lar
cau'li·flow'er	cease	cel'lu·li'tis
caus'al	ceased	cel'lu·loid

cel'lu·lose

Celt'ic

ce·ment'

ce'men·ta'tion

cem'e·ter'y

cen'a·cle

cen'o·bite

cen'o·taph

cen'ser

cen'sor

cen'sored

cen·so'ri·al

cen·so'ri·ous

cen'sor·ship

cen'sur·a·ble

cen'sure

cen'sured

cen'sus

cent

cen'taur

cen'te·nar'i·an

cen'te·nar'y

cen·ten'ni·al

cen'ter

cen'ter·board'

cen'tered

cen'ter·piece'

cen'ti·grade

cen'ti·me'ter

cen'ti·pede

cen'tral

cen'tral·i·za'tion

cen'tral·ize

cen'tral·ized

cen·trif'u·gal

cen'tri·fuge

cen·trip'e·tal

cen'trist

cen·tu'ri·on

cen'tu·ry

ce·phal'ic

ce·ram'ic

ce're·al

cer'e·bel'lum

cer'e·bral

cer'e·bra'tion

cer'e·brum

cere'ment

cer'e·mo'ni·al

cer'e·mo'ni·al·ly

cer'e·mo'ni·ous

cer'e·mo'ni·ous·ly

cer'e·mo'ni·ous·ness

cer'e·mo'ny

ce·rise'

ce'ri·um

cer'tain

cer'tain·ly

cer'tain·ty

cer·tif'i·cate

cer·tif'i·cat'ed

cer·tif'i·ca'tion

cer'ti·fied

cer'ti·fy

cer'ti·o·ra'ri

cer'ti·tude

cer'vi·cal

cer'vix

ce'si·um

ces·sa'tion

ces'sion

cess'pool'

ces'tus

ce·ta'cean

chafe

chaf'fer

chaf'fered

chaf'finch

chaff'weed'

cha·grin'

cha·grined'

chain

chained

chain'work'

chair

chair'man

chaise

chal·ced'o·ny

cha·let'

chal'ice

chalk

chalk'i·ness

chal'lenge

chal'lenged

cham'ber

cham'bered

cham'ber·lain

cham'ber·maid'

cha·me'le·on

cham'ois

cham·pagne'

cham'per·ty

cham'pi·on

cham'pi·on·ship'

chance

chanced

chan'cel

chan'cel·ler·y

chan'cel·lor

chan'cer·y

chan'de·lier'

chan'dler

chan'dler·y

change

change'a·ble

changed

change'less

change'ling

chan'nel

chan'neled

chant

chant'ed

cha'os

cha·ot'ic

cha·ot'i·cal·ly

chap'ar·ral'

chap'el

chap'er·on

chap'lain

chap'let

chap'ter

char

char'ac·ter

char'ac·ter·is'tic

char'ac·ter·is'ti·cal·ly

char'ac·ter·i·za'tion

char'ac·ter·ize

char'ac·ter·ized

cha·rade'

char'coal'

chard

charge

charge'a·ble

charged

charg'er

char'i·ly

char'i·ness

char'i·ot

char'i·ot·eer'

char'i·ta·ble

char'i·ta·bly

char'i·ty

char'la·tan

charm

charmed

charm'ing·ly

char'nel

charred

chart

chart'ed

char'ter

char'tered

char·treuse'

char'y

chase

chased

chasm

chas'sis

chaste

chas'ten

chas'tened

chas'ten·ing·ly

chas·tise'

chas·tised'

chas'tise·ment

chas'ti·ty

chas'u·ble

châ·teau'

chat'e·laine

chat'tel

chat'ter

chat'tered

chat'ter·er

chat'ty

chauf·feur'

chau'vin·ism

cheap

cheap'en

cheap'ened

cheap'er

cheap'est

cheap'ly

cheap'ness	chem'is·try	child
cheat	che·nille'	child'hood
cheat'ed	cher'ish	child'ish
cheat'er	che·root'	child'ish·ly
check	cher'ry	child'ish·ness
check'book'	cher'ub	child'less
checked	che·ru'bic	child'like'
check'er	cher'u·bim	chil'dren
check'er·board'	cher'vil	chil'i
check'ered	chess	chill
check'mate'	chess'board'	chilled
check'mat'ed	chess'man	chill'i·er
check'off'	chest	chill'i·est
check'rein'	ches'ter·field'	chill'ing·ly
cheek'y	chest'nut	chill'y
cheer	chev'ron	chime
cheered	chew	chimed
cheer'ful	chic	chi·me'ra
cheer'ful·ly	chi·can'er·y	chi·mer'i·cal
cheer'ful·ness	chick'a·dee	chim'ney
cheer'i·ly	chick'en	chim'pan·zee'
cheer'less	chick'weed'	chin
cheer'less·ly	chic'le	chi'na
cheer'y	chic'o·ry	chinch
cheese	chide	chin·chil'la
cheese'cake'	chief	chine
cheese'cloth'	chief'ly	Chi'nese'
chef	chief'tain	chink
chem'i·cal	chif'fon	chintz
chem'i·cal·ly	chif'fo·nier'	chip
che·mise'	chig'ger	chip'munk
chem'ist	chil'blain'	chipped

chip'per

chi·rog'ra·phy

chi·rop'o·dist

chi'ro·prac'tor

chirp

chis'el

chis'eled

chit'chat'

chit'ter·ling

chiv'al·ric

chiv'al·rous

chiv'al·ry

chive

chlo'ral

chlo'rate

chlo'ride

chlo'rin·ate

chlo'rine

chlo'rite

chlo'ro·form

chlo'ro·phyll

chlo·ro'sis

choc'o·late

choice

choir

choir'boy'

choke

chok'er

chol'er

chol'er·a

chol'er·ic

choose

chop

chop'house'

chopped

chop'per

cho·ral'

chord

cho·re'a

cho're·og'ra·phy

chor'is·ter

chor'tle

cho'rus

chose

cho'sen

chow

chow'der

chrism

chris'ten

Chris'ten·dom

chris'tened

chris'ten·ings

Chris'tian

Chris'ti·an'i·ty

Christ'mas

chro'mate

chro·mat'ics

chrome

chro'mic

chro'mite

chro'mi·um

chro'mo·some

chron'ic

chron'i·cal·ly

chron'i·cle

chron'i·cled

chron'i·cler

chron'i·cles

chron'o·graph

chron'o·log'i·cal

chron'o·log'i·cal·ly

chro·nol'o·gy

chro·nom'e·ter

chron'o·met'ric

chrys'a·lis

chrys·an'the·mum

chrys'o·lite

chub'bi·ness

chub'by

chuck

chuck'le

chuck'led

chuck'le·head'

chuck'ling·ly

chum

chum'my

chump

chunk

chunk'i·ness

chunk'y

church

church'man

churl

churl'ish

churl'ish·ly

churl'ish·ness

churn	cir'cu·lat'ed	cite
churned	cir·cu·la'tion	cit'ed
chute	cir'cu·la·to'ry	cit'i·zen
chut'ney	cir'cum·am'bi·ent	cit'i·zen·ry
chyle	cir·cum'fer·ence	cit'i·zen·ship'
ci·ca'da	cir·cum'fer·en'tial	cit'rate
cic'a·trix	cir'cum·flex	cit'ric
ci'der	cir'cum·lo·cu'tion	cit'ron
ci·gar'	cir'cum·loc'u·to'ry	cit'y
cig'a·rette'	cir'cum·nav'i·gate	civ'ic
cinch	cir'cum·scribe'	civ'il
cinc'ture	cir'cum·scribed'	ci·vil'ian
cinc'tured	cir'cum·spect	ci·vil'i·ty
cin'der	cir'cum·spec'tion	civ'i·li·za'tion
cin'e·ma	cir'cum·spect'ly	civ'i·lize
cin'e·mat'o·graph	cir'cum·spect'ness	civ'i·lized
cin'na·bar	cir'cum·stance	civ'il·ly
cin'na·mon	cir'cum·stanc·es	clack
cinque'foil'	cir'cum·stan'tial	claim
ci'on	cir·cum·stan'ti·al'i·ty	claim'ant
ci'pher	cir'cum·stan'ti·ate	claimed
ci'phered	cir'cum·stan'ti·at'ed	clair·voy'ance
cir'cle	cir'cum·vent'	clair·voy'ant
cir'cled	cir'cum·vent'ed	cla'mant
cir'cuit	cir'cum·ven'tion	clam'bake'
cir·cu'i·tous	cir'cus	clam'ber
cir·cu'i·tous·ly	cir·rho'sis	clam'bered
cir·cu'i·tous·ness	cir·rhot'ic	clam'my
cir'cu·lar	cir'rus	clam'or
cir'cu·lar·i·za'tion	cis'tern	clam'ored
cir'cu·lar·ize	cit'a·del	clam'or·ous
cir'cu·late	ci·ta'tion	clamp

clam'shell'

clan

clan·des'tine

clang

clanged

clang'or

clank

clanked

clan'nish

clan'ship

clans'man

clap

clapped

clap'per

clap'trap'

claque

clar'et

clar'i·fi·ca'tion

clar'i·fied

clar'i·fy

clar'i·net'

clar'i·on

clar'i·ty

clash

clasp

class

clas'sic

clas'si·cal

clas'si·cal·ism

clas'si·cal·ist

clas'si·cal·ly

clas'si·cist

clas'si·fi·ca'tion

clas'si·fied

clas'si·fi'er

clas'si·fy

class'mate'

class'room'

class'work'

clat'ter

clat'tered

clause

claus'tro·pho'bi·a

clav'i·chord

clav'i·cle

claw

clay

clean

cleaned

clean'er

clean'est

clean'li·ness

clean'ly

clean'ness

cleanse

cleans'er

clean'up'

clear

clear'ance

cleared

clear'er

clear'est

clear'head'ed

clear'ing·house'

clear'ly

clear'ness

cleat

cleat'ed

cleav'age

cleave

cleav'er

clef

cleft

clem'a·tis

clem'en·cy

clem'ent

clench

clere'sto'ry

cler'gy

cler'gy·man

cler'i·cal

cler'i·cal·ism

clerk

clev'er

clev'er·er

clev'er·est

clev'er·ness

clew

cli·ché'

click

cli'ent

cli'en·tele'

cliff

cli·mac'ter·ic

cli·mac'tic

cli'mate

cli·mat'ic

cli'max

climb

climbed

climb'er

clinch

clinch'er

cling

cling'ing·ly

clin'ic

clin'i·cal

cli·ni'cian

clink

clinked

clink'er

clip

clip'per

clip'pings

clique

cloak

clock

clock'wise'

clock'work'

clod

clog

cloi'son'né'

clois'ter

clois'tered

clon'ic

close

closed

close'ly

close'ness

clos'er

clos'est

clos'et

clos'et·ed

clo'sure

clot

cloth

clothed

clothes

clothes'pin'

cloth'ier

clot'ted

cloud

cloud'i·er

cloud'i·est

cloud'i·ness

cloud'less

cloud'y

clout

clout'ed

clove

clo'ven

clo'ver

clown

clowned

clown'ish

cloy

cloyed

club

clubbed

club'house'

club'man

cluck

clump

clum'si·er

clum'si·est

clum'si·ly

clum'si·ness

clum'sy

clus'ter

clus'tered

clutch

clut'ter

clut'tered

coach

coach'man

co·ad'ju·tor

co·ag'u·late

co·ag'u·lat'ed

co·ag'u·lates

co·ag'u·la'tion

co·ag'u·la'tive

coal

co'a·lesce'

co'a·lesced'

co'a·les'cence

co'a·les'cent

co'a·li'tion

coal'sack'

coarse

coars'en

coars'ened

coars'er

coars'est

coast

coast'al

coast'er

coast'wise'

coat

coat'ed

coat'ings

co·au'thor

coax

coaxed

co·ax'i·al

coax'ing·ly

co'balt

cob'ble

cob'bled

co'bra

cob'web'

co·caine'

coc'cyx

coch'i·neal'

cock·ade'

cock'a·too'

cock'le

cock'le·shell'

cock'ney

cock'pit'

cock'roach'

cock'sure'

cock'sure'ness

cock'tail'

co'coa

co'co·nut'

co·coon'

co'da

code

cod'ed

co'de·fend'ant

co'de·ine

co'dex

cod'fish'

cod'i·cil

cod'i·fi·ca'tion

cod'i·fy

co'ed'

co'ed·u·ca'tion

co'ef·fi'cient

co·erce'

co·erced'

co·er'cion

co·er'cive

co·e'val

co'ex·ec'u·tor

cof'fee

cof'fer

cof'fin

cog

co'gen·cy

co'gent

cog'i·tate

cog'i·tat'ed

cog'i·ta'tion

cog'i·ta'tive

co'gnac

cog'nate

cog·ni'tion

cog'ni·zance

cog'ni·zant

cog·no'men

co·hab'it

co·here'

co·hered'

co·her'ence

co·her'ent

co·her'ent·ly

co·her'er

co·he'sion

co·he'sive

co'hort

coif

coif·fure'

coign

coil

coiled

coin

coin'age

co'in·cide'

co'in·cid'ed

co·in'ci·dence

co·in'ci·den'tal

coined

coin'er

co'in·sur'ance

co'in·sure'

co'in·sur'er

coke

col'an·der	col·lec'tor·ship	col'or·less
cold	col'lege	co·los'sal
cold'er	col·le'gi·ate	Col'os·se'um
cold'est	col·lide'	co·los'sus
cold'ly	col·lid'ed	col'por'teur
cole'slaw'	col'lie	colt
col'ic	col'lier	col'um·bine
col'i·se'um	col·li'sion	col'umn
co·li'tis	col'lo·ca'tion	co·lum'nar
col·lab'o·rate	col·lo'di·on	co'ma
col·lab'o·rat'ed	col'loid	com'a·tose
col·lab'o·ra'tion	col·loi'dal	comb
col·lapse'	col·lo'qui·al	com'bat
col·lapsed'	col'lo·quy	com'bat·ant
col·laps'i·ble	col'lo·type	com'ba·tive
col'lar	col·lu'sion	com·bat'ive·ness
col'lar·band'	col·lu'sive	combed
col'lar·bone'	co·logne'	com'bi·na'tion
col·late'	co'lon	com'bine
col·lat'ed	colo'nel	com·bined'
col·lat'er·al	co·lo'ni·al	comb'ings
col·la'tion	col'o·nist	com·bust'
col·la'tor	col'o·ni·za'tion	com·bus'ti·ble
col·league'	col'o·nize	com·bus'tion
col'lect	col'o·nized	come
col·lect'ed	col'on·nade'	co·me'di·an
col·lect'i·ble	col'o·ny	com'e·dy
col·lec'tion	col'o·phon	come'li·ness
col·lec'tive	col'or	come'ly
col·lec'tiv·ism	col'or·a'tion	co·mes'ti·ble
col·lec'tiv·ist	col'o·ra·tu'ra	com'et
col·lec'tor	col'ored	com'fit

com′fort	com·men′su·rate	com′mon·al·ty
com′fort·a·ble	com′ment	com′mon·er
com′fort·a·bly	com′men·tar′y	com′mon·est
com′fort·ed	com′men·ta′tor	com′mon·ly
com′fort·er	com′ment·ed	com′mon·place′
com′fort·less	com′merce	com′mon·wealth′
com′ic	com·mer′cial	com·mo′tion
com′i·cal	com·mer′cial·ism	com′mu·nal
com′ings	com·mer′cial·i·za′tion	com·mune′
com′ma	com·mer′cial·ize	com·mu′ni·ca·ble
com·mand′	com·min′a·to′ry	com·mu′ni·cant
com′man·dant′	com·min′gle	com·mu′ni·cate
com·mand′ed	com·min′gled	com·mu′ni·cat′ed
com′man·deer′	com′mi·nute	com·mu′ni·ca′tion
com·mand′er	com′mi·nut′ed	com·mu′ni·ca′tive
com·mand′er·y	com′mi·nu′tion	com·mun′ion
com·mand′ing·ly	com·mis′er·ate	com·mu′ni·qué′
com·mand′ment	com·mis′er·a′tion	com′mu·nism
com·man′do	com′mis·sar′	com′mu·nist
com·mem′o·rate	com′mis·sar′i·at	com·mu·nis′tic
com·mem′o·rat′ed	com′mis·sar′y	com·mu′ni·ty
com·mem′o·ra′tion	com·mis′sion	com′mu·ni·za′tion
com·mem′o·ra′tive	com·mis′sioned	com′mu·nize
com·mence′	com·mis′sion·er	com′mu·ta′tion
com·menced′	com·mit′	com′mu·ta′tor
com·mence′ment	com·mit′ment	com·mute′
com·mend′	com·mit′ted	com·mut′ed
com·mend′a·ble	com·mit′tee	com·mut′er
com′men·da′tion	com·mo′di·ous	com·pact′
com·mend′a·to′ry	com·mod′i·ty	com·pan′ion
com·mend′ed	com′mo·dore′	com·pan′ion·a·ble
com·men′su·ra·ble	com′mon	com·pan′ion·ship

com·pan'ion·way'

com'pa·ny

com'pa·ra·bil'i·ty

com'pa·ra·ble

com·par'a·tive

com·pare'

com·pared'

com·par'i·son

com·part'ment

com'pass

com·pas'sion

com·pas'sion·ate

com·pas'sion·ate·ly

com·pat'i·bil'i·ty

com·pat'i·ble

com·pa'tri·ot

com·peer'

com·pel'

com·pelled'

com·pel'ling·ly

com'pend

com·pen'di·ous

com·pen'di·um

com'pen·sate

com'pen·sat'ed

com'pen·sa'tion

com'pen·sa'tor

com·pen'sa·to'ry

com·pete'

com·pet'ed

com'pe·tence

com'pe·tent

com'pe·tent·ly

com'pe·ti'tion

com·pet'i·tive

com·pet'i·tor

com·pi·la'tion

com·pile'

com·piled'

com·pil'er

com·pla'cence

com·pla'cen·cy

com·pla'cent

com·plain'

com·plain'ant

com·plained'

com·plain'ing·ly

com·plaint'

com·plai'sance

com·plai'sant

com'ple·ment

com'ple·men'tal

com'ple·men'ta·ry

com'ple·ment·ed

com·plete'

com·plet'ed

com·ple'tion

com·plex'

com·plex'ion

com·plex'i·ty

com·pli'ance

com·pli'ant

com'pli·cate

com'pli·cat'ed

com'pli·ca'tion

com·plic'i·ty

com·plied'

com'pli·ment

com'pli·men'ta·ry

com'plin

com·ply'

com·po'nent

com·port'

com·pose'

com·posed'

com·pos'er

com·pos'ite

com·po·si'tion

com·pos'i·tor

com'post

com·po'sure

com'pote

com'pound

com'pre·hend'

com'pre·hend'ed

com'pre·hen'si·bil'i·ty

com'pre·hen'si·ble

com'pre·hen'sion

com'pre·hen'sive

com·press'

com·press'i·bil'i·ty

com·press'ible

com·pres'sion

com·pres'sor

com·prise'

com'pro·mise

com'pro·mis'ing·ly
Comp·tom'e·ter
comp·trol'ler
com·pul'sion
com·pul'sive
com·pul'so·ry
com·punc'tion
com'pu·ta'tion
com·pute'
com·put'ed
com'rade
con·cat'e·na'tion
con'cave
con·cav'i·ty
con·ceal'
con·cealed'
con·ceal'ment
con·cede'
con·ced'ed
con·ceit'
con·ceit'ed
con·ceit'ed·ly
con·ceiv'a·ble
con·ceiv'a·bly
con·ceive'
con·ceived'
con'cen·trate
con'cen·trat'ed
con'cen·tra'tion
con·cen'tric
con'cept
con·cep'tion

con·cep'tu·al
con·cern'
con·cerned'
con'cert
con·cert'ed
con'cer·ti'na
con·ces'sion
con·ces'sion·aire'
conch
con·cil'i·ate
con·cil'i·at'ed
con·cil'i·a'tion
con·cil'i·a·to'ry
con·cise'
con·cise'ness
con'clave
con·clude'
con·clud'ed
con·clu'sion
con·clu'sive
con·clu'sive·ly
con·coct'
con·coct'ed
con·coc'tion
con·com'i·tant
con'cord
con·cord'ance
con'course
con·crete'
con·cur'
con·curred'
con·cur'rence

con·cur'rent
con·cus'sion
con·demn'
con·dem·na'tion
con·dem'na·to'ry
con·demned'
con'den·sa'tion
con·dense'
con·densed'
con·dens'er
con'de·scend'
con'de·scend'ing·ly
con'de·scen'sion
con·dign'
con'di·ment
con·di'tion
con·di'tion·al
con·di'tion·al·ly
con·di'tioned
con·dole'
con·do'lence
con'do·min'i·um
con'do·na'tion
con·done'
con·doned'
con'dor
con·du'cive
con·duct'
con·duct'ed
con·duc'tion
con'duc·tiv'i·ty
con·duc'tor

con′duit

con′dyle

cone

con·fec′tion

con·fec′tion·er

con·fec′tion·er′y

con·fed′er·a·cy

con·fed′er·ate

con·fed′er·a′tion

con·fer′

con′fer·ee′

con′fer·ence

con·ferred′

con·fess′

con·fess′ed·ly

con·fes′sion

con·fes′sion·al

con·fes′sor

con·fide′

con·fid′ed

con′fi·dence

con′fi·dent

con′fi·den′tial

con′fi·den′tial·ly

con′fi·dent·ly

con·fid′ing·ly

con·fig′u·ra′tion

con·fine′

con·fined′

con·fine′ment

con·firm′

con′fir·ma′tion

con·firmed′

con′fis·cate

con′fis·cat′ed

con′fis·ca′tion

con·fis′ca·to′ry

con′fla·gra′tion

con·flict′

con·flict′ed

con·flic′tion

con′flu·ence

con′flu·ent

con·form′

con·form′a·ble

con′for·ma′tion

con·formed′

con·form′er

con·form′i·ty

con·found′

con·found′ed

con′frere

con·front′

con′fron·ta′tion

con·front′ed

con·fuse′

con·fused′

con·fus′ed·ly

con·fus′ing·ly

con·fu′sion

con′fu·ta′tion

con·fute′

con·fut′ed

con·geal′

con·gealed′

con′ge·la′tion

con′ge·ner

con·gen′ial

con·ge′ni·al′i·ty

con·gen′i·tal

con·gest′

con·gest′ed

con·ges′tion

con·glom′er·ate

con·glom′er·a′tion

con·grat′u·late

con·grat′u·lat′ed

con·grat′u·lates

con·grat′u·la′tion

con·grat′u·la·to′ry

con′gre·gate

con′gre·gat′ed

con′gre·ga′tion

con′gre·ga′tion·al

con′gress

con·gres′sion·al

con′gru·ence

con′gru·ent

con·gru′i·ty

con′gru·ous

con′ic

con′i·cal

co′ni·fer

co·nif′er·ous

con·jec′tur·al

con·jec′ture

con·jec′tured

con′ju·gal

con′ju·gate

con′ju·gat′ed

con′ju·ga′tion

con·junc′tion

con·junc′tive

con·junc′ti·vi′tis

con′ju·ra′tion

con·jure′

con·jured′

con′jur·er

con·nect′

con·nect′ed·ly

con·nec′tion

con·nec′tive

con·nec′tor

con·niv′ance

con·nive′

con·nived′

con′nois·seur′

con′no·ta′tion

con·note′

con·not′ed

con·nu′bi·al

con′quer

con′quered

con′quer·or

con′quest

con′san·guin′i·ty

con′science

con′sci·en′tious

con′sci·en′tious·ly

con′scious

con′scious·ly

con′scious·ness

con′script

con·scrip′tion

con′se·crate

con′se·crat′ed

con′se·cra′tion

con′se·cra′tive

con·sec′u·tive

con·sen′sus

con·sent′

con·sent′ed

con′se·quence

con′se·quent

con′se·quen′tial

con′se·quent·ly

con′ser·va′tion

con·serv′a·tism

con·serv′a·tive

con·serv′a·to′ry

con·serve′

con·served′

con·sid′er

con·sid′er·a·ble

con·sid′er·ate

con·sid′er·a′tion

con·sid′ered

con·sign′

con·signed′

con·sign·ee′

con·sign′ment

con·sign′or

con·sist′

con·sist′en·cy

con·sist′ent

con·sis′to·ry

con·so·la′tion

con·sole′

con·soled′

con·sol′i·date

con·sol′i·dat′ed

con·sol′i·da′tion

con·sol′ing·ly

con′sols

con′som·mé′

con′so·nance

con′so·nant

con′so·nan′tal

con·sort′

con·sort′ed

con·spic′u·ous

con·spic′u·ous·ly

con·spir′a·cy

con·spir′a·tor

con·spir′a·to′ri·al

con·spire′

con·spired′

con′sta·ble

con·stab′u·lar′y

con′stan·cy

con′stant

con′stant·ly

con'stel·la'tion

con'ster·na'tion

con'sti·pa'tion

con·stit'u·en·cy

con·stit'u·ent

con'sti·tute

con'sti·tut'ed

con'sti·tu'tion

con'sti·tu'tion·al

con'sti·tu'tion·al'i·ty

con'sti·tu'tion·al·ly

con·strain'

con·strained'

con·straint'

con·strict'

con·strict'ed

con·stric'tion

con·struct'

con·struct'ed

con·struc'tive

con·strue'

con·strued'

con'sul

con'su·lar

con'su·late

con'su·lates

con·sult'

con·sult'ant

con'sul·ta'tion

con·sult'a·tive

con·sult'ed

con·sum'a·ble

con·sume'

con·sumed'

con·sum'er

con'sum·mate

con'sum·ma'tion

con·sump'tion

con·sump'tive

con'tact

con·ta'gion

con·ta'gious

con·tain'

con·tained'

con·tain'er

con·tam'i·nate

con·tam'i·nat'ed

con·tam'i·na'tion

con'tem·plate

con'tem·plat'ed

con'tem·pla'tion

con·tem'pla·tive

con·tem'po·ra'ne·ous

con·tem'po·rar'y

con·tempt'

con·tempt'i·ble

con·temp'tu·ous

con·tend'

con·tend'ed

con·tend'er

con·tent'

con·tent'ed

con·ten'tion

con·ten'tious

con·tent'ment

con'test

con·test'ant

con'tes·ta'tion

con'text

con·tex'tu·al

con'ti·gu'i·ty

con·tig'u·ous

con'ti·nence

con'ti·nent

con'ti·nen'tal

con·tin'gen·cy

con·tin'gent

con·tin'u·al

con·tin'u·al·ly

con·tin'u·ance

con·tin'u·ant

con·tin'u·a'tion

con·tin'ue

con·tin'ued

con'ti·nu'i·ty

con·tin'u·ous

con·tin'u·ous·ly

con·tin'u·um

con·tort'

con·tort'ed

con·tor'tion

con·tor'tion·ist

con'tour

con'tra·band

con'tra·bass'

con'tract

con·tract'ed

con·trac'tile

con·trac'tion

con·trac'tor

con·trac'tu·al

con'tra·dict'

con'tra·dic'tion

con'tra·dic'to·ry

con'tra·dis·tinc'tion

con'tra·in'di·cate

con'tra·in'di·ca'tion

con·tral'to

con·trap'tion

con'tra·ri·ly

con'tra·ri·ness

con'tra·ri·wise'

con'tra·ry

con'trast

con'tra·vene'

con'tra·ven'tion

con·trib'ute

con'tri·bu'tion

con·trib'u·tive

con·trib'u·tor

con·trib'u·to'ry

con'trite

con'trite·ly

con·tri'tion

con·triv'ance

con·trive'

con·trol'

con·trol'la·ble

con·trolled'

con·trol'ler

con'tro·ver'sial

con'tro·ver·sy

con'tro·vert

con'tu·ma'cious

con'tu·ma·cy

con'tu·me'li·ous

con'tu·me'ly

con·tuse'

con·tused'

con·tu'sion

co·nun'drum

con'va·lesce'

con'va·les'cence

con'va·les'cent

con·vec'tion

con·vene'

con·vened'

con·ven'ience

con·ven'ienc·es

con·ven'ient

con·ven'ient·ly

con·vent'

con·ven'tion

con·ven'tion·al

con·ven'tion·al'i·ty

con·ven'tion·al·ize

con·ven'tion·al·ly

con·ven'tu·al

con·ven'tu·al·ly

con·verge'

con·verged'

con·ver'gence

con·ver'gent

con·ver'sant

con'ver·sa'tion

con'ver·sa'tion·al

con'ver·sa'tion·al·ist

con·verse'

con·ver'sion

con·vert'

con·vert'ed

con·vert'i·bil'i·ty

con·vert'i·ble

con'vex

con·vex'i·ty

con·vey'

con·vey'ance

con·veyed'

con·vey'er

con·vict'

con·vict'ed

con·vic'tion

con·vince'

con·vinc'ing·ly

con·viv'i·al

con·viv'i·al'i·ty

con·viv'i·al·ly

con'vo·ca'tion

con·voke'

con·voked'

con'vo·lute

con'vo·lut'ed

con'vo·lu'tion
con·voy'
con·voyed'
con·vulse'
con·vul'sion
con·vul'sive
cook'book'
cook'er
cook'er·y
cook'house'
cool
cooled
cool'er
cool'est
cool'head'ed
cool'house'
coo'lie
cool'ly
cool'ness
coop
coop'er
coop'er·age
co-op'er·ate
co-op'er·at'ed
co-op'er·a'tion
co-op'er·a'tive
co-opt'
co-opt'ed
co-or'di·nate
co-or'di·nat'ed
co-or'di·na'tion
co-or'di·na'tor

coot
co'pal
co·part'ner
co·part'ner·ship
cope
coped
Co·per'ni·can
cop'ied
cop'i·er
cop'ing
co'pi·ous
co'pi·ous·ly
co'pi·ous·ness
cop'per
cop'per·head'
cop'per·plate'
cop'per·smith'
cop'pice
cop'ra
cop'y
cop'y·hold'er
cop'y·ist
cop'y·read'er
cop'y·right'
co'quet·ry
co·quette'
co·quet'tish
cor'a·cle
cor'a·coid
cor'al
cor'al·line
cord

cord'age
cord'ed
cor'dial
cor·dial'i·ty
cor'dial·ly
cord'ite
cor'don
Cor'do·van
cor'du·roy
cord'wood'
core
cored
co're·spond'ent
co·ri·an'der
Co·rin'thi·an
cork
cork'age
cork'screw'
cork'wood'
cor'mo·rant
corn
cor'ne·a
cor'ner
cor'nered
cor'ner·stone'
cor'net
corn'field'
corn'flow'er
cor'nice
corn'stalk'
cor'nu·co'pi·a
cor·ol·lar'y

co·ro'na	cor're·spond'ed	cor'us·cate
cor'o·nar'y	cor're·spond'ence	cor'us·cat'ed
cor'o·na'tion	cor're·spond'ent	cor'us·ca'tion
cor'o·ner	cor·re·spond'ing·ly	cor·vette'
cor'o·net	cor're·sponds'	co·ry'za
cor'po·ral	cor'ri·dor	co·sig'na·to'ry
cor'po·rate	cor·rob'o·rate	co·sign'er
cor'po·rate·ly	cor·rob'o·ra'tion	cos'i·ly
cor'po·ra'tion	cor·rob'o·ra'tive	co'sine
cor'po·ra'tive	cor·rob'o·ra·to'ry	cos·met'ic
cor·po're·al	cor·rode'	cos'me·ti'cian
corps	cor·rod'ed	cos'mic
corpse	cor·ro'si·ble	cos·mog'o·ny
cor'pu·lence	cor·ro'sion	cos·mol'o·gy
cor'pu·lent	cor·ro'sive	cos·mop'o·lis
cor'pus	cor'ru·gate	cos'mo·pol'i·tan
cor'pus·cle	cor'ru·gat'ed	cos·mop'o·lite
cor·pus'cu·lar	cor'ru·ga'tion	cos'mos
cor·ral'	cor·rupt'	Cos'sack
cor·rect'	cor·rupt'ed	cost
cor·rect'ed	cor·rupt'i·bil'i·ty	cos'tal
cor·rec'tion	cor·rupt'i·ble	cos'tive
cor·rec'tion·al	cor·rup'tion	cost'li·ness
cor·rec'tive	cor·rupt'ly	cost'ly
cor·rect'ly	cor·sage'	cos'tume
cor·rect'ness	cor'sair	cos·tum'er
cor·rec'tor	corse'let	co'sy
cor're·late	cor'set	cot
cor're·lat'ed	cor·tege'	co'te·rie
cor're·la'tion	cor'tex	co·ter'mi·nous
cor·rel'a·tive	cor'ti·cal	co·til'lion
cor're·spond'	co·run'dum	cot'tage

cot'ter

cot'ton

cot'ton·tail'

cot'ton·wood'

couch

cou'gar

cough

could

coun'cil

coun'ci·lor

coun'sel

coun'seled

count

count'ed

coun'te·nance

count'er

coun'ter·act'

coun'ter·at·tack'

coun'ter·bal'ance

coun'ter·blast'

coun'ter·change'

coun'ter·check'

coun'ter·claim'

coun'ter·clock'wise'

count'ered

coun'ter·feit

coun'ter·feit'er

coun'ter·foil'

coun'ter·ir'ri·tant

coun'ter·mand'

coun'ter·march'

coun'ter·mine'

coun'ter·of·fen'sive

coun'ter·pane'

coun'ter·part'

coun'ter·plot'

coun'ter·point'

coun'ter·shaft'

coun'ter·sign'

coun'ter·sink'

coun'ter·vail'

coun'ter·weight'

count'ess

count'less

coun'try

coun'try·man

coun'try·side'

coun'ty

coup

cou'pé'

cou'ple

cou'pler

cou'plet

cou'pling

cou'pon

cour'age

cou·ra'geous

cour'i·er

course

coursed

cours'er

court

court'ed

cour'te·ous

cour'te·sy

court'house'

cour'ti·er

court'li·ness

court'ly

court'-mar'tial

court'ship

court'yard'

cous'in

cove

cov'e·nant

cov'er

cov'er·age

cov'ered

cov'er·let

cov'ert

cov'et

cov'et·ed

cov'et·ous

cov'ey

cow'ard

cow'ard·ice

cow'ard·ly

cow'bell'

cow'boy'

cow'catch'er

cow'er

cowl

cow'lick'

co-work'er

cow'slip

cox'comb'

cox'swain	crane	craze
coy	craned	cra'zi·er
coy'ly	cra'ni·al	cra'zi·est
coy'ness	cra'ni·om'e·try	cra'zi·ly
coy'ote	cra'ni·ot'o·my	cra'zi·ness
coz'en	cra'ni·um	cra'zy
co'zi·er	crank	creak
co'zi·est	crank'case'	creak'ing·ly
co'zi·ly	cranked	cream
co'zi·ness	crank'i·ly	creamed
co'zy	crank'i·ness	cream'er·y
crab	crank'y	cream'i·er
crack	cran'ny	cream'i·est
cracked	crape	cream'y
crack'er	crash	crease
crack'le	crass	cre·ate'
crack'led	crass'ly	cre·at'ed
cra'dle	crass'ness	cre·a'tion
cra'dled	crate	cre·a'tive
craft	crat'ed	cre·a'tive·ly
craft'i·er	cra'ter	cre·a'tive·ness
craft'i·est	cra·vat'	cre'a·tiv'i·ty
craft'i·ly	crave	cre·a'tor
craft'i·ness	craved	crea'ture
crafts'man	cra'ven	crèche
craft'y	cra'ven·ette'	cre'dence
crag	crav'ings	cre·den'tial
cram	craw'fish'	cre·den'za
crammed	crawl	cred'i·bil'i·ty
cramp	crawled	cred'i·ble
cram'pon	cray'fish'	cred'it
cran'ber'ry	cray'on	cred'it·a·bil'i·ty

cred'it·a·ble

cred'it·ed

cred'i·tor

cre'do

cre·du'li·ty

cred'u·lous

cred'u·lous·ness

creed

creek

creel

creep

creep'er

creep'i·ness

cre'mate

cre'mat·ed

cre·ma'tion

cre'ma·to'ry

Cre·mo'na

cre'ole

cre'o·sote

crepe

crep'i·tant

crep'i·tate

crep'i·ta'tion

cre·scen'do

cres'cent

crest

crest'ed

crest'fall'en

cre'tin

cre'tin·ism

cre'tin·oid

cre'tin·ous

cre·tonne'

cre·vasse'

crev'ice

crew

crew'el

crib

crib'bage

crib'work'

crick'et

crime

crim'i·nal

crim'i·nal'i·ty

crim'i·nal·ly

crim'i·nol'o·gist

crim'i·nol'o·gy

crimp

crim'son

cringe

cringed

crin'kle

crin'kled

crin'o·line

crip'ple

crip'pled

cri'ses

cri'sis

crisp

crisp'er

crisp'est

crisp'ly

crisp'ness

criss'cross'

cri·te'ri·a

cri·te'ri·on

crit'ic

crit'i·cal

crit'i·cal·ly

crit'i·cism

crit'i·cize

crit'i·cized

cri·tique'

croak

croaked

croak'er

croak'ing·ly

croch'et

crock

crock'er·y

croc'o·dile

cro'cus

crook

crook'ed

crook'ed·ness

croon

crooned

croon'er

crop

cro·quet'

cro·quette'

cro'sier

cross

cross'bar'

cross'bow'

cross'bow'man

cross'bred'

cross'cut'

cross'hatch'

cross'ings

cross'o'ver

cross'road'

cross'walk'

cross'wise'

cross'word'

crotch'et

crouch

crouched

croup

crou'pi·er

crow

crow'bar'

crowd

crowd'ed

crown

crowned

crown'work'

cru'cial

cru'cial·ly

cru'ci·ble

cru'ci·fied

cru'ci·fix

cru'ci·fix'ion

cru'ci·form

cru'ci·fy

crude

crud'er

crud'est

cru'di·ty

cru'el

cru'el·ly

cru'el·ty

cru'et

cruise

cruis'er

crul'ler

crumb

crum'ble

crum'bled

crump

crum'pet

crum'ple

crum'pled

crunch

crup'per

cru·sade'

cru·sad'er

cruse

crush

crushed

crush'er

crush'ing·ly

crust

crust'ed

crust'i·er

crust'i·est

crust'y

crutch

crux

cry

cry'o·lite

crypt

cryp'tic

cryp'ti·cal

cryp'ti·cal·ly

cryp'to·gram

cryp'to·graph

cryp·tog'ra·phy

crys'tal

crys'tal·line

crys'tal·li·za'tion

crys'tal·lize

crys'tal·lized

crys'tal·loid

cub

cub'by·hole'

cube

cu'beb

cu'bic

cu'bi·cle

cub'ism

cu'bit

cuck'oo

cu'cum·ber

cud'dle

cud'dled

cudg'el

cudg'eled

cue

cuff

cuffed

cui·rass′	cup′board	cu′ri·ous·ly
cui·sine′	cup′cake′	curl
cu′li·nar′y	cu′pel	curled
cull	cu′pel·la′tion	curl′er
culled	cup′ful	cur′lew
cul′mi·nate	Cu′pid	curl′i·cue
cul′mi·nat′ed	cu·pid′i·ty	curl′y
cul′mi·na′tion	cu′po·la	cur·mudg′eon
cul′pa·bil′i·ty	cupped	cur′rant
cul′pa·ble	cu′pric	cur′ren·cy
cul′prit	cu′prous	cur′rent
cult	cur	cur′rent·ly
cul′ti·vate	cur′a·ble	cur·ric′u·la
cul′ti·vat′ed	cu′ra·çao′	cur·ric′u·lar
cul′ti·va′tion	cu′ra·cy	cur·ric′u·lum
cul′ti·va′tor	cu·ra′re	cur′ry
cul′tur·al	cu′rate	curse
cul′tur·al·ly	cur′a·tive	curs′ed
cul′ture	cu·ra′tor	cur′sive
cul′tured	curb	cur′so·ry
cul′vert	curbed	curt
cum′ber	curd	cur·tail′
cum′bered	cure	cur·tailed′
cum′ber·some	cured	cur′tain
cum′brous	cu·ret′tage	cur′te·sy
cum′mer·bund′	cu·rette′	curt′ly
cu′mu·la′tive	cur′few	cur′va·ture
cu′mu·lus	cu′rie	curve
cu·ne′i·form	cu′ri·o	curved
cun′ning	cu·ri·os′i·ties	cur′vi·lin′e·ar
cun′ning·ly	cu·ri·os′i·ty	cush′ion
cup	cu′ri·ous	cush′ioned

cusp

cus'pi·dor

cuss'ed·ness

cus'tard

cus·to'di·al

cus·to'di·an

cus'to·dy

cus'tom

cus'tom·ar'i·ly

cus'tom·ar'y

cus'tom·er

cut

cu·ta'ne·ous

cut'a·way'

cut'back'

cute

cu'ti·cle

cut'lass

cut'ler·y

cut'let

cut'off'

cut'out'

cut'purse'

cut'ter

cut'tings

cut'tle·fish'

cut'weed'

cut'worm

cy'a·nate

cy·an'ic

cy'a·nide

cy'a·nite

cy·an'o·gen

cy'a·no'sis

cyc'la·men

cy'cle

cy'clic

cy'cloid

cy·clom'e·ter

cy'clone

cy·clon'ic

cy'clo·pe'di·a

cy'clo·pe'dic

Cy'clops

cy'clo·ra'ma

cyg'net

cyl'in·der

cy·lin'dric

cy·lin'dri·cal

cym'bal

cyn'ic

cyn'i·cal

cyn'i·cal·ly

cyn'i·cism

cy'no·sure

cy'press

Cy·ril'lic

cyst

cys·ti'tis

cyst'oid

cys'to·lith

czar

Czech

D

dab'ble

dachs'hund'

da·coit'

dae'dal

dae'mon

daf'fo·dil

daft

dag'ger

da·guerre'o·type

dahl'ia

dai'ly

dain'ti·er

dain'ti·est

dain'ti·ly

dain'ti·ness

dain'ty

dair'y

dair'y·maid'

dair'y·man

da'is

dai'sy

dal'li·ance

dal'ly

dal·ma'tian

dam

dam'age

dam'aged

dam'a·scene'

dam'a·scened'

da·mas'cus

dam'ask

dammed

dam'na·ble

dam·na'tion

damp

damp'en

damp'ened

damp'er

damp'est

damp'ness

dam'sel

dance

danc'er

dan'de·li'on

dan'dle

dan'dled

dan'druff

dan'dy

dan'ger

dan'ger·ous

dan'ger·ous·ly

dan'gle

dan'gled

Dan'ish

dank

dap'per

dap'ple

dap'pled

dare

dared

dar'ing·ly

dark

dark'en

dark'er

dark'est

dark'ly

dark'ness
dar'ling
darned
dart
dart'ed
dash
dash'board'
dashed
dash'ing·ly
das'tard·ly
da'ta
date
dat'ed
da'tive
da'tum
daub
daubed
daugh'ter
daugh'ter-in-law'
daunt
daunt'ed
daunt'less
dau'phin
dav'en·port
dav'it
daw'dle
daw'dled
dawn
dawned
day
day'book'
day'break'

day'dream'
day'light'
day'time'
daz'zle
daz'zled
dea'con
dead
dead'en
dead'ened
dead'fall'
dead'head'
dead'light'
dead'li·ness
dead'lock
dead'ly
deaf
deaf'en
deaf'ened
deaf'en·ing·ly
deaf'er
deaf'est
deal
deal'er
deal'ings
dean
dean'er·y
dear
dear'er
dear'est
dear'ly
dear'ness
dearth

death
death'bed'
death'blow'
death'less
death'like'
death'ly
de·ba'cle
de·bar'
de·bark'
de·barred'
de·base'
de·based'
de·base'ment
de·bat'a·ble
de·bate'
de·bat'ed
de·bat'er
de·bauch'
de·bauched'
de·bauch'er·y
de·ben'ture
de·bil'i·tate
de·bil'i·tat'ed
de·bil'i·ty
deb'it
deb'it·ed
de·bris'
debt
debt'or
de·bunk'
de'but
deb'u·tante'

dec'ade

de·ca'dence

de·ca'dent

de·cal'co·ma'ni·a

de·camp'

de·cant'

de·cant'er

de·cap'i·tate

de·cap'i·ta'tion

de-car'bon·ize

de·cath'lon

de·cay'

de·cayed'

de·cease'

de·ceased'

de·ce'dent

de·ceit'

de·ceit'ful

de·ceit'ful·ness

de·ceive'

de·ceived'

de·cel'er·a'tion

De·cem'ber

de'cen·cy

de·cen'ni·al

de'cent

de'cent·ly

de·cen'tral·i·za'tion

de·cen'tral·ize

de·cep'tion

de·cep'tive

de·cep'tive·ly

de·cep'tive·ness

de·cide'

de·cid'ed·ly

de·cid'u·ous

dec'i·mal

dec'i·mate

dec'i·mat'ed

dec'i·ma'tion

de·ci'pher

de·ci'pher·a·ble

de-ci'phered

de·ci'sion

de·ci'sive

de·ci'sive·ly

de·ci'sive·ness

deck

decked

deck'house'

deck'le

de·claim'

de·claimed'

dec'la·ma'tion

de·clam'a·to'ry

dec'la·ra'tion

de-clar'a·tive

de·clar'a·to'ry

de·clare'

de·clared'

de·clen'sion

dec'li·na'tion

de·cline'

de·clined'

de·cliv'i·ty

de·coc'tion

dé·col'le·tage

dé·col'le·té

de·com'pen·sate

de·com'pen·sa'tion

de'com·pose'

de·com·posed'

de'com·po·si'tion

dec'o·rate

dec'o·rat'ed

dec'o·ra'tion

dec'o·ra'tive

dec'o·ra'tor

dec'o·rous

dec'o·rous·ly

dec'o·rous·ness

de·co'rum

de·coy'

de·crease'

de·creased'

de·creas'ing·ly

de·cree'

de·creed'

de·crep'it

de·crep'i·tude

de·cre'tal

de·cried'

de·cry'

ded'i·cate

ded'i·cat'ed

ded'i·ca'tion

ded'i·ca·to'ry

de·duce'

de·duced'

de·duc'i·ble

de·duct'

de·duct'ed

de·duct'i·ble

de·duc'tion

de·duc'tive·ly

deed

deed'ed

deem

deemed

deep

deep'en

deep'ened

deep'er

deep'est

deep'ly

deep'ness

deer

deer'hound'

deer'skin'

deer'stalk'er

deer'weed'

de·face'

de·faced'

de·fal'cate

de·fal'cat·ed

de'fal·ca'tion

def'a·ma'tion

de·fam'a·to'ry

de·fame'

de·famed'

de·fault'

de·fault'ed

de·fault'er

de·fea'si·ble

de·feat'

de·feat'ed

de·feat'ism

de·fect'

de·fec'tion

de·fec'tive

de·fec'tor

de·fend'

de·fend'ant

de·fend'ed

de·fend'er

de·fense'

de·fen'si·ble

de·fen'sive

de·fen'sive·ly

de·fen'sive·ness

de·fer'

def'er·ence

def'er·en'tial

def'er·en'tial·ly

de·fer'ment

de·fer'ral

de·ferred'

de·fi'ance

de·fi'ant

de·fi'ant·ly

de·fi'cien·cy

de·fi'cient

def'i·cit

def'i·lade'

def'i·lad'ed

de·file'

de·filed'

de·file'ment

de·fin'a·ble

de·fine'

de·fined'

def'i·nite

def'i·nite·ly

def'i·nite·ness

def'i·ni'tion

de·fin'i·tive

de·fin'i·tive·ly

de·fin'i·tive·ness

de·fin'i·tize

de·flate'

de·flat'ed

de·fla'tion

de·fla'tion·ar'y

de·flect'

de·flect'ed

de·flec'tion

de·for'est·a'tion

de·form'

de'for·ma'tion

de·formed'

de·form'i·ty

de·fraud'

de·fraud'ed

de·fray'

de·frayed'

deft

deft'ly

deft'ness

de·funct'

de·fied'

de·fy'

de·gen'er·a·cy

de·gen'er·ate

de·gen'er·at'ed

de'gen·er·a'tion

deg'ra·da'tion

de·grade'

de·grad'ed

de·grad'ing·ly

de·gree'

de·hy'drate

de·hy'drat·ed

de'i·fi·ca'tion

de'i·fied

de'i·fy

deign

deigned

de'ism

de'ist

de'i·ty

de·ject'ed

de·ject'ed·ly

de·jec'tion

de·lay'

de·layed'

de·lec'ta·bil'i·ty

de·lec'ta·ble

de'lec·ta'tion

del'e·gate

del'e·gat'ed

del'e·ga'tion

de·lete'

de·let'ed

del'e·te'ri·ous

del'e·te'ri·ous·ly

de·le'tion

delft'ware'

de·lib'er·ate

de·lib'er·at'ed

de·lib'er·a'tion

de·lib'er·a'tive

del'i·ca·cy

del'i·cate

del'i·cate·ly

del'i·ca·tes'sen

de·li'cious

de·li'cious·ly

de·light'

de·light'ed

de·light'ful

de·light'ful·ly

de·lim'it

de·lim'i·ta'tion

de·lin'e·ate

de·lin'e·at'ed

de·lin'e·a'tion

de·lin'e·a'tive

de·lin'e·a'tor

de·lin'quen·cy

de·lin'quent

del'i·quesce'

del'i·ques'cence

del'i·ques'cent

de·lir'i·ous

de·lir'i·um

de·liv'er

de·liv'er·ance

de·liv'ered

de·liv'er·er

de·liv'er·y

del·phin'i·um

del'ta

del'toid

de·lude'

de·lud'ed

del'uge

del'uged

de·lu'sion

de·lu'sive

de luxe'

delve

de·mag'net·ize

dem'a·gog'ic

dem'a·gogue

de·mand'

de·mand'ed

de·mand'ing·ly

de'mar·ca'tion

de·mean'

de·meaned'

de·mean'or

de·ment'ed

de·men'ti·a

de·mer'it

dem'i·god'

de·mil'i·ta·rize

de·mise'

de·mo'bi·li·za'tion

de·mo'bi·lize

de·mo'bi·lized

de·moc'ra·cy

dem'o·crat

dem'o·crat'ic

dem'o·crat'i·cal·ly

de·moc'ra·ti·za'tion

de·moc'ra·tize

de·mol'ish

de·mol'ished

dem'o·li'tion

de'mon

de·mon'e·ti·za'tion

de·mon'e·tize

de'mo·ni'a·cal

de·mon'stra·ble

dem'on·strate

dem'on·strat'ed

dem'on·stra'tion

de·mon'stra·tive

dem'on·stra'tor

de·mor'al·i·za'tion

de·mor'al·ize

de·mor'al·ized

de·mot'ic

de·mount'able

de·mur'

de·mure'

de·mure'ly

de·mur'rage

de·murred'

de·mur'rer

den

de·na'ture

de·na'tured

den·drol'o·gy

de·ni'al

de·nied'

den'i·grate

den'i·zen

de·nom'i·nate

de·nom'i·nat'ed

de·nom'i·na'tion

de·nom'i·na'tion·al

de·nom'i·na'tor

de'no·ta'tion

de·note'

de·not'ed

de·noue'ment

de·nounce'

de·nounced'

dense

dens'er

dens'est

den'si·ty

dent

den'tal

den·tal'gi·a

dent'ed

den'ti·frice

den'tine

den'tist

den'tist·ry

den·ti'tion

den'u·da'tion

de·nude'

de·nun'ci·a'tion

de·nun'ci·a·to'ry

de·ny'

de·o'dor·ant

de·o'dor·ize

de·o'dor·ized

de·part'

de·part'ed

de·part'ment

de'part·men'tal

de'part·men'tal·ize

de·par'ture

de·pend'

de·pend'ed

de·pend'en·cy

de·pend'ent

de·per'son·al·ize

de·pict'

de·pict'ed

de·pic'tion

de·pil'a·to'ry

de·plete'

de·plet'ed

de·ple'tion

de·plor'a·ble

de·plore'

de·plored'

de·ploy'

de·ployed'

de·ploy'ment

de·po'lar·i·za'tion

de·po'lar·ize

de·po'nent

de·pop'u·late

de·pop'u·lat'ed

de·port'

de'por·ta'tion

de·port'ed

de·port'ment

de·pose'

de·posed'

de·pos'it

de·pos'i·tar'y

de·pos'it·ed

dep'o·si'tion

de·pos'i·tor

de·pos'i·to'ry

de'pot

dep'ra·va'tion

de·prave'

de·praved'

de·prav'i·ty

dep're·cate

dep're·cat'ed

dep're·ca'tion

dep're·ca·to'ry

de·pre'ci·ate

de·pre'ci·at'ed

de·pre'ci·a'tion

dep're·da'tion

de·press'

de·pres'sant

de·pressed'

de·press'ing·ly

de·pres'sion

de·pres'sive

dep'ri·va'tion

de·prive'

de·prived'

depth

dep'u·ta'tion

de·pute'

de·put'ed

dep'u·tize

dep'u·tized

dep'u·ty

de·rail'

de·railed'

de·rail'ment

de·range'

de·ranged'

de·range'ment

der'by

der'e·lict

der'e·lic'tion

de·ride'

de·rid'ed

de·ri'sion

de·ri'sive

de·riv'a·ble

der'i·va'tion

de·riv'a·tive

de·rive'

de·rived'

der'mal

der'ma·ti'tis

der'ma·tol'o·gy

der'ma·to'sis

der'o·gate

der'o·gat'ed

der'o·ga'tion

de·rog'a·to'ry

der'rick

der'vish

des'cant

de·scend'

de·scend'ant

de·scent'

de·scribe'

de·scribed'

de·scrip'tion

de·scrip'tive

de·scry'

des'e·crate

des'e·crat'ed

des'e·cra'tion

de·sen'si·tize

de·sen'si·tiz'er

de·sert'

de·sert'ed

de·sert'er

de·ser'tion

de·serve'

de·served'

des'ic·cant

des'ic·cate

des'ic·cat·ed

des'ic·ca'tion

des'ic·ca'tive

de·sid'er·a'ta

de·sid'er·a'tum

de·sign'

des'ig·nate

des'ig·nat'ed

des'ig·na'tion

de·signed'

de·sign'ed·ly

de·sign'er

de·sir'a·bil'i·ty

de·sir'a·ble

de·sire'

de·sired'

de·sires'

de·sir'ous

de·sist'

de·sists'

desk

des'o·late

des'o·lat'ed

des'o·late·ly

des'o·la'tion

de·spair'

de·spaired'

de·spair'ing·ly

des'per·a'do

des'per·ate

des'per·ate·ly

des'per·a'tion

des'pi·ca·ble

de·spise'

de·spised'

de·spite'

de·spoil'

de·spoiled'

de·spond'en·cy

de·spond'ent

de·spond'ing·ly

des'pot

des·pot'ic

des'pot·ism

des'qua·ma'tion

des·sert'

des'ti·na'tion

des'tine

des'tined

des'ti·ny

des'ti·tute

des'ti·tu'tion

de·stroy'

de·stroyed'

de·stroy'er

de·struct'i·ble

de·struc'tion

de·struc'tive

des'ue·tude

des'ul·to'ri·ly

des'ul·to'ry

de·tach'

de·tach'a·ble

de·tached'

de·tach'ment

de·tail'

de·tailed'

de·tain'

de·tained'

de·tect'

de·tect'ed

de·tec'tion

de·tec'tive

de·tec'tor

de·ten'tion

de·ter'

de·ter'gent

de·te'ri·o·rate

de·te'ri·o·rat'ed

de·te'ri·o·ra'tion

de·ter'mi·na·ble

de·ter'mi·nant

de·ter'mi·na'tion

de·ter'mi·na'tive

de·ter'mine

de·ter'mined

de·ter'min·ism

de·terred'

de·ter'rent

de·test'

de·test'a·ble

de'tes·ta'tion

de·test'ed

de·throne'

de·throned'

det'o·nate

det'o·nat'ed

det'o·na'tion

det'o·na'tor

de·tour'

de·toured'

de·tract'

de·tract'ed

de·trac'tion

de·trac'tor

det'ri·ment

det'ri·men'tal

de·tri'tus

de·val'u·ate

de·val'u·at'ed

de·val'u·a'tion

dev'as·tate

dev'as·tat'ed

dev'as·tat'ing·ly

dev'as·ta'tion

de·vel'op

de·vel'oped

de·vel'op·ment

de·vel'op·men'tal

de'vi·ate

de'vi·at'ed

de'vi·a'tion

de·vice'

dev'il

dev'il·try

de'vi·ous

de'vi·ous·ness

de·vise'

de·vised'

de·vi'tal·ize

de·void'

de·volve'

de·volved'

de·vote'

de·vot'ed

de·vot'ed·ly

dev'o·tee'

de·vo'tion

de·vo'tion·al

de·vour'

de·voured'

de·vout'ly

dew

dew'y

dex'ter

dex·ter'i·ty

dex'ter·ous

dex'ter·ous·ly

dex'trose

di'a·be'tes

di'a·bet'ic

di'a·bol'ic

di'a·bol'i·cal

di·ac'o·nal

di'a·crit'i·cal

di'a·dem

di·aer'e·sis

di'ag·nose'

di'ag·nosed'

di'ag·no'ses

di'ag·no'sis

di'ag·nos'tic

di'ag·nos·ti'cian

di·ag'o·nal

di·ag'o·nal·ly

di'a·gram

di'al

di'a·lect

di'a·lec'tic

di'aled

di'a·logue

di·al'y·sis

di·am'e·ter

di'a·met'ric

di'a·met'ri·cal·ly

di'a·mond

di'a·pa'son

di'a·per

di·aph'a·nous

di'a·phragm

di'a·rist

di'a·ry

Di·as'po·ra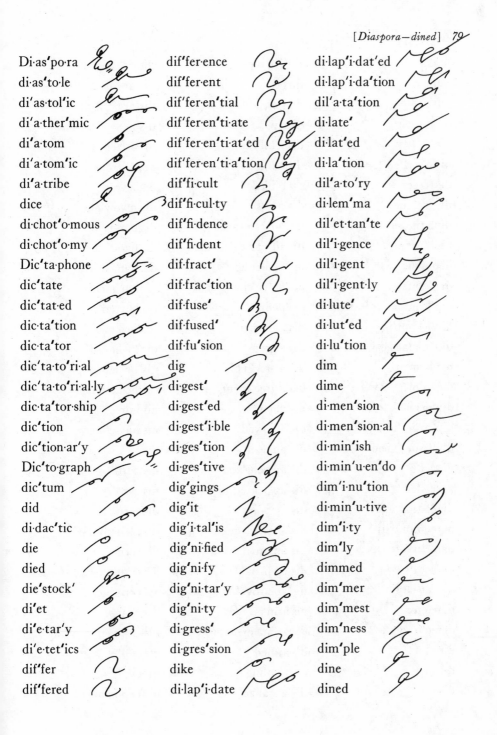

di·as'to·le

di·as·tol'ic

di'a·ther'mic

di'a·tom

di'a·tom'ic

di'a·tribe

dice

di·chot'o·mous

di·chot'o·my

Dic'ta·phone

dic'tate

dic'tat·ed

dic·ta'tion

dic·ta'tor

dic'ta·to'ri·al

dic'ta·to'ri·al·ly

dic·ta'tor·ship

dic'tion

dic'tion·ar'y

Dic'to·graph

dic'tum

did

di·dac'tic

die

died

die'stock'

di'et

di'e·tar'y

di'e·tet'ics

dif'fer

dif'fered

dif'fer·ence

dif'fer·ent

dif'fer·en'tial

dif'fer·en'ti·ate

dif'fer·en'ti·at·ed

dif'fer·en'ti·a'tion

dif'fi·cult

dif'fi·cul·ty

dif'fi·dence

dif'fi·dent

dif·fract'

dif·frac'tion

dif·fuse'

dif·fused'

dif·fu'sion

dig

di·gest'

di·gest'ed

di·gest'i·ble

di·ges'tion

di·ges'tive

dig'gings

dig'it

dig'i·tal'is

dig'ni·fied

dig'ni·fy

dig'ni·tar'y

dig'ni·ty

di·gress'

di·gres'sion

dike

di·lap'i·date

di·lap'i·dat'ed

di·lap'i·da'tion

dil'a·ta'tion

di·late'

di·lat'ed

di·la'tion

dil'a·to'ry

di·lem'ma

dil'et·tan'te

dil'i·gence

dil'i·gent

dil'i·gent·ly

di·lute'

di·lut'ed

di·lu'tion

dim

dime

di·men'sion

di·men'sion·al

di·min'ish

di·min'u·en'do

dim'i·nu'tion

di·min'u·tive

dim'i·ty

dim'ly

dimmed

dim'mer

dim'mest

dim'ness

dim'ple

dine

dined

din'er

din'gy

din'ner

di'no·saur

dint

di·oc'e·san

di'o·cese

di'o·ra'ma

diph·the'ri·a

diph'thong

di·plo'ma

di·plo'ma·cy

dip'lo·mat

dip'lo·mat'ic

dip'lo·mat'i·cal·ly

di·plo'ma·tist

di·plo'pi·a

dip'per

dip'so·ma'ni·a

dip'so·ma'ni·ac

di·rect'

di·rect'ed

di·rec'tion

di·rec'tion·al

di·rec'tive

di·rect'ly

di·rect'ness

di·rec'tor

di·rec'to·ry

dire'ful

dir'est

dirge

dir'i·gi·ble

dirt

dirt'i·ly

dirt'y

dis'a·bil'i·ty

dis·a'ble

dis·a'bled

dis·a·buse'

dis'ad·van'tage

dis·ad'van·ta'geous

dis'af·fect'ed

dis'af·fec'tion

dis'af·firm'

dis'af·firmed'

dis'a·gree'

dis'a·gree'a·ble

dis'a·gree'ment

dis'al·low'

dis'al·lowed'

dis'ap·pear'

dis'ap·pear'ance

dis'ap·peared'

dis'ap·point'

dis'ap·point'ment

dis'ap·pro·ba'tion

dis'ap·prov'al

dis'ap·prove'

dis·arm'

dis·ar'ma·ment

dis·armed'

dis·arm'ing·ly

dis'ar·range'

dis'ar·ranged'

dis'ar·ray'

dis'ar·tic'u·late

dis·as·so'ci·a'tion

dis·as'ter

dis·as'trous

dis'a·vow'

dis'a·vow'al

dis·band'

dis·band'ed

dis·bar'

dis·bar'ment

dis·barred'

dis·be·lieve'

dis·be·lieved'

dis·be·liev'er

dis·be·liev'ing·ly

dis·burse'

dis·burse'ment

disc

dis'card

dis·card'ed

dis·cern'

dis·cerned'

dis·cern'i·ble

dis·cern'ing·ly

dis·cern'ment

dis·charge'

dis·charged'

dis·ci'ple

dis·ci'ple·ship

dis'ci·pli·nar'y

dis'ci·pline

dis'ci·plined

dis·claim'

dis·claimed'

dis·close'

dis·clo'sure

dis·col'or

dis·col'or·a'tion

dis·col'ored

dis·com'fit

dis·com'fi·ture

dis·com'fort

dis'com·pose'

dis'com·posed'

dis'com·po'sure

dis'con·cert'

dis'con·nect'

dis'con·nect'ed

dis'con·so·late

dis'con·tent'

dis'con·tent'ed

dis'con·tin'u·ance

dis'con·tin'ue

dis'con·tin'ued

dis'cord

dis·cord'ance

dis·cord'ant

dis'count

dis'count·ed

dis·coun'te·nance

dis·cour'age

dis·cour'aged

dis·cour'age·ment

dis·cour'ag·ing·ly

dis·course'

dis·cour'te·ous

dis·cour'te·sy

dis·cov'er

dis·cov'ered

dis·cov'er·er

dis·cov'er·y

dis·cred'it

dis·cred'it·a·ble

dis·cred'it·ed

dis·creet'

dis·crep'an·cy

dis·crete'

dis·cre'tion

dis·cre'tion·ar'y

dis·crim'i·nate

dis·crim'i·nat'ed

dis·crim'i·na'tion

dis·crim'i·na'tive

dis·crim'i·na·to'ry

dis·cur'sive

dis'cus

dis·cuss'

dis·cuss'es

dis·dain'

dis·dained'

dis·dain'ful

dis·ease'

dis·eased'

dis·em'bar·ka'tion

dis'em·bar'rass

dis'em·bod'y

dis'en·chant'

dis'en·gage'

dis'es·tab'lish

dis'es·teem'

dis·fa'vor

dis·fea'ture

dis·fig'ure

dis·fig'ured

dis·fig'ure·ment

dis·fran'chise

dis·gorge'

dis·grace'

dis·grace'ful

dis·grun'tle

dis·guise'

dis·gust'

dis·gust'ed

dis·gust'ed·ly

dis·gust'ing·ly

dish

dis'ha·bille'

dis·har'mo·ny

dis·heart'en

di·shev'el

di·shev'eled

dis·hon'est

dis·hon'est·ly

dis·hon'or

dis·hon'or·a·ble

dis·hon'ored

dis·il·lu'sion

dis·in'cli·na'tion

dis·in·cline'

dis·in·clined'

dis'in·fect'

dis'in·fect'ant

dis'in·gen'u·ous

dis'in·her'it

dis·in'te·grate

dis·in'te·gra'tion

dis·in'ter·est·ed

dis·join'

dis·joined'

dis·join'ings

dis·joint'ed

dis·junc'tion

dis·junc'tive

disk

dis·like'

dis'lo·cate

dis'lo·cat'ed

dis'lo·ca'tion

dis·lodge'

dis·loy'al

dis·loy'al·ty

dis'mal

dis'mal·ly

dis·man'tle

dis·man'tled

dis·mast'

dis·mast'ed

dis·may'

dis·mayed'

dis·mem'ber

dis·mem'bered

dis·mem'ber·ment

dis·miss'

dis·miss'al

dis·mount'

dis·mount'ed

dis'o·be'di·ence

dis'o·be'di·ent

dis'o·bey'

dis'o·beyed'

dis'o·blige'

dis'o·blig'ing·ly

dis·or'der

dis·or'dered

dis·or'der·ly

dis·or'gan·ize

dis·or'gan·ized

dis·own'

dis·par'age

dis·par'age·ment

dis·par'ag·ing·ly

dis'pa·rate

dis'par'i·ty

dis·pas'sion·ate

dis·patch'

dis·patched'

dis·patch'er

dis·pel'

dis·pelled'

dis·pen'sa·ble

dis·pen'sa·ry

dis·pen·sa'tion

dis·pense'

dis·pensed'

dis·per'sal

dis·perse'

dis·persed'

dis·per'sion

dis·pir'it·ed

dis·place'

dis·place'ment

dis·play'

dis·please'

dis·pleas'ure

dis·port'

dis·pos'al

dis·pose'

dis·posed'

dis'po·si'tion

dis'pos·sess'

dis'pos·sessed'

dis·po'sure

dis·praise'

dis·proof'

dis'pro·por'tion

dis'pro·por'tion·ate

dis'pu·ta·ble

dis'pu·tant

dis'pu·ta'tion

dis'pu·ta'tious

dis·pute'

dis·put'ed

dis·qual'i·fi·ca'tion

dis·qual'i·fy

dis·qui'et·ed

dis·qui'e·tude

dis'qui·si'tion

dis're·gard'

dis·re·pair'

dis·rep'u·ta·ble

dis're·pute'

dis're·spect'

dis're·spect'ful

dis·robe'

dis·root'

dis·rupt'

dis·rup'tion

dis·rup'tive

dis'sat·is·fac'tion

dis·sat'is·fied

dis·sect'

dis·sect'ed

dis·sem'ble

dis·sem'i·nate

dis·sem'i·nat'ed

dis·sem'i·na'tion

dis·sen'sion

dis·sent'

dis·sent'er

dis·sen'tient

dis'ser·ta'tion

dis·serv'ice

dis'si·dence

dis'si·dent

dis·sim'i·lar

dis·sim'i·lar'i·ty

dis·sim'u·late

dis·sim'u·lat'ed

dis·sim'u·la'tion

dis'si·pate

dis'si·pat'ed

dis'si·pa'tion

dis·so'ci·ate

dis·so'ci·at'ed

dis·so'ci·a'tion

dis'so·lute

dis'so·lu'tion

dis·solv'a·ble·ness

dis·solve'

dis·solved'

dis'so·nance

dis'so·nant

dis·suade'

dis·sua'sion

dis'taff

dis'tal

dis'tance

dis'tant

dis·taste'

dis·taste'ful

dis·tem'per

dis·tend'

dis·ten'si·ble

dis·till'

dis'til·late

dis'til·la'tion

dis·tilled'

dis·till'er

dis·till'er·y

dis·tinct'

dis·tinc'tion

dis·tinc'tive

dis·tinct'ly

dis·tinct'ness

dis·tin'guish

dis·tin'guished

dis·tort'

dis·tort'ed

dis·tor'tion

dis·tract'

dis·tract'ing·ly

dis·trac'tion

dis·train'

dis·trained'

dis·traught'

dis·tress'

dis·trib'ute

dis'tri·bu'tion

dis·trib'u·tive

dis·trib'u·tor

dis'trict

dis·trust'

dis·trust'ful

dis·turb'

dis·turb'ance

dis·turbed'

dis·turb'er

dis·un'ion

dis'u·nite'	di·vine'ly	dodge
dis·use'	di·vin'i·ty	dodged
ditch	di·vis'i·bil'i·ty	do'do
ditched	di·vis'i·ble	doe
dith'y·ram'bic	di·vi'sion	doe'skin'
dit'to	di·vi'sor	doff
dit'ty	di·vorce'	dog
di·ur'nal	di·vor'cee'	dog'cart'
di'va·gate	di·vorce'ment	doge
di'van	di·vulge'	dog'ged
dive	di·vulged'	dog'ger·el
dived	diz'zi·er	dog'ma
div'er	diz'zi·est	dog·mat'ic
di·verge'	diz'zi·ly	dog'ma·tism
di·verged'	diz'zi·ness	dog'ma·tize
di·ver'gence	diz'zy	dog'trot'
di·ver'gent	do	dog'wood'
di·verg'ing·ly	doc'ile	doi'ly
di·verse'	do·cil'i·ty	do'ings
di·ver'si·fi·ca'tion	dock	dol'drums
di·ver'si·fy	dock'et	dole
di·ver'sion	dock'yard'	doled
di·ver'sion·ar·y	doc'tor	dole'ful
di·ver'si·ty	doc'tor·ate	doll
di·vert'	doc'tri·naire'	dol'lar
di·vest'	doc'tri·nal	dol'man
di·vide'	doc'trine	dol'phin
di·vid'ed	doc'u·ment	dolt
div'i·dend	doc'u·men'ta·ry	do·main'
di·vid'er	doc'u·men·ta'tion	dome
di·vine'	doc'u·ment'ed	domed
di·vined'	dod'der	do·mes'tic

do·mes'ti·cal·ly
do·mes'ti·cate
do·mes'ti·cat'ed
do'mes·tic'i·ty
dom'i·cile
dom'i·cil'i·ar'y
dom'i·nance
dom'i·nant
dom'i·nate
dom'i·nat'ed
dom'i·na'tion
dom'i·neer'
dom'i·neered'
dom'i·neer'ing·ly
dom'i·nie
do·min'ion
dom'i·no
do'nate
do'nat·ed
do·na'tion
don'a·tive
done
don'key
do'nor
doom
doomed
door
door'bell'
door'frame'
door'knob'
door'nail'
door'sill'

door'stop'
door'way'
door'yard'
dope
dor'mant
dor'mer
dor'mi·to'ry
dor'mouse'
dor'sal
do'ry
dos'age
dose
dos'si·er
dot
dot'age
do'tard
dote
dot'ing·ly
dot'ted
dou'ble
dou'bled
dou'bly
doubt
doubt'ed
doubt'ful
doubt'ful·ly
doubt'ing·ly
doubt'less
dough
dough'boy'
dough'nut'
dough'ty

dough'y
dour
dove
dove
dove'cot'
dove'tail'
dow'a·ger
dow'di·er
dow'di·est
dow'di·ly
dow'dy
dow'el
dow'eled
dow'er
down
down'cast'
down'fall'
down'heart'ed
down'hill'
down'pour'
down'right'
down'stairs'
down'town'
down'ward
down'y
dow'ry
dows'er
dox·ol'o·gy
doze
doz'en
drab
drach'ma

draft	dra'per·y	drear'i·er
draft'ed	dras'tic	drear'i·est
draft'ee'	draught	drear'i·ly
draft'i·er	draw	drear'i·ness
draft'i·est	draw'back'	drear'y
draft'i·ly	draw'bar'	dredge
draft'y	draw'bridge'	dredged
drag	draw'ee'	dreg
drag'gle	draw'er	drench
drag'gled	draw'ings	drenched
drag'net'	drawl	dress
drag'on	drawled	dressed
drag'on·fly'	drawn	dress'er
dra·goon'	draw'plate'	dress'ings
dra·gooned'	draw'string'	dress'mak'er
drain	dray	dress'y
drain'age	dray'age	drew
drained	dray'man	drib'ble
drain'er	dread	drib'bled
drake	dread'ed	dried
dra'ma	dread'ful	dri'er
dra·mat'ic	dream	dri'est
dra·mat'i·cal·ly	dreamed	drift
dra·mat'ics	dream'er	drift'wood'
dram'a·tist	dream'i·er	drill
dram'a·ti·za'tion	dream'i·est	drilled
dram'a·tize	dream'i·ly	drill'er
dram'a·tized	dream'i·ness	drink
dram'a·tur'gy	dream'land	drink'a·ble
drank	dream'less	drink'er
drape	dream'like	drip
drap'er	dream'y	drip'pings

drive

driv'el

driv'en

driv'er

drive'way'

driz'zle

driz'zled

droll

droll'er·y

drom'e·dar'y

drone

dron'ing·ly

drool

drool'ings

droop

drop

drop'out'

drop'per

drop'pings

drop'si·cal

drop'sy

dross

drought

drove

drown

drowned

drown'ings

drowse

drow'si·ly

drow'si·ness

drow'sy

drudge

drudg'er·y

drug

drug'gist

drug'store'

dru'id

dru·id'i·cal

drum

drum'head'

drummed

drum'mer

drum'stick'

drunk

drunk'ard

drunk'en

dry

dry'ly

dry'ness

du'al

du'al·ism

du'al·is'tic

du·al'i·ty

du·bi'e·ty

du'bi·ous

du'cal

duc'at

duch'ess

duch'y

duck

duck'ling

duck'pin'

duck'weed'

duct

duc'tile

duc·til'i·ty

dudg'eon

due

du'el

du'el·ist

du·en'na

du·et'

duf'fel

duff'er

dug

du'gong

dug'out'

duke

duke'dom

dul'cet

dul'ci·mer

dull

dull'ard

dull'er

dull'est

dull'ness

du'ly

dumb

dumb'bell'

dum'my

dump

dump'ing

dump'ling

dun

dunce

dune

dun'ga·ree'

dun'geon

dun'nage

dunned

dupe

du'plex

du'pli·cate

du'pli·cat'ed

du'pli·ca'tion

du'pli·ca'tor

du·plic'i·ty

du'ra·bil'i·ty

du'ra·ble

du·ral'u·min

dur'ance

du·ra'tion

du'ress

dur'ing

dusk'y

dust

dust'ed

dust'er

dust'i·er

dust'i·est

dust'y

du'te·ous

du'ties

du'ti·ful

du'ty

dwarf

dwarf'ish

dwell

dwel'lings

dwelt

dwin'dle

dwin'dled

dy·nam'ic

dy'na·mism

dy'na·mite

dy'na·mit'ed

dy'na·mo

dy'nas·ty

dys'en·ter'y

dys·func'tion

dys·pep'si·a

dys·pep'tic

dys'tro·phy

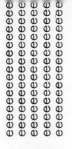

each	ear'shot'	East'er
ea'ger	earth	east'er·ly
ea'ger·ly	earth'en	east'ern
ea'ger·ness	earth'en·ware'	east'ern·er
ea'gle	earth'li·ness	east'ward
ea'glet	earth'ling	east'ward·ly
ear	earth'ly	eas'y
earl	earth'quake'	eas'y·go'ing
earl'dom	earth'ward	eat
ear'li·er	earth'work'	eat'a·ble
ear'li·est	earth'worm'	eat'en
ear'ly	ear'wax'	eat'er
ear'mark'	ear'wig'	eaves'drop'
earn	ease	ebb
earned	eased	ebbed
earn'er	ea'sel	eb'on·ize
ear'nest	ease'ment	eb'on·ized
ear'nest·ly	eas'i·er	eb'on·y
ear'nest·ness	eas'i·est	e·bul'li·ence
earn'ings	eas'i·ly	e·bul'li·ent
ear'ring'	eas'i·ness	eb'ul·li'tion
ear'rings'	east	ec·cen'tric

89

ec'cen·tric'i·ty

ec'chy·mo'sis

ec·cle'si·as'tic

ec·cle'si·as'ti·cal

ech'e·lon

ech'o

ech'oed

é·clair'

é·clat'

ec·lec'tic

ec·lec'ti·cism

e·clipse'

ec'logue

e'co·nom'ic

e'co·nom'i·cal

e'co·nom'i·cal·ly

e·con'o·mist

e·con'o·mize

econ'omized

econ'omy

ec'ru

ec'sta·sy

ec·stat'ic

ec·stat'i·cal·ly

ec'ze·ma

ed'dy

e'del·weiss

e·de'ma

edge

edged

edg'er

edge'ways'

edge'wise'

ed'i·bil'i·ty

ed'i·ble

e'dict

ed'i·fi·ca'tion

ed'i·fice

ed'i·fied

ed'i·fy

ed'it

ed'it·ed

e·di'tion

ed'i·tor

ed'i·to'ri·al

ed'i·to'ri·al·ize

ed'i·to'ri·al·ly

ed'u·ca·ble

ed'u·cate

ed'u·cat'ed

ed'u·ca'tion

ed'u·ca'tion·al

ed'u·ca'tion·al·ly

ed'u·ca'tor

e·duce'

eel

eel'pot'

eel'worm'

ee'rie

ef·face'

ef·face'ment

ef·fect'

ef·fect'ed

ef·fec'tive

ef·fec'tu·al

ef·fec'tu·al·ly

ef·fec'tu·ate

ef·fem'i·na·cy

ef·fem'i·nate

ef'fer·ent

ef'fer·vesce'

ef'fer·ves'cence

ef'fer·ves'cent

ef·fete'

ef'fi·ca'cious

ef'fi·ca·cy

ef·fi'cien·cy

ef·fi'cient

ef'fi·gies

ef'fi·gy

ef'flo·resce'

ef'flo·res'cence

ef'flo·res'cent

ef·flu'vi·a

ef·flu'vi·um

ef'flux

ef'fort

ef'fort·less

ef·fron'ter·y

ef·ful'gence

ef·ful'gent

ef·fu'sion

ef·fu'sive

ef·fu'sive·ly

ef·fu'sive·ness

e·gal'i·tar'i·an

egg'nog'

egg'plant'

egg'shell'

eg'lan·tine

e'go

e'go·cen'tric

e'go·cen·tric'i·ty

e'go·ism

e'go·is'tic

e'go·tism

e'go·tis'tic

e'go·tis'ti·cal

e·gre'gious

e'gress

e'gret

E·gyp'tian

ei'der

ei'ther

e·jac'u·late

e·jac'u·la'tion

e·ject'

e·jec'tion

e·ject'ment

e·jec'tor

e·lab'o·rate

e·lab'o·rate·ly

e·lab'o·ra'tion

e·lapse'

e·lapsed'

e·las'tic

e·las'tic'i·ty

e·lat'ed

e·la'tion

el'bow

el'bowed

el'bow·room'

eld'er

el'der·ber'ry

eld'er·ly

eld'est

e·lect'

e·lect'ed

e·lec'tion

e·lec'tion·eer'

e·lec'tive

e·lec'tor

e·lec'tor·al

e·lec'tor·ate

e·lec'tric

e·lec'tri·cal

e·lec'tri·cal·ly

e·lec'tri'cian

e·lec'tric'i·ty

e·lec'tri·fi·ca'tion

e·lec'tri·fy

e·lec'tro·cute

e·lec'tro·cu'tion

e·lec'trode

e·lec'tro·lier'

e·lec'trol'y·sis

e·lec'tro·lyt'ic

e·lec'tro·lyt'i·cal

e·lec'tro·lyze

e·lec'tro·mag'net

e·lec'trom'e·ter

e·lec'tro·mo'tive

e·lec'tron

e·lec'tron'ic

e·lec'tro·plate'

e·lec'tro·pos'i·tive

e·lec'tro·scope

e·lec'tro·type

e·lec'tro·typ'er

el'ee·mos'y·nar'y

el'e·gance

el'e·gant

el'e·gy

el'e·ment

el'e·men'tal

el'e·men'tal·ly

el'e·men'ta·ry

el'e·phant

el'e·phan·ti'a·sis

el'e·phan'tine

el'e·vate

el'e·vat'ed

el'e·va'tion

el'e·va'tor

elf'in

e·lic'it

e·lic'it·ed

e·lide'

el'i·gi·bil'i·ty

el'i·gi·ble

e·lim'i·nate

e·lim'i·nat'ed

e·lim′i·na′tion	e·lu′so·ry	em·bez′zle·ment
e·lim′i·na′tive	e·ma′ci·ate	em·bez′zler
e·li′sion	e·ma′ci·at′ed	em·bit′ter
e·lite′	e·ma′ci·a′tion	em·bit′tered
e·lix′ir	em′a·nate	em·bla′zon
E·liz′a·be′than	em′a·nat′ed	em′blem
elk	e·man′ci·pate	em′blem·at′ic
el·lip′sis	e·man′ci·pat′ed	em′blem·at′i·cal
el·lips′oid	e·man′ci·pa′tion	em·bod′ied
el·lip′tic	e·man′ci·pa′tor	em·bod′i·ment
el·lip′ti·cal	e·mas′cu·late	em·bod′y
elm	e·mas′cu·la′tion	em·bold′en
el′o·cu′tion	em·balm′	em·bold′ened
el′o·cu′tion·ist	em·balmed′	em′bo·lism
e·lon′gate	em·balm′er	em′bo·lus
e·lon′gat·ed	em·bank′ment	em·boss′
e·lon′ga′tion	em·bar′go	em·bossed′
e·lope′	em·bar′goed	em·brace′
e·lope′ment	em·bark′	em·braced′
el′o·quence	em′bar·ka′tion	em·bra′sure
el′o·quent	em·bar′rass	em′bro·cate
el′o·quent·ly	em·bar′rassed	em′bro·ca′tion
else	em·bar′rass·ment	em·broi′der
else′where	em′bas·sy	em·broi′dered
else′wise	em·bat′tle	em·broi′der·y
e·lu′ci·date	em·bat′tled	em·broil′
e·lu′ci·dat′ed	em·bel′lish	em·broiled′
e·lu′ci·da′tion	em·bel′lished	em′bry·o
e·lude′	em·bel′lish·ment	em′bry·ol′o·gy
e·lud′ed	em′ber	em′bry·on′ic
e·lu′sive	em·bez′zle	e·mend′
e·lu′sive·ness	em·bez′zled	e′men·da′tion

e·mend'ed

em'er·ald

e·merge'

e·merged'

e·mer'gence

e·mer'gen·cy

e·mer'gent

e·mer'i·tus

em'er·y

e·met'ic

em'i·grant

em'i·grate

em'i·grat·ed

em'i·gra'tion

em'i·nence

em'i·nent

em'is·sar'y

e·mis'sion

e·mit'

e·mit'ted

e·mol'li·ent

e·mol'u·ment

e·mo'tion

e·mo'tion·al

e·mo'tion·al·ly

em·pan'el

em'per·or

em'pha·ses

em'pha·sis

em'pha·size

em'pha·sized

em·phat'ic

em·phat'i·cal·ly

em'pire

em·pir'ic

em·pir'i·cal

em·pir'i·cism

em·place'ment

em·ploy'

em·ployed'

em·ploy'ee

em·ploy'er

em·ploy'ment

em·po'ri·um

em·pow'er

em·pow'ered

em'press

emp'tied

emp'ti·ly

emp'ti·ness

emp'ty

em·py·re'an

e'mu

em'u·late

em'u·lat'ed

em'u·lates

em'u·la'tion

em'u·la'tive

em'u·la·to'ry

em'u·lous

e·mul'si·fi·ca'tion

e·mul'si·fi'er

e·mul'si·fy

e·mul'sion

en·a'ble

en·a'bled

en·act'

en·act'ed

en·act'ment

en·am'el

en·am'eled

en·am'ored

en·camp'

en·camp'ment

en·cap'su·late

en·caus'tic

en'ce·phal'ic

en·ceph'a·li'tis

en·chant'

en·chant'ed

en·chant'ing·ly

en·chant'ment

en·cir'cle

en·cir'cled

en·cir'cle·ment

en'clave

en·close'

en·closed'

en·clo'sure

en·co'mi·a

en·co'mi·as'tic

en·co'mi·um

en·com'pass

en·core'

en·coun'ter

en·coun'tered

en·cour'age

en·cour'aged

en·cour'age·ment

en·cour'ag·ing·ly

en·croach'

en·croached'

en·croach'ment

en·cum'ber

en·cum'bered

en·cum'brance

en·cy'cli·cal

en·cy'clo·pe'di·a

en·cy'clo·pe'dic

en·cyst'

en·cyst'ed

end

en·dan'ger

en·dan'gered

en·dear'

en·deared'

en·deav'or

en·deav'ored

end'ed

en·dem'ic

end'ings

en'dive

end'less

end'less·ly

end'long'

en'do·crine

en'do·cri·nol'o·gy

en'do·derm

en·dog'e·nous

en·dorse'

en·dorse'ment

en·dow'

en·dowed'

en·dow'ment

en·due'

en·dued'

en·dur'a·ble

en·dur'ance

en·dure'

en·dured'

en·dur'ing·ly

end'ways

end'wise

en'e·my

en'er·get'ic

en'er·gize

en'er·gized

en'er·vate

en'er·va'tion

en·fee'ble

en·fee'bled

en'fi·lade'

en·fold'

en·force'

en·force'a·ble

en·forced'

en·force'ment

en·forc'er

en·fran'chise

en·fran'chised

en·gage'

en·gaged'

en·gage'ment

en·gag'ing·ly

en·gen'der

en·gen'dered

en'gine

en'gi·neer'

Eng'lish

Eng'lish·man

en·gorge'

en·gorge'ment

en·grain'

en·grained'

en·grave'

en·graved'

en·grav'er

en·gross'

en·grossed'

en·gross'er

en·gulf'

en·hance'

en·hanced'

en·hance'ment

en·har·mon'ic

e·nig'ma

e'nig·mat'ic

e'nig·mat'i·cal

en·join'

en·joined'

en·joy'

en·joy'a·ble

en·joyed'

en·joy'ment

en·large'

en·larged'

en·large'ment

en·larg'er

en·light'en

en·light'ened

en·light'en·ing·ly

en·light'en·ment

en·list'

en·list'ed

en·list'ment

en·liv'en

en·liv'ened

en·mesh'

en'mi·ty

en·no'ble

en·no'bled

e·nor'mi·ty

e·nor'mous

e·nough'

en·rage'

en·raged'

en·rap'ture

en·rap'tured

en·rich'

en·riched'

en·rich'ment

en·roll'

en·rolled'

en·roll'ment

en·shrine'

en·shrined'

en'sign

en'si·lage

en·slave'

en·slave'ment

en·sue'

en·sued'

en·sure'

en·sured'

en·tab'la·ture

en·tail'

en·tailed'

en·tan'gle

en·tan'gled

en·tan'gle·ment

en'ter

en'tered

en'ter·i'tis

en'ter·prise

en'ter·tain'

en'ter·tained'

en'ter·tain'er

en'ter·tain'ing·ly

en'ter·tain'ment

en·thrall'

en·thralled'

en·throne'

en·throned'

en·thu'si·asm

en·thu'si·ast

en·thu'si·as'tic

en·thu'si·as'ti·cal·ly

en·tice'

en·ticed'

en·tice'ment

en·tic'ing·ly

en·tire'

en·tire'ly

en·tire'ty

en·ti'tle

en·ti'tled

en'ti·ty

en·tomb'

en·tombed'

en·tomb'ment

en'to·mol'o·gist

en'to·mol'o·gy

en'trails

en'trance

en·tranc'ing·ly

en'trant

en·trap'

en·treat'

en·treat'ed

en·treat'y

en·trench'

en·trust'

en'try

en'try·way'

en·twine'

e·nu'cle·ate

e·nu'cle·a'tion

e·nu'mer·ate

e·nu'mer·at'ed

e·nu'mer·a'tion

e·nu'mer·a'tor

e·nun'ci·ate

e·nun'ci·at'ed

e·nun'ci·a'tion

e·nun'ci·a'tor

en·vel'op

en've·lope

en·ven'om

en'vi·a·ble

en'vi·ous

en·vi'ron·ment

en·vi'ron·men'tal

en·vi'ron·men'tal·ly

en·vi'rons

en·vis'age

en·vis'aged

en'voy

en'voys

en'vy

en'zyme

e'on

e·phem'er·al

ep'ic

ep'i·cure

ep'i·cu·re'an

ep'i·dem'ic

ep'i·der'mal

ep'i·der'mic

ep'i·der'mis

ep'i·der'moid

ep'i·gas'tric

ep'i·glot'tis

ep'i·gram

ep'i·gram·mat'ic

ep'i·graph

ep'i·lep'sy

ep'i·lep'tic

ep'i·lep'toid

ep'i·logue

e·piph'y·sis

e·pis'co·pa·cy

e·pis'co·pal

e·pis'co·pa'li·an

e·pis'co·pate

ep'i·sode

ep'i·sod'ic

e·pis'te·mol'o·gy

e·pis'tle

e·pis'to·lar'y

e·pis'to·la·to'ry

ep'i·taph

ep'i·tha·la'mi·um

ep'i·the'li·um

ep'i·thet

e·pit'o·me

e·pit'o·mize

ep'i·zo·ot'ic

ep'och

ep'och·al

ep'o·nym

ep·ox'y

eq'ua·ble

eq'ua·bly

e'qual

e'qualed

e·qual'i·tar'i·an

e·qual'i·ty

e'qual·i·za'tion

e'qual·ize

e'qual·ized

e'qual·iz'er

e'qual·ly

e'qua·nim'i·ty

e·quate'

e·quat'ed

e·qua'tion

e·qua'tor

e'qua·to'ri·al

eq'uer·ry

e·ques'tri·an

e·ques'tri·enne'

e'qui·an'gu·lar

e'qui·dis'tance

e'qui·dis'tant

e'qui·lat'er·al

e'qui·lib'ri·um

e'quine

e'qui·noc'tial

e'qui·nox

e·quip'

eq'ui·page

e·quip'ment

e'qui·poise

eq'ui·ta·ble

eq'ui·ta'tion

eq'ui·ty

e·quiv'a·lence

e·quiv'a·len·cy

e·quiv'a·lent

e·quiv'o·cal

e·quiv'o·cal·ly

e·quiv'o·cate

e·quiv'o·ca'tion

e'ra

e·rad'i·cate

e·rad'i·cat'ed

e·rad'i·ca'tion

e·rase'

e·rased'

e·ras'er

e·ra'sure

e·rect'

e·rect'ed

e·rec'tile

e·rec'tion

e·rect'ness

erg

er'go

er'got

er'mine

e·rode'

e·ro'sion

e·rot'ic

err

er'rand

er·ra'ta

er·rat'ic

er·rat'i·cal·ly

er·ra'tum

erred

er·ro'ne·ous

er'ror

erst'while'

er'u·dite

er'u·di'tion

e·rupt'

e·rup'tion

e·rup'tive

er'y·sip'e·las

es'ca·lade'

es'ca·la'tor

es'ca·pade'

es·cape'

es·cape'ment

es·cap'ist

es·carp'ment

es·cheat'

es·chew'

es'cort

es·cort'ed

es'cri·toire'

es·crow'

es·cutch'eon

Es'ki·mo

e·soph'a·gus

es'o·ter'ic

es·par'to

es·pe'cial

es·pe'cial·ly

Es'pe·ran'to

es'pi·o·nage

es'pla·nade'

es·pous'al

es·pouse'

es'prit'

es·py'

es·quire'

es·say'

es·sayed'

es'say·ist

es'sence

es·sen'tial

es·sen'tial·ly

es·tab'lish

es·tab'lished

es·tab'lish·ment

es·tate'

es·teem'

es·teemed'

es'ter

es·thet'ic

es'ti·ma·ble

es'ti·mate

es'ti·mat'ed

es'ti·ma'tion

es'ti·ma'tor

es'ti·vate

es·top'pel

es·trange'

es·tranged'

es·trange'ment

es'tu·ar'y

e·su'ri·ent

etch

etch'er

etch'ings

e·ter'nal

e·ter'nal·ly

e·ter'ni·ty

eth'ane

e'ther

e·the're·al

e·the're·al·ly

eth'i·cal

eth'i·cal·ly

eth'ics

eth·nol'o·gy

eth'yl

e'ti·ol'o·gy

et'i·quette

e'tude

et'y·mo·log'i·cal

et'y·mol'o·gy

eu'ca·lyp'tus

Eu'cha·rist

eu'chre

Eu·clid'e·an

eu·gen'ics

eu'lo·gis'tic

eu'lo·gize

eu'lo·gy

eu'phe·mism

eu'phe·mis'tic

eu·pho'ni·ous

eu·pho'ny

Eur·a'sian

eu·re'ka

Eu'ro·pe'an

Eu·sta'chi·an

eu·tec'tic

eu·tha·na'si·a

e·vac'u·ate

e·vac'u·at'ed

e·vac'u·a'tion

e·vade'

e·vad'ed

e·val'u·ate

e·val'u·a'tion

ev'a·nesce'

ev'a·nes'cence

ev'a·nes'cent

e·van·gel'i·cal

e·van'ge·list

e·vap'o·rate

e·vap'o·rat'ed

e·vap'o·ra'tion

e·vap'o·ra'tor

e·va'sion

e·va'sive

e·va'sive·ly

e·va'sive·ness

e'ven

eve'ning

eve'nings

e'ven·ly

e'ven·ness

e·vent'

e·vent'ful

e·vent'ful·ly

e·ven'tu·al

e·ven'tu·al'i·ty

e·ven'tu·al·ly

e·ven'tu·ate

ev'er

ev'er·glade

ev'er·green'

ev'er·last'ing

ev'er·last'ing·ly

ev'er·y

ev'er·y·bod'y

ev'er·y·day'

ev'er·y·one'

ev'er·y·thing'

ev'er·y·where'

e·vict'

e·vict'ed

e·vic'tion

ev'i·dence

ev'i·dent

ev'i·den'tial

ev'i·den'tial·ly

e'vil

e'vil·ly

e·vince'

e·vinced'

e·vis'cer·ate

ev'o·ca'tion

e·voc'a·tive

e·voke'

e·voked'

ev'o·lu'tion

ev'o·lu'tion·ar'y

ev'o·lu'tion·ist

e·volve'

ewe

ew'er

ex·ac'er·bate

ex·ac'er·ba'tion

ex·act'

ex·act'ed

ex·ac'tion

ex·act'i·tude

ex·act'ly

ex·act'ness

ex·ag'ger·ate

ex·ag'ger·at'ed

ex·ag'ger·a'tion

ex·alt'

ex'al·ta'tion

ex·alt'ed

ex·a'men

ex·am'i·na'tion

ex·am'ine

ex·am'ined

ex·am'in·er

ex·am'ple

ex·as'per·ate

ex·as'per·at'ed

ex·as'per·a'tion

ex'ca·vate

ex'ca·vat'ed

ex'ca·va'tion

ex'ca·va'tor

ex·ceed'

ex·ceed'ed

ex·ceed'ing·ly

ex·cel'

ex·celled'

ex'cel·lence

ex'cel·len·cy

ex'cel·lent

ex·cel'si·or

ex·cept'

ex·cept'ed

ex·cep'tion

ex·cep'tion·al

ex·cep'tion·al·ly

ex·cerpt'

ex·cess'

ex·cess'es

ex·ces'sive

ex·ces'sive·ly

ex·change'

ex·change'a·ble

ex·cheq'uer

ex·cip'i·ent

ex'cise

ex·ci'sion

ex·cit'a·bil'i·ty

ex·cit'a·ble

ex·cit'ant

ex'ci·ta'tion

ex·cite'

ex·cit'ed·ly

ex·cite'ment

ex·claim'

ex·claimed'

ex'cla·ma'tion

ex·clam'a·to'ry

ex·clude'

ex·clud'ed

ex·clu'sion

ex·clu'sive

ex'com·mu'ni·cate

ex'com·mu'ni·ca'tion

ex·co'ri·ate

ex·co'ri·at'ed

ex·co'ri·a'tion

ex·cres'cence

ex·cres'cent

ex·crete'

ex·cret'ed

ex·cre'tion

ex'cre·to'ry

ex·cru'ci·ate

ex·cru'ci·at'ing·ly

ex·cru'ci·a'tion

ex'cul·pate

ex'cul·pat'ed

ex'cul·pa'tion

ex·cur'sion

ex·cus'a·ble

ex·cuse'

ex·cused'

ex·cus'es

ex'e·cra·ble

ex'e·crate

ex'e·crat'ed

ex'e·cra'tion

ex·ec'u·tant

ex'e·cute

ex'e·cut'ed

ex'e·cu'tion

ex'e·cu'tion·er

ex·ec'u·tive

ex·ec'u·tor

ex·ec'u·trix

ex'e·ge'sis

ex·em'plar

ex·em'pla·ry

ex·em'pli·fi·ca'tion

ex·em'pli·fy

ex·empt'

ex·empt'ed

ex·emp'tion

ex'e·qua'tur

ex'er·cise

ex'er·cised

ex'er·cis'er

ex·ert'

ex·ert'ed

ex·er'tion

ex'ha·la'tion

ex·hale'

ex·haled'

ex·haust'

ex·haus'tion

ex·haus'tive

ex·haust'less

ex·hib'it

ex·hib'it·ed

ex'hi·bi'tion

ex·hib'i·tor

ex·hil'a·rate

ex·hil'a·rat'ed

ex·hil'a·ra'tion

ex·hort'

ex'hor·ta'tion

ex·hort'ed

ex·hu·ma'tion

ex·hume'

ex·humed'

ex'i·gen·cy

ex'i·gent

ex·ig'u·ous

ex'ile

ex'iled

ex·ist'

ex·ist'ed

ex·ist'ence

ex·ist'ent

ex'it

ex'o·dus

ex·on'er·ate

ex·on'er·at'ed

ex·on'er·a'tion

ex·or'bi·tant

ex·or'bi·tant·ly

ex'or·cise

ex'or·cised

ex'or·cism

ex·or'di·um

ex'o·ter'ic

ex·ot'ic

ex·ot'i·cism

ex·pand'

ex·pand'ed

ex·panse'

ex·pan'sion

ex·pan'sive

ex·pa'ti·ate

ex·pa'ti·at'ed

ex·pa'tri·ate

ex·pa'tri·a'tion

ex·pect'

ex·pect'an·cy

ex·pect'ant

ex'pec·ta'tion

ex·pect'ed

ex·pec'to·rant

ex·pec'to·rate

ex·pec'to·ra'tion

ex·pe'di·en·cy

ex·pe'di·ent

ex'pe·dite

ex'pe·dit'ed

ex'pe·di'tion

ex'pe·di'tion·ar'y

ex'pe·di'tious

ex'pe·di'tious·ly

ex·pel'

ex·pelled'

ex·pend'

ex·pend'ed

ex·pend'i·ture

ex·pense'

ex·pen'sive·ly

ex·pe'ri·ence

ex·pe'ri·enced

ex·pe'ri·enc·es

ex·per'i·ment

ex·per'i·men'tal

ex·per'i·men'tal·ly

ex·per'i·men·ta'tion

ex·per'i·ment·er

ex·pert'

ex·pert'ly

ex·pert'ness

ex'per'tise'

ex'pi·ate

ex'pi·a'tion

ex'pi·ra'tion

ex·pire'

ex·pired'

ex·plain'

ex·plained'

ex'pla·na'tion

ex·plan'a·to'ry

ex'ple·tive

ex'pli·ca·ble

ex'pli·cate

ex·plic'it

ex·plic'it·ly

ex·plode'

ex·plod'ed

ex'ploit

ex'ploi·ta'tion

ex·ploit'ed

ex'plo·ra'tion

ex·plor'a·to'ry

ex·plore'

ex·plored'

ex·plor'er

ex·plor'ing·ly

ex·plo'sion

ex·plo'sive

ex·po'nent

ex'po·nen'tial

ex·port'

ex'por·ta'tion

ex·pose'

ex·posed'

ex'po·si'tion

ex·pos'i·to'ry

ex·pos'tu·late

ex·pos'tu·lat'ed

ex·pos'tu·la'tion

ex·po'sure

ex·pound'

ex·press'

ex·pres'sion

ex·pres'sive

ex·pres'sive·ly

ex·press'ly

ex·press'man

ex·pro'pri·ate

ex·pro'pri·a'tion

ex·pul'sion

ex·punge'

ex·punged'

ex'pur·gate

ex'pur·gat'ed

ex'pur·ga'tion

ex'qui·site

ex'tant

ex·tem'po·ra'ne·ous

ex·tem'po·rar'y

ex·tem'po·re

ex·tem'po·ri·za'tion

ex·tem'po·rize

ex·tend'

ex·tend'ed

ex·ten'si·ble

ex·ten'sion

ex·ten'sive

ex·tent'

ex·ten'u·ate

ex·ten'u·at'ed

ex·ten'u·a'tion

ex·te'ri·or

ex·ter'mi·nate

ex·ter'mi·nat'ed

ex·ter'mi·na'tion

ex·ter'mi·na'tor

ex·ter'nal

ex·ter'nal·i·za'tion

ex·ter'nal·ly

ex·tinct'

ex·tinc'tion

ex·tin'guish

ex·tin'guished

ex·tin'guish·er

ex'tir·pate

ex'tir·pat'ed

ex'tir·pa'tion

ex·tol'

ex·tolled'

ex·tort'

ex·tort'ed

ex·tor'tion

ex·tor'tion·ate

ex'tra

ex·tract'

ex·tract'ed

ex·trac'tion

ex·trac'tive

ex'tra·cur-
ric'u·lar

ex'tra·dite

ex'tra·dit'ed

ex'tra·di'tion

ex·tra'ne·ous

ex·traor'di·nar'i·ly

ex·traor'di·nar'y

ex·trap'o·late

ex'tra·ter'ri·to'ri·al'i·ty

ex·trav'a·gance

ex·trav'a·gant

ex·trav'a·gan'za

ex·trav'a·sate

ex·trav'a·sa'tion

ex·treme'

ex·trem'ist

ex·trem'i·ty

ex'tri·cate

ex'tri·cat'ed

ex'tri·ca'tion

ex·trin'sic

ex'tro·ver'sion

ex'tro·vert'

ex·trude'

ex·trud'ed

ex·tru'sion

ex·u'ber·ance

ex·u'ber·ant

ex'u·date

ex'u·da'tion

ex·ude'

ex·ud'ed

ex·ult'

ex·ult'ant

ex'ul·ta'tion

ex·ult'ed

ex·ult'ing·ly

eye

eye'ball'

eye'brow'

eye'cup'

eyed

eye'lash'

eye'let

eye'lid'

eye'piece'

eyes

eye'shot'

eye'sight'

eye'strain'

eye'tooth'

eye'wash'

eye'wit'ness

F

Fa'bi·an
fa'ble
fa'bled
fab'ric
fab'ri·cate
fab'ri·cat'ed
fab'ri·ca'tion
fab'u·lous
fa·çade'
face
faced
fac'et
fa·ce'tious
fa'cial
fac'ile
fa·cil'i·tate
fa·cil'i·tat'ed
fa·cil'i·ty
fac'ings
fac·sim'i·le
fact
fac'tion

fac'tion·al
fac'tious
fac·ti'tious
fac'tor
fac'to·ry
fac·to'tum
fac'tu·al
fac'tu·al·ly
fac'ul·ta'tive
fac'ul·ty
fad'dist
fade
fad'ed
fad'ing·ly
Fahr'en·heit
fail
failed
fail'ing·ly
fail'ings
faille
fail'ure
faint

faint'ed
faint'heart'ed
faint'ly
faint'ness
fair
fair'er
fair'est
fair'ly
fair'ness
fair'way'
fair'y
fair'y·land'
faith
faith'ful
faith'less
faith'less·ly
fake
fak'er
fal'con
fall
fal·la'cious
fal'la·cy

fall'en

fal'li·bil'i·ty

fal'li·ble

fal'low

false

false'hood

false'ly

false'ness

fal·set'to

fal'si·fi·ca'tion

fal'si·fi'er

fal'si·fy

fal'si·ty

fal'ter

fal'tered

fal'ter·ing·ly

fame

famed

fa·mil'ial

fa·mil'iar

fa·mil'i·ar'i·ty

fa·mil'iar·ize

fa·mil'iar·ly

fam'i·lies

fam'i·ly

fam'ine

fam'ish

fa'mous

fa'mous·ly

fan

fa·nat'ic

fa·nat'i·cal

fa·nat'i·cism

fan'cied

fan'ci·er

fan'ci·est

fan'ci·ful

fan'cy

fan'fare

fang

fanged

fan'light'

fanned

fan'tail'

fan·ta'sia

fan·tas'tic

fan'ta·sy

far

far'ad

farce

far'cial

far'ci·cal

far'cy

fare

fared

fare'well'

far'fetched'

fa·ri'na

far'i·na'ceous

farm

farmed

farm'er

farm'house'

farm'yard'

far'o

far'ri·er

far'see'ing

far'sight'ed

far'ther

far'thest

far'thing

fas'ci·nate

fas'ci·nat'ed

fas'ci·na'tion

fas'ci·nat'ing·ly

fas'ci·na'tor

fas'cism

fas'cist

fash'ion

fash'ion·a·ble

fash'ioned

fast

fas'ten

fas'tened

fas'ten·ings

fast'er

fast'est

fas·tid'i·ous

fast'ness

fat

fa'tal

fa'tal·ism

fa'tal·ist

fa'tal·is'tic

fa'tal'i·ty

fa'tal·ly

fate

fat'ed

fate'ful

fa'ther

fa'thered

fa'ther·hood

fa'ther-in-law'

fa'ther·land'

fa'ther·less

fa'ther·li·ness

fa'ther·ly

fath'om

fath'omed

fath'om·less

fa·tigue'

fat'ness

fat'ten

fat'tened

fat'ter

fat'test

fat'ty

fa·tu'i·ty

fat'u·ous

fau'cet

fault

fault'i·ly

fault'less

fault'less·ly

fault'y

fau'na

fa'vor

fa'vor·a·ble

fa'vored

fa'vor·ite

fa'vor·it·ism

fawn

fawned

fe'al·ty

fear

feared

fear'ful

fear'less

fear'less·ly

fear'some

fea'si·bil'i·ty

fea'si·ble

feast

feat

feath'er

feath'ered

feath'er·edge'

feath'er·weight'

feath'er·y

fea'ture

fea'tured

fe'brile

Feb'ru·ar'y

fe'cund

fe'cun·date

fe·cun'di·ty

fed'er·al

fed'er·al·ism

fed'er·al·ist

fed'er·al·i·za'tion

fed'er·al·ize

fed'er·al·ized

fed'er·ate

fed'er·at'ed

fed'er·a'tion

fed'er·a'tive

fe·do'ra

fee

fee'ble

fee'ble·ness

fee'blest

fee'bly

feed

feed'-back'

feed'ings

feel

feel'er

feel'ing·ly

feel'ings

feer

feered

feet

feign

feigned

feint

feld'spar'

fe·lic'i·tate

fe·lic'i·tat'ed

fe·lic'i·ta'tion

fe·lic'i·tous

fe·lic'i·tous·ly

fe·lic'i·ty

fe'line	fe·roc'i·ty	fet'id
fel'low	fer'ret	fe'tish
fel'low·ship	fer'ret·ed	fe'tish·ism
fel'on	fer'ric	fet'lock
fe·lo'ni·ous	fer'ro·chrome	fet'ter
fel'o·ny	fer'ro·type	fet'tered
felt	fer'rous	fet'tle
fe·luc'ca	fer'rule	feud
fe'male	fer'ry	feu'dal
fem'i·nine	fer'ry·boat'	feu'dal·ism
fem'i·nin'i·ty	fer'tile	feu'da·to'ry
fem'i·nism	fer·til'i·ty	fe'ver
fem'i·nist	fer'ti·li·za'tion	fe'ver·ish
fem'o·ral	fer'ti·lize	fe'ver·ish·ly
fe'mur	fer'ti·lized	few
fen	fer'ti·liz'er	few'er
fence	fer'ule	few'est
fenc'er	fer'vent	fez
fend	fer'vent·ly	fi·as'co
fend'ed	fer'vid	fi'at
fend'er	fer'vid·ly	fib
fe·nes'trat·ed	fer'vor	fi'ber
fen·es·tra'tion	fes'cue	fi'broid
Fe'ni·an	fes'tal	fib'u·la
fen'nel	fes'ter	fick'le
fe'ral	fes'tered	fic'tion
fer·ment'	fes'ti·val	fic'tion·al
fer'men·ta'tion	fes'tive	fic·ti'tious
fer·ment'ed	fes·tiv'i·ty	fid'dle
fern	fes·toon'	fid'dled
fe·ro'cious	fes·tooned'	fid'dler
fe·ro'cious·ly	fetch	fi·del'i·ty

fidg'et

fi·du'ci·ar'y

fief

field

field'ed

field'piece'

fiend

fiend'ish

fiend'ish·ly

fierce

fierce'ness

fierc'er

fierc'est

fi'er·y

fife

fig

fight

fig'ment

fig'u·ra'tion

fig'ur·a·tive

fig'ur·a·tive·ly

fig'ure

fig'ured

fig'ure·head'

fig'u·rine'

fil'a·ment

fil'a·ri'a·sis

fil'a·ture

fil'bert

filch

filched

file

filed

fil'i·al

fil'i·bus'ter

fil'i·gree

fil'ings

fill

filled

fill'er

fil'let

fill'ings

film

filmed

film'y

fil'ter

fil'tered

filth

filth'i·er

filth'i·est

filth'i·ness

filth'y

fil'trate

fil·tra'tion

fin

fi'nal

fi'nal·ist

fi·nal'i·ty

fi'nal·ly

fi·nance'

fi·nan'cial

fi·nan'cial·ly

fin'an·cier'

finch

find

find'er

find'ings

fine

fined

fine'ly

fine'ness

fin'er

fin'er·y

fine'spun'

fi·nesse'

fin'est

fin'ger

fin'gered

fin'ger·print'

fin'i·al

fi'nis

fin'ish

fin'ished

fin'ish·er

fi'nite

fiord

fir

fire

fire'arm'

fire'boat'

fire'box'

fire'brand'

fire'break'

fire'brick'

fired

fire'fly'

fire'man

fire'place'

fire'proof'

fire'side'

fire'weed'

fire'wood'

fire'works'

fir'kin

firm

fir'ma·ment

firm'er

firm'est

firm'ly

firm'ness

first

first'ly

firth

fis'cal

fish

fish'er·man

fish'er·y

fish'hook'

fish'wife'

fish'y

fis'sile

fis'sion

fis'sure

fist

fist'ic

fist'i·cuffs

fis'tu·la

fit

fit'ful

fit'ful·ly

fit'ness

fit'ted

fit'ter

fit'ting·ly

fit'tings

fix

fix·a'tion

fix'a·tive

fixed

fix'er

fix'ings

fix'i·ty

fix'ture

fiz'zle

fiz'zled

flab'bi·er

flab'bi·est

flab'bi·ness

flab'by

flac'cid

flag

flag'el·lant

flag'el·late

flag'el·la'tion

flag'eo·let'

flag'eo·lets'

fla·gi'tious

flag'on

flag'pole'

fla'grance

fla'grant

fla'grant·ly

flag'ship'

flag'staff'

flag'stone'

flail

flailed

flair

flake

flak'i·ness

flak'y

flam'beau

flam·boy'ant

flame

flamed

fla·men'co

flame'proof'

flam'ing·ly

fla·min'go

flan

flange

flanged

flank

flanked

flan'nel

flan'nel·ette'

flap

flap'jack'

flare

flare'back'

flared

flash

flash'board'	flaunt'ed	fleur'-de-lis'
flash'er	flaunt'ing·ly	flew
flash'i·ly	flau'tist	flex
flash'i·ness	fla'vor	flexed
flash'ing·ly	fla'vored	flex'i·bil'i·ty
flash'light'	fla'vor·ings	flex'i·ble
flash'y	fla'vors	flex'ure
flask	flaw	flick
flat	flawed	flicked
flat'-bed'	flax	flick'er
flat'boat'	flax'en	flick'er·ing·ly
flat'fish'	flax'seed'	fli'er
flat'-foot'ed	flay	flight
flat'head'	flea	flight'i·ness
flat'i'ron	flea'bite'	flight'y
flat'ly	fleck	flim'si·er
flat'ness	fledge	flim'si·est
flat'ten	fledg'ling	flim'si·ly
flat'tened	flee	flim'si·ness
flat'ter	fleece	flim'sy
flat'tered	fleeced	flinch
flat'ter·er	fleec'i·ness	flinched
flat'ter·ing·ly	fleec'y	flinch'ing·ly
flat'ter·y	fleet	fling
flat'test	fleet'ing·ly	flint
flat'u·lence	Flem'ish	flint'i·ness
flat'u·lent	flesh	flint'lock'
flat'ware'	flesh'i·ness	flint'y
flat'wise'	flesh'ings	flip'pan·cy
flat'work'	flesh'pot'	flip'pant
flat'worm'	flesh'y	flip'pant·ly
flaunt	Fletch'er·ism	flip'per

flirt

flir·ta'tion

flir·ta'tious

flirt'ed

flit

flitch

fliv'ver

float

float'ed

float'er

floc'cu·lence

floc'cu·lent

flock

floe

flog

flogged

flog'gings

flood

flood'ed

flood'gate'

flood'light'

flood'wa'ter

floor

floor'walk'er

flop'pi·ness

flop'py

flo'ral

Flor'en·tine

flo'ret

flo'ri·cul'ture

flor'id

flo·rid'i·ty

flor'id·ly

flor'in

flo'rist

floss

floss'i·er

floss'i·est

floss'y

flo·ta'tion

flo·til'la

flot'sam

flounce

floun'der

floun'dered

floun'der·ing·ly

flour

flour'ish

flour'ish·ing·ly

flour'y

flout

flout'ed

flow

flowed

flow'er

flow'ered

flow'er·i·ness

flow'er·pot'

flow'er·y

flow'ing·ly

flown

fluc'tu·ate

fluc'tu·at'ed

fluc'tu·a'tion

flue

flu'en·cy

flu'ent

flu'ent·ly

fluff

fluff'i·ness

fluff'y

flu'id

flu'id·ly

flu'id·ex'tract

flu·id'i·ty

fluke

flume

flung

flunk

flunked

flunk'y

flu'o·res'cence

flu'o·res'cent

flu·or'ic

flu'o·ri·date

flu'o·ri·da'tion

flu'o·ride

flu'o·ri·nate

flu'o·rine

flu'o·ro·scope

flu'or·os'co·py

flur'ry

flush

flushed

flus'ter

flus'tered

flute

flut'ed

flut'ings

flut'ist

flut'ter

flut'tered

flut'ter·ing·ly

flut'ter·y

flux

flux'ion

fly

fly'er

fly'leaf'

fly'trap'

fly'wheel'

foal

foaled

foam

foamed

foam'i·er

foam'i·est

foam'i·ness

foam'y

fob

fobbed

fo'cal

fo'cal·i·za'tion

fo'cal·ize

fo'cal·ized

fo'cus

fo'cused

fod'der

foe

foe'man

fog

fog'gi·er

fog'gi·est

fog'gy

fog'horn'

foi'ble

foil

foiled

foist

foist'ed

fold

fold'ed

fold'er

fo'li·age

fo'li·ate

fo'li·a'tion

fo'li·o

folk

folk'way'

fol'li·cle

fol·lic'u·lar

fol'low

fol'lowed

fol'low·er

fol'ly

fo·ment'

fo'men·ta'tion

fo·ment'ed

fond

fon'dant

fond'er

fond'est

fon'dle

fon'dled

fond'ly

fond'ness

fon·due'

font

food

fool

fooled

fool'har'di·ness

fool'har'dy

fool'ish

fool'ish·ly

fool'ish·ness

fool'proof'

fools'cap'

foot

foot'age

foot'ball'

foot'board'

foot'bridge'

foot'ed

foot'fall'

foot'gear'

foot'hill'

foot'hold'

foot'ings

foot'less

foot'lights'

foot'-loose'

foot'man	for'ci·ble	fore'mast'
foot'mark'	ford	fore'most
foot'note'	ford'ed	fore'name'
foot'pace'	fore'arm'	fore'noon'
foot'pad'	fore'bear	fo·ren'sic
foot'path'	fore·bode'	fore'or·dain'
foot'print'	fore·bod'ing·ly	fore'or·dained'
foot'rest'	fore·bod'ings	fore'quar'ter
foot'sore'	fore·bore'	fore·run'ner
foot'step'	fore-cast'	fore·saw'
foot'stool'	fore'cas·tle	fore·see'
foot'wear'	fore·close'	fore·see'ing·ly
foot'work'	fore·closed'	fore·shad'ow
foot'worn'	fore·clo'sure	fore·shore'
foo'zle	fore'deck'	fore·short'en
foo'zled	fore·doom'	fore'sight'
fop'per·y	fore·doomed'	fore'sight'ed·ness
fop'pish	fore·fa'ther	for'est
for	fore'fin'ger	fore·stall'
for'age	fore'foot'	fore·stalled'
fo·ra'men	fore'front'	for'est·a'tion
for'as·much'	fore·gone'	for'est·ed
for'ay	fore'ground'	for'est·er
for·bear'	fore'hand'ed	for'est·ry
for·bear'ance	fore'head	fore·taste'
for·bid'	for'eign	fore·tell'
for·bid'den	for'eign·er	fore'thought'
for·bid'ding·ly	for'eign·ism	fore·told'
force	fore·knowl'edge	for·ev'er
force'ful	fore'leg'	fore·warn'
force'meat'	fore'lock'	fore·warned'
for'ceps	fore'man	fore'wom'an

fore'word'

for'feit

for'feit·ed

for'fei·ture

for·gath'er

for·gave'

forge

forged

for'ger

for'ger·y

for·get'

for·get'ful

for·get'ful·ly

for·get'ful·ness

for·give'

for·giv'en

for·give'ness

for·giv'ing·ly

for·go'

for·got'

for·got'ten

fork

forked

for·lorn'

form

for'mal

form·al'de·hyde

for'mal·ism

for·mal'i·ty

for'mal·i·za'tion

for'mal·ize

for'mal·ly

for'mat

for·ma'tion

form'a·tive

formed

form'er

for'mer·ly

for'mic

for'mi·da·ble

form'less

for'mu·la

for'mu·lar'y

for'mu·late

for'mu·lat'ed

for'mu·la'tion

for·sake'

for·sak'en

for·sook'

for·sooth'

for·swear'

for·syth'i·a

fort

for'ta·lice

forte

for'te

forth

forth'com'ing

forth'right'

forth'right'ness

forth'with'

for'ti·fi·ca'tion

for'ti·fy

for·tis'si·mo

for'ti·tude

fort'night

fort'night·ly

for'tress

for·tu'i·tous

for·tu'i·ty

for'tu·nate

for'tune

for'tune·tell'er

fo'rum

for'ward

for'ward·ed

for'ward·er

for'ward·ness

fos'sil

fos'sil·if'er·ous

fos'sil·i·za'tion

fos'sil·ize

fos'sil·ized

fos'ter

fos'tered

fought

foul

fou·lard'

foul'er

foul'est

foul'ly

foul'ness

found

foun·da'tion

found'ed

found'er

found'ling

found'lings

found'ry

fount

foun'tain

foun'tain·head'

four'some

four'square'

fourth

fowl

fox

foxes

fox'glove'

fox'i·er

fox'i·est

fox'y

fra'cas

frac'tion

frac'tion·al

frac'tion·al·ly

frac'tion·ate

frac'tion·a'tion

frac'tious

frac'ture

frac'tured

frag'ile

frag'ile·ly

fra·gil'i·ty

frag'ment

frag'men·tar'i·ly

frag'men·tar'y

frag'men·ta'tion

frag'ment·ed

fra'grance

fra'grant

fra'grant·ly

frail

frail'er

frail'est

frail'ty

frame

framed

frame'work'

franc

fran'chise

Fran·cis'can

frank

frank'er

frank'est

frank'furt·er

frank'ly

frank'ness

fran'tic

frap'pé'

fra·ter'nal

fra·ter'nal·ly

fra·ter'ni·ty

frat'er·ni·za'tion

frat'er·nize

frat'er·nized

frat'ri·cid'al

frat'ri·cide

fraud

fraud'u·lent

fraught

fray

fraz'zle

fraz'zled

freak

freak'ish

freck'le

freck'led

free

free'board'

free'born'

free'dom

free'hand'

free'hold'

free'ly

free'man

free'ma'son

free'ma'son·ry

fre'er

fre'est

free'stone'

free'think'er

free'wheel'ing

freeze

freez'er

freight

freight'er

French

fren'zied

fren'zy

fre'quen·cy

fre'quent

fre'quent·ly

fres'co

fresh

fresh'en

fresh'en·er

fresh'er

fresh'est

fresh'ly

fresh'man

fresh'ness

fret

fret'ful

fret'ted

fret'work'

fri'a·bil'i·ty

fri'a·ble

fri'ar

fric'as·see'

fric'tion

fric'tion·al

Fri'day

fried

friend

friend'less

friend'li·er

friend'li·est

friend'li·ness

friend'ly

friend'ship

frieze

frig'ate

fright

fright'en

fright'ened

fright'en·ing·ly

fright'ful

fright'ful·ly

fright'ful·ness

frig'id

Frig'id·aire'

fri·gid'i·ty

frig'id·ly

frill

frilled

frill'i·ness

frill'y

fringe

fringed

frip'per·y

frisk

frit'ter

frit'tered

fri·vol'i·ty

friv'o·lous

friv'o·lous·ly

friz'zi·ness

friz'zle

friz'zled

frock

frog

frog'fish'

frol'ic

frol'icked

from

frond

frond'ed

front

front'age

fron'tal

front'ed

fron·tier'

fron'tis·piece

frost

frost'bite'

frost'ed

frost'fish'

frost'i·er

frost'i·est

frost'i·ly

frost'i·ness

frost'work'

frost'y

froth

frothed

froth'y

fro'ward

frown

frowned

frown'ing·ly

frowz'i·ly

frowz'y

froze

fro'zen

fruc·tif'er·ous

fruc'ti·fy

fru'gal

fru·gal′i·ty

fru′gal·ly

fruit

fruit′er·er

fruit′ful

fruit′ful·ly

fruit′i·ness

fru·i′tion

fruit′less

fruit′less·ly

fruit′less·ness

fruit′worm′

fruit′y

frump

frus′trate

frus·tra′tion

fry

fry′er

fuch′sia

fud′dle

fud′dled

fudge

fu′el

fu′eled

fu·ga′cious

fu′gi·tive

fugue

ful′crum

ful·fill′

ful·filled′

ful·fill′ment

full

full′er

full′est

full′ness

ful′ly

ful′mi·nate

ful′mi·nat′ed

ful′mi·na′tion

ful′some

fum′ble

fum′bling

fume

fumed

fu′mi·gate

fu′mi·gat′ed

fu′mi·ga′tion

fu′mi·ga′tor

fun

func′tion

func′tion·al

func′tion·al·ly

func′tion·ar′y

fund

fun′da·men′tal

fun′da·men′tal·ly

fund′ed

fu′ner·al

fu·ne′re·al

fu·ne′re·al·ly

fun′gi

fun′gi·ble

fun′gi·cide

fun′goid

fun′gus

fu·nic′u·lar

fun′nel

fun′ni·er

fun′ni·est

fun′ny

fur

fur′be·low

fur′bish

fu′ri·ous

fu′ri·ous·ly

furl

furled

fur′long

fur′lough

fur′loughed

fur′nace

fur′nish

fur′nished

fur′nish·ings

fur′ni·ture

fu′ror

fur′ri·er

fur′ri·est

fur′row

fur′rowed

fur′ry

fur′ther

fur′ther·ance

fur′ther·more′

fur′thest

fur′tive

fur'tive·ly

fu'run·cle

fu'ry

furze

fuse

fused

fu'sel

fu'se·lage

fus'es

fu'si·bil'i·ty

fu'si·ble

fu'sil·lade'

fu'sion

fuss

fussed

fuss'i·er

fuss'y

fus'tian

fu'tile

fu'tile·ly

fu·til'i·ty

fu'ture

fu'tur·is'tic

fu·tu'ri·ty

fuzz

fuzz'i·ly

fuzz'i·ness

G

gab'ar·dine'
ga'ble
gad'fly'
gad'o·lin'i·um
ga·droon'
gaff
gag
gage
gagged
gag'gle
gai'e·ty
gai'ly
gain
gained
gain'er
gain'ful
gain'ful·ly
gain'say'
gait'ed
gai'ter
ga'la
gal'an·tine

gal'ax·y
gale
ga·le'na
gall
gal'lant
gal'lant·ry
galled
gal'ler·y
gal'ley
Gal'lic
gall'ing·ly
gal'li·um
gal'lon
gal'lop
gal'lows
gall'stone'
ga·lore'
gal'va·nism
gal'va·ni·za'tion
gal'va·nize
gal'va·nized
gal'va·nom'e·ter

gam'bit
gam'ble
gam'bled
gam'bler
gam·boge'
gam'bol
gam'brel
game
game'ness
gam'mon
gam'ut
gan'der
gang
ganged
gan'gli·a
gan'gli·on
gang'plank'
gan'grene
gan'gre·nous
gang'ster
gang'way'
gan'try

gap	gashed	gay'ly
gaped	gas'house'	gay'ness
ga·rage'	gas'ket	gaze
garb	gas'o·line	ga·ze'bo
gar'bage	gasp	ga·zelle'
gar'ble	gas'tight'	ga·zette'
gar'den	gas·tral'gi·a	ga·zet'ted
gar'den·er	gas'tric	gaz'et·teer'
gar·de'ni·a	gas·tri'tis	gear
gar'gle	gas'tro·nom'ic	geared
gar'goyle	gas·tron'o·my	gear'shift'
gar'ish	gate	gei'sha
gar'land	gate'house'	gel'a·tin
gar'lic	gate'post'	ge·lat'i·nize
gar'ment	gate'way'	ge·lat'i·noid
gar'ner	gath'er	ge·lat'i·nous
gar'nered	gath'ered	gem
gar'net	gath'er·er	gen'der
gar'nish	gau'che·rie'	gen'e·a·log'i·cal
gar'nished	gaud'i·er	gen'e·al'o·gist
gar'nish·ee'	gaud'i·est	gen'e·al'o·gy
gar'nish·er	gaud'y	gen'er·al
gar'nish·ment	gauge	gen'er·al·is'si·mo
gar'ni·ture	gauged	gen'er·al·ist
gar'ret	gaunt'let	gen'er·al'i·ty
gar'ri·son	gauze	gen'er·al·i·za'tion
gar'ri·soned	gave	gen'er·al·ize
gar'ru·lous	gav'el	gen'er·al·ized
gar'ter	ga·votte'	gen'er·al·ly
gas	gawk'y	gen'er·al·ship'
gas'e·ous	gay	gen'er·ate
gash	gay'e·ty	gen'er·at'ed

gen'er·a'tion

gen'er·a'tive

gen'er·a'tor

ge·ner'ic

gen'er·os'i·ty

gen'er·ous

gen'er·ous·ly

gen'e·sis

ge·net'ics

ge·ni'al

ge'ni·al'i·ty

gen'ial·ly

gen'i·tive

gen'ius

gen·teel'

gen·teel'ly

gen'tian

gen'tile

gen·til'i·ty

gen'tle

gen'tle·man

gen'tle·men

gen'tle·ness

gen'tler

gen'tlest

gen'tly

gen'try

gen'u·flect

gen'u·flec'tion

gen'u·ine

gen'u·ine·ly

gen'u·ine·ness

ge'nus

ge·od'e·sy

ge'o·det'ic

ge·og'ra·pher

ge·og'ra·phy

ge'o·log'i·cal

ge·ol'o·gist

ge·ol'o·gy

ge'o·met'ric

ge'o·met'ri·cal

ge·om'e·try

ge·ra'ni·um

ge'rent

ger'i·a·tri'cian

ger'i·at'rics

germ

Ger'man

ger·mane'

ger'mi·cide

ger'mi·nal

ger'mi·nant

ger'mi·nate

ger'mi·nat'ed

ger'mi·na'tion

ger'mi·na'tive

ger'und

ge·run'di·al

ge·run'dive

ges'so

Ge·stalt'

ges·tic'u·late

ges·tic'u·la'tion

ges'ture

ges'tured

get

gew'gaw

gey'ser

ghast'li·ness

ghast'ly

gher'kin

ghet'to

ghost

ghost'li·ness

ghost'ly

ghoul

gi'ant

gi'ant·ism

gib'ber

gib'ber·ish

gib'bet

gib'bon

gibe

gib'let

gid'di·ly

gid'di·ness

gid'dy

gift

gift'ed

gig

gi·gan'tic

gi·gan'ti·cal·ly

gi·gan'tism

gig'gle

gig'gled

gild	gla'cier	gleam
gild'ed	glad	gleamed
gild'er	glad'den	glean
gill	glad'dened	glean'er
gill	glade	glean'ings
gilt	glad'i·a'tor	glee'ful
gim'bals	glad'i·a·to'ri·al	glib
gim'crack'	glad'i·o'lus	glib'ly
gim'let	glad'ly	glide
gin	glad'ness	glid'ed
gin'ger	Glad'stone	glid'er
gin'ger·ly	glam'or·ous	glim'mer
ging'ham	glam'our	glim'mered
gin'gi·vi'tis	glance	glim'mer·ings
gi·raffe'	gland	glimpse
gir'an·dole	glan'dered	glimpsed
gird	glan'ders	glint
gird'er	glan'du·lar	glint'ed
gir'dle	glare	gli·o'ma
gir'dled	glared	glis·san'do
gir'dler	glar'ing·ly	glis'ten
girl	glass	glis'tened
girl'hood	glass'ful	glis'ter
girl'ish	glass'house'	glit'ter
girt	glass'i·ly	glit'tered
girth	glass'i·ness	gloat
gist	glass'ware'	gloat'ed
give	glass'y	glob'al
giv'en	glau·co'ma	glob'al·ly
giv'er	glaze	globe
giz'zard	glazed	glob'u·lar
gla'cial	gla'zier	glob'ule

glock'en·spiel'

gloom

gloom'i·ly

gloom'i·ness

glo'ri·fi·ca'tion

glo'ri·fy

glo'ri·ous

glo'ry

gloss

glos'sal

glos'sa·ry

gloss'i·ly

gloss'i·ness

glos·si'tis

gloss'y

glot'tis

glove

glov'er

glow

glowed

glow'er

glow'ered

glow'ing·ly

glow'worm'

glu·ci'num

glu'cose

glue

glued

glue'y

glum

glut

glut'ted

glut'ton

glut'ton·ize

glut'ton·ous

glut'ton·y

glyc'er·in

gnarl

gnarled

gnash

gnashed

gnat

gnath'ic

gnaw

gnawed

gnaw'ings

gneiss

gnome

gno'mic

gno'mon

gnu

go

goad

goal

goat

goat'fish'

goat'herd'

goat'skin'

goat'weed'

gob'ble

gob'bled

gob'let

gob'lin

go'cart'

god

god'child'

god'dess

god'fa'ther

god'head

god'hood

god'less

god'like'

god'li·ness

god'ly

god'moth'er

god'par'ent

god'send'

god'son'

gog'gle

go'ings

goi'ter

gold

gold'en

gold'en·rod'

gold'finch'

gold'smith'

gold'weed'

golf

golf'er

gon'do·la

gon'do·lier'

gone

gong

goo'ber

good

good'-by'

good'ly

good'-na'tured

good'ness

goose

goose'ber'ry

goose'neck'

go'pher

Gor'di·an

gore

gored

gorge

gorged

gor'geous

gor'get

gor'gon

go·ril'la

gos'hawk'

gos'ling

gos'pel

gos'sa·mer

gos'sip

got

Goth'ic

got'ten

gouache

gouge

gouged

gou'lash

gourd

gour'mand

gour'met

gout

gov'ern

gov'ern·ance

gov'erned

gov'ern·ess

gov'ern·ment

gov'ern·men'tal

gov'er·nor

gown

grab

grabbed

grace

grace'ful

grace'less

gra'cious

gra'cious·ly

grack'le

gra·da'tion

grade

grad'ed

gra'di·ent

grad'u·al

grad'u·al·ly

grad'u·ate

grad'u·at'ed

grad'u·a'tion

graft

graft'ed

graft'er

grail

grain

grained

grain'field'

gram'mar

gram·mar'i·an

gram·mat'i·cal

gram·mat'i·cal·ly

gram'pus

gran'a·ry

grand

grand'child'

gran·dee'

gran'deur

grand'fa'ther

gran·dil'o·quence

gran·dil'o·quent

gran'di·ose

grand'ly

grand'moth'er

grand'ness

grand'par'ent

grand'sire'

grand'son'

grand'stand'

grange

gran'ite

gran'it·oid

gra·niv'o·rous

grant

grant'ed

gran'u·lar

gran'u·late

gran'u·lat'ed

gran'u·la'tion

gran'ule

grape	grav'en	greed
grape'shot'	grav'er	greed'i·er
graph	grav'est	greed'i·est
graph'ic	grave'stone'	greed'i·ly
graph'ics	grave'yard'	greed'i·ness
graph'ite	grav'i·tate	greed'y
grap'nel	grav'i·tat'ed	Greek
grap'ple	grav'i·ta'tion	green
grap'pled	grav'i·ta'tion·al	green'back'
grasp	grav'i·ty	green'er
grasp'ing·ly	gra·vure'	green'er·y
grass	gra'vy	green'est
grass'hop'per	gray	green'horn'
grass'plot'	gray'beard'	green'house'
grate	gray'ish	green'ish
grat'ed	gray'ness	green'ness
grate'ful	graze	green'room'
grat'er	grazed	green'stick'
grat'i·fi·ca'tion	gra'zier	green'sward'
grat'i·fy	grease	green'wood'
grat'i·fy'ing·ly	greased	greet
grat'i·nate	grease'wood'	greet'ed
grat'ings	greas'i·er	greet'ings
gra'tis	greas'i·est	gre·gar'i·ous
grat'i·tude	greas'i·ly	Gre·go'ri·an
gra·tu'i·tous	greas'i·ness	gre·nade'
gra·tu'i·ty	greas'y	gren'a·dier'
gra·va'men	great	gren'a·dine'
grave	great'er	grew
grave'dig'ger	great'est	grey'hound'
grav'el	great'ly	grid
grav'el·ly	great'ness	grid'dle

grid′i′ron

grief

griev′ance

grieve

grieved

griev′ous

griev′ous·ly

grif′fin

grill

grilled

grim

gri·mace′

grime

grim′i·er

grim′i·est

grim′i·ly

grim′i·ness

grim′y

grin

grind

grind′er

grind′ing·ly

grind′stone′

grinned

grip

gripe

grip′per

gris′ly

grist

gris′tle

grist′mill′

grit

grit′ti·ness

grit′ty

griz′zle

griz′zled

griz′zly

groan

groaned

groan′ing·ly

gro′cer

gro′cer·y

grog

grog′gy

groin

grom′met

groom

groomed

groove

grooved

grope

grop′ing·ly

gros′beak′

gros′grain′

gross

gross′er

gross′est

gross′ly

gross′ness

gro·tesque′

gro·tesque′ly

grot′to

grouch

grouch′i·ly

grouch′y

ground

ground′ed

ground′less

ground′lings

ground′work′

group

group′ings

grouse

grout

grout′ed

grove

grov′el

grov′eled

grow

grow′er

growl

growled

grown

growth

grub

grubbed

grub′bi·ness

grub′by

grudge

grudg′ing·ly

gru′el

grue′some

gruff

gruff′er

gruff′est

gruff′ly

grum′ble

grum′bled

grump′i·ly

grump′i·ness

grump′y

grunt

grunt′ed

guar′an·tee′

guar′an·tor

guar′an·ty

guard

guard′ed

guard′i·an

guard′i·an·ship′

guard′room′

guards′man

gua′va

gu′ber·na·to′ri·al

gudg′eon

guer′don

guer·ril′la

guess

guess′work′

guest

guid′ance

guide

guide′book′

guid′ed

guide′line′

gui′don

guild

guile

guile′ful

guile′less

guil′lo·tine

guilt

guilt′i·er

guilt′i·est

guilt′i·ly

guilt′i·ness

guilt′y

guin′ea

guise

guis′es

gui·tar′

gulch

gul′den

gulf

gull

gul′let

gul′li·bil′i·ty

gul′li·ble

gul′ly

gulp

gum

gum′bo

gum′boil′

gummed

gum·mo′sis

gum′my

gump′tion

gum′shoe′

gum′weed′

gum′wood′

gun

gun′boat′

gun′cot′ton

gun′fire′

gun′lock′

gun′man

gun′ner

gun′ner·y

gun′ny

gun′pa′per

gun′pow′der

gun′run′ning

gun′shot′

gun′smith′

gun′stock′

gun′wale

gur′gle

gu′ru

gush

gush′er

gush′y

gus′set

gust

gus′ta·to′ry

gust′i·ly

gus′to

gust′y

gut′ter

gut′ter·snipe′

gut′tur·al

gut′tur·al·ly

guy

guz′zle

guz′zled

guz′zler

gym·kha′na

gym·na′si·um

gym′nast

gym·nas′tic

gyn′e·col′o·gist

gyn′e·col′o·gy

gyp′sum

gyp′sy

gy′rate

gy′rat·ed

gy·ra′tion

gy′ra·to′ry

gyr′fal′con

gy′ro

gy′ro·com′pass

gy′ro·scope

gy′ro·stat

gyves

hab′er·dash′er	hag′gard	half′heart′ed
hab′er·dash′er·y	hag′gle	half′tone′
ha·bil′i·ment	hag′gled	half′way′
hab′it	hail	half′-wit′ted
hab′it·a·ble	hailed	hal′i·but
hab′i·tat	hail′stone′	hal′ide
hab′i·ta′tion	hail′storm′	hal′ite
hab′it·ed	hair	hal′i·to′sis
ha·bit′u·al	hair′breadth′	hall
ha·bit′u·al·ly	hair′brush′	hall′mark′
ha·bit′u·ate	hair′cut′	hal′low
ha·bit′u·at′ed	hair′line′	hal′lowed
hab′i·tude	hair′pin′	Hal′low·een′
hack′le	hair′split′ter	hal·lu′ci·na′tion
hack′man	hair′spring′	hal·lu′ci·na·to′ry
hack′ney	hair′y	hal·lu′ci·no′sis
hack′neyed	hake	ha′lo
hack saw	ha·la′tion	hal′o·gen
had	hal′berd	halt
had′dock	hal′cy·on	halt′ed
haft	hale	hal′ter
hag	half	halt′ing·ly

halves	hand'some	hard
hal'yard	hand'spring'	hard'en
ham	hand'work'	hard'ened
ham'let	hand'writ'ing	hard'en·er
ham'mer	hand'y	hard'er
ham'mered	hang	hard'est
ham'mer·less	hang'ar	hard'fist'ed
ham'mock	hanged	hard'head'ed
ham'per	hang'er	har'di·hood
ham'pered	hang'ings	har'di·ness
ham'ster	hang'man	hard'ly
ham'string'	han'ker	hard'ness
ham'strung'	han'kered	hard'pan'
hand	han'som	hard'ship
hand'bag'	hap'haz'ard	hard'ware'
hand'ball'	hap'less	har'dy
hand'bill'	hap'loid	hare
hand'book'	hap'pen	hare'brained'
hand'cuff'	hap'pened	hare'lip'
hand'ed	hap'pen·ings	ha'rem
hand'ful	hap'pi·er	hark
hand'i·cap	hap'pi·est	har'le·quin
hand'i·capped	hap'pi·ly	har'le·quin·ade'
hand'i·craft	hap'pi·ness	harm
hand'i·er	hap'py	harmed
hand'i·est	ha·rangue'	harm'ful
hand'i·ly	ha·rangued'	harm'ful·ly
hand'i·ness	har'ass	harm'ful·ness
hand'ker·chief	har'ass·ment	harm'less
han'dle	har'bin·ger	harm'less·ly
han'dled	har'bor	harm'less·ness
hand'rail	har'bored	har·mon'ic

har·mon'i·ca	hasp	hauled
har·mo'ni·ous	has'sock	haunch
har·mo'ni·ous·ly	haste	haunt
har·mo'ni·ous·ness	has'ten	haunt'ed
har·mo'ni·um	has'tened	haunt'ing·ly
har'mo·ni·za'tion	hast'i·er	haut'boy
har'mo·nize	hast'i·est	hau·teur'
har'mo·nized	hast'i·ly	have
har'mo·ny	hast'i·ness	ha'ven
har'ness	hast'y	hav'er·sack
har'nessed	hat	hav'oc
harp	hat'band'	Ha·wai'ian
harp'er	hatch	hawk
harp'ist	hatched	hawk'er
har·poon'	hatch'er·y	hawk'weed'
har·pooned'	hatch'et	hawse
harp'si·chord	hatch'ment	haw'ser
har'ri·er	hatch'way'	haw'thorn
har'row	hate	hay
harsh	hat'ed	hay'cock'
harsh'er	hate'ful	hay'fork'
harsh'est	hate'ful·ly	hay'loft'
harsh'ly	hate'ful·ness	hay'mow'
harsh'ness	hat'pin'	hay'rack'
har'te·beest'	ha'tred	hay'seed'
har'vest	hat'ter	hay'stack'
har'vest·ed	haugh'ti·er	haz'ard
har'vest·er	haugh'ti·est	haz'ard·ed
has	haugh'ti·ly	haz'ard·ous
hash	haugh'ty	haz'ard·ous·ly
hashed	haul	haze
hash'ish	haul'age	ha'zel

ha′zel·nut′

ha′zi·er

ha′zi·est

ha′zi·ly

ha′zi·ness

ha′zy

he

head

head′ache′

head′band′

head′board′

head′cheese′

head′dress′

head′ed

head′er

head′first′

head′fore′most

head′gear′

head′i·ly

head′ings

head′land′

head′less

head′light′

head′line′

head′lock′

head′long

head′mas′ter

head′phone′

head′piece′

head′quar′ters

heads′man

head′spring′

head′stone′

head′strong

head′wa′ter

head′way′

head′work′

head′y

heal

healed

heal′er

health

health′ful

health′ful·ness

health′i·er

health′i·est

health′i·ly

health′y

heap

heaped

hear

heard

hear′er

hear′ings

hark′en

hark′ened

hear′say′

hearse

heart

heart′ache′

heart′beat′

heart′break′

heart′bro′ken

heart′burn′

heart′en

heart′ened

heart′felt′

hearth

hearth′stone′

heart′i·er

heart′i·est

heart′i·ly

heart′less

heart′sick′

heart′sore′

heart′string′

heart′wood′

heart′y

heat

heat′ed

heat′er

heath

hea′then

hea′then·ish

hea′then·ish·ly

heath′er

heat′stroke′

heave

heav′en

heav′en·ly

heav′en·ward

heav′i·er

heav′i·est

heav′i·ly

heav′i·ness

heav′y

He·bra'ic

He'brew

hec'a·tomb

heck'le

heck'led

heck'ler

hec'tic

hec'to·graph

hedge

hedged

hedge'hog'

hedge'row'

he'don·ism

heed

heed'ed

heed'ful·ly

heed'ful·ness

heed'less

heed'less·ness

heel

heft

he·gem'o·ny

he·gi'ra

heif'er

height

height'en

height'ened

hei'nous

heir

heir'ess

heir'loom'

hel'i·cal

hel'i·coid

hel'i·cop'ter

he'li·o·trope

he'li·um

he'lix

helm

hel'met

hel'met·ed

helms'man

help

help'er

help'ful

help'ful·ly

help'ful·ness

help'ing

help'less

help'less·ly

help'less·ness

help'mate'

hem

hem'a·tite

hem'i·cy'cle

hem'i·ple'gi·a

hem'i·sphere

hem'i·spher'i·cal

hem'lock

hemmed

hem'or·rhage

hemp

hemp'en

hem'stitch'

hem'stitched'

hence

hence'forth'

hence'for'ward

hench'man

hen'e·quen

hen'na

he·pat'ic

he·pat'i·ca

hep'a·ti'tis

hep'ta·gon

hep·tam'e·ter

her

her'ald

her'ald·ed

he·ral'dic

her'ald·ry

herb

her·ba'ceous

herb'age

herb'al

her·bar'i·um

her'bi·cide

her·biv'o·rous

Her·cu'le·an

herd

herd'ed

here

here'a·bouts'

here·aft'er

here·by'

he·red'i·ta·bil'i·ty

he·red'i·ta·ble

he·red'i·ta·bly

her'e·dit'a·ment

he·red'i·tar'y

he·red'i·ty

here'in·aft'er

here·in·be·fore'

here·on'

her'e·sy

her'e·tic

he·ret'i·cal

here·to'

here'to·fore'

here'un·to'

here'up·on'

here·with'

her'it·a·bil'i·ty

her'it·a·ble

her'it·a·bly

her'it·age

her·met'ic

her·met'i·cal·ly

her'mit

her'mit·age

her'ni·a

he'ro

he·ro'ic

he·ro'i·cal

her'o·ine

her'o·ism

her'on

her'pes

her'pe·tol'o·gy

her'ring

her'ring·bone'

hers

her·self'

hes'i·tance

hes'i·tan·cy

hes'i·tant

hes'i·tate

hes'i·tat'ed

hes'i·tat'ing·ly

hes'i·ta'tion

hes'i·ta'tive·ly

het'er·o·dox

het'er·o·ge·ne'i·ty

het'er·o·ge'ne·ous

het'er·o·nym'

heu·ris'tic

hew

hewed

hew'er

hewn

hex'a·gon

hex·ag'o·nal

hex·am'e·ter

hex·an'gu·lar

hex'a·pod

hey'day'

hi·a'tus

hi'ber·nate

hi'ber·na'tion

hi·bis'cus

hick'o·ry

hid

hid'den

hide

hide'bound'

hid'e·ous

hid'e·ous·ly

hid'e·ous·ness

hi'er·arch'y

hi'er·at'ic

hi'er·o·glyph'ic

high

high'born'

high'boy'

high'er

high'est

high'land

high'land·er

high'ly

high'ness

high'road'

high'way'

high'way'man

hike

hiked

hik'er

hi·lar'i·ous

hi·lar'i·ty

hill

hill'i·er

hill'i·est

hill'i·ness

hill'ock

hill'side'

hilt

him

him·self'

hind

hin'der

hin'dered

hin'drance

hinge

hinged

hint

hint'ed

hin'ter·land'

hip'po·drome

hip'po·pot'a·mus

hire

hired

hire'ling

hir'sute

his

hiss

his·tol'o·gist

his·tol'o·gy

his·to'ri·an

his·tor'ic

his·tor'i·cal

his'to·ry

his'tri·on'ic

hit

hitch

hitched

hitch'hike'

hith'er

hith'er·to'

hive

hoar

hoard

hoard'ed

hoard'er

hoar'frost'

hoarse

hoars'er

hoars'est

hoax

hob'ble

hob'bled

hob'by

hob'gob'lin

hob'nail'

hob'nailed'

hob'nob'

ho'bo

hock

hock'ey

hod

hoe

hog

hog'back'

hog'fish'

hog'gish

hogs'head

hog'weed'

hoist

hoist'ed

hoist'way'

ho'kum

hold

hold'er

hold'ings

hole

hol'i·day

ho'li·ly

ho'li·ness

Hol'land

hol'low

hol'lowed

hol'ly

hol'ly·hock

hol'o·caust

hol'o·graph

hol'o·graph'ic

hol'ster

ho'ly

ho'ly·stone'

hom'age

home

home'land'

home'like'

home'li·ness

home'ly

ho'me·o·path'ic

ho'me·op'a·thy

home'sick'ness

home'site'

home'spun'

home'stead

home'ward

home'work'

hom'i·cid'al

hom'i·cide

hom'i·let'ics

hom'i·lies

hom'i·ly

hom'i·ny

ho'mo·ge·ne'i·ty

ho'mo·ge'ne·ous

ho'mo·ge'ne·ous·ly

ho·mog'e·nize

ho·mol'o·gous

hom'o·nym

ho·mun'cu·lus

hone

honed

hon'est

hon'est·ly

hon'es·ty

hon'ey

hon'ey·bee'

hon'ey·comb'

hon'ey·dew'

hon'eyed

hon'ey·moon'

hon'ey·suck'le

honk

hon'or

hon'or·a·ble

hon'or·a·bly

hon'o·rar'i·um

hon'or·ar'y

hon'ored

hood

hood'ed

hood'lum

hoo'doo

hood'wink

hoof

hook

hooked

hook'er

hook'worm'

hoop

Hoo'sier

hope

hope'ful

hope'ful·ly

hope'ful·ness

hope'less

hope'less·ly

hope'less·ness

hop'lite

hop'per

hop'scotch'

horde

hore'hound'

ho·ri'zon

hor'i·zon'tal

hor'mone

horn

horn'book'

horned

hor'net

horn'pipe'

ho·rol'o·gy

hor'o·scope

hor·ren'dous

hor'ri·ble

hor'rid

hor'ri·fi·ca'tion

hor'ri·fied

hor'ri·fy

hor'ror

horse

horse'back'

horse chest'nut

horse'hair'

horse'man

horse'man·ship

horse'pow'er

horse'shoe'

horse'weed'

horse'whip'

horse'wom'an

hor'ta·tive

hor'ta·to'ry

hor'ti·cul'ture

hose

ho'sier

ho'sier·y

hos'pice

hos'pi·ta·ble

hos'pi·tal

hos'pi·tal'i·ty

hos'pi·tal·i·za'tion

hos'pi·tal·ize

host

hos'tage

hos'tel

host'ess

hos'tile

hos'tile·ly

hos·til'i·ty

hot

hot'bed'

hot'box'

ho·tel'

hot'head'ed

hot'house'

hot'ly

hot'ness

hot'ter

hot'test

hound

hound'ed

hour

hour'ly

house

housed

house'fly'

house'fur'nish·ings

house'hold

house'hold'er

house'keep'er

house'maid'

house'man

house'moth'er

house'room'

house'wares'

house'warm'ing

house'wife'

house'work'

hov'el

hov'er

hov'ered

hov'er·ing·ly

how

how·ev'er

how'itz·er

howl

how'so·ev'er

hoy'den

hub

hub'bub

huck'le·ber'ry

huck'ster

hud'dle

hud'dled

hue

huff

hug

huge

hug'er

hug'est

Hu'gue·not

hulk

hull

hulled

hum

hu'man

hu·mane'

hu·mane'ly

hu·mane'ness

hu'man·ism

hu'man·ist

hu'man·is'tic

hu·man'i·tar'i·an

hu·man'i·tar'i·an·ism

hu·man'i·ty

hu'man·i·za'tion

hu'man·ize

hu'man·ized

hu'man·kind'

hu'man·ly

hum'ble

hum'bled

hum'ble·ness

hum'bler

hum'blest

hum'bly

hum'bug'

hum'drum'

hu'mer·us

hu'mid

hu·mid'i·fi·ca'tion

hu·mid'i·fied

hu·mid'i·fi'er

hu·mid'i·fy

hu·mid'i·ty

hu'mi·dor

hu·mil′i·ate	hurl	hy′drant
hu·mil′i·at′ed	hurled	hy′drate
hu·mil′i·a′tion	hur′ri·cane	hy·drau′lic
hu·mil′i·ty	hur′ry	hy′dro·car′bon
hummed	hurt	hy′dro·chlo′ric
hum′ming·bird′	hurt′ful	hy′dro·cy·an′ic
hum′mock	hurt′ful·ly	hy′dro·e·lec′tric
hu′mor	hurt′ful·ness	hy′dro·flu·or′ic
hu′mored	hur′tle	hy′dro·foil′
hu′mor·esque′	hur′tled	hy′dro·gen
hu′mor·ist	hus′band	hy·drom′e·ter
hu′mor·ous	hus′band·ry	hy′dro·pho′bi·a
hu′mor·ous·ness	hush	hy′dro·plane
hump	hushed	hy′dro·stat′ics
hu′mus	husk	hy·drox′ide
hunch	husk′i·ly	hy·e′na
hun′dred	husk′i·ness	hy′giene
hun′dred·fold′	hus′ky	hy′gi·en′ic
hun′dredth	hus′sy	hy′gi·en′i·cal·ly
Hun·gar′i·an	hus′tings	hy′gi·en·ist
hun′ger	hus′tle	hy·grom′e·ter
hun′gered	hus′tled	hy′gro·scop′ic
hun′gri·er	hus′tler	hymn
hun′gri·est	hut	hym′nal
hun′gry	hutch	hymn′book′
hunk	hy′a·cinth	hy·per′bo·la
hunt	hy′a·loid	hy·per′bo·le
hunt′ed	hy′brid	hy′per·bol′ic
hunt′er	hy′brid·ism	hy′per·crit′i·cal
hunts′man	hy′brid·i·za′tion	hy′per·e′mi·a
hur′dle	hy′brid·ize	hy′per·o′pi·a
hur′dled	hy·dran′ge·a	hy′per·sen′si·tive

hy'per·thy'roid

hy·per'tro·phy

hy'phen

hy'phen·ate

hy'phen·at'ed

hy'phen·a'tion

hyp·no'sis

hyp·not'ic

hyp'no·tist

hyp'no·tize

hyp'no·tized

hy'po·chon'dri·a

hy'po·chon'dri·ac

hy·poc'ri·sy

hyp'o·crite

hyp'o·crit'i·cal

hy'po·der'mic

hy'po·der'mi·cal·ly

hy·pot'e·nuse

hy·poth'e·cate

hy·poth'e·ca'tion

hy·poth'e·ses

hy·poth'e·sis

hy·poth'e·size

hy'po·thet'i·cal

hy'po·thet'i·cal·ly

hys·te'ri·a

hys·ter'i·cal

hys·ter'ics

hys'ter·oid

I

i·am'bic

I·be'ri·an

i'bex

i'bis

ice

ice'berg'

ice'boat'

ice'box'

ice'break'er

ice'house'

ice'man'

ich·neu'mon

i'chor

ich'thy·ol'o·gy

i'ci·cle

i'ci·er

i'ci·est

i'ci·ly

i'ci·ness

i'con

i'cy

i·de'a

i·de'al

i·de'al·ism

i·de'al·ist

i·de'al·is'tic

i·de'al·i·za'tion

i·de'al·ize

i·de'al·ly

i'de·a'tion

i'de·a'tion·al

i·den'ti·cal

i·den'ti·fi·ca'tion

i·den'ti·fy

i·den'ti·ty

id'e·o·log'i·cal

id'e·ol'o·gy

id'i·o·cy

id'i·om

id'i·o·mat'ic

id'i·o·mat'i·cal·ly

id'i·o·syn'cra·sy

id'i·o·syn·crat'ic

id'i·ot

id'i·ot'ic

id'i·ot'i·cal·ly

i'dle

i'dled

i'dle·ness

i'dler

i'dlest

i'dly

i'dol

i·dol'a·ter

i·dol'a·trize

i·dol'a·trous

i·dol'a·try

i'dol·ize

i'dyl

i·dyl'lic

if

ig'loo

ig'ne·ous

ig·nite'

ig·nit'ed

ig·ni'tion

ig·no′ble	il·lu′mine	im′i·ta′tion
ig′no·min′i·ous	il·lu′mined	im′i·ta′tive
ig′no·min·y	il·lu′sion	im′i·ta′tor
ig′no·ra′mus	il·lu′sive	im·mac′u·late
ig′no·rance	il·lu′so·ry	im·mac′u·late·ly
ig′no·rant	il′lus·trate	im′ma·nent
ig′no·rant·ly	il′lus·trat′ed	im′ma·te′ri·al
ig·nore′	il′lus·tra′tion	im′ma·ture′
ig·nored′	il·lus′tra·tive	im′ma·ture′ly
i·gua′na	il′lus·tra′tor	im′ma·tu′ri·ty
i′lex	il·lus′tri·ous	im·meas′ur·a·ble
Il′i·ad	im′age	im·me′di·a·cy
ilk	im′age·ry	im·me′di·ate
ill	im·ag′i·na·ble	im·me′di·ate·ly
il·le′gal	im·ag′i·nar′y	im·me′di·ate·ness
il′le·gal′i·ty	im·ag′i·na′tion	im′me·mo′ri·al
il·leg′i·ble	im·ag′i·na′tive	im·mense′
il·leg′i·bly	im·ag′ine	im·mense′ly
il′le·git′i·ma·cy	im·ag′ined	im·men′si·ty
il′le·git′i·mate	im·ag′in·ings	im·merse′
il·lib′er·al	i·ma′go	im·mersed′
il·lic′it	i·mam′	im·mer′sion
il·lim′it·a·ble	im′be·cile	im′mi·grant
il·lit′er·a·cy	im′be·cil′i·ty	im′mi·grate
il·lit′er·ate	im·bibe′	im′mi·grat′ed
ill′ness	im·bibed′	im′mi·gra′tion
il·log′i·cal	im·bro′glio	im′mi·nence
il·lu′mi·nant	im·bue′	im′mi·nent
il·lu′mi·nate	im·bued′	im·mo′bile
il·lu′mi·nat′ed	im′i·ta·ble	im·mo′bil′i·ty
il·lu′mi·na′tion	im′i·tate	im·mo′bi·li·za′tion
il·lu′mi·na′tor	im′i·tat′ed	im·mo′bi·lize

im·mod'er·ate

im·mod'est

im'mo·late

im'mo·la'tion

im·mor'al

im'mo·ral'i·ty

im·mor'al·ly

im·mor'tal

im'mor·tal'i·ty

im·mor'tal·ize

im·mor'tal·ly

im'mor·telle'

im·mov'a·bil'i·ty

im·mov'a·ble

im·mov'a·ble·ness

im·mov'a·bly

im·mune'

im·mu'ni·ty

im'mu·ni·za'tion

im'mu·nize

im'mu·nol'o·gy

im·mure'

im'mu·ta·bil'i·ty

im·mu'ta·ble

imp

im'pact

im·pac'tion

im·pair'

im·paired'

im·pair'ment

im·pa'la

im·pale'

im·paled'

im·pale'ment

im·pal'pa·bil'i·ty

im·pal'pa·ble

im·pan'el

im·pan'eled

im·part'

im·part'ed

im·par'tial

im'par·ti·al'i·ty

im·par'tial·ly

im·pass'a·bil'i·ty

im·pass'a·ble

im·passe'

im·pas'sion

im·pas'sioned

im·pas'sive

im·pas'sive·ly

im'pas·siv'i·ty

im·pa'tience

im·pa'tient

im·peach'

im·peach'ment

im·pec'ca·bil'i·ty

im·pec'ca·ble

im'pe·cu'ni·os'i·ty

im'pe·cu'ni·ous

im·ped'ance

im·pede'

im·ped'ed

im·ped'i·ment

im·ped'i·men'ta

im·pel'

im·pelled'

im·pend'

im·pend'ed

im·pen'e·tra·bil'i·ty

im·pen'e·tra·ble

im·pen'i·tent

im·per'a·tive

im'per·cep'ti·ble

im'per·cep'tive

im·per'fect

im'per·fec'tion

im·per'fo·rate

im·pe'ri·al

im·pe'ri·al·ism

im·pe'ri·al·ist

im·pe'ri·al·is'tic

im·pe'ri·ous

im·per'ish·a·ble

im·per'ma·nent

im·per'me·a·ble

im'per·scrip'ti·ble

im·per'son·al

im·per'son·ate

im·per'son·at'ed

im·per'son·a'tion

im·per'ti·nence

im·per'ti·nent

im'per·turb'a·ble

im·per'vi·ous

im'pe·ti'go

im·pet'u·os'i·ty

im·pet′u·ous

im·pet′u·ous·ly

im·pet′u·ous·ness

im′pe·tus

im·pi′e·ty

im·pinge′

im·pinged′

im·pinge′ment

im′pi·ous

im′pi·ous·ly

imp′ish

im·pla′ca·bil′i·ty

im·pla′ca·ble

im·plant′

im·plant′ed

im·plau′si·bil′i·ty

im·plau′si·ble

im′ple·ment

im′ple·ment′ed

im′pli·cate

im′pli·cat′ed

im′pli·ca′tion

im·plic′it

im·plic′it·ly

im·plied′

im′plo·ra′tion

im·plore′

im·plored′

im·plor′ing·ly

im·plo′sion

im·ply′

im′po·lite′

im′po·lite′ly

im′po·lite′ness

im·pol′i·tic

im·pon′der·a·ble

im·port′

im·por′tance

im·por′tant

im′por·ta′tion

im′port′er

im·por′tu·nate

im′por·tune′

im′por·tu′ni·ty

im·pose′

im·posed′

im·pos′ing·ly

im′po·si′tion

im·pos′si·bil′i·ty

im·pos′si·ble

im′post

im·pos′tor

im·pos′ture

im′po·tence

im′po·tent

im·pound′

im·pov′er·ish

im·pov′er·ish·ment

im·pow′er

im·prac′ti·ca·ble

im·prac′ti·cal′i·ty

im′pre·cate

im′pre·ca′tion

im′pre·ca·to′ry

im·preg′na·bil′i·ty

im·preg′na·ble

im·preg′nate

im′preg·na′tion

im′pre·sa′ri·o

im′pre·scrip′ti·ble

im·press′

im·pressed′

im·pres′sion

im·pres′sion·a·ble

im·pres′sion·ism

im·pres′sive

im′pri·ma′tur

im·print′

im·print′ed

im·pris′on

im·pris′oned

im·pris′on·ment

im′prob·a·bil′i·ty

im·prob′a·ble

im·prob′a·bly

im·promp′tu

im·prop′er

im′pro·pri′e·ty

im·prov′a·ble

im·prove′

im·prove′ment

im·prov′i·dence

im·prov′i·dent

im′pro·vi·sa′tion

im′pro·vise

im′pro·vised

im·pru'dence

im·pru'dent

im·pru'dent·ly

im'pu·dence

im'pu·dent

im·pugn'

im·pugn'a·ble

im·pugned'

im·pugn'ment

im'pulse

im·pul'sion

im·pul'sive

im·pu'ni·ty

im·pure'

im·pure'ly

im·pu'ri·ty

im·put'a·ble

im'pu·ta'tion

im·put'a·tive

im·pute'

im·put'ed

in'a·bil'i·ty

in'ac·ces'si·bil'i·ty

in'ac·ces'si·ble

in·ac'cu·ra·cy

in·ac'cu·rate

in·ac'tion

in·ac'ti·vate

in·ac'tive

in'ac·tiv'i·ty

in·ad'e·qua·cy

in·ad'e·quate

in'ad·mis'si·bil'i·ty

in'ad·mis'si·ble

in'ad·vert'ence

in'ad·vert'ent

in'ad·vis'a·bil'i·ty

in'ad·vis'a·ble

in·al'ien·a·ble

in·am'o·ra'ta

in·ane'

in·an'i·mate

in'a·ni'tion

in·an'i·ty

in·ap'pli·ca·ble

in·ap'po·site

in'ap·pro'pri·ate

in·apt'

in·apt'i·tude

in'ar·tic'u·late

in'ar·tis'tic

in'as·much'

in'at·ten'tion

in'at·ten'tive

in·au'di·bil'i·ty

in·au'di·ble

in·au'di·bly

in·au'gu·ral

in·au'gu·rate

in·au'gu·rat'ed

in·au'gu·ra'tion

in'aus·pi'cious

in'board'

in'born'

in'bred'

in·cal'cu·la·ble

in'can·desce'

in'can·des'cence

in'can·des'cent

in'can·ta'tion

in'ca·pa·bil'i·ty

in·ca'pa·ble

in'ca·pac'i·tate

in'ca·pac'i·tat'ed

in'ca·pac'i·ta'tion

in'ca·pac'i·ty

in·car'cer·ate

in·car'cer·at'ed

in·car'cer·a'tion

in·car'nate

in'car·na'tion

in·cen'di·a·rism

in·cen'di·ar'y

in·cense'

in·censed'

in·cen'tive

in·cep'tion

in·cer'ti·tude

in·ces'sant

in·ces'sant·ly

in'cest

in·ces'tu·ous

inch

in·cho'ate

inch'worm'

in'ci·dence

in'ci·dent

in'ci·den'tal

in'ci·den'tal·ly

in·cin'er·ate

in·cin'er·at'ed

in·cin'er·a'tion

in·cin'er·a'tor

in·cip'i·ent

in·cise'

in·cised'

in·ci'sion

in·ci'sive

in·ci'sive·ly

in·ci'sive·ness

in·ci'sor

in'ci·ta'tion

in·cite'

in·cite'ment

in'ci·vil'i·ty

in·clem'en·cy

in·clem'ent

in'cli·na'tion

in·cline'

in·clined'

in·close'

in·closed'

in·clo'sure

in·clude'

in·clud'ed

in·clu'sive

in·clu'sive·ly

in·clu'sive·ness

in·cog'ni·to

in'co·her'ence

in'co·her'ent

in'com·bus'ti·bil'i·ty

in'com·bus'ti·ble

in'come

in'com·men'su·ra·ble

in'com·men'su·rate

in'com·mode'

in'com·mu'ni·ca'do

in·com'pa·ra·ble

in·com'pa·ra·bly

in'com·pat'i·bil'i·ty

in'com·pat'i·ble

in·com'pe·tence

in·com'pe·tent

in·com'pe·tent·ly

in'com·plete'

in'com·pre·hen'si·bil'i·ty

in'com·pre·hen'si·ble

in'com·press'i·bil'i·ty

in'com·press'i·ble

in'con·ceiv'a·bil'i·ty

in'con·ceiv'a·ble

in'con·clu'sive

in'con·clu'sive·ness

in'con·gru'i·ty

in·con'gru·ous

in'con·se·quen'tial

in'con·sid'er·a·ble

in'con·sid'er·ate

in'con·sid'er·ate·ly

in'con·sist'en·cy

in'con·sist'ent

in'con·sol'a·ble

in'con·spic'u·ous

in'con·spic'u·ous·ly

in·con'stan·cy

in·con'stant

in'con·test'a·ble

in·con'ti·nence

in·con'ti·nent

in'con·tro·vert'i·ble

in'con·ven'ience

in'con·ven'ienced

in'con·ven'ient

in'con·ven'ient·ly

in'con·ver'si·bil'i·ty

in'con·vert'i·bil'i·ty

in'con·vert'i·ble

in·cor'po·rate

in·cor'po·rat'ed

in·cor'po·ra'tion

in·cor'po·ra'tor

in'cor·rect'

in·cor'ri·gi·bil'i·ty

in·cor'ri·gi·ble

in'cor·rupt'i·bil'i·ty

in'cor·rupt'i·ble

in·crease'

in·creased'

in·creas'ing·ly

in·cred'i·bil'i·ty

in·cred'i·ble

in·cre·du'li·ty

in·cred'u·lous

in'cre·ment

in'cre·men'tal

in·cre'tion

in·crim'i·nate

in·crim'i·nat'ed

in·crim'i·na'tion

in·crim'i·na·to'ry

in'crus·ta'tion

in'cu·bate

in'cu·bat'ed

in'cu·ba'tion

in'cu·ba'tor

in'cu·bus

in·cul'cate

in·cul'cat·ed

in·cul·ca'tion

in·cul'pate

in·cul'pat·ed

in·cul·pa'tion

in·cul'pa·to'ry

in·cum'ben·cy

in·cum'bent

in·cu·nab'u·la

in·cur'

in·cur'a·ble

in·cur'a·bly

in·curred'

in·cur'sion

in·debt'ed

in·debt'ed·ness

in·de'cen·cy

in·de'cent

in·de'cent·ly

in'de·ci'sion

in'de·ci'sive

in'de·ci'sive·ly

in'de·ci'sive·ness

in·dec'o·rous

in·de·co'rum

in·deed'

in'de·fat'i·ga·bil'i·ty

in'de·fat'i·ga·ble

in'de·fea'si·ble

in'de·fen'si·ble

in'de·fin'a·ble

in·def'i·nite

in·def'i·nite·ly

in·def'i·nite·ness

in·del'i·bil'i·ty

in·del'i·ble

in·del'i·bly

in·del'i·ca·cy

in·del'i·cate

in·del'i·cate·ly

in·dem'ni·fi·ca'tion

in·dem'ni·fied

in·dem'ni·fy

in·dem'ni·ty

in·dent'

in'den·ta'tion

in·dent'ed

in·den'tion

in·den'ture

in·den'tured

in'de·pend'ence

in'de·pend'ent

in'de·scrib'a·ble

in'de·struct'i·ble

in'de·ter'mi·na·ble

in'de·ter'mi·nate

in'dex

in'dexed

in'dex·er

in'dex·es

In'di·an

in'di·cate

in'di·cat'ed

in'di·ca'tion

in·dic'a·tive

in'di·ca'tor

in'di·ca·to'ry

in'di·ces

in·di'ci·a

in·dict'

in·dict'a·ble

in·dict'ed

in·dict'ment

in·dif'fer·ence

in·dif'fer·ent

in·dif'fer·ent·ly

in'di·gence

in·dig'e·nous

in'di·gent

in'di·gest'i·bil'i·ty

in'di·gest'i·ble

in'di·ges'tion

in·dig'nant

in·dig'nant·ly

in'dig·na'tion

in·dig'ni·ty

in'di·go

in'di·rect'

in'di·rec'tion

in'di·rect'ly

in'di·rect'ness

in'dis·creet'

in'dis·creet'ly

in'dis·cre'tion

in'dis·crim'i·nate

in'dis·crim'i·nate·ly

in'dis·pen'sa·bil'i·ty

in'dis·pen'sa·ble

in'dis·pose'

in'dis·posed'

in'dis·po·si'tion

in·dis'pu·ta·ble

in·dis'so·lu·ble

in·dis'so·lu·bly

in'dis·tinct'

in'dis·tinct'ly

in·dis·tin'guish·a·ble

in·dite'

in·dit'ed

in'di·um

in'di·vid'u·al

in'di·vid'u·al·ism

in'di·vid'u·al·ist

in'di·vid'u·al'i·ty

in'di·vid'u·al·ize

in'di·vid'u·al·ly

in'di·vis'i·bil'i·ty

in'di·vis'i·ble

in·doc'tri·nate

in·doc'tri·nat'ed

in·doc'tri·na'tion

in'do·lence

in'do·lent

in'do·lent·ly

in·dom'i·ta·ble

in'doors'

in·dorse'

in·dorsed'

in·dorse'ment

in·dors'er

in·du'bi·ta·ble

in·duce'

in·duced'

in·duce'ment

in·duct'

in·duct'ance

in·duct'ed

in·duc'tion

in·duc'tive

in·duc'tor

in·due'

in·dued'

in·dulge'

in·dul'gence

in·dul'gent

in·dul'gent·ly

in'du·rate

in'du·rat'ed

in·dus'tri·al

in·dus'tri·al·ly

in·dus'tri·al·ism

in·dus'tri·al·ist

in·dus'tri·al·i·za'tion

in·dus'tri·al·ize

in·dus'tri·al·ized

in·dus'tri·ous

in·dus'tri·ous·ly

in·dus'tri·ous·ness

in'dus·try

in·e'bri·ate

in·e'bri·at'ed

in·e'bri·a'tion

in'e·bri'e·ty

in·ed'i·ble

in·ef'fa·ble

in·ef'fa·bly

in'ef·fec'tive

in'ef·fec'tu·al

in'ef·fec'tu·al·ly

in'ef·fi·ca'cious

in'ef·fi'cien·cy

in'ef·fi'cient

in'ef·fi'cient·ly

in'e·las'tic

in'e·las·tic'i·ty

in·el'e·gance

in·el'e·gant

in·el'e·gant·ly

in·el'i·gi·bil'i·ty

in·el'i·gi·ble

in·e·luc'ta·ble

in·ept'

in·ept'i·tude

in·e·qual'i·ty

in·eq'ui·ta·ble

in·eq'ui·ty

in·e·rad'i·ca·ble

in·e·rad'i·ca·bly

in·er'ran·cy

in·er'rant

in·ert'

in·er'tia

in·ert'ly

in·ert'ness

in·es·sen'tial

in·es'ti·ma·ble

in·es'ti·ma·bly

in·ev'i·ta·bil'i·ty

in·ev'i·ta·ble

in·ev'i·ta·bly

in'ex·act'

in'ex·act'i·tude

in'ex·cus'a·ble

in'ex·cus'a·bly

in'ex·haust'i·ble

in'ex·haust'i·bly

in·ex'o·ra·ble

in'ex·pe'di·ence

in'ex·pe'di·en·cy

in'ex·pe'di·ent

in'ex·pen'sive

in'ex·pe'ri·ence

in'ex·pert'

in·ex'pli·ca·ble

in·ex'pli·ca·bly

in·ex'tri·ca·ble

in·fal'li·bil'i·ty

in·fal'li·ble

in'fa·mous

in'fa·my

in'fan·cy

in'fant

in·fan'ti·cide

in'fan·tile

in'fan'ti·lism

in'fan·try

in'fan·try·man

in·farct'

in·farc'tion

in·fat'u·ate

in·fat'u·at'ed

in·fat'u·a'tion

in·fea'si·ble

in·fect'

in·fect'ed

in·fec'tion

in·fec'tious

in·fec'tious·ly

in·fec'tious·ness

in'fe·lic'i·tous

in'fe·lic'i·ty

in·fer'

in'fer·ence

in'fer·en'tial

in·fe'ri·or

in·fe'ri·or'i·ty

in·fer'nal

in·fer'nal·ly

in·fer'no

in·ferred'

in·fer'tile

in'fer·til'i·ty

in·fest'

in'fes·ta'tion

in'fi·del

in'fi·del'i·ty

in'field'

in'field'er

in·fil'trate

in·fil'trat·ed

in'fil·tra'tion

in'fi·nite

in'fin·i·tes'i·mal

in'fin·i·tes'i·mal·ly

in·fin'i·tive

in·fin'i·tude

in·fin'i·ty

in·firm'

in·fir'ma·ry

in·fir'mi·ty

in·flame'

in·flamed'

in·flam′ma·bil′i·ty

in·flam′ma·ble

in·flam′ma·bly

in′flam·ma′tion

in·flam′ma·to′ry

in·flate′

in·flat′ed

in·fla′tion

in·fla′tion·ar′y

in·fla′tion·ist

in·flect′

in·flect′ed

in·flec′tion

in·flex′i·bil′i·ty

in·flex′i·ble

in·flict′

in·flict′ed

in·flic′tion

in′flu·ence

in′flu·enced

in′flu·en′tial

in′flu·en′tial·ly

in′flu·en′za

in′flux

in·form′

in·for′mal

in′for·mal′i·ty

in·for′mal·ly

in·form′ant

in′for·ma′tion

in·form′a·tive

in·formed′

in·form′er

in·form′ing·ly

in·frac′tion

in·fran′gi·ble

in′fra·red′

in·fre′quent

in·fre′quent·ly

in·fringe′

in·fringed′

in·fringe′ment

in·fu′ri·ate

in·fu′ri·at′ed

in·fuse′

in·fused′

in·fus′es

in·fu′sion

in·gen′ious

in·gen′ious·ly

in′ge·nu′i·ty

in·gen′u·ous

in·gest′

in·gest′ed

in·ges′tion

in·ges′tive

in·glo′ri·ous

in′got

in·grain′

in·grained′

in′grate

in·gra′ti·ate

in·gra′ti·a′tion

in·gra′ti·a·to′ry

in·grat′i·tude

in·gre′di·ent

in′gress

in′grown′

in·hab′it

in·hab′it·a·ble

in·hab′it·ance

in·hab′it·ant

in·hab′i·ta′tion

in·hab′it·ed

in′ha·la′tion

in·hale′

in·haled′

in·hal′er

in′har·mo′ni·ous.

in·here′

in·hered′

in·her′ence

in·her′ent

in·her′ent·ly

in·her′it

in·her′it·a·ble

in·her′it·ance

in·her′it·ed

in·her′i·tor

in·hib′it

in·hib′it·ed

in′hi·bi′tion

in·hib′i·to′ry

in·hos′pi·ta·ble

in·hos′pi·ta·bly

in·hos′pi·tal′i·ty

in·hu′man

in′hu·mane′

in′hu·man′i·ty

in′hu·ma′tion

in·hume′

in·humed′

in·im′i·cal

in·im′i·ta·ble

in·im′i·ta·bly

in·iq′ui·tous

in·iq′ui·tous·ly

in·iq′ui·ty

in·i′tial

in·i′tialed

in·i′tial·ly

in·i′ti·ate

in·i′ti·at′ed

in·i′ti·a′tion

in·i′ti·a′tive

in·i′ti·a′tor

in·i′ti·a·to′ry

in·ject′

in·ject′ed

in·jec′tion

in·jec′tor

in′ju·di′cious

in′ju·di′cious·ly

in·junc′tion

in·junc′tive

in′jure

in′jured

in·ju′ri·ous

in′ju·ry

in·jus′tice

in·jus′tic·es

ink

inked

ink′horn′

ink′ling

ink′lings

ink′stand′

ink′well′

ink′y

in·laid′

in′land

in·lay′

in·let′

in′mate

in′most

inn

in′nate

in′nate·ly

in′ner

in′ner·most

in′ning

in′nings

inn′keep′er

in′no·cence

in′no·cent

in′no·cent·ly

in·noc′u·ous

in·noc′u·ous·ly

in′no·vate

in′no·va′tion

in′no·va′tive

in′no·va′tor

in′nu·en′do

in·nu′mer·a·ble

in′ob·serv′ant

in·oc′u·late

in·oc′u·lat′ed

in·oc′u·la′tion

in′of·fen′sive

in·op′er·a·ble

in·op′er·a′tive

in·op′por·tune′

in·or′di·nate

in′or·gan′ic

in′pa′tient

in′put′

in′quest

in·qui′e·tude

in·quire′

in·quired′

in·quir′er

in·quires′

in·quir′ies

in·quir′ing·ly

in·quir′y

in′qui·si′tion

in·quis′i·tive

in·quis′i·tor

in·quis′i·to′ri·al

in·road′

in·rush′

in·sane′

in·sane'ly

in·san'i·tar'y

in·san'i·ta'tion

in·san'i·ty

in·sa'ti·a·bil'i·ty

in·sa'ti·a·ble

in·scribe'

in·scribed'

in·scrib'er

in·scrip'tion

in·scru'ta·bil'i·ty

in·scru'ta·ble

in'sect

in·sec'ti·cide

in'sec·tiv'o·rous

in'se·cure'

in'se·cu'ri·ty

in·sen'sate

in·sen'si·bil'i·ty

in·sen'si·ble

in·sen'si·tive

in·sen'si·tive·ness

in·sen'ti·ence

in·sen'ti·ent

in·sep'a·ra·ble

in·sep'a·ra·bly

in·sert'

in·sert'ed

in·ser'tion

in'set'

in'shore'

in'side'

in'sid'er

in·sides'

in·sid'i·ous

in·sid'i·ous·ly

in'sight'

in·sig'ne

in·sig'ni·a

in'sig·nif'i·cance

in'sig·nif'i·cant

in'sig·nif'i·cant·ly

in'sin·cere'

in'sin·cere'ly

in'sin·cer'i·ty

in·sin'u·ate

in·sin'u·at'ed

in·sin'u·at'ing·ly

in·sin'u·a'tion

in·sin'u·a'tive

in·sip'id

in'si·pid'i·ty

in·sip'id·ly

in·sist'

in·sist'ed

in·sist'ence

in·sist'ent

in·sist'ent·ly

in'so·bri'e·ty

in'sole'

in'so·lence

in'so·lent

in'so·lent·ly

in·sol'u·bil'i·ty

in·sol'u·ble

in·solv'a·ble

in·sol'ven·cy

in·sol'vent

in·som'ni·a

in·som'ni·ac

in'so·much'

in·sou'ci·ance

in·sou'ci·ant

in·spect'

in·spect'ed

in·spec'tion

in·spec'tor

in·spec'tor·ate

in'spi·ra'tion

in'spi·ra'tion·al

in'spi·ra'tion·al·ly

in·spir'a·to'ry

in·spire'

in·spired'

in·spir'er

in·spir'ing·ly

in·spir'it·ing·ly

in'sta·bil'i·ty

in·stall'

in'stal·la'tion

in·stalled'

in·stall'ment

in'stance

in'stant

in'stan·ta'ne·ous

in·stan'ter

in'stant·ly

in·state'

in·stat'ed

in·stead'

in'step

in'sti·gate

in'sti·gat·ed

in'sti·ga'tion

in'sti·ga'tor

in·still'

in·stilled'

in·stinct'

in·stinc'tive

in·stinc'tive·ly

in·stinc'tu·al

in'sti·tute

in'sti·tut'ed

in'sti·tu'tion

in'sti·tu'tion·al

in'sti·tu'tion·al·ize

in'sti·tu'tion·al·ly

in·struct'

in·struct'ed

in·struc'tion

in·struc'tion·al

in·struc'tive

in·struc'tor

in'stru·ment

in'stru·men'tal

in'stru·men'tal·ist

in'stru·men·tal'i·ty

in'stru·men'tal·ly

in'stru·men·ta'tion

in'sub·or'di·nate

in'sub·or'di·na'tion

in·suf'fer·a·ble

in'suf·fi'cien·cy

in'suf·fi'cient

in'su·lar

in'su·lar'i·ty

in'su·late

in'su·lat'ed

in'su·la'tion

in'su·la'tor

in'su·lin

in·sult'

in·sult'ed

in·sult'ing·ly

in·su'per·a·ble

in'sup·port'a·ble

in'sup·press'i·ble

in·sur'a·bil'i·ty

in·sur'a·ble

in·sur'ance

in·sure'

in·sured'

in·sur'er

in·sur'gen·cy

in·sur'gent

in'sur·mount'a·ble

in'sur·rec'tion

in'sur·rec'tion·ar'y

in'sur·rec'tion·ist

in·tact'

in·tagl'io

in'take'

in·tan'gi·bil'i·ty

in·tan'gi·ble

in·tar'si·a

in'te·ger

in'te·gral

in'te·gral·ly

in'te·grate

in'te·grat'ed

in'te·gra'tion

in·teg'ri·ty

in·teg'u·ment

in'tel·lect

in'tel·lec'tu·al

in'tel·lec'tu·al·ism

in'tel·lec'tu·al·ize

in'tel·lec'tu·al·ly

in·tel'li·gence

in·tel'li·gent

in·tel'li·gent'si·a

in·tel'li·gi·bil'i·ty

in·tel'li·gi·ble

in·tem'per·ance

in·tem'per·ate

in·tem'per·ate·ly

in·tend'

in·tend'ant

in·tend'ed

in·tense'

in·ten'si·fi·ca'tion

in·ten'si·fi'er

in·ten'si·fy	in'ter·de·pend'ent	in'ter·mar'riage
in·ten'si·ty	in'ter·dict	in'ter·mar'ry
in·ten'sive	in'ter·dic'tion	in'ter·me'di·ar'y
in·tent'	in'ter·est	in'ter·me'di·ate
in·ten'tion	in'ter·est·ed	in·ter'ment
in·ten'tion·al	in'ter·est·ed·ly	in'ter·mez'zo
in·ten'tion·al·ly	in'ter·est·ing·ly	in·ter'mi·na·ble
in·tent'ly	in'ter·fere'	in·ter'mi·na·bly
in·tent'ness	in'ter·fered'	in'ter·min'gle
in'ter·act'	in'ter·fer'ence	in'ter·min'gled
in'ter·ac'tion	in'ter·fer'ing·ly	in'ter·mis'sion
in'ter·bor'ough	in'ter·im	in'ter·mit'
in'ter·breed'	in·te'ri·or	in'ter·mit'tence
in'ter·cede'	in'ter·ject'	in'ter·mit'tent
in'ter·ced'ed	in'ter·ject'ed	in'ter·mit'tent·ly
in'ter·cept'	in'ter·jec'tion	in'ter·mix'ture
in'ter·cept'ed	in'ter·lace'	in·tern'
in'ter·cep'tion	in'ter·laced'	in·ter'nal
in'ter·cep'tor	in'ter·lard'	in·ter'nal·ly
in'ter·ces'sion	in'ter·leaf'	in'ter·na'tion·al
in'ter·ces'so·ry	in'ter·leave'	in'ter·na'tion·al·ize
in'ter·change'	in'ter·line'	in'ter·na'tion·al·ly
in'ter·change'a·bil'i·ty	in'ter·lin'e·al	in'terne
in'ter·change'a·ble	in'ter·lin'e·ar	in'ter·ne'cine
in'ter·col·le'gi·ate	in'ter·lin'e·a'tion	in·terned'
in'ter·com·mu'ni·cate	in'ter·lined'	in·tern'ment
in'ter·con·nect'	in'ter·lock'	in'ter·pel'late
in'ter·cos'tal	in'ter·locked'	in'ter·pel·la'tion
in'ter·course	in'ter·loc'u·tor	in'ter·plan'e·tar'y
in'ter·de·nom'i·na'tion·al	in'ter·loc'u·to'ry	in·ter'po·late
in'ter·de'part·men'tal	in'ter·lop'er	in·ter'po·lat'ed
in'ter·de·pend'ence	in'ter·lude	in·ter'po·la'tion

in'ter·pose'

in'ter·posed'

in'ter·po·si'tion

in·ter'pret

in·ter'pre·ta'tion

in·ter'pre·ta'tive

in·ter'pret·ed

in·ter'pret·er

in'ter·reg'num

in'ter·re·la'tion

in·ter'ro·gate

in·ter'ro·ga'tion

in·ter'rog'a·tive

in·ter'rog'a·to'ry

in'ter·rupt'

in'ter·rupt'ed·ly

in'ter·rup'tion

in'ter·scap'u·lar

in'ter·scho·las'tic

in'ter·sect'

in'ter·sect'ed

in'ter·sperse'

in'ter·spersed'

in'ter·state'

in'ter·stel'lar

in·ter'stice

in·ter'stic·es

in'ter·sti'tial

in'ter·sti'tial·ly

in'ter·twine'

in'ter·twined'

In'ter·type

in'ter·ur'ban

in'ter·val

in'ter·vene'

in'ter·vened'

in'ter·ven'tion

in'ter·ven'tion·ist

in'ter·ver'te·bral

in'ter·view

in'ter·viewed

in'ter·view'er

in'ter·weave'

in'ter·wo'ven

in·tes'ta·cy

in·tes'tate

in·tes'ti·nal

in·tes'tine

in'ti·ma·cy

in'ti·mate

in'ti·mat'ed

in'ti·mate·ly

in'ti·ma'tion

in·tim'i·date

in·tim'i·dat'ed

in·tim'i·da'tion

in'to

in·tol'er·a·ble

in·tol'er·ance

in·tol'er·ant

in'to·na'tion

in·tone'

in·toned'

in·tox'i·cate

in·tox'i·cat'ed

in·tox'i·cat'ing·ly

in·tox'i·ca'tion

in·trac'ta·bil'i·ty

in·trac'ta·ble

in'tra·mu'ral

in·tran'si·gence

in·tran'si·gent

in·tran'si·tive

in'tra·state'

in·trench'ment

in·trep'id

in·tre·pid'i·ty

in·trep'id·ly

in'tri·ca·cies

in'tri·ca·cy

in'tri·cate

in'tri·cate·ly

in·trigue'

in·trigued'

in·trin'sic

in·trin'si·cal

in·trin'si·cal·ly

in'tro·duce'

in'tro·duced'

in'tro·duc'tion

in'tro·duc'to·ry

in·tro'it

in'tro·jec'tion

in'tro·spect'

in'tro·spec'tion

in'tro·spec'tive

in·tro·ver·sion

in·tro·vert'

in·tro·vert'ed

in·trude'

in·trud'ed

in·trud'er

in·tru'sion

in·tru'sive

in·tru'sive·ly

in·tu·i'tion

in·tu·i'tion·al

in·tu'i·tive

in·tu'i·tive·ly

in·tu·mesce'

in·tu·mes'cence

in·tu·mes'cent

in·unc'tion

in'un·date

in'un·dat'ed

in'un·da'tion

in·ure'

in·ured'

in·ur'ed·ness

in·urn'

in·vade'

in·vad'ed

in'va·lid

in·val'i·date

in·val'i·dat'ed

in·val'i·da'tion

in'va·lid'i·ty

in·val'u·a·ble

In·var'

in·var'i·a·bil'i·ty

in·var'i·a·ble

in·var'i·a·ble·ness

in·va'sion

in·va'sive

in·vec'tive

in·veigh'

in·vei'gle

in·vei'gled

in·vent'

in·vent'ed

in·ven'tion

in·ven'tive

in·ven'tive·ly

in·ven'tive·ness

in·ven'tor

in'ven·to·ry

in·verse'

in·ver'sion

in·vert'

in·vert'ed

in·vert'i·ble

in·vest'

in·vest'ed

in·ves'ti·gate

in·ves'ti·gat'ed

in·ves'ti·ga'tion

in·ves'ti·ga'tive

in·ves'ti·ga'tor

in·ves'ti·ture

in·vest'ment

in·ves'tor

in·vet'er·ate

in·vid'i·ous

in·vid'i·ous·ly

in·vig'i·late

in·vig'or·ate

in·vig'or·at'ed

in·vig'or·at'ing·ly

in·vig'or·a'tion

in·vig'or·a'tive

in·vin'ci·bil'i·ty

in·vin'ci·ble

in·vi'o·la·bil'i·ty

in·vi'o·la·ble

in·vi'o·late

in·vis'i·bil'i·ty

in·vis'i·ble

in·vis'i·bly

in'vi·ta'tion

in'vi·ta'tion·al

in·vite'

in·vit'ed

in·vit'ing·ly

in'vo·ca'tion

in'voice

in'voiced

in'voic·es

in·voke'

in·voked'

in·vol'un·tar'i·ly

in·vol'un·tar'y

in'vo·lute

in'vo·lu'tion
in·volve'
in·volved'
in·vul'ner·a·bil'i·ty
in·vul'ner·a·ble
in'ward
in'ward·ly
in'ward·ness
i'o·date
i·od'ic
i'o·dide
i'o·dine
i'o·dize
i·o'do·form
i'on
I·on'ic
i'on·i·za'tion
i'on·ize
i·o'ta
ip'e·cac
I·ra'ni·an
i·ras'ci·bil'i·ty
i·ras'ci·ble
i'rate
i'rate·ly
ire
ir'i·des'cence
ir'i·des'cent
i·rid'i·um
i'ris
I'rish
I'rish·man

i·ri'tis
irk
irked
irk'some
i'ron
i'ron·bound'
i'ron·clad'
i'roned
i·ron'ic
i·ron'i·cal
i·ron'i·cal·ly
i'ron·ings
i'ron·side'
i'ron·ware'
i'ron·weed'
i'ron·wood'
i'ron·work'
i'ron·work'er
i'ro·ny
Ir'o·quois
ir·ra'di·ate
ir·ra'di·at'ed
ir·ra'di·a'tion
ir·ra'tion·al
ir·ra'tion·al'i·ty
ir·ra'tion·al·ly
ir're·claim'a·ble
ir'rec'on·cil'a·ble
ir'rec'on·cil'i·a·bil'i·ty
ir'rec'on·cil'i·a·ble
ir're·cov'er·a·ble
ir're·deem'a·ble

ir're·den'ta
ir're·duc'i·ble
ir·ref'ra·ga·ble
ir're·fran'gi·ble
ir·ref'u·ta·ble
ir·reg'u·lar
ir·reg'u·lar'i·ty
ir·reg'u·lar·ly
ir·rel'e·vance
ir·rel'e·vant
ir're·li'gious
ir·re·me'di·a·ble
ir're·mis'si·ble
ir're·mov'a·ble
ir·rep'a·ra·ble
ir're·place'a·ble
ir're·press'i·ble
ir're·proach'a·ble
ir're·sist'i·ble
ir·res'o·lute
ir·res'o·lu'tion
ir're·solv'a·ble
ir're·spec'tive
ir're·spon'si·bil'i·ty
ir're·spon'si·ble
ir're·spon'si·bly
ir're·trace'a·ble
ir're·triev'a·ble
ir·rev'er·ence
ir·rev'er·ent
ir're·vers'i·ble
ir·rev'o·ca·ble

ir'ri·ga·ble	i'so·late	i·tal'i·cize
ir'ri·gate	i'so·lat'ed	itch
ir'ri·gat'ed	i·so·la'tion	itched
ir'ri·ga'tion	i'so·la'tion·ism	itch'i·er
ir'ri·ta·bil'i·ty	i'so·la'tion·ist	itch'i·est
ir'ri·ta·ble	i'so·mer	itch'y
ir'ri·tant	i'so·mer'ic	i'tem
ir'ri·tate	i'so·mor'phic	i'tem·ize
ir'ri·tat'ed	i·sos'ce·les	i'tem·ized
ir'ri·ta'tion	i'so·therm	it'er·ate
ir'ri·ta'tive	i'so·tope	it'er·a'tion
ir·rup'tion	is'su·ance	it'er·a'tive
ir·rup'tive	is'sue	i·tin'er·a·cy
is'chi·um	is'sued	i·tin'er·an·cy
i'sin·glass'	is'sues	i·tin'er·ant
Is'lam	isth'mi·an	i·tin'er·ar'y
is'land	isth'mus	i·tin'er·ate
is'land·er	it	its
isle	I·tal'ian	it·self'
is'let	I·tal'ian·ate	i'vo·ry
i'so·bar	i·tal'ic	i'vy

J

jab'ber	jal'ou·sie	jaun'ty
jab'ber·ing·ly	jam	jave'lin
ja'bot'	jam'bo·ree'	jaw
jack	jammed	jaw'bone'
jack'al	jan'gle	jazz
jack'a·napes'	jan'i·tor	jazz'y
jack'daw'	jan'i·tress	jeal'ous
jack'et	Jan'u·ar'y	jeal'ous·y
jack'et·ed	Ja·pan'	jeer
jack'knife'	Jap'a·nese'	jeered
jack'stone'	ja·panned'	jeer'ing·ly
jack'straw'	jar	Je·ho'vah
jack'weed'	jar'gon	je·june'
Jac·o·be'an	jarred	je·ju'num
jade	jas'mine	jel'lied
jad'ed	jas'per	jel'ly
jade'ite	jaun'dice	jel'ly·fish'
jagged	jaunt	jen'net
jag'uar	jaun'ti·er	jeop'ard·ize
jail	jaun'ti·est	jeop'ard·y
jailed	jaun'ti·ly	jer'e·mi'ad
jail'er	jaun'ti·ness	jerk

jerked	jit'ney	jol'li·er
jerk'i·ly	jit'ters	jol'li·est
jer'kin	jit'ter·y	jol'li·fi·ca'tion
jerk'y	job	jol'li·ty
jer'sey	job'ber	jol'ly
jest	jock'ey	jolt
jest'er	jo·cose'	jolt'ed
jest'ing·ly	jo·cose'ly	jon'quil
Jes'u·it	jo·cos'i·ty	jos'tle
Je'sus	joc'u·lar	jos'tled
jet	joc'u·lar'i·ty	jot
jet'sam	joc'u·lar·ly	jot'ted
jet'ti·son	joc'und	jounce
jet'ty	jo·cun'di·ty	jour'nal
jew'el	jodh'purs	jour'nal·ism
jew'eled	jog	jour'nal·ist
jew'el·er	jogged	jour'nal·is'tic
jew'el·ry	jog'gle	jour'nal·ize
Jew'ish	jog'gled	jour'nal·ized
Jew'ry	join	jour'ney
jibe	join'der	jour'neyed
jig	joined	jour'ney·man
jig'ger	join'er	jo'vi·al
jig'gle	join'ings	jo'vi·al'i·ty
jig'gled	joint	jo'vi·al·ly
jig'saw'	joint'ed	jowl
jin'gle	joint'ly	joy
jin'gled	join'ture	joy'ful
jin'go	joist	joy'ful·ly
jin'go·ism	joke	joy'ful·ness
jin·rik'i·sha	jok'er	joy'less
jinx	jok'ing·ly	joy'ous

ju'bi·lance

ju'bi·lant

ju'bi·late

ju'bi·la'tion

ju'bi·lee

Ju'da·ism

judge

judged

judge'ship

judg'ment

ju'di·ca'tive

ju'di·ca·to'ry

ju'di·ca·ture

ju·di'cial

ju·di'cial·ly

ju·di'ci·ar'y

ju·di'cious

jug'gle

jug'gled

jug'gler

jug'u·lar

juice

juic'y

ju'lep

ju'li·enne'

Ju·ly'

jum'ble

jum'bled

jum'bo

jump

jumped

jump'er

junc'tion

junc'ture

June

jun'gle

jun'ior

ju'ni·per

junk

jun'ket

jun'ta

ju'rat

ju·rid'i·cal

ju'ris·con·sult'

ju'ris·dic'tion

ju'ris·pru'dence

ju'rist

ju'ror

ju'ry

ju'ry·man

just

jus'tice

jus·ti'ci·a·ble

jus'ti·fi'a·ble

jus'ti·fi·ca'tion

jus'ti·fi·ca·to'ry

jus'ti·fied

jus'ti·fy

just'ly

just'ness

jut

jute

jut'ted

ju've·nile

ju've·nil'i·ty

jux'ta·po·si'tion

K

kai'ser

kale

ka·lei'do·scope

ka·lei'do·scop'ic

kal'so·mine

kan'ga·roo'

ka'o·lin

ka'pok

kar'ma

kay'ak

keel

keen

keen'er

keen'est

keen'ly

keen'ness

keep

keep'er

keep'sake'

keg

kelp

ken'nel

kept

ker'a·tin

ker'chief

ker'nel

ker'o·sene'

ker'sey

ketch

ke·to'sis

ket'tle

key

key'board'

keyed

key'hole'

key'note'

key'stone'

khak'i

khe·dive'

kib'itz·er

ki'bosh

kick

kick'back'

kick'er

kick'off'

kick'shaw'

kid

kid'nap

kid'naped

kid'ney

kid'skin'

kill

killed

kill'er

kill'ings

kiln

kil'o·cy'cle

kil'o·gram

kil'o·me'ter

kilt

kilt'ed

kin

kind

kind'er

kind'est

kin'der·gar'ten

kin'dle

kin'dled

kind'li·ness

kind'ly

kind'ness

kin'dred

kine

kin'es·thet'ic

ki·net'ic

king

king'bird'

king'bolt'

king'craft

king'dom

king'fish'

king'fish'er

king'let

king'li·ness

king'ly

king'pin'

king'ship

kink

kinked

kink'y

kin'ship

kins'man

ki·osk'

kip'per

kiss

kissed

kitch'en

kitch'en·ette'

kite

kith

kit'ten

klep'to·ma'ni·a

klep'to·ma'ni·ac

knap'sack'

knave

knav'er·y

knav'ish

knead

knead'ed

knee'cap'

kneel

kneeled

knelt

knew

knick'ers

knick'knack'

knife

knifed

knight

knight'ed

knight'hood

knight'li·ness

knight'ly

knit

knit'ter

knives

knob

knock

knock'down'

knock'er

knock'out'

knoll

knot

knot'hole'

knot'ted

knot'ty

knot'work'

knout

know

know'a·ble

know'ing·ly

know'ing·ness

knowl'edge

known

knuck'le

knuck'led

knurl

knurled

knurl'y

ko'bold

ko'dak

kohl'ra'bi

ko'peck

Ko·ran'

Ko·re'an

ko'sher

kraft

krem'lin

kryp'ton

ku·lak'

ky'mo·graph

ky·pho'sis

L

la'bel

la'beled

la'bi·al

la'bor

lab'o·ra·to'ry

la'bored

la'bor·er

la·bo'ri·ous

la·bur'num

lab'y·rinth

lab'y·rin'thine

lace

laced

lac'er·ate

lac'er·at'ed

lac'er·a'tion

lac'er·a'tive

lace'wing'

lace'wood'

lace'work'

lach'es

lach'ry·mal

lach'ry·mose

lac'ings

lack

lack'a·dai'si·cal

lack'ey

lack'lus'ter

la·con'ic

lac'quer

lac'quered

la·crosse'

lac'tase

lac'tate

lac·ta'tion

lac'te·al

lac'tic

lac'tose

la·cu'na

la·cu'nae

lad'der

lad'en

la'dle

la'dled

la'dy

la'dy·like'

la'dy·ship

lag

la'ger

lag'gard

lagged

la·goon'

lair

laird

la'i·ty

lake

lamb'doid

lam'bent

lamb'kin

lamb'like'

lam'bre·quin

la'mé'

lame

lamed

lame'ly

lame'ness

la·ment'	land'slip'	large
lam'en·ta·ble	lands'man	large'ly
lam'en·ta'tion	land'ward	large'ness
la·ment'ed	lan'guage	larg'er
lam'i·na	lan'guid	lar'gess
lam'i·nae	lan'guish	larg'est
lam'i·nate	lan'guor	lar'i·at
lam'i·nat'ed	lan'guor·ous	lark
lam'i·na'tion	lank	lark'spur
lamp	lank'er	lar'va
lamp'black'	lank'est	lar'vae
lam·poon'	lank'y	lar'val
lam·pooned'	lan'o·lin	la·ryn'ge·al
lam'prey	lans'downe	lar'yn·gi'tis
lance	lan'tern	lar'ynx
lanc'er	lan'tha·num	las'car
lan'cet	lan'yard	las·civ'i·ous
lan'ci·nate	lap	lash
lan'ci·nat'ed	la·pel'	lashed
lan'ci·na'tion	lap'ful	lash'ings
land	lap'i·dar'y	lass
lan'dau	lap'i·da'tion	las'si·tude
land'ed	lapse	las'so
land'fall'	lapsed	last
land'hold'er	lap'wing'	last'ed
land'la'dy	lar'board	last'ing·ly
land'locked'	lar'ce·nous	last'ly
land'lord'	lar'ce·ny	lasts
land'mark'	larch	Lat'a·ki'a
land'own'er	lard	latch
land'scape	lard'ed	latched
land'slide'	lard'er	latch'key'

latch'string'	laud'a·to'ry	lawn
late	laud'ed	law'suit'
la·teen'	laugh	law'yer
late'ly	laugh'a·ble	lax
la'ten·cy	laugh'ing·ly	lax'a·tive
late'ness	laugh'ing·stock'	lax'i·ty
la'tent	laugh'ter	lax'ly
lat'er	launch	lax'ness
lat'er·al	launch'ings	lay'er
lat'er·al·ly	laun'der	lay'man
lat'est	laun'dered	laz'a·ret'to
la'tex	laun'der·ings	la'zi·er
lath	laun'dress	la'zi·est
lath'er	laun'dry	la'zi·ly
laths	laun'dry·man	la'zi·ness
Lat'in	lau're·ate	la'zy
Lat'in·ism	lau'rel	leach
La·tin'i·ty	la'va	leached
Lat'in·i·za'tion	lav'a·liere'	lead
Lat'in·ize	lav'a·to'ry	lead'en
lat'i·tude	lav'en·der	lead'er
lat'i·tu'di·nal	lav'ish	lead'er·ship
lat'i·tu'di·nar'i·an	lav'ished	leads'man
lat'ter	lav'ish·ness	leaf
lat'ter·most	law	leaf'let
lat'tice	law'break'er	league
lat'tice·work'	law'ful	leagued
laud	law'ful·ly	leak
laud'a·bil'i·ty	law'giv'er	leak'age
laud'a·ble	law'less	leak'i·ness
lau'da·num	law'less·ness	leak'y
lau·da'tion	law'mak'er	lean

leaned	leered	le·git′i·ma·cy
lean′ings	leer′ing·ly	le·git′i·mate
leap	lee′ward	le·git′i·mate·ly
leaped	lee′way′	le·git′i·mate·ness
learn	left	le·git′i·ma′tion
learned	left′-hand′ed	le·git′i·mist
learnt	leg	le·git′i·mize
lease	leg′a·cy	leg′ume
leased	le′gal	le·gu′mi·nous
lease′hold′	le′gal·ism	lei′sure
lease′hold′er	le′gal·is′tic	lei′sure·li·ness
leash	le·gal′i·ty	lei′sure·ly
leashed	le′gal·i·za′tion	lem′mings
least	le′gal·ize	lem′on
leath′er	le′gal·ly	lem′on·ade′
leath′ern	leg′ate	lem′on·weed′
leath′er·oid	leg′a·tee′	le′mur
leath′er·y	le·ga′tion	lend
leave	le·ga′to	length
leav′en	leg′end	length′en
leav′ened	leg′end·ar′y	length′ened
leav′ing	leg′er·de·main′	length′i·er
lec′i·thin	leg′gings	length′i·est
lec′tern	leg′i·bil′i·ty	length′i·ly
lec′ture	leg′i·ble	length′i·ness
lec′tured	le′gion	length′ways
lec′tur·er	le′gion·ar′y	length′wise
ledge	leg′is·late	length′y
ledg′er	leg′is·la′tion	le′ni·ence
leech	leg′is·la′tive	le′ni·en·cy
leek	leg′is·la′tor	le′ni·ent
leer	leg′is·la′ture	le′ni·ent·ly

Len'in·ism	let'tered	li'beled
len'i·tive	let'ter·head'	li'bel·ous
len'i·ty	let'ter·press'	lib'er·al
lens	let'ter·space'	lib'er·al·ism
lent	let'tuce	lib'er·al'i·ty
Lent'en	leu'co·cyte	lib'er·al·i·za'tion
len·tic'u·lar	leu'co·cy·to'sis	lib'er·al·ize
len'til	leu'co·der'ma	lib'er·al·ized
len'toid	leu·ke'mi·a	lib'er·al·ly
le'o·nine	lev'ant	lib'er·ate
leop'ard	lev'ee	lib'er·at'ed
le'o·tard	lev'el	lib'er·a'tion
lep'er	lev'eled	lib'er·a'tor
lep're·chaun'	lev'el·head'ed	lib'er·tar'i·an
lep'ro·sy	le'ver	lib'er·tine
lep'rous	le'ver·age	lib'er·ty
le'sion	lev'i·tate	li·bi'do
less	lev'i·tat'ed	li·brar'i·an
les·see'	lev'i·ta'tion	li'brar'y
less'en	lev'i·ty	li·bret'to
less'ened	lev'u·lose	lice
less'er	lev'y	li'cense
les'son	lex'i·cog'ra·pher	li'cen·see'
les'sor	lex'i·cog'ra·phy	li·cen'ti·ate
lest	lex'i·con	li·cen'tious
let	li'a·bil'i·ty	li·cen'tious·ness
le'thal	li'a·ble	li'chen
le·thar'gic	li·a'na	li'chen·oid
le·thar'gi·cal	li'ar	lic'it
leth'ar·gy	li·ba'tion	lick
let's	li'bel	lic'o·rice
let'ter	li'bel·ant	lic'tor

lie

liege

li'en

lieu

lieu·ten'an·cy

lieu·ten'ant

life

life'guard'

life'less

life'like'

life'long'

life'time'

life'work'

lift

lift'ed

lig'a·ment

li'gate

li·ga'tion

lig'a·ture

lig'a·tured

light

light'ed

light'en

light'ened

light'er

light'er·age

light'est

light'face'

light'head'ed

light'heart'ed

light'house'

light'ly

light'ness

light'ning

light'ship'

light'weight'

lig'ne·ous

lig'ni·fy

lig'nite

lik'a·ble

like

liked

like'li·er

like'li·est

like'li·hood

like'ly

lik'en

like'ness

like'wise'

lik'ings

li'lac

lil'i·a'ceous

lilt

lilt'ing·ly

lil'y

limb

lim'ber

lim'bo

lime

lime'kiln'

lime'light'

li'men

Lim'er·ick

lime'stone'

lime'wa'ter

lim'i·nal

lim'it

lim'it·a·ble

lim'i·ta'tion

lim'it·ed

lim'it·less

limn

limned

lim·nol'o·gy

lim'ou·sine'

limp

limped

limp'er

limp'est

lim'pet

lim'pid

lim·pid'i·ty

lim'pid·ly

limp'ly

limp'ness

lin'age

lin'den

line

lin'e·age

lin'e·al

lin'e·al'i·ty

lin'e·a·ment

lin'e·ar

lined

line'man

lin'en

lin'er

lines'man

lin'ger

lin'gered

lin'ge·rie'

lin'ger·ing·ly

lin'go

lin'gual

lin'guist

lin·guis'tic

lin·guis'ti·cal·ly

lin·guis'tics

lin'i·ment

lin'ings

link

link'age

linked

Lin·nae'an

lin'net

li·no'le·um

Lin'o·type

lin'seed'

lint

lin'tel

li'on

li'on·ess

li'on·ize

lip'oid

li·po'ma

liq'ue·fa'cient

liq'ue·fac'tion

liq'ue·fac'tive

liq'ue·fi'a·ble

liq'ue·fied

liq'ue·fy

li'ques'cence

li·queur'

liq'uid

liq'ui·date

liq'ui·dat'ed

liq'ui·da'tion

liq'ui·da'tor

liq'uor

li'ra

lisp

lisped

lisp'ing·ly

lis'some

list

list'ed

lis'ten

lis'tened

lis'ten·er

list'ings

list'less

lit'a·ny

li'ter

lit'er·a·cy

lit'er·al

lit'er·al·ism

lit'er·al'i·ty

lit'er·al·ize

lit'er·al·ly

lit'er·ar'y

lit'er·ate

lit'er·a·ture

lith'arge

lithe

lithe'some

lith'i·a

lith'i·um

lith'o·graph

li·thog'ra·pher

lith'o·graph'ic

li·thog'ra·phy

li·tho'sis

li·thot'o·my

lit'i·ga·ble

lit'i·gant

lit'i·gate

lit'i·gat'ed

lit'i·ga'tion

li·ti'gious

lit'mus

lit'ter

lit'tered

lit'tle

lit'tlest

lit'to·ral

li·tur'gi·cal

lit'ur·gist

lit'ur·gy

liv'a·ble

live

live

lived

live'li·er

live'li·est

live'li·hood

live'li·ness

live'long'

live'ly

liv'er

liv'er·y

liv'er·y·man

liv'id

li·vid'i·ty

liv'ings

liz'ard

lla'ma

lla'no

load

load'ed

load'ings

loaf

loaf'er

loam

loan

loaned

loathe

loathed

loath'er

loath'ful

loath'ly

loath'some

lo'bar

lob'bied

lob'by

lob'by·ist

lob'ster

lo'cal

lo'cal·ism

lo·cal'i·ty

lo'cal·i·za'tion

lo'cal·ize

lo'cal·ized

lo'cal·ly

lo'cate

lo'cat·ed

lo·ca'tion

lo'ci

lock

lock'age

lock'er

lock'et

lock'jaw'

lock'out'

lock'smith'

lock'up'

lo'co·mo'tion

lo'co·mo'tive

lo'cus

lo'cust

lo·cu'tion

lode

lode'star'

lodge

lodged

lodg'er

lodg'ings

lodg'ment

loft

loft'i·ly

loft'i·ness

loft'y

log

lo'gan·ber'ry

log'a·rithm

log'book'

loge

log'ger·heads'

log'gia

log'ic

log'i·cal

log'i·cal·ly

lo·gi'cian

lo·gis'tics

log'or·rhe'a

log'o·type

log'wood'

loin

loi'ter

loi'tered

loi'ter·er

loll

lolled

lol'li·pop

lone

lone'li·ness

lone'ly

lone'some

lone'some·ly

lone'some·ness	lop'sid'ed	lov'a·ble
long	lo·qua'cious	love
long'boat'	lo·qua'cious·ly	love'less
longed	lo·quac'i·ty	love'li·ness
lon'ger	lord	love'lorn'
long'est	lord'li·ness	love'ly
lon·gev'i·ty	lord'ly	lov'er
long'hand'	lor·do'sis	love'sick'
long'horn'	lord'ship	lov'ing·ly
long'ing·ly	lore	low
long'ings	lor'gnette'	low'born'
lon'gi·tude	lor'ry	low'boy'
lon'gi·tu'di·nal	los'a·ble	low'bred'
long'shore'man	lose	low'er
look	los'er	low'est
look'out'	los'es	low'land
loom	los'ings	low'li·er
loomed	loss	low'li·est
loon	lost	low'li·ness
loon'y	lo'tion	low'ly
loop	lot'ter·y	low'most
loop'hole'	lo'tus	loy'al
loose	loud	loy'al·ism
loose'ly	loud'er	loy'al·ist
loos'en	loud'est	loy'al·ly
loos'ened	loud'ly	loy'al·ty
loose'ness	loud'ness	loz'enge
loos'er	lounge	lu'bri·cant
loos'est	louse	lu'bri·cate
loot	lout	lu'bri·ca'tion
loot'ed	lout'ish	lu'bri·ca'tor
lop	lou'ver	lu·bric'i·ty

lu'cent	lu'mi·nif'er·ous	lus'ter
lu'cid	lu'mi·nos'i·ty	lust'ful
lu·cid'i·ty	lu'mi·nous	lust'i·ly
lu'cid·ly	lump	lust'i·ness
lu'cid·ness	lump'i·er	lus'trous
luck	lump'i·est	lus'trous·ly
luck'i·ly	lump'y	lus'trum
luck'i·ness	lu'na·cy	lust'y
luck'less	lu'nar	lute
luck'y	lu'na·tic	Lu'ther·an
lu'cra·tive	lunch	lux·u'ri·ance
lu'cre	lunch'eon	lux·u'ri·ant
lu'cu·bra'tion	lunch'eon·ette'	lux·u'ri·ate
lu'di·crous	lunch'room'	lux·u'ri·at'ed
lug	lu·nette'	lux·u'ri·ous
lug'gage	lung	lux'u·ry
lugged	lunge	ly·ce'um
lug'ger	lunged	lydd'ite
lu·gu'bri·ous	lurch	lymph
luke'warm'	lurched	lym·phat'ic
lull	lurch'ing	lymph'oid
lull'a·by'	lure	lynx
lulled	lured	ly'on·naise'
lum·ba'go	lu'rid	lyre
lum'ber	lurk	lyre'bird'
lum'ber·yard'	lurked	lyr'ic
lu'mi·nar'y	lus'cious	lyr'i·cal
lu'mi·nes'cence	lush	lyr'i·cism
lu'mi·nes'cent	lust	

M

ma·ca′bre	mac′u·late	mag′is·te′ri·al
mac·ad′am	mad	mag′is·tra·cy
mac·ad′am·ize	mad′am	mag′is·tral
mac′a·ro′ni	mad′den·ing·ly	mag′is·trate
mac′a·roon′	mad′der	mag′is·tra·ture
ma·caw′	mad′dest	mag′na·nim′i·ty
mac′er·ate	mad′house′	mag·nan′i·mous
mac′er·at′ed	mad′ly	mag′nate
mac′er·a′tion	mad′man	mag·ne′sia
Mach	mad′ness	mag·ne′si·um
ma·che′te	ma·don′na	mag′net
ma·chic′o·la′tion	mad′ri·gal	mag·net′ic
mach′i·nate	mael′strom	mag·net′i·cal·ly
mach′i·na′tion	maf′fi·a	mag′net·ism
ma·chine′	mag′a·zine′	mag′net·i·za′tion
ma·chined′	ma·gen′ta	mag′net·ize
ma·chin′er·y	mag′got	mag′net·ized
ma·chin′ist	Ma′gi	mag·ne′to
mack′er·el	mag′ic	mag′ni·fi·ca′tion
mac′ro·cosm	mag′i·cal	mag·nif′i·cence
mac′ro·cyte	mag′i·cal·ly	mag·nif′i·cent
ma′cron	ma·gi′cian	mag·nif′i·co

172

mag'ni·fi'er

mag'ni·fy

mag·nil'o·quent

mag'ni·tude

mag·no'li·a

mag'num

mag'pie

mag'uey

ma·ha'ra'ja

ma·ha'ra'ni

ma·hat'ma

ma·hog'a·ny

maid

maid'en

maid'en·hair'

maid'en·hood

maid'en·ly

maid'serv'ant

mail

mail'a·ble

mail'bag'

mail'box'

mailed

mail'er

mail'ings

maim

maimed

main

main'land'

main'ly

main'mast'

main'sail'

main'sheet'

main'spring'

main'stay'

main·tain'

main·tain'a·ble

main'te·nance

ma·jes'tic

maj'es·ty

ma·jol'i·ca

ma'jor

ma·jor'i·ty

ma·jus'cule

make

make'-be·lieve'

mak'er

make'shift'

mak'ings

mal'a·chite

mal'ad·just'ed

mal'ad·just'ment

mal'a·droit'

mal'a·dy

mal'a·pert

mal'a·prop·ism

mal'ap·ro·pos'

ma·lar'i·a

ma·lar'i·al

mal'as·sim'i·la'tion

Ma·lay'

mal'con·tent'

male

mal'e·dic'tion

mal'e·dic'to·ry

mal'e·fac'tor

ma·lef'i·cence

ma·lef'i·cent

ma·lev'o·lence

ma·lev'o·lent

mal·fea'sance

mal·fea'sor

mal'for·ma'tion

mal·formed'

mal'ice

ma·li'cious

ma·li'cious·ly

ma·li'cious·ness

ma·lign'

ma·lig'nan·cy

ma·lig'nant

ma·lig'nant·ly

ma·ligned'

ma·lig'ni·ty

ma·lign'ly

ma·lin'ger

ma·lin'ger·er

mall

mal'lard

mal'le·a·bil'i·ty

mal'le·a·ble

mal·le'o·lar

mal·le'o·lus

mal'let

mal'low

malm'sey

mal'nu·tri'tion	man'da·to'ry	man'i·fold'er
mal·o'dor·ous	man'di·ble	man'i·kin
mal'po·si'tion	man·dib'u·lar	ma·nip'u·late
mal'prac'tice	man'do·lin	ma·nip'u·lat'ed
malt	man'drake	ma·nip'u·lates
malt'ase	man'drel	ma·nip'u·la'tion
Mal'tese'	ma·neu'ver	ma·nip'u·la'tive
malt'ose	ma·neu'vered	ma·nip'u·la'tor
mal·treat'	man'ga·nate	ma·nip'u·la·to'ry
mal·ver·sa'tion	man'ga·nese	man'kind'
mam'ba	mange	man'like'
mam'mal	man'ger	man'li·ness
mam·ma'li·an	man'gi·ly	man'ly
mam'ma·ry	man'gi·ness	man'na
mam'mon	man'gle	man'ner
mam'moth	man'gled	man'nered
man	man'go	man'ner·ism
man'a·cle	man'grove	man'ner·ly
man'a·cled	man'gy	man'nish
man'age	man'hole'	ma·nom'e·ter
man'age·a·ble	man'hood	man'o·met'ric
man'aged	ma'ni·a	man'or
man'age·ment	ma'ni·ac	ma·no'ri·al
man'ag·er	ma·ni'a·cal	man'sard
man'a·ge'ri·al	man'i·cure	man'serv'ant
man'a·ge'ri·al·ly	man'i·cur'ist	man'sion
man'ag·er·ship'	man'i·fest	man'slaugh'ter
man'a·tee'	man'i·fes·ta'tion	man'teau
man·da'mus	man'i·fest·ed	man'tel
man'da·rin	man'i·fes'to	man·til'la
man'date	man'i·fold	man'tis
man'dat·ed	man'i·fold'ed	man·tis'sa

man'tle

man'u·al

man'u·al·ly

man'u·fac'to·ry

man'u·fac'ture

man'u·fac'tured

man'u·fac'tur·er

man'u·mis'sion

ma·nure'

man'u·script

Manx

man'y

Ma'o·ri

map

ma'ple

mapped

mar

mar'a·bou

mar'a·schi'no

ma·raud'

ma·raud'er

mar'ble

mar'bled

mar'ca·site

march

march'er

mar'chion·ess

mar·co'ni·gram

mare

mar'ga·rine

mar'gin

mar'gin·al

mar'gi·na'li·a

mar'gin·al·ly

mar'grave

mar'i·gold

mar'i·jua'na

ma·rim'ba

ma·ri'na

mar'i·nade'

mar'i·nate

mar'i·nat'ed

ma·rine'

mar'i·ner

mar'i·o·nette'

Mar'ist

mar'i·tal

mar'i·tal·ly

mar'i·time

mar'jo·ram

mark

marked

mark'ed·ly

mark'er

mar'ket

mar'ket·a·bil'i·ty

mar'ket·a·ble

mark'ings

marks'man

marks'man·ship

mark'weed'

marl

mar'lin

mar'ma·lade

mar'mo·set

mar'mot

ma·roon'

ma·rooned'

mar'plot'

mar·quee'

mar'qui·sette'

marred

mar'riage

mar'riage·a·ble

mar'ried

mar'row

mar'row·bone'

mar'row·fat'

mar'row·y

mar'ry

Mars

mar'shal

mar'shaled

marsh'i·ness

marsh'mal'low

marsh'y

mar·su'pi·al

mart

mar'ten

mar'tial

mar'tial·ly

Mar'ti·an

mar'ti·net'

mar'tin·gale

mar'tyr

mar'tyr·dom

mar'tyred

mar'vel

mar'veled

mar'vel·ous

mar'zi·pan

mas·car'a

mas'cot

mas'cu·line

mas'cu·lin'i·ty

mash

mashed

mash'er

mash'ie

mask

masked

mask'er

ma'son

ma·son'ic

ma'son·ry

mas'quer·ade'

mas'quer·ad'ed

mass

mas'sa·cre

mas·sage'

mas·seur'

mas'sive

mast

mas'ter

mas'tered

mas'ter·ful

mas'ter·ful·ly

mas'ter·ful·ness

mas'ter·ly

mas'ter·piece'

mas'ter·ship

mas'ter·work'

mas'ter·y

mast'head'

mas'tic

mas'ti·cate

mas'ti·cat'ed

mas'ti·ca'tion

mas'ti·ca'tor

mas'ti·ca·to'ry

mas'tiff

mas'to·don

mas'toid

mas'toid·i'tis

mat

mat'a·dor

match

matched

match'less

match'less·ly

match'mak'er

match'wood'

ma·té'

ma·te'ri·al

ma·te'ri·al·ism

ma·te'ri·al·ist

ma·te'ri·al·is'tic

ma·te'ri·al'i·ty

ma·te'ri·al·i·za'tion

ma·te'ri·al·ize

ma·te'ri·al·ized

ma·te'ri·al·ly

ma·ter'nal

ma·ter'nal·ly

ma·ter'ni·ty

math'e·mat'i·cal

math'e·ma·ti'cian

math'e·mat'ics

mat'in

mat'i·nee'

ma'tri·arch

ma'tri·arch'y

ma'tri·ces

ma'tri·cide

ma·tric'u·lant

ma·tric'u·late

ma·tric'u·lat'ed

ma·tric'u·lates

ma·tric'u·la'tion

mat'ri·mo'ni·al

mat'ri·mo'ni·al·ly

mat'ri·mo'ny

ma'trix

ma'tron

ma'tron·li·ness

ma'tron·ly

matte

mat'ted

mat'ter

mat'tered

mat'tings

mat'tock

mat'tress	maze	me·a'tus
mat'u·rate	ma·zur'ka	me·chan'ic
mat'u·rat'ed	me	me·chan'i·cal
mat'u·ra'tion	mead'ow	me·chan'i·cal·ly
ma·tur'a·tive	mead'ow·land'	mech'a·ni'cian
ma·ture'	mea'ger	me·chan'ics
ma·tured'	meal	mech'a·nism
ma·ture'ly	meal'i·er	mech'a·ni·za'tion
ma·ture'ness	meal'i·est	mech'a·nize
ma·tu'ri·ty	meal'time'	med'al
ma·tu'ti·nal	meal'y	med'al·ist
maud'lin	meal'y·mouthed'	me·dal'lion
maul	mean	med'dle
mauled	me·an'der	med'dled
maun'der	mean'ing·ful	med'dle·some
mau'so·le'um	mean'ing·less	me'di·a
mauve	mean'ing·ly	me'di·al
mav'er·ick	mean'ings	me'di·an
ma'vis	mean'ly	me'di·ate
maw	mean'ness	me'di·at'ed
mawk'ish	mean'time'	me'di·a'tion
max'il·lar'y	mean'while'	me'di·a'tive
max'im	mea'sles	me'di·a'tor
max'i·mal	meas'ur·a·ble	med'i·cal
max'i·mize	meas'ur·a·bly	med'i·cal·ly
max'i·mum	meas'ure	me·dic'a·ment
may	meas'ured	med'i·cate
may'be	meas'ure·less	med'i·cat'ed
may'hem	meas'ure·ment	med'i·ca'tion
may'on·naise'	meas'ur·er	med'i·ca'tive
may'or	meat	me·dic'i·nal
may'or·al·ty	meat'cut'ter	me·dic'i·nal·ly

med'i·cine

me'di·e'val

me'di·e'val·ist

me'di·e'val·ly

me'di·o'cre

me'di·oc'ri·ty

med'i·tate

med'i·tat'ed

med'i·ta'tion

med'i·ta'tive

me'di·um

med'lar

me·dul'la

meek

meek'er

meek'est

meek'ly

meek'ness

meer'schaum

meet

meet'ings

meet'ing·house'

meg'a·cy'cle

meg'a·phone

mei·o'sis

mei·ot'ic

mel'an·cho'li·a

mel'an·chol'ic

mel'an·chol'y

mel'a·nism

mel'a·no'sis

meld

mel'io·rate

mel'io·rat'ed

mel'io·ra'tion

mel'io·ra'tive

me·lis'ma

mel'is·mat'ic

mel·lif'lu·ous

mel'low

mel'lowed

mel'low·er

mel'low·est

me·lo'de·on

me·lod'ic

me·lo'di·on

me·lo'di·ous

me·lo'di·ous·ly

mel'o·dra'ma

mel'o·dra·mat'ic

mel'o·dy

mel'on

me'los

melt

melt'ed

melt'ing·ly

mem'ber

mem'ber·ship

mem'brane

mem'bra·nous

me·men'to

mem'oir

mem'o·ra·bil'i·a

mem'o·ra·ble

mem'o·ran'da

mem'o·ran'dum

mem'o·ran'dums

me·mo'ri·al

me·mo'ri·al·i·za'tion

me·mo'ri·al·ize

mem'o·ri·za'tion

mem'o·rize

mem'o·rized

mem'o·ry

men'ace

men'aced

me·nage'

me·nag'er·ie

mend

men·da'cious

men·dac'i·ty

mend'ed

Men·de'li·an

men'di·can·cy

men'di·cant

men'folk'

men·ha'den

me'ni·al

me'ni·al·ly

me·nin'ges

men'in·gi'tis

me·nis'cus

Men'non·ite

men'su·ra'tion

men'su·ra'tive

men'tal

men·tal'i·ty

men'tal·ly

men'thol

men'tion

men'tioned

men'tor

men'u

me·phit'ic

mer'can·tile

mer'ce·nar'y

mer'cer·ize

mer'cer·ized

mer'chan·dise

mer'chan·dis'er

mer'chant

mer'chant·man

mer'ci·ful

mer'ci·less

mer'ci·less·ly

mer·cu'ri·al

mer'cu·ry

mer'cy

mere'ly

mer'est

mer'e·tri'cious

merge

merged

merg'er

me·rid'i·an

me·ringue'

me·ri'no

mer'it

mer'it·ed

mer'i·to'ri·ous

mer'i·to'ri·ous·ly

mer'lin

mer'maid'

mer'ri·er

mer'ri·est

mer'ri·ly

mer'ri·ment

mer'ri·ness

mer'ry

mer'ry·mak'ing

me'sa

mes·cal'

mes·cal'ine

mesh

mesh'work'

mes'mer·ism

mes'on

mess

mes'sage

mes'sen·ger

Mes·si'ah

mess'man

mess'mate'

mes·ti'zo

met'a·bol'ic

me·tab'o·lism

met'a·car'pal

met'a·car'pus

met'al

me·tal'lic

me·tal'li·cal·ly

met'al·loid

met'al·lur'gic

met'al·lur'gi·cal

met'al·lur'gy

met'al·ware'

met'al·work'

met'al·work'er

met'a·mor'phose

met'a·mor'phoses

met'a·mor'pho·sis

met'a·phor

met'a·phor'ic

met'a·phor'i·cal

met'a·phor'i·cal·ly

met'a·phys'i·cal

met'a·phys'i·cal·ly

met'a·phy·si'cian

met'a·phys'ics

me·tas'ta·sis

me·tas'ta·size

met'a·tar'sal

met'a·tar'sus

mete

met'ed

me'te·or

me'te·or'ic

me'te·or·ite

me'te·or·oid'

me'te·or·ol'o·gy

me'ter

me'tered

meth'ane	mi·crom'e·ter	mid'year'
me·thinks'	mi'cron	mien
meth'od	mi'cro·phone	might
me·thod'i·cal	mi'cro·scope	might'i·ly
me·thod'i·cal·ly	mi·cro·scop'ic	might'i·ness
meth'od·ist	mi·cros'co·py	might'y
meth'od·ize	mi'cro·spore	mi'graine
meth'od·ol'o·gy	mi'cro·struc'ture	mi'grant
meth'yl	mi'cro·tome	mi'grate
me·tic'u·lous	mi·crot'o·my	mi'grat·ed
mé·tier'	Mi'das	mi·gra'tion
me·ton'y·my	mid'brain'	mi'gra·to'ry
met'ric	mid'day'	mi·ka'do
met'ri·cal	mid'dle	milch
me·trol'o·gy	mid'dle·man'	mild
met'ro·nome	mid'dle·weight'	mild'er
me·trop'o·lis	midge	mild'est
met'ro·pol'i·tan	midg'et	mil'dew
met'tle	mid'i'ron	mild'ly
met'tled	mid'land	mild'ness
met'tle·some	mid'most	mile
Mex'i·can	mid'night'	mile'age
mez'za·nine	mid'riff	mile'post'
mi·as'ma	mid'ship'man	mil'er
mi·as'mal	mid'ships'	mile'stone'
mi'as·mat'ic	midst	mil'i·tant
mi'ca	mid'stream'	mil'i·ta·rism
mi·ca'ce·ous	mid'sum'mer	mil'i·ta·rist
mi'crobe	mid'way'	mil'i·ta·ris'tic
mi'cro·cosm	mid'week'	mil'i·ta·rize
mi'cro·de·ter'mi·na'tion	mid'wife'	mil'i·tar'y
mi'cro·dis·sec'tion	mid'win'ter	mil'i·tate

mil'i·tat'ed

mi·li'tia

milk

milk'maid'

milk'man'

milk'weed'

milk'y

mill

mill'board'

milled

mil'le·nar'y

mil·len'ni·al

mil·len'ni·um

mil'le·pede

mill'er

mil'let

mil'line'

mil'li·ner

mil'li·ner'y

mil'lion

mil'lion·aire'

mil'lion·fold'

mil'lionth

mill'pond'

mill'race'

mill'stone'

mill'work'

mill'wright'

Mil·ton'ic

mime

mim'e·o·graph'

mi·met'ic

mim'ic

mim'ic·ry

mi·mo'sa

min'a·ret'

min'a·to'ry

mince

minced

mince'meat'

minc'ing·ly

mind

mind'ed

mind'ful

mind'less

mine

min'er

min'er·al

min'er·al'o·gy

min'gle

min'gled

min'i·a·ture

min'i·a·tur·ist

min'im

min'i·mal

min'i·mi·za'tion

min'i·mize

min'i·mum

min'ion

min'is·ter

min'is·tered

min'is·te'ri·al

min'is·te'ri·al·ly

min'is·tra'tion

min'is·try

min'i·ver

mink

min'now

mi'nor

mi·nor'i·ty

min'ster

min'strel

min'strel·sy

mint

mint'ed

min'u·end

min'u·et'

mi'nus

mi·nus'cule

min'ute

mi·nute'

mi·nute'ness

mi·nu'ti·a

mi·nu'ti·ae

minx

mir'a·cle

mi·rac'u·lous

mi·rage'

mire

mired

mir'ror

mir'rored

mirth

mirth'ful

mirth'ful·ly

mirth'less

mis'ad·ven'ture

mis'al·li'ance

mis'an·thrope

mis'an·throp'ic

mis'an·throp'i·cal

mis·an'thro·pism

mis·an'thro·pist

mis·an'thro·py

mis'ap·pli·ca'tion

mis'ap·ply'

mis'ap·pre·hen'sion

mis'ap·pro'pri·ate

mis'ap·pro'pri·a'tion

mis'ar·range'

mis'be·got'ten

mis'be·have'

mis'be·haved'

mis'be·hav'ior

mis'be·liev'er

mis·brand'

mis·cal'cu·late

mis·cal'cu·lat'ed

mis·call'

mis·car'riage

mis·car'ried

mis·car'ry

mis·cast'

mis'ce·ge·na'tion

mis'cel·la'ne·a

mis'cel·la'ne·ous

mis'cel·la'nist

mis'cel·la'ny

mis·chance'

mis'chief

mis'chie·vous

mis'ci·ble

mis'con·ceive'

mis'con·cep'tion

mis'con·duct'

mis'con·struc'tion

mis'con·strue'

mis·count'

mis'cre·ant

mis·cue'

mis·date'

mis·deal'

mis·deed'

mis'de·mean'or

mis'di·rect'

mis'di·rect'ed

mis'di·rec'tion

mis·doubt'

mi'ser

mis'er·a·ble

mi'ser·li·ness

mi'ser·ly

mis'er·y

mis·fea'sance

mis·fire'

mis·fired'

mis·fit'

mis·formed'

mis·for'tune

mis·giv'ings

mis·gov'ern

mis·gov'erned

mis·guide'

mis·guid'ed

mis·hap'

mish'mash'

mis'in·form'

mis'in·formed'

mis'in·ter'pret

mis'in·ter'pre·ta'tion

mis'in·ter'pret·ed

mis·judge'

mis·judged'

mis·laid'

mis·lay'

mis·lead'

mis·lead'ing·ly

mis·like'

mis·liked'

mis·made'

mis·man'age

mis·man'age·ment

mis·mate'

mis·mat'ed

mis·name'

mis·named'

mis·no'mer

mi·sog'y·nist

mis·place'

mis·placed'

mis·print'

mis·pri'sion

mis'pro·nounce'

mis·pro·nun'ci·a'tion

mis'quo·ta'tion

mis·quote'

mis·read'

mis're·mem'ber

mis're·mem'brance

mis'rep·re·sent'

mis'rep·re·sen·ta'tion

mis·rule'

miss

mis'sal

missed

mis·shap'en

mis'sile

mis'sion

mis'sion·ar'y

mis'sion·er

mis'sive

mis·spell'

mis·spelled'

mis·spell'ings

mis·spend'

mis·spent'

mis·state'

mis·stat'ed

mis·state'ment

mis·step'

mist

mis·take'

mis·tak'en

mis·tak'en·ly

mis·taught'

mis·teach'

mist'i·er

mist'i·est

mist'i·ly

mist'i·ness

mis'tle·toe

mis·took'

mis·treat'

mis·treat'ment

mis'tress

mis·tri'al

mis·trust'

mis·trust'ful

mist'y

mis'un·der·stand'

mis'un·der·stand'ings

mis'un·der·stood'

mis·us'age

mis·use'

mis·used'

mite

mi'ter

mi'tered

mit'i·ga·ble

mit'i·gate

mit'i·gat'ed

mit'i·ga'tion

mit'i·ga'tive

mit'i·ga·to'ry

mi·to'sis

mi·tot'ic

mi'tral

mit'ten

mit'tened

mix

mixed

mix'er

mix'ture

miz'zen·mast'

mne·mon'ic

mo'a

moan

moaned

moat

mob

mob'cap'

mo'bile

mo·bil'i·ty

mo'bi·li·za'tion

mo'bi·lize

mo'bi·lized

mob·oc'ra·cy

moc'ca·sin

Mo'cha

mock

mock'er·y

mock'ing·ly

mod'al

mo·dal'i·ty

mode

mod'el

mod'eled

mod'er·ate

mod'er·at'ed

mod'er·ate·ly

mod'er·ate·ness

mod'er·a'tion

mod'er·a'tion·ist

mod'er·a'tor

mod'ern

mod'ern·ism

mod'ern·ist

mod'ern·is'tic

mo·der'ni·ty

mod'ern·i·za'tion

mod'ern·ize

mod'ern·ized

mod'est

mod'est·ly

mod'es·ty

mod'i·cum

mod'i·fi·ca'tion

mod'i·fi·ca'tion·ist

mod'i·fied

mod'i·fi'er

mod'i·fy

mod'ish

mod'ish·ly

mod'ish·ness

mod'u·lar

mod'u·late

mod'u·lat'ed

mod'u·la'tion

mod'u·la'tive

mod'u·la'tor

mod'u·la·to'ry

mod'ule

mod'u·lus

mog'a·dore'

Mo·gul'

mo'hair'

Mo·ham'med·an

Mo'hawk

mo'ho

moi'e·ty

moil

moiled

moi·re'

moist

mois'ten

mois'tened

mois'ten·er

mois'ture

mo'lal

mo'lar

mo·lar'i·ty

mo·las'ses

mold

mold'board'

mold'ed

mold'er

mold'ings

mold'y

mole

mo·lec'u·lar

mol'e·cule

mole'hill'

mole'skin'

mo·lest'

mo'les·ta'tion

mo·lest'ed

mol'li·fi·ca'tion

mol'li·fied

mol'li·fy

mol'lusk

mol'ly·cod'dle

molt

molt'ed

mol'ten

mo'ly

mo·lyb'de·num

mo'ment

mo'men·tar'i·ly

mo'men·tar'y

mo'ment·ly

mo·men'tous

mo·men'tum

mon'ad

mo·nad'nock

mon'arch

mo·nar'chi·al

mo·nar'chi·an·ism

mo·nar'chic

mon'arch·ism

mon'arch·ist

mon'arch·is'tic

mon'arch·y

mon'as·te'ri·al

mon'as·te'ri·al·ly

mon'as·ter'y

mo·nas'tic

mo·nas'ti·cism

mon'a·tom'ic

Mon'day

mo·nel'

mon'e·tar'y

mon'e·ti·za'tion

mon'e·tize

mon'ey

mon'eyed

mon'goose

mon'grel

mon'ism

mon'i·tor

mon'i·tored

mon'i·to'ri·al

mon'i·to'ry

monk

mon'key

monk'hood

monk'ish

mon'o·bas'ic

mon'o·cle

mon'o·cled

mo·noc'u·lar

mon'o·dy

mo·nog'a·mous

mo·nog'a·my

mon'o·gram

mon'o·graph

mon'o·lith

mon'o·lith'ic

mon'o·logue

mon'o·ma'ni·a

mon'o·ma'ni·ac

mon'o·ma·ni'a·cal

mon'o·mor'phic

mon'o·plane

mon'o·ple'gi·a

mo·nop'o·lism

mo·nop'o·list

mo·nop'o·lis'tic

mo·nop'o·lis'ti·cal·ly

mo·nop'o·li·za'tion

mo·nop'o·lize

mo·nop'o·lized

mo·nop'o·ly

mon'o·rail'

mon'o·syl·lab'ic

mon'o·syl'la·ble

mon'o·the·ism

mon'o·the·is'tic

mon'o·tone

mo·not'o·nous

mo·not'o·ny

mon'o·type

mon·ox'ide

mon·si'gnor

mon·soon'

mon'ster

mon'strance

mon·stros'i·ty

mon'strous

month

month'ly

mon'u·ment

mon'u·men'tal

mon'u·men'tal·ly

mood

mood'i·ly

mood'i·ness

mood'y

moon

moon'beam'

moon'faced'

moon'fish'

moon'flow'er

moon'light'

moon'light'ed

moon'light'er

moon'light'ing

moon'rise'

moon'shine'

moon'stone'

moon'-struck

moor

moor'age

moored

moor'ings

Moor'ish

moor'land'

moose

moot

mop

mopped

mop'pet	mor'phine	most'ly
mo·raine'	mor'phin·ism	mote
mor'al	mor'phin·ize	mo·tet'
mo·rale'	mor·phol'o·gy	moth
mor'al·ist	mor'ris	moth'er
mor'al·is'tic	mor'row	moth'er·hood
mo·ral'i·ty	mor'sel	moth'er-in-law'
mor'al·i·za'tion	mor'tal	moth'er·land'
mor'al·ize	mor·tal'i·ty	moth'er·less
mor'al·ized	mor'tal·ly	moth'er·li·ness
mor'al·ly	mor'tar	moth'er·ly
mo·rass'	mor'tar·board'	moth'er-of-pearl'
mor'a·to'ri·um	mort'gage	mo·tif'
mo·ray'	mort'gaged	mo'tile
mor'bid	mort'ga·gee'	mo'tion
mor·bid'i·ty	mort'ga·gor'	mo'tioned
mor·bid·ly	mor·ti'cian	mo'tion·less
mor'dant	mor'ti·fi·ca'tion	mo'ti·vate
more	mor'ti·fied	mo'ti·vat'ed
more·o'ver	mor'ti·fy	mo'ti·va'tion
mo'res	mor'tise	mo'ti·va'tion·al
mor'ga·nat'ic	mort'main	mo'tive
morgue	mor'tu·ar'y	mot'ley
mor'i·bund	mo·sa'ic	mo'tor
Mor'mon	Mos'lem	mo'tor·boat'
morn	mosque	mo'tor·cy'cle
morn'ing	mos·qui'to	mo'tored
morn'ings	moss	mo'tor·ist
mo·roc'co	moss'back'	mo'tor·ize
mo'ron	moss'i·ness	mo'tor·man
mo·rose'	moss'y	mot'tle
mo·rose'ly	most	mot'tled

mot'to	mow	mug
mound	mow	mug'gi·ness
mount	mow'er	mug'gy
moun'tain	much	mug'wump'
moun'tain·eer'	mu'ci·lage	mu·lat'to
moun'tain·ous	mu'ci·lag'i·nous	mul'ber'ry
moun'tain·ous·ly	muck	mulch
moun'te·bank	muck'er	mulched
mount'ed	muck'rak'er	mulct
mount'ings	muck'weed'	mulct'ed
mourn	muck'worm'	mule
mourned	mu'coid	mu'le·teer'
mourn'er	mu·co'sa	mu'li·eb'ri·ty
mourn'ful	mu'cous	mul'ish
mouse	mu'cus	mull
mous'er	mud	mulled
mouse'trap'	mud'di·er	mul'let
mousse	mud'di·est	mul'li·ga·taw'ny
mouth	mud'di·ly	mul'lion
mouthed	mud'di·ness	mul'ti·far'i·ous
mouth'ful	mud'dle	mul'ti·fold
mouth'fuls	mud'dled	mul'ti·form
mouth'piece'	mud'dle-head'ed	mul'ti·for'mi·ty
mov'a·bil'i·ty	mud'dy	Mul'ti·graph
mov'a·ble	mud'fish'	Mul'ti·lith'
mov'a·bly	mud'weed'	mul'ti·mil'lion·aire'
move	muff	mul'ti·ped
moved	muf'fin	mul'ti·ple
move'ment	muf'fle	mul'ti·plex
mov'er	muf'fled	mul'ti·pli·cand'
mov'ie	muf'fler	mul'ti·pli·cate
mov'ing·ly	muf'ti	mul'ti·pli·ca'tion

mul'ti·pli·ca'tive	mu'rex	musk
mul'ti·plic'i·ty	mu'ri·at'ic	mus'keg
mul'ti·plied	murk	mus'kel·lunge
mul'ti·pli'er	murk'i·ly	mus'ket
mul'ti·ply	murk'i·ness	mus'ket·eer'
mul'ti·tude	murk'y	mus'ket·ry
mul'ti·tu'di·nous	mur'mur	musk'mel'on
mul'ti·va'lent	mur'mured	musk'rat'
mum'ble	mur'mur·er	mus'lin
mum'bled	mur'mur·ous	muss
mum'mer	mus'ca·dine	mussed
mum'mer·y	mus'cat	mus'sel
mum'mi·fi·ca'tion	mus'ca·tel'	muss'i·er
mum'mi·fied	mus'cle	muss'i·est
mum'mi·fy	mus'cu·lar	muss'y
mum'my	mus'cu·lar'i·ty	must
mumps	mus'cu·lar·ly	mus·tache'
munch	mus'cu·la·ture	mus·ta'chio
munched	muse	mus'tang
mun'dane	mused	mus'tard
mu·nic'i·pal	mu·sette'	mus'ter
mu·nic'i·pal'i·ty	mu·se'um	mus'tered
mu·nic'i·pal·ly	mush	mus'ti·ness
mu·nif'i·cence	mush'room	mus'ty
mu·nif'i·cent	mush'roomed	mu'ta·bil'i·ty
mu'ni·ment	mush'y	mu'ta·ble
mu·ni'tion	mu'sic	mu'tate
mu'ral	mu'si·cal	mu·ta'tion
mur'der	mu'si·cale'	mu'ta·tive
mur'dered	mu'si·cal·ly	mute
mur'der·er	mu·si'cian	mut'ed
mur'der·ous	mu·si'cian·ly	mute'ness

mu'ti·late	muz'zle	mys·te'ri·ous·ly
mu'ti·lat'ed	muz'zled	mys'ter·y
mu'ti·la'tion	my	mys'tic
mu'ti·la'tor	my·col'o·gy	mys'ti·cal
mu'ti·neer'	my·co'sis	mys'ti·cal·ly
mu'ti·nied	my·dri'a·sis	mys'ti·cism
mu'ti·nous	myd'ri·at'ic	mys'ti·fi·ca'tion
mu'ti·ny	my'e·loid	mys'ti·fied
mut'ism	my·o'ma	mys'ti·fy
mut'ter	my·o'pi·a	myth
mut'tered	my·op'ic	myth'i·cal
mut'ter·ings	myr'i·ad	myth'o·log'i·cal
mut'ton	myrrh	my·thol'o·gist
mu'tu·al	myr'tle	my·thol'o·gy
mu'tu·al'i·ty	my·self'	
mu'tu·al·ly	mys·te'ri·ous	

na·celle′

na′cre

na′cre·ous

na′dir

nai′ad

nail

nailed

nail′head′

nain′sook

na·ïve′

na·ïve·té′

na′ked

na′ked·ly

na′ked·ness

nam′a·ble

name

named

name′less

name′less·ly

name′ly

name′sake′

nan·keen′

nap

na′per·y

naph′tha

naph′tha·lene

nap′kin

na·po′le·on

Na·po′le·on·a′na

Na·po′le·on′ic

napped

nar·cis′sism

nar·cis′sus

nar·co′sis

nar·cot′ic

nar·cot′i·cism

nar′co·tize

nar′co·tized

nar·rate′

nar·rat′ed

nar·ra′tion

nar′ra·tive

nar·ra′tor

nar′row

nar′rowed

nar′row·er

nar′row·est

nar′row·ly

nar′row·ness

nar′whal

na′sal

na·sal′i·ty

na′sal·ize

na′sal·ly

nas′cent

nas′ti·er

nas′ti·est

nas′ti·ly

nas′ti·ness

nas·tur′tium

nas′ty

na′tal

na·ta′tion

na′ta·to′ri·um

na′ta·to′ry

na′tion

na'tion·al

na'tion·al·ism

na'tion·al·is'tic

na'tion·al'i·ty

na'tion·al·i·za'tion

na'tion·al·ize

na'tion·al·ized

na'tion·al·ly

na'tive

na·tiv'i·ty

nat'u·ral

nat'u·ral·ism

nat'u·ral·ist

nat'u·ral·is'tic

nat'u·ral·i·za'tion

nat'u·ral·ize

nat'u·ral·ized

nat'u·ral·ly

nat'u·ral·ness

na'ture

na'tur·is'tic

naught

naugh'ti·ly

naugh'ti·ness

naugh'ty

nau'se·a

nau'se·ate

nau'se·at'ed

nau'seous

nau'ti·cal

nau'ti·lus

na'val

nave

na'vel

nav'i·ga·ble

nav'i·gate

nav'i·gat'ed

nav'i·ga'tion

nav'i·ga'tion·al

nav'i·ga'tor

na'vy

Naz'a·rene'

neap

Ne'a·pol'i·tan

near

near'by'

neared

near'er

near'est

near'ly

near'ness

near'sight'ed

neat

neat'er

neat'est

neat'herd'

neat'ly

neat'ness

neb'u·la

neb'u·lar

neb'u·los'i·ty

neb'u·lous

neb'u·lous·ly

nec'es·sar'i·ly

nec'es·sar'y

ne·ces'si·tar'i·an

ne·ces'si·tate

ne·ces'si·tat'ed

ne·ces'si·tous

ne·ces'si·ty

neck

neck'band'

neck'cloth'

neck'er·chief

neck'lace

neck'tie'

neck'wear'

nec'ro·log'i·cal

ne·crol'o·gy

nec'ro·man'cy

nec'ro·man'tic

nec'ro·pho'bi·a

ne·crop'o·lis

nec'rop·sy

ne·cro'sis

ne·crot'ic

nec'tar

nec'tar·ine'

need

need'ed

need'ful

need'ful·ly

need'i·er

need'i·est

need'i·ness

nee'dle

nee'dled

nee'dle·ful

need'less

need'less·ly

need'less·ness

nee'dle·work'

need'y

ne·far'i·ous

ne·gate'

ne·gat'ed

ne·ga'tion

neg'a·tive

neg'a·tived

neg'a·tiv·ism

neg·lect'

neg·lect'ed

neg·lect'ful

neg'li·gee'

neg'li·gence

neg'li·gent

neg'li·gi·ble

ne·go'ti·a·bil'i·ty

ne·go'ti·a·ble

ne·go'ti·ate

ne·go'ti·at'ed

ne·go'ti·a'tion

ne·go'ti·a'tor

Ne'gro

Ne'gro·phile

neigh'bor

neigh'bor·hood

neigh'bor·li·ness

neigh'bor·ly

nei'ther

nem'a·tode

Nem'e·sis

ne'o·for·ma'tion

ne'o·lith'ic

ne·ol'o·gism

ne·ol'o·gy

ne'on

ne'o·phyte

ne'o·plasm

ne·pen'the

neph'ew

ne·phrec'to·my

ne·phri'tis

nep'o·tism

nerve

nerve'less

ner'vous

nerv'ous·ly

nerv'ous·ness

nes'ci·ence

nes'ci·ent

nest

nest'ed

nes'tle

nes'tled

nest'lings

net

neth'er

neth'er·most

net'su·ke

net'ted

net'tings

net'tle

net'tled

net'work'

neu'ral

neu·ral'gia

neu'ras·the'ni·a

neu'ras·then'ic

neu·ri'tis

neu·ro'ses

neu·ro'sis

neu·rot'ic

neu'ter

neu'tral

neu'tral·ism

neu'tral·ist

neu·tral'i·ty

neu'tral·i·za'tion

neu'tral·ize

neu'tral·ized

neu'tral·iz'er

neu'tral·ly

neu'tron

nev'er

nev'er·more'

nev'er·the·less'

new

new'com'er

new'el

new'er

new'est

new'fan'gled

new'ly

new'ness

news'i·er

news'i·est

news'let'ter

news'pa'per

news'reel'

news'stand'

news'y

newt

next

nex'us

nib'ble

nib'bled

nib'lick

nice

nice'ly

nice'ness

nic'er

nic'est

ni'ce·ty

niche

nick

nicked

nick'el

nick'el·if'er·ous

nick'el·o'de·on

nick'name'

nick'named'

nic'o·tine

nic'o·tin'ic

niece

ni·el'lo

nig'gard

nig'gard·li·ness

nig'gard·ly

nig'gle

nig'gling·ly

nigh

night

night'cap'

night'fall'

night'fish'

night'gown'

night'hawk'

night'in·gale

night'ly

night'mare'

night'mar'ish

night'shade'

night'shirt'

night'time'

night'wear'

night'work'

night'work'er

ni'hil·ism

ni'hil·ist

ni'hil·is'tic

nim'ble

nim'bus

nin'com·poop

nine'pins'

nip'per

nip'ple

nip'py

nir·va'na

ni'ter

ni'trate

ni'tric

ni'tride

ni'tri·fi·ca'tion

ni'tri·fy

ni'tro·gen

ni·trog'e·nous

ni'tro·glyc'er·in

ni'trous

nit'wit'

no

no·bil'i·ty

no'ble

no'ble·man

no'bler

no'blest

no'bly

no'bod·y

noc·tur'nal

noc·tur'nal·ly

nod

nod'ded

node

nod'ule

no·el'

noise

noise'less

nois'i·er

nois'i·est

nois'i·ly

nois'i·ness

noi'some

nois'y

no'mad

no·mad'ic

no'men·cla'ture

nom'i·nal

nom'i·nal·ism

nom'i·nal·ly

nom'i·nate

nom'i·nat'ed

nom'i·na'tion

nom'i·na·tive

nom'i·nee'

non'a·ge·nar'i·an

non'a·gon

non'ap·pear'ance

non·call'a·ble

nonce

non'cha·lance

non'cha·lant

non'cha·lant·ly

non·com'bat·ant

non·com·mis'sioned

non·com·mit'tal

non·com·mu'ni·cant

non·con·duc'tor

non·con·form'ism

non·con·form'ist

non'con·form'i·ty

non'-co-op'er·a'tion

non'de·script

non·en'ti·ty

non·es·sen'tial

none'such'

non·ex·ist'ence

non·fea'sance

non·fea'sor

non·for'feit·ure

non'in·ter·ven'tion

non'met'al

non'me·tal'lic

non'pa·reil'

non'par·tic'i·pat'ing

non·par'ti·san

non·per'ma·nent

non'plus

non'plused

non·res'i·dence

non·res'i·dent

non're·sist'ance

non're·sist'ant

non'sense

non·sen'si·cal

non'skid'

non'stop'

non'sub·scrib'er

non'suit'

non'sup·port'

non·un'ion

noo'dle

nook

noon

noon'day'

noon'time'

noose

nor

norm

nor'mal

nor'mal'i·ty

nor'mal·ize

nor'mal·ized

nor'mal·ly

Nor'man

nor'ma·tive

Norse

north

north'east'

north'east'er

north'east'er·ly

north'east'ern

north'east'ward

north'east'ward·ly

north'er·ly

north'ern

north'ern·er

north'land

north'ward

north'west'

north'west'er·ly

north'west'ern

Nor·we'gian

nose	no'ti·fied	noz'zle
nose'band'	no'ti·fy	nu·ance'
nose'bleed'	no'tion	nu'cle·ar
nose'gay'	no·to·ri'e·ty	nu'cle·ate
nose'piece'	no·to'ri·ous	nu'cle·at'ed
nos'ings	no·to'ri·ous·ly	nu'cle·a'tion
no·sol'o·gy	not'with·stand'ing	nu'cle·i
nos·tal'gi·a	nou'gat	nu·cle'o·lus
nos·tal'gic	nou'ga·tine	nu'cle·us
nos'tril	nought	nude
nos'trum	nou'me·non	nudge
not	noun	nudged
no·ta·bil'i·ty	nour'ish	nud'ism
no'ta·ble	nour'ished	nud'ist
no·tar'i·al	nour'ish·ing·ly	nu'di·ty
no·tar'i·al·ly	nour'ish·ment	nu'ga·to'ry
no'ta·ry	nov'el	nug'get
no·ta'tion	nov'el·ette'	nui'sance
notch	nov'el·ist	null
notched	nov'el·ize	nul'li·fi·ca'tion
notch'weed'	no·vel'la	nul'li·fi·ca'tion·ist
note	nov'el·ty	nul'li·fied
note'book'	No·vem'ber	nul'li·fy
not'ed	no·ve'na	nul'li·ty
note'wor'thi·ly	nov'ice	numb
note'wor'thy	no·vi'ti·ate	numbed
noth'ing	No'vo·cain'	num'ber
noth'ing·ness	now	num'bered
no'tice	now'a·days'	num'ber·less
no'tice·a·ble	no'where	numb'ness
no'ticed	nox'ious	nu'mer·al
no'ti·fi·ca'tion	nox'ious·ness	nu'mer·ate

nu'mer·a'tion

nu'mer·a'tor

nu·mer'ic

nu·mer'i·cal

nu'mer·ous

nu'mis·mat'ics

nu·mis'ma·tist

num'skull'

nun

nun'ci·a·ture

nun'ci·o

nun'ner·y

nup'tial

nurse

nursed

nurse'maid'

nurs'er·y

nurs'er·y·maid'

nurs'er·y·man

nurs'lings

nur'ture

nur'tured

nut

nut'hatch'

nut'meg

nu'tri·a

nu'tri·ent

nu'tri·ment

nu·tri'tion

nu·tri'tion·al

nu·tri'tion·al·ly

nu·tri'tion·ist

nu·tri'tious

nu·tri'tious·ly

nu'tri·tive

nu'tri·tive·ly

nut'shell'

nuz'zle

nuz'zled

nyc'ta·lo'pi·a

nymph

nys·tag'mus

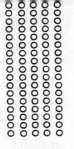

oaf

oak

oak'en

oa'kum

oar

oar'lock'

oars'man

o·a'sis

oat'en

oath

oat'meal'

ob'bli·ga'to

ob'du·ra·cy

ob'du·rate

o·be'di·ence

o·be'di·ent

o·bei'sance

ob'e·lisk

o·bese'

o·bes'i·ty

o·bey'

o·beyed'

o·bit'u·ar'y

ob·ject'

ob·ject'ed

ob·jec'tion

ob·jec'tion·a·ble

ob·jec'tive

ob·jec'tive·ly

ob·jec'tive·ness

ob'jec·tiv'i·ty

ob·jec'tor

ob'jur·gate

ob'late

ob·la'tion

ob'li·gate

ob'li·gat'ed

ob'li·ga'tion

ob·lig'a·to'ry

o·blige'

o·bliged'

o·blig'ing·ly

ob·lique'

ob·lique'ly

ob·lique'ness

ob·liq'ui·ty

ob·lit'er·ate

ob·lit'er·at'ed

ob·lit'er·a'tion

ob·liv'i·on

ob·liv'i·ous

ob·liv'i·ous·ly

ob·liv'i·ous·ness

ob'long

ob'lo·quy

ob·nox'ious

ob·nox'ious·ly

o'boe

ob·scene'

ob·scen'i·ty

ob·scure'

ob·scure'ness

ob·scu'ri·ty

ob·se'qui·ous

ob·se'qui·ous·ly

ob·se'qui·ous·ness

197

ob·se·quy

ob·serv'a·ble

ob·serv'ance

ob·serv'ant

ob·ser·va'tion

ob·serv'a·to'ry

ob·serve'

ob·served'

ob·serv'er

ob·serv'ing·ly

ob·sess'

ob·sessed'

ob·ses'sion

ob·ses'sion·al

ob·ses'sive

ob·sid'i·an

ob'so·les'cence

ob'so·les'cent

ob'so·lete

ob'so·lete·ly

ob'so·lete·ness

ob'sta·cle

ob·stet'ri·cal

ob'ste·tri'cian

ob·stet'rics

ob'sti·na·cy

ob'sti·nate

ob'sti·nate·ly

ob·strep'er·ous

ob·struct'

ob·struct'ed

ob·struc'tion

ob·struc'tion·ism

ob·struc'tion·ist

ob·struc'tive

ob·struc'tor

ob·tain'

ob·tain'a·ble

ob·tained'

ob·trude'

ob·trud'ed

ob·trud'er

ob·tru'sion

ob·tru'sive

ob·tuse'

ob·tuse'ly

ob·tuse'ness

ob'verse

ob'vi·ate

ob'vi·at'ed

ob'vi·a'tion

ob'vi·ous

ob'vi·ous·ly

oc·a·ri'na

oc·ca'sion

oc·ca'sion·al

oc·ca'sion·al·ly

oc·ca'sioned

oc'ci·dent

oc'ci·den'tal

oc'ci·den'tal·ly

oc·cip'i·tal

oc'ci·put

oc·clude'

oc·clud'ed

oc·clu'sion

oc·cult'

oc'cul·ta'tion

oc·cult'ism

oc·cult'ist

oc'cu·pan·cy

oc'cu·pant

oc'cu·pa'tion

oc'cu·pa'tion·al

oc'cu·pa'tion·al·ly

oc'cu·pied

oc'cu·py

oc·cur'

oc·curred'

oc·cur'rence

o'cean

o'ce·an'ic

o'ce·a·nog'ra·phy

o'ce·lot

o'cher

och·loc'ra·cy

oc'ta·gon

oc·tag'o·nal

oc·tag'o·nal·ly

oc·tam'e·ter

oc·tan'gu·lar

oc'tave

oc·ta'vo

oc·tet'

Oc·to'ber

oc'to·ge·nar'i·an

oc'to·pus

oc'u·lar

oc'u·list

odd

odd'er

odd'est

odd'i·ty

odd'ly

odd'ment

odd'ness

ode

o·de'um

o'di·ous

o'di·ous·ly

o'di·ous·ness

o'di·um

o·dom'e·ter

o'dor

o'dor·if'er·ous

o'dor·less

o'dor·ous

oe·nol'o·gy

of

off

off'fal

off'cast'

of·fend'

of·fend'ed

of·fense'

of·fen'sive

of'fer

of'fered

of'fer·ings

of'fer·to'ry

off'hand'

of'fice

of'fi·cer

of·fi'cial

of·fi'cial·ly

of·fi'ci·ate

of·fi'ci·at'ed

of·fi'ci·a'tion

of·fi'cious

of·fi'cious·ly

of·fi'cious·ness

off'ish

off'set'

off'shoot'

off'shore'

of'ten

of'ten·er

of'ten·est

of'ten·times'

o·gee'

o'give

o'gle

o'gled

o'gre

ohm

ohm'age

ohm'me'ter

oil

oiled

oil'er

oil'hole'

oil'i·er

oil'i·est

oil'i·ly

oil'i·ness

oil'man

oil'pa'per

oil'proof'

oil'seed'

oil'skin'

oil'stone'

oil'tight'

oil'y

oint'ment

o·ka'pi

o'kra

old

old'en

old'er

old'est

old'-fash'ioned

old'ish

old'ness

old'ster

o'le·ag'i·nous

o'le·an'der

o'le·ate

o·lec'ra·non

o'le·o

o'le·o·mar'ga·rine

ol·fac'to·ry

ol'i·garch'y

ol'ive

o·me'ga

om'e·let

o'men

o·men'tum

om'i·nous

o·mis'sion

o·mit'

o·mit'ted

om'ni·bus

om·nip'o·tence

om·nip'o·tent

om'ni·pres'ent

om·nis'cience

om·nis'cient

om·niv'o·rous

on

on'a·ger

once

one

one'ness

on'er·ous

one·self'

one'time'

on'ion

on'look'er

on'ly

on'o·mat'o·poe'ia

on'set'

on'slaught'

on'to

on·tog'e·ny

on·tol'o·gy

o'nus

on'ward

on'yx

o·öl'o·gy

oo'long

ooze

oozed

o·pac'i·ty

o'pal

o'pal·esce'

o'pal·es'cence

o'pal·es'cent

o·paque'

o'pen

o'pened

o'pen·er

o'pen·ings

o'pen·ly

o'pen·ness

o'pen·work'

op'er·a

op'er·a·ble

op'er·a·logue'

op'er·ate

op'er·at'ed

op'er·at'ic

op'er·at'i·cal·ly

op'er·a'tion

op'er·a'tive

op'er·a'tor

op'er·et'ta

oph'thal·mol'o·gist

oph'thal·mol'o·gy

o'pi·ate

o·pin'ion

o·pin'ion·at'ed

o·pin'ion·a'tive

o'pi·um

o·pos'sum

op·po'nent

op'por·tune'

op'por·tun'ism

op'por·tu'ni·ty

op·pos'a·ble

op·pose'

op·posed'

op·pos'er

op·pos'ing

op'po·site

op'po·si'tion

op·press'

op·pressed'

op·pres'sion

op·pres'sive

op·pres'sive·ly

op·pres'sive·ness

op·pres'sor

op·pro'bri·ous

op·pro'bri·ous·ly

op·pro'bri·ous·ness

op·pro'bri·um

opt

opt'ed

op'ta·tive

op'tic

op'ti·cal

op·ti'cian

op'tics

op'ti·mism

op'ti·mist

op'ti·mis'tic

op'ti·mis'ti·cal·ly

op'ti·mum

op'tion

op'tion·al

op'tion·al·ly

op·tom'e·trist

op·tom'e·try

op'u·lence

op'u·lent

o'pus

or

or'a·cle

o·rac'u·lar

o·rac'u·lar·ly

o'ral

o'ral·ly

or'ange

o·rang'u·tan'

o·ra'tion

or'a·tor

or'a·tor'i·cal

or'a·to'ri·o

or'a·to'ry

orb

or'bit

or'bit·al

or'bit·ed

or'chard

or'ches·tra

or·ches'tral

or'ches·trate

or'ches·trat'ed

or·ches·tra'tion

or'chid

or'chi·da'ceous

or·dain'

or·dained'

or·deal'

or'der

or'dered

or'der·li·ness

or'der·ly

or'di·nal

or'di·nance

or'di·nar'i·ly

or'di·nar'y

or'di·na'tion

ord'nance

ore

or'gan

or·gan'ic

or·gan'i·cal·ly

or'gan·ism

or'gan·ist

or'gan·i·za'tion

or'gan·i·za'tion·al

or'gan·ize

or'gan·ized

or'gy

o'ri·el

o'ri·ent

o'ri·en'tal

o'ri·en'tal·ism

o'ri·en'tal·ist

o'ri·en'tal·ly

o'ri·en·tate'

o'ri·en·ta'tion

o'ri·ent'ed

or'i·fice

or'i·gin

o·rig'i·nal

o·rig'i·nal'i·ty

o·rig'i·nal·ly

o·rig'i·nate

o·rig'i·nat'ed

o·rig'i·na'tion

o·rig'i·na'tive

o·rig'i·na'tor

o'ri·ole

O·ri'on

or'i·son

or'lop

or'mo·lu

or'na·ment

or'na·men'tal

or'na·men'tal·ly

or'na·men·ta'tion

or·nate'

or·nate'ly	os'se·ous	out'crop'
or'ni·tho·log'i·cal	os'si·fi·ca'tion	out'cry'
or'ni·thol'o·gist	os'si·fied	out·curve'
or'ni·thol'o·gy	os'si·fy	out·dis'tance
o'ro·tund	os·ten'si·ble	out·do'
o'ro·tun'di·ty	os·ten'si·bly	out'doors'
or'phan	os'ten·ta'tion	out'er
or'phan·age	os'ten·ta'tious	out'er·most
or'phaned	os'ten·ta'tious·ly	out·face'
or'phan·hood	os'te·o·path	out'field'
or'phe·um	os'te·op'a·thy	out'fit
or'rer·y	os'tra·cism	out'fit'ter
or'tho·dox	os'tra·cize	out·flank'
or'tho·ëp'y	os'tra·cized	out'flow'
or·thog'ra·phy	os'trich	out·go'
or'tho·pe'dic	o·tal'gi·a	out'growth'
or·thop'tic	oth'er	out'ings
or'to·lan	oth'er·wise'	out·land'ish
os'cil·late	o'ti·ose	out·land'ish·ness
os'cil·lat'ed	ot'ter	out·last'
os'cil·la'tion	Ot'to·man	out'law'
os'cil·la'tor	ought	out'law'ry
os·cil·la·to'ry	ounce	out'lay'
os·cil'lo·scope	our	out'let
os'cu·late	ours	out'lets
os'cu·la'tion	our·selves'	out'line'
os'cu·la·to'ry	oust	out'lined'
o'sier	oust'er	out·live'
os'mi·um	out	out·lived'
os·mo'sis	out'cast'	out·look'
os·mot'ic	out·class'	out'ly'ing
os'prey	out·come'	out'march'

out·mod'ed

out·num'ber

out'put'

out'rage

out·ra'geous

out·ra'geous·ly

out·ra'geous·ness

out·rank'

out·ranked'

out·reach'

out'rid·er

out'rig'ger

out'right'

out·run'

out'set'

out'side'

out'sid'er

out'size'

out'skirt'

out·stand'ing·ly

out·stay'

out·strip'

out·vote'

out'ward

out'ward·ly

out·wear'

out·wit'

out·work'

o'val

o'vate

o·va'tion

ov'en

ov'en·bird'

ov'en·ware'

o'ver

o'ver·age

o'ver·age'

o'ver·alls'

o'ver·awe'

o'ver·awed'

o'ver·bal'ance

o'ver·bear'

o'ver·bear'ing·ly

o'ver·bid'

o'ver·board'

o'ver·build'

o'ver·built'

o'ver·bur'den

o'ver·cap'i·tal·ize

o'ver·cast'

o'ver·charge'

o'ver·charged'

o'ver·clothes'

o'ver·coat'

o'ver·come'

o'ver·com'pen·sa'tion

o'ver·cor·rect'

o'ver·count'

o'ver·de·vel'op

o'ver·do'

o'ver·done'

o'ver·dose'

o'ver·draft'

o'ver·draw'

o'ver·drawn'

o'ver·dress'

o'ver·drew'

o'ver·drive'

o'ver·driv'en

o'ver·due'

o'ver·eat'

o'ver·es'ti·mate

o'ver·ex·pose'

o'ver·ex·po'sure

o'ver·flow'

o'ver·flow'ing·ly

o'ver·grown'

o'ver·hand'

o'ver·hang'

o'ver·haul'

o'ver·head'

o'ver·heat'

o'ver·is'sue

o'ver·land'

o'ver·lap'

o'ver·look'

o'ver·lord'

o'ver·ly

o'ver·mas'ter·ing·ly

o'ver·mod'u·la'tion

o'ver·night'

o'ver·pass'

o'ver·pay'

o'ver·pop'u·la'tion

o'ver·pow'er

o'ver·pow'ered

o'ver·pow'er·ing·ly	o'ver·sub·scribe'	o'vule
o'ver·pro·duc'tion	o'ver·sup·ply'	o'vum
o'ver·rate'	o'vert	owe
o'ver·rat'ed	o'ver·take'	owed
o'ver·reach'	o'ver·tax'	owl
o'ver·ride'	o'ver·taxed'	owl'et
o'ver·ripe'	o'ver·threw'	owl'ish
o'ver·rule'	o'ver·throw'	own
o'ver·ruled'	o'ver·thrown'	owned
o'ver·run'	o'ver·time'	own'er
o'ver·seas'	o'ver·tone'	own'er·ship
o'ver·see'	o'ver·ture	ox
o'ver·se'er	o'ver·turn'	ox'a·late
o'ver·sell'	o'ver·turned'	ox·al'ic
o'ver·shad'ow	o'ver·val'ue	ox'i·da'tion
o'ver·shad'owed	o'ver·ween'ing·ly	ox'ide
o'ver·shoe'	o'ver·weight'	ox'i·diz'a·ble
o'ver·side'	o'ver·whelm'	ox'i·dize
o'ver·sight'	o'ver·whelmed'	ox'i·dized
o'ver·size'	o'ver·whelm'ing·ly	ox'tongue'
o'ver·spread'	o'ver·wind'	ox'y·gen
o'ver·state'	o'ver·work'	ox'y·gen·ate
o'ver·state'ment	o'ver·worked'	oys'ter
o'ver·stay'	o'ver·wrought'	oys'ter·shell'
o'ver·step'	o'vi·duct	o'zone
o'ver·stock'	o·vip'a·rous	o'zo·nize
o'ver·strain'	o'vi·pos'i·tor	o'zo·nized

P

pab'u·lum	pack'sack'	paid
pace	pack'sad'dle	pail
pace'mak'er	pack'thread'	pain
pac'er	pact	pained
pach'y·derm	pad	pain'ful
pach'y·san'dra	pad'ded	pain'kill'er
pa·cif'ic	pad'dings	pain'less
pa·cif'i·cal·ly	pad'dle	pains'tak'ing·ly
pa·cif'i·cate	pad'dled	paint
pac'i·fi·ca'tion	pad'dle·fish'	paint'ed
pa·cif'i·ca·to'ry	pad'dock	paint'er
pac'i·fied	pad'lock'	paint'ings
pac'i·fi'er	pae'an	paint'pot'
pac'i·fism	pa'gan	pair
pac'i·fist	pa'gan·ism	paired
pac'i·fy	pa'gan·ize	pair'ings
pack	page	pa·ja'ma
pack'age	pag'eant	pal'ace
pack'aged	pag'eant·ry	pal'a·din
pack'er	paged	pal'an·quin'
pack'et	pag'i·na'tion	pal'at·a·bil'i·ty
pack'ings	pa·go'da	pal'at·a·ble

pal'a·tal

pal'a·tal·ize

pal'ate

pa·la'tial

pa·la'tial·ly

pa·lat'i·nate

pal'a·tine

pa·lav'er

pale

paled

pa'le·og'ra·phy

pal'er

pal'est

pal'ette

pal'frey

pal'imp·sest

pal'in·drome

pal'ings

pal'i·node

pal'i·sade'

pall

pal·la'di·um

pall'bear'er

palled

pal'let

pal'li·ate

pal'li·at'ed

pal'li·a'tion

pal'li·a'tive

pal'lid

pal·lid'i·ty

pal'lid·ly

pal'li·um

pal'lor

palm

pal'mate

palmed

palm'er

palm·met'to

palm'ist

palm'is·try

pal'pa·bil'i·ty

pal'pa·ble

pal'pate

pal'pat·ed

pal·pa'tion

pal'pa·to'ry

pal'pi·tant

pal'pi·tate

pal'pi·tat'ed

pal'pi·tat'ing·ly

pal'pi·ta'tion

pal'sied

pal'sy

pal'ter

pal'tered

pal'try

pam'pas

pam'per

pam'pered

pam'phlet

pam'phlet·eer'

pam'phlet·ize

pan

pan'a·ce'a

pan'a·ma'

Pan'-A·mer'i·can

Pan'-A·mer'i-can·ism

pan'cake'

pan'chro·mat'ic

pan'cre·as

pan'cre·at'ic

pan'da

pan·dem'ic

pan'de·mo'ni·um

pan'der

pan'dered

pane

pan'e·gyr'ic

pan'e·gyr'i·cal

pan'e·gy·rize

pan'e·gy·rized

pan'el

pan'eled

pang

Pan'hel·len'ic

pan'ic

pan'icked

pan'ick·y

pan·jan'drum

panned

pan'nier

pan'ni·kin

pan'o·ply

pan'o·ra'ma

pan'o·ram'ic

pan'sy

pant

pan'ta·loon'

pant'ed

pan'the·ism

pan'the·ist

pan'the·is'tic

pan'the·on

pan'ther

pan'to·graph

pan'to·mime

pan'try

pan'try·man

pa'pa·cy

pa'pal

pa·pay'a

pa'per

pa'per·back'

pa'per·board'

pa'pered

pa'per·er

pap'e·terie

pa·poose'

pa·pri'ka

Pap'u·an

pap'ule

pa·py'rus

par

par'a·ble

pa·rab'o·la

par'a·bol'ic

par'a·bol'i·cal

pa·rab'o·loid

par'a·chute

pa·rade'

pa·rad'ed

par'a·digm

par'a·dise

par'a·dox

par'a·dox'i·cal

par'af·fin

par'a·gon

par'a·graph

par'a·graphed

par'a·keet

par'al·lax

par'al·lel

par'al·leled

par'al·lel·ism

par'al·lel'o·gram

pa·ral'y·sis

par'a·lyt'ic

par'a·lyt'i·cal·ly

par'a·lyze

par'a·lyzed

pa·ram'e·ter

par'a·mount

par'a·noi'a

par'a·noi'ac

par'a·noid

par'a·pet

par'a·pher·na'li·a

par'a·phrase

par'a·phrased

par'a·phras'tic

par'a·ple'gi·a

par'a·pleg'ic

par'a·site

par'a·sit'ic

par'a·sit'i·cal

par'a·sit'i·cide

par'a·sit·ism

par'a·sit·ize

par'a·sol

par'a·thy'roid

par'a·ty'phoid

par'a·vane

par'boil'

par'boiled'

par'cel

par'celed

parch

parched

parch'ment

par'don

par'don·a·ble

par'doned

pare

pared

par'e·gor'ic

pa·ren'chy·ma

par'ent

par'ent·age

pa·ren'tal

pa·ren'tal·ly

pa·ren'the·ses

par·en'the·sis

par·en'the·size

par'en·thet'i·cal

par'en·thet'i·cal·ly

par'ent·hood

pa·re'sis

par·fait'

pa·ri'ah

pa·ri'e·tal

par'ings

par'ish

pa·rish'ion·er

par'i·ty

park

par'ka

parked

park'way'

par'lance

par·lan'do

par'lay

par'ley

par'leyed

par'lia·ment

par'lia·men·tar'i·an

par'lia·men'ta·ri·ly

par'lia·men'ta·ry

par'lor

par'lous

Par'me·san'

Par·nas'sus

pa·ro'chi·al

pa·ro'chi·al·ism

pa·ro'chi·al·ly

par'o·dy

pa·role'

par'o·no·ma'si·a

pa·rot'id

par'ox·ysm

par'ox·ys'mal

par'ox·ys'mal·ly

par·quet'

par'ri·cid'al

par'ri·cid'al·ly

par'ri·cide

par'ried

par'rot

par'rot·ed

par'ry

parse

parsed

par'si·mo'ni·ous

par'si·mo'ny

pars'ley

pars'nip

par'son

par'son·age

part

par·take'

par·tak'er

part'ed

par·terre'

par'the·no·gen'e·sis

Par'the·non

Par'thi·an

par'tial

par'ti·al'i·ty

par'tial·ly

par·tic'i·pant

par·tic'i·pate

par·tic'i·pat'ed

par·tic'i·pa'tion

par·tic'i·pa'tive

par·tic'i·pa'tor

par'ti·cip'i·al

par'ti·cip'i·al·ly

par'ti·ci·ple

par'ti·cle

par·tic'u·lar

par·tic'u·lar'i·ty

par·tic'u·lar·ize

par·tic'u·lar·ized

par·tic'u·lar·ly

part'ings

par'ti·san

par'ti·san·ship'

par·ti'tion

par·ti'tioned

par'ti·tive

part'ner

part'ner·ship

par'tridge

par'ty

par've·nu

pas'chal

pa·sha'

pass

pass'a·ble

pas'sage

pas'sage·way'

pass'book'

passed

pas'sen·ger

pas'sion

pas'sion·ate

pas'sion·ate·ly

Pas'sion·ist

pas'sion·less

pas'sive

pas'sive·ness

pas'siv·ism

pas'siv·ist

pas·siv'i·ty

pass'key'

pass'o·ver

pass'port

pass'word'

past

paste

paste'board'

past'ed

pas·tel'

pas'tern

pas'teur·i·za'tion

pas'teur·ize

pas'teur·ized

pas·tiche'

pas·tille'

pas'time'

past'i·ness

pas'tor

pas'to·ral

pas'to·ral·ly

pas'tor·ate

pas'try

pas'try·man

pas'tur·age

pas'ture

pas'tured

past'y

pat

Pat·a·go'ni·an

patch

patched

patch'ou·li

patch'work'

patch'y

pa·tel'la

pa·tel'lar

pat'ent

pat'ent·a·ble

pat'ent·ed

pat'ent·ee'

pa'ter·fa·mil'i·as

pa·ter'nal

pa·ter'nal·ism

pa·ter'nal·is'tic

pa·ter'nal·ly

pa·ter'ni·ty

path

pa·thet'ic

pa·thet'i·cal·ly

path'less

pa·thol'o·gist

pa·thol'o·gy

pa'thos

path'way'

pa'tience

pa'tient

pat'i·na

pa'ti·o

pat'ness

pat'ois

pa'tri·arch

pa'tri·ar'chal

pa'tri·arch'ate

pa'tri·arch'y

pa·tri'cian

pat'ri·cide

pat'ri·mo'ni·al

pat'ri·mo'ny

pa'tri·ot

pa'tri·ot'ic

pa'tri·ot'i·cal·ly

pa'tri·ot·ism

pa·tris'tic

pa·trol'

pa·trolled'

pa·trol'man

pa'tron

pa'tron·age

pa'tron·ess

pa'tron·ize

pa'tron·ized

pat'ro·nym'ic

pa·troon'

pat'ted

pat'ten

pat'ter

pat'tered

pat'tern

pat'terned

pau'ci·ty

Paul'ist

paunch

paunch'i·ness

pau'per

pau'per·ism

pau'per·i·za'tion

pau'per·ize

pau'per·ized

pause

paused

pave

paved

pave'ment

pav'er

pa·vil'lion

paw

pawed

pawl

pawn

pawn'bro'ker

pawned

pawn'shop'

pay

pay'a·ble

pay'day'

pay'ee'

pay'ees'

pay'er

pay'mas'ter

pay'ment

pay'roll'

pea

peace

peace'a·ble

peace'a·bly

peace'ful

peace'mak'er

peach

pea'cock'

peak

peaked

peal

pealed

pea'nut'

pear

pearl

pearl'ite

pearl'y

peas'ant

peas'ant·ry

pea'shoot'er

peat

pea'vey

peb'ble

peb'bled

peb'ble·ware'

peb'bly

pe·can'

pec'ca·dil'lo

pec'can·cy

pec'cant

pec'ca·ry

peck

pec'tase

pec'tin

pec'to·ral

pec'u·late

pec'u·lat'ed

pec'u·la'tion

pec'u·la'tor

pe·cul'iar

pe·cu'li·ar'i·ty

pe·cul'iar·ly

pe·cu'ni·ar'y

ped'a·gog'ic

ped'a·gog'i·cal

ped'a·gog'i·cal·ly

ped'a·gogue

ped'a·go'gy

ped'al

ped'aled

ped'ant

pe·dan'tic

pe·dan'ti·cal

pe·dan'ti·cism

ped'ant·ry

ped'dle

ped'dled

ped'dler

ped'es·tal

pe·des'tri·an

pe·des'tri·an·ism

pe'di·a·tri'cian

pe'di·at'rics

pe·dic'u·lar

pe·dic'u·lo'sis

ped'i·cure

ped'i·gree

ped'i·greed

ped'i·ment

pe·dom'e·ter

peek

peel

peeled

peel'ings

peen

peep

peer

peer'age

peered

peer'less

pee'vish

peg

Peg'a·sus

pegged

pe'jo·ra'tive

pe'koe

pe·lag'ic

pelf

pel'i·can

pe·lisse'

pel·la'gra

pel'let

pel·lu'cid

pe·lo'ta

pelt

pelt'ed

pel'try

pel'vic

pel'vis

pem'mi·can

pen

pe'nal

pe'nal·i·za'tion

pe'nal·ize

pe'nal·ized

pen'al·ty

pen'ance

pen'chant'

pen'cil

pen'ciled

pend'ant

pend'en·cy

pend'ing

pen'du·lous

pen'du·lum

pen'e·tra·bil'i·ty

pen'e·tra·ble

pen'e·trant

pen'e·trate

pen'e·trat'ed

pen'e·trat'ing·ly

pen'e·tra'tion

pen'e·tra'tive

pen'guin

pen'hold'er

pen'i·cil'lin

pen·in'su·la

pen·in'su·lar

pen'i·tence

pen'i·tent

pen'i·ten'tial

pen'i·ten'tial·ly

pen'i·ten'tia·ry

pen'i·tent·ly

pen'knife'

pen'man

pen'man·ship

pen'nant

pen'ni·less

pen'non

pen'ny

pen'ny·roy'al

pen'ny·weight'

pe·nol'o·gist

pe·nol'o·gy

pen'sion

pen'sion·ar'y

pen'sioned

pen'sion·er

pen'sive

pen'stock'

pent	per·bo'rate	per·en'ni·al·ly
pen'ta·gon	per·cale'	per'fect
pen·tag'o·nal	per·ceiv'a·ble	per·fect'ed
pen·tam'e·ter	per·ceive'	per·fect'i·bil'i·ty
Pen'ta·teuch	per·ceived'	per·fect'i·ble
pen·tath'lon	per cent	per·fec'tion
pen·ta·ton'ic	per·cent'age	per·fec'tion·ism
Pen'te·cost	per·cen'tile	per·fec'tion·ist
pent'house'	per'cept	per'fect·ly
pent·ox'ide	per·cep'ti·bil'i·ty	per·fec'to
pe'nult	per·cep'ti·ble	per·fid'i·ous
pe·nul'ti·mate	per·cep'tion	per'fi·dy
pe·num'bra	per·cep'tive	per'fo·rate
pe·nu'ri·ous	per·cep'tu·al	per'fo·rat'ed
pen'u·ry	per·cep'tu·al·ly	per'fo·ra'tion
pe'on	perch	per'fo·ra'tive
pe'on·age	per·chance'	per'fo·ra'tor
pe'o·ny	per·cip'i·en·cy	per·force'
peo'ple	per·cip'i·ent	per·form'
peo'pled	per'co·late	per·form'a·ble
pep'lum	per'co·la'tion	per·form'ance
pep'per	per'co·la'tor	per·formed'
pep'pered	per·cus'sion	per·form'er
pep'per·i·ness	per·cus'sive	per·fume'
pep'per·mint	per·di'tion	per·fumed'
pep'per·y	per·du'	per·fum'er
pep'sin	per·dur'a·ble	per·fum'er·y
pep'tic	per'e·gri·na'tion	per·func'to·ri·ly
pep'tone	per·emp'to·ri·ly	per·func'to·ri·ness
per'ad·ven'ture	per·emp'to·ri·ness	per·func'to·ry
per·am'bu·late	per·emp'to·ry	per·fuse'
per·am'bu·la'tor	per·en'ni·al	per·fused'

per'go·la

per·haps'

per'i·car'di·al

per'i·car·di'tis

per'i·car'di·um

per'il

per'il·ous

per'il·ous·ly

per·im'e·ter

pe'ri·od

per·i'o·date

pe'ri·od'ic

pe'ri·od'i·cal

pe'ri·od'i·cal·ly

pe'ri·o·dic'i·ty

per'i·os'te·um

per'i·pa·tet'ic

pe·riph'er·al

pe·riph'er·al·ly

pe·riph'er·y

per'i·phras'tic

per'i·scope

per'i·scop'ic

per'ish

per'ish·a·ble

per'ished

per'i·stal'sis

per'i·stal'tic

per'i·stal'ti·cal·ly

per'i·style

per'i·to·ne'um

per'i·to·ni'tis

per'i·win'kle

per'jure

per'jured

per'jur·er

per·ju'ri·ous·ly

per'ju·ry

perk'y

perm'al·loy'

per'ma·nence

per'ma·nent

per'ma·nent·ly

per·man'ga·nate

per'me·a·bil'i·ty

per'me·a·ble

per'me·ate

per'me·at'ed

per'me·a'tion

per·mis'si·bil'i·ty

per·mis'si·ble

per·mis'sion

per·mis'sive

per·mit'

per·mit'ted

per'mu·ta'tion

per·mute'

per·mut'ed

per·ni'cious

per'o·ra'tion

per·ox'ide

per'pen·dic'u·lar

per'pen·dic'u·lar'i·ty

per'pe·trate

per'pe·trat'ed

per'pe·tra'tion

per'pe·tra'tor

per·pet'u·al

per·pet'u·al·ly

per·pet'u·ate

per·pet'u·at'ed

per·pet'u·a'tion

per·pet'u·a'tor

per·pe·tu'i·ty

per·plex'

per·plexed'

per·plex'ed·ly

per·plex'ing·ly

per·plex'i·ty

per'qui·site

per'qui·si'tion

per'se·cute

per'se·cut'ed

per'se·cu'tion

per'se·cu'tor

per'se·ver'ance

per·sev'er·a'tion

per'se·vere'

per'se·vered'

per'si·flage

per·sim'mon

per·sist'

per·sist'ence

per·sist'en·cy

per·sist'ent

per·sist'ing·ly

per'son

per'son·a·ble

per'son·age

per'son·al

per'son·al'i·ty

per'son·al·ize

per'son·al·ly

per'son·al·ty

per·son'i·fi·ca'tion

per·son'i·fied

per·son'i·fy

per'son·nel'

per·spec'tive

per'spi·ca'cious

per'spi·cac'i·ty

per·spic'u·ous

per'spi·ra'tion

per·spir'a·to'ry

per·spire'

per·spired'

per·suade'

per·suad'ed

per·suad'er

per·sua'sion

per·sua'sive

per·sua'sive·ness

per·sul'phate

pert

per·tain'

per·tained'

per'ti·na'cious

per'ti·nac'i·ty

per'ti·nence

per'ti·nent

per·turb'

per·turb'a·ble

per'tur·ba'tion

per·turbed'

pe·rus'al

pe·ruse'

pe·rused'

Pe·ru'vi·an

per·vade'

per·vad'ed

per·vad'ing·ly

per·va'sion

per·va'sive

per·verse'

per·ver'sion

per·ver'si·ty

per·ver'sive

per·vert'

per·vert'ed

per'vi·ous

pes'si·mism

pes'si·mist

pes'si·mis'tic

pes'si·mis'ti·cal·ly

pest

pes'ter

pes'tered

pest'hole'

pest'house'

pes·tif'er·ous

pes'ti·lence

pes'ti·lent

pes'ti·len'tial

pes'ti·len'tial·ly

pes'tle

pet

pet'al

pe·tard'

pe·tite'

pe·ti'tion

pe·ti'tioned

pe·ti'tion·er

pet'rel

pet'ri·fac'tion

pet'ri·fac'tive

pet'ri·fy

pet'rol

pet'ro·la'tum

pe·tro'le·um

pe·trol'o·gy

pet'ted

pet'ti·coat

pet'ti·er

pet'ti·est

pet'ti·fog'ger

pet'ti·ly

pet'ti·ness

pet'tish

pet'ty

pet'u·lance

pet'u·lant

pe·tu'ni·a

pew

pew'ter

pha'e·ton

phag'o·cyte

phal'ange

phal'an·ster'y

pha'lanx

phan'tasm

phan·tas'ma·go'ri·a

phan'tom

Phar'aoh

phar'ma·ceu'tic

phar'ma·ceu'ti·cal

phar'ma·ceu'tics

phar'ma·cist

phar'ma·col'o·gy

phar'ma·co·poe'ia

phar'ma·cy

phar'yn·gi'tis

phar'ynx

phase

phased

pheas'ant

phe'nol

phe·nom'e·na

phe·nom'e·nal

phe·nom'e·nol'o·gy

phe·nom'e·non

phi'al

phi·lan'der

phi·lan'der·er

phil'an·throp'ic

phil'an·throp'i·cal

phi·lan'thro·pist

phi·lan'thro·py

phil'a·tel'ic

phi·lat'e·list

phi·lat'e·ly

phil'har·mon'ic

phi·lip'pic

Phil'ip·pine

Phil·is'tine

phi·lol'o·gist

phi·lol'o·gy

phi·los'o·pher

phil'o·soph'ic

phil'o·soph'i·cal

phi·los'o·phize

phi·los'o·phy

phil'ter

phle·bi'tis

phle·bot'o·my

phlegm

phleg·mat'ic

phleg·mat'i·cal·ly

phlo'em

phlox

pho'bi·a

phoe'nix

phone

pho·net'ic

pho·net'i·cal·ly

pho'ne·ti'cian

pho·net'ics

phon'ic

pho'no·graph

phos'phate

phos'phide

phos'phite

phos'pho·resce'

phos'pho·res'cence

phos·phor'ic

phos'pho·rous

phos'pho·rus

pho'to·cop'i·er

pho'to·e·lec'tric

pho'to·en·grav'ing

pho'to·gen'ic

pho'to·graph

pho'to·graphed

pho·tog'ra·pher

pho'to·graph'ic

pho·tog'ra·phy

pho'to·gra·vure'

pho'to·lith'o·graph

pho'to·mi'cro·graph

pho'ton

pho'to·play'

pho'to·sen'si·tize

Pho'to·stat

pho'to·syn'the·sis

phrase

phrased

phra'se·ol'o·gy

phre·net'ic

phren'ic

phre·nol'o·gist	pick'led	pig'let
phre·nol'o·gy	pick'lock'	pig'ment
phthi'sis	pick'pock'et	pig'men·tar'y
phy·lac'ter·y	pick'up'	pig'men·ta'tion
phys'ic	pic'nic	pig'ment·ed
phys'i·cal	pic'nick·er	pig'nut'
phys'i·cal·ly	pic'ric	pig'pen'
phy·si'cian	pic'to·graph	pig'skin'
phys'i·cist	pic·to'ri·al	pig'stick'er
phys'ics	pic·to'ri·al·ly	pig'sty'
phys'i·og'no·my	pic'ture	pig'tail'
phys'i·o·log'i·cal	pic'tured	pig'weed'
phys'i·o·log'i·cal·ly	pic'tur·esque'	pike
phys'i·ol'o·gy	pie	pik'er
phy·sique'	pie'bald'	pike'staff'
pi·a·nis'si·mo	piece	pi·las'ter
pi·an'ist	piece'meal'	pil'chard
pi·a'no	piece'work'	pile
pi·an'o·for'te	pie'crust'	piled
pi·az'za	pied	pile'work'
pi'ca	pie'plant'	pile'worm'
pic'a·resque'	pier	pil'fer
pic'co·lo	pierce	pil'fer·age
pick	pierced	pil'fered
pick'ax	pi'e·ty	pil'fer·ings
picked	pig	pil'grim
pick'er	pi'geon	pil'grim·age
pick'er·el	pi'geon·hole'	pill
pick'et	pig'fish'	pil'lage
pick'et·ed	pig'ger·y	pil'laged
pick'ings	pig'gish	pil'lar
pick'le	pig'head'ed	pil'lion

pil'lo·ry

pil'low

pil'low·case'

pil'lowed

pi'lot

pi'lot·ed

pi·men'to

pim'per·nel

pim'ple

pin

pin'a·fore'

pin'cers

pinch

pinched

pin'cush'ion

pine

pine'ap'ple

pined

pin'feath'er

pin'fish'

ping'-pong'

pin'guid

pin'hole'

pin'ion

pink

pink'ish

pink'weed'

pink'wood'

pin'nace

pin'na·cle

pinned

pi'noch'le

pin'prick'

pint

pin'to

pin'weed'

pin'worm'

pi'o·neer'

pi'o·neered'

pi'ous

pi'ous·ly

pip

pip'age

pipe

piped

pipe'line'

pip'er

pipe'stem'

pipe'stone'

pi·pette'

pipe'wood'

pip'ing·ly

pip'ings

pip'it

pip'kin

pip·sis'se·wa

pi'quan·cy

pi'quant

pique

pi·qué'

piqued

pi'ra·cy

pi'rate

pi'rat·ed

pi·rat'ic

pi·rat'i·cal

pi·rogue'

pir'ou·ette'

pir·ou·et'ted

pis'ca·tol'o·gy

pis'ca·to'ri·al

pis'ca·to'ri·al·ly

pis·tach'i·o

pis'tol

pis·tole'

pis'ton

pit

pitch

pitched

pitch'er

pitch'fork'

pit'e·ous

pit'e·ous·ness

pit'fall'

pith

pith'i·ly

pith'i·ness

pith'y

pit'i·a·ble

pit'i·ful

pit'i·less

pit'i·less·ly

pit'i·less·ness

pit'tance

pit'ted

pi·tu'i·tar'y

pit'y	plain'ly	plas'ma
pit'y·ing·ly	plain'ness	plas'ter
piv'ot	plaint	plas'tered
piv'ot·al	plain'tiff	plas'ter·er
piv'ot·ed	plain'tive	plas'ter·work'
pla'ca·bil'i·ty	plait	plas'tic
pla'ca·ble	plait'ed	plas·tic'i·ty
plac'ard	plait'ings	plas'tron
pla'cate	plan	plate
pla'cat·ed	plan·chette'	pla·teau'
pla'ca·tive·ly	plane	plat'ed
pla'ca·to'ry	plan'et	plate'hold'er
place	plan'e·tar'i·an	plate'let
pla·ce'bo	plan'e·tar'i·um	plat'en
place'man	plan'e·tar'y	plat'er
place'ment	plan'et·oid	plat'form'
pla·cen'ta	plan'gent	plat'i·na
plac'er	plan'i·sphere	plat'i·nate
plac'id	plank	plat'ings
pla·cid'i·ty	planked	pla·tin'ic
plac'id·ly	plank'ton	plat'i·nize
plack'et	plan'less	plat'i·noid
pla'gi·a·rism	planned	plat'i·num
pla'gi·a·rist	pla'no·graph'ic	plat'i·tude
pla'gi·a·rize	plant	plat'i·tu'di·nize
pla'gi·a·ry	plan'tain	plat'i·tu'di- nous
plague	plan'tar	pla·toon'
plagued	plan·ta'tion	plat'ter
plaid	plant'ed	plat'y·pus
plain	plant'er	plau'dit
plain'er	plant'ings	plau'si·bil'i·ty
plain'est	plaque	plau'si·ble

play	pleat	plinth
play'back'	ple·be'ian	plod
play'bill'	pleb'i·scite	plod'ded
play'boy'	pledge	plod'der
played	pledged	plod'ding·ly
play'er	pledg'ee'	plot
play'ful	pledge'or'	plot'ted
play'ful·ness	pledg'er	plot'ter
play'ground'	pledg'et	plough
play'ings	ple'na·ri·ly	plov'er
play'mate'	ple'na·ry	plow
play'read'er	plen'i·po·ten'ti·ar'y	plow'boy
play'room'	plen'i·tude	plow'ings
play'script'	plen'te·ous	plow'man
play'thing'	plen'ti·ful	plow'share'
play'time'	plen'ty	pluck
play'wright'	ple'num	plucked
pla'za	ple'o·nasm	pluck'i·er
plea	ple'o·nas'tic	pluck'i·est
plead	pleth'o·ra	pluck'i·ly
plead'ed	ple·thor'ic	pluck'i·ness
plead'er	pleu'ra	pluck'y
plead'ing·ly	pleu'ral	plug
plead'ings	pleu'ri·sy	plugged
pleas'ant	plex'us	plum
pleas'ant·ly	pli'a·bil'i·ty	plum'age
pleas'ant·ness	pli'a·ble	plumb
pleas'ant·ry	pli'an·cy	plum·ba'go
please	pli'ant	plum'bate
pleased	pli'ers	plumbed
pleas'ur·a·ble	plight	plumb'er
pleas'ure	plight'ed	plum'bic

plum'bous	plu·to'ni·um	point'less
plume	ply	point'less·ly
plumed	pneu·mat'ic	poise
plum'met	pneu·mat'i·cal·ly	poised
plum'met·ed	pneu·mat'ics	poi'son
plump	pneu·mo'ni·a	poi'soned
plump'er	poach	poi'son·er
plump'est	poach'er	poi'son·ous
plump'ly	pock'et	poke
plump'ness	pock'et·book'	poked
plun'der	pock'et·knife'	pok'er
plun'dered	pock'mark'	poke'weed'
plun'der·er	pod	po'lar
plunge	po·dag'ra	po·lar'i·ty
plunged	po·di'a·try	po'lar·i·za'tion
plung'er	po'di·um	po'lar·ize
plunk	po'em	po'lar·ized
plunked	po'e·sy	po'lar·iz'er
plu'ral	po'et	pole
plu'ral·ism	po'et·as'ter	pole'cat'
plu'ral·ist	po·et'ic	po·lem'ic
plu·ral·is'tic	po·et'i·cal	po·lem'i·cal
plu·ral'i·ty	po'et·ry	po·lem'i·cist
plu'ral·ize	po'i	po·lem'ics
plu'ral·ized	poign'an·cy	pole'star'
plus	poign'ant	po·lice'
plush	poin'ci·an'a	po·liced'
plu·toc'ra·cy	poin·set'ti·a	po·lice'man
plu'to·crat	point	pol'i·cy
plu'to·crat'ic	point'ed	pol'ish
plu'to·crat'i·cal·ly	point'ed·ly	pol'ished
plu·ton'ic	point'er	pol'ish·er

po·lite'

po·lite'ly

po·lite'ness

pol'i·tic

po·lit'i·cal

po·lit'i·cal·ly

pol'i·ti'cian

pol'i·tics

pol'ka

poll

pol'lard

pol'lard·ed

polled

pol'len

pol'li·nate

pol'li·na'tion

pol'li·nif'er·ous

pol·lute'

pol·lut'ed

pol·lu'tion

po'lo

pol'o·naise'

po·lo'ni·um

pol·troon'

pol'y·an'drous

pol'y·an'dry

pol'y·chrome

pol'y·clin'ic

po·lyg'a·mist

po·lyg'a·mous

po·lyg'a·my

pol'y·glot

pol'y·gon

po·lyg'o·nal

pol'y·mer'ic

po·lym'er·ism

pol'y·mer·i·za'tion

pol'y·mer·ize

pol'y·no'mi·al

pol'yp

po·lyph'o·ny

pol'y·syl·lab'ic

pol'y·tech'nic

po·made'

po·man·der

po·ma'tum

pome'gran'ate

Pom·er·a'ni·an

pom'mel

pom'meled

po·mol'o·gy

pomp

pom'pa·dour

pom'pa·no

Pom·pe'ian

pom'pon

pom·pos'i·ty

pomp'ous

pon'cho

pond

pon'der

pon'der·a·ble

pon'dered

pon'der·o'sa

pon'der·os'i·ty

pon'der·ous

pond'fish'

pond'weed'

pon·gee'

pon'iard

pon'tiff

pon·tif'i·cal

pon·tif'i·cal·ly

pon·tif'i·cate

pon·toon'

po'ny

poo'dle

pool

pooled

pool'room'

poor

poor'er

poor'est

poor'house'

poor'ly

poor'ness

pop

pop'corn'

pop'gun'

pop'in·jay

pop'lar

pop'lin

pop'o'ver

popped

pop'pet

pop'py

pop′u·lace

pop′u·lar

pop′u·lar′i·ty

pop′u·lar·i·za′tion

pop′u·lar·ize

pop′u·lar·ized

pop′u·late

pop′u·lat′ed

pop′u·la′tion

pop′u·lous

por′ce·lain

porch

por′cu·pine

pore

pored

por′gy

pork

por·nog′ra·phy

po·ros′i·ty

po′rous

por′phy·ry

por′poise

por′ridge

por′rin·ger

port

port′a·ble

por′tage

por′tal

port·cul′lis

por·tend′

por·tend′ed

por′tent

por·ten′tous

por′ter

por′ter·house′

port·fo′li·o

port′hole′

por′ti·co

por·tiere′

por′tion

por′tioned

port·man′teau

por′trait

por′trait·ist

por′trai·ture

por·tray′

por·tray′al

por·trayed′

Por′tu·guese

por′tu·la′ca

pose

posed

po·si′tion

pos′i·tive

pos′i·tiv·ism

pos′i·tiv·is′tic

pos′i·tron

pos′se

pos·sess′

pos·sessed′

pos·ses′sion

pos·ses′sive

pos·ses′sor

pos·ses′sor·ship

pos′si·bil′i·ty

pos′si·ble

pos′si·bly

pos′sum

post

post′age

post′al

post′box′

post′date′

post′dat′ed

post′ed

post′er

pos·te′ri·or

pos·ter′i·ty

pos′tern

post·grad′u·ate

post′haste′

post′hole′

post′hu·mous

pos·til′ion

post′im·pres′sion·ism

post′ings

post′lude

post′man

post·mar′i·tal

post′mark′

post′mas′ter

post′me·rid′i·an

post′mis′tress

post′-mor′tem

post·nup′tial

post′op′er·a·tive

post'paid'

post·pone'

post·poned'

post·pone'ment

post·pran'di·al

post'script

pos'tu·lant

pos'tu·late

pos'tu·lat'ed

pos'tu·la'tion

pos'ture

pos'tured

pos'tur·ings

po'sy

pot

po'ta·bil'i·ty

po'ta·ble

pot'ash'

po·tas'si·um

po·ta'tion

po·ta'to

pot'boil'er

po'ten·cy

po'tent

po'ten·tate

po·ten'tial

po·ten'ti·al'i·ty

po·ten'tial·ly

po·ten'ti·om'e·ter

pot'herb'

pot'hole'

pot'hook'

pot'house'

po'tion

pot'latch'

pot'luck'

pot'pie'

pot'pour'ri'

pot'sherd'

pot'tage

pot'ter

pot'ter·y

pouch

poult

poul'ter·er

poul'tice

poul'ticed

poul'try

pounce

pounced

pound

pound'age

pound'cake'

pound'ed

pound'ings

pour

poured

pout

pout'ed

pov'er·ty

pow'der

pow'dered

pow'der·y

pow'er

pow'ered

pow'er·ful

pow'er·ful·ly

pow'er·less

pow'er·less·ly

pow'er·less·ness

pow'wow'

prac'ti·ca·bil'i·ty

prac'ti·ca·ble

prac'ti·ca·bly

prac'ti·cal

prac'ti·cal'i·ty

prac'ti·cal·ly

prac'tice

prac'ticed

prac'ti·cum

prac·ti'tion·er

prag·mat'ic

prag·mat'i·cal

prag·mat'i-cal·ly

prag'ma·tism

prag'ma·tist

prai'rie

praise

praised

praise'wor·thy

pra'line

prance

pranced

pranc'ing·ly

prank

prank'ster

prate	pre·cep′tress	pre·cool′
prat′ed	pre·ces′sion	pre·cur′sor
prat′ings	pre·chill′	pre·cur′so·ry
pra·tique′	pre′cinct	pre·da′ceous
prat′tle	pre′ci·os′i·ty	pre·dac′i·ty
prat′tling·ly	pre′cious	pre·date′
prawn	pre′cious·ly	pre·da′tion
pray	prec′i·pice	pred′a·tive
prayed	pre·cip′i·tan·cy	pred′a·tor
prayer	pre·cip′i·tant	pred′a·to′ry
prayer′ful	pre·cip′i·tate	pre′de·cease′
prayer′ful·ly	pre·cip′i·tat′ed	pred′e·ces′sor
preach	pre·cip′i·ta′tion	pre′de·cide′
preached	pre·cip′i·tous	pre·des′ig·nat′ed
preach′er	pré·cis′	pre′des·ig·na′tion
preach′ment	pre·cise′	pre·des′ti·nar′i·an
preach′y	pré·cised′	pre·des′ti·nar-i·an·ism
pre′ad·o·les′cent	pre·cise′ly	pre·des′ti·na′tion
pre′am′ble	pre·cise′ness	pre·des′tine
pre′ar·range′	pre·ci′sion	pre·des′tined
pre′ar·range′ment	pre·ci′sion·ist	pre′de·ter′mi·nant
preb′en·dar′y	pre·clin′i·cal	pre′de·ter′mi·nate
pre·can′celed	pre·clude′	pre′de·ter′mi·na-tion
pre·car′i·ous	pre·clud′ed	pre′de·ter′mine
pre·cau′tion	pre·clu′sion	pre′de·ter′mined
pre·cau′tion·ar′y	pre·co′cious	pre′di·as·tol′ic
pre·cede′	pre·co′cious·ly	pre·dic′a·ment
pre·ced′ed	pre·coc′i·ty	pred′i·cate
pre·ced′ence	pre·con·ceived′	pred′i·cat′ed
prec′e·dent	pre′con·cep′tion	pred′i·ca′tion
pre′cept	pre·cook′	pred′i·ca′tive
pre·cep′tor		pre·dict′

pre·dict'a·ble

pre·dict'ed

pre·dic'tion

pre·dic'tion·al

pre·dic'tive

pre'di·gest'

pre'di·gest'ed

pre'di·ges'tion

pre'di·lec'tion

pre'dis·clo'sure

pre'dis·pose'

pre'dis·posed'

pre'dis·po·si'tion

pre·dom'i·nance

pre·dom'i·nant

pre·dom'i·nate

pre·dom'i·nat'ed

pre·dom'i·nate·ly

pre·dom'i·nat'ing·ly

pre·draft'

pre·dry'

pre-em'i·nence

pre-em'i·nent

pre-empt'

pre-empt'ed

pre-emp'tion

pre-emp'tive

preen

preened

pre-es'ti·mate

pre'-ex·ist'

pre'-ex·ist'ent

pref'ace

pref'aced

pre·fash'ion

pref'a·to'ry

pre'fect

pre'fec·ture

pre·fer'

pref'er·a·ble

pref'er·a·bly

pref'er·ence

pref'er·en'tial

pref'er·en'tial·ly

pre·fer'ment

pre·ferred'

pre·fig'ure

pre·fig'ured

pre'fix

pre'fix·al

pre·fixed'

pre·form'

pre·formed'

pre·gath'er

preg'nan·cy

preg'nant

pre·har'vest

pre·hen'sile

pre'hen·sil'i·ty

pre'his·tor'ic

pre'im·ag'ine

pre'in·au'gu·ral

pre'in·cline'

pre'in·clined'

pre·in'ven·to'ry

pre·judge'

pre·judged'

prej'u·diced

prej'u·di'cial

prej'u·di'cial·ly

prel'a·cy

prel'ate

pre·lim'i·nar'y

pre·lit'er·ate

prel'ude

pre'ma·ter'ni·ty

pre'ma·ture'

pre·med'i·cal

pre·med'i·tate

pre·med'i·tat'ed

pre'med·i·ta'tion

pre'mi·er

prem'ise

prem'is·es

pre'mi·um

pre'mo·ni'tion

pre·mon'i·to'ry

pre·na'tal

pre·na'tal·ly

pre·oc'cu·pa'tion

pre·oc'cu·pied

pre·oc'cu·py

pre·op'er·a·tive

pre'or·dain'

pre'or·dained'

pre·paid'

prep'a·ra'tion

pre·par'a·tive

pre·par'a·to'ry

pre·pare'

pre·pared'

pre·par'ed·ness

pre·pay'

pre·pay'ment

pre·pense'

pre·pon'der·ance

pre·pon'der·ant

pre·pon'der·ate

pre·pon'der·at'ing·ly

prep'o·si'tion

prep'o·si'tion·al

pre'pos·sess'

pre'pos·ses'sion

pre·pos'ter·ous

pre·print'

pre're·lease'

pre·req'ui·site

pre·rog'a·tive

pre·sage'

pre·saged'

pres'by·ter

Pres'by·te'ri·an

pres'by·ter'y

pre'sci·ence

pre'sci·ent

pre·scribe'

pre·scribed'

pre·scrip'tion

pre·scrip'tive

pres'ence

pres'ent

pre·sent'a·bil'i·ty

pre·sent'a·ble

pres'en·ta'tion

pre·sent'ed

pre·sen'ti·ment

pres'ent·ly

pre·sent'ment

pres'er·va'tion

pre·serv'a·tive

pre·serve'

pre·serv'er

pre·side'

pre·sid'ed

pres'i·den·cy

pres'i·dent

pres'i·den'tial

press

press'board'

pressed

pres'sings

press'man

press'room'

pres'sure

press'work'

pres'ti·dig'i·ta'tor

pres·tige'

pres·tig'i·ous

pres'to

pre·sum'a·ble

pre·sume'

pre·sumed'

pre·sum'ed·ly

pre·sump'tion

pre·sump'tive

pre·sump'tu·ous

pre'sup·pose'

pre'sys·tol'ic

pre·tend'

pre·tend'ed

pre·tend'er

pre·tense'

pre·ten'sion

pre·ten'tious

pre·ten'tious·ly

pre·ten'tious·ness

pret'er·it

pre'ter·mit'

pre'ter·mit'ted

pre'ter·nat'u·ral

pre'text

pret'ti·er

pret'ti·est

pret'ti·ly

pret'ti·ness

pret'ty

pret'zel

pre·vail'

pre·vailed'

pre·vail'ing·ly

prev'a·lence

prev'a·lent

prev'a·lent·ly

pre·var'i·cate

pre·var'i·cat'ed

pre·var'i·ca'tion

pre·var'i·ca'tor

pre·vent'

pre·vent'a·bil'i·ty

pre·vent'a·ble

pre·vent'ed

pre·ven'tion

pre·ven'tive

pre'view'

pre'vi·ous

pre·vi'sion

pre'vo·ca'tion·al

prey

price

priced

price'less

prick

pricked

prick'le

prick'led

prick'li·ness

prick'ly

pride

pride'ful

priest

priest'ess

priest'hood

priest'ly

prig'gish

prim

pri'ma·cy

pri'mal

pri'ma·ri·ly

pri'ma·ry

pri'mate

pri'mate·ship

prime

primed

prim'er

pri·me'val

prim'i·tive

prim'i·tiv·ism

prim'ly

prim'ness

pri'mo·gen'i·ture

pri·mor'di·al

prim'rose'

prince

prince'li·ness

prince'ling

prince'ly

prin'ces

prin'cess

prin'ci·pal

prin'ci·pal'i·ty

prin'ci·pal·ly

prin'ci·ple

prin'ci·pled

print

print'a·ble

print'ed

print'er

print'er·y

print'ings

pri'or

pri·or'i·ty

pri'o·ry

prism

pris·mat'ic

pris'on

pris'on·er

pris'tine

pri'va·cy

pri'vate

pri'va·teer'

pri'vate·ly

pri'vate·ness

pri·va'tion

priv'et

priv'i·lege

priv'i·ly

priv'i·ty

priv'y

prize

prized

prob'a·bil'i·ty

prob'a·ble

prob'a·bly

pro'bate

pro·ba'tion

pro·ba'tion·ar'y

probe

prob'i·ty

prob'lem	prod'ded	prof'fered
prob'lem·at'ic	prod'i·gal	pro·fi'cien·cy
pro·bos'cis	prod'i·gal'i·ty	pro·fi'cient
pro·ce'dur·al	prod'i·gal·ly	pro·fi'cient·ly
pro·ce'dure	pro·di'gious	pro'file
pro·ceed'	pro·di'gious·ly	prof'it
pro·ceed'ed	prod'i·gy	prof'it·a·ble
pro·ceed'ings	pro·duce'	prof'it·a·bly
proc'ess	pro·duced'	prof'it·ed
proc'essed	pro·duc'er	prof'it·eer'
proc'ess·es	prod'uct	prof'it·less
pro·ces'sion	pro·duc'tion	prof'li·ga·cy
pro·ces'sion·al	pro·duc'tive	prof'li·gate
pro·claim'	pro'duc·tiv'i·ty	pro·found'
pro·claimed'	pro'em	pro·found'ness
proc'la·ma'tion	prof'a·na'tion	pro·fun'di·ty
pro·cliv'i·ty	pro·fan'a·to'ry	pro·fuse'
pro·con'sul	pro·fane'	pro·fuse'ly
pro·cras'ti·nate	pro·faned'	pro·fuse'ness
pro·cras'ti·nat'ed	pro·fan'i·ty	pro·fu'sion
pro·cras'ti·na'tion	pro·fess'	pro·gen'i·tor
pro·cras'ti·na'tor	pro·fessed'	prog'e·ny
pro'cre·a'tion	pro·fess'ed·ly	prog·no'sis
pro'cre·a'tive	pro·fes'sion	prog·nos'tic
proc'tor	pro·fes'sion·al	prog·nos'ti·cate
pro·cur'a·ble	pro·fes'sion·al·ism	prog·nos'ti-cat'ed
proc'u·ra'tion	pro·fes'sion·al·ize	prog·nos'ti-ca'tion
proc'u·ra'tor	pro·fes'sion·al·ly	pro'gram
pro·cure'	pro·fes'sor	pro'gramed
pro·cured'	pro'fes·so'ri·al	pro·gress'
pro·cure'ment	pro·fes'sor·ship	pro·gressed'
prod	prof'fer	pro·gres'sion

pro·gres'sive

pro·hib'it

pro·hib'it·ed

pro'hi·bi'tion

pro'hi·bi'tion·ist

pro·hib'i·tive

pro·hib'i·to'ry

pro·ject'

pro·ject'ed

pro·jec'tile

pro·jec'tion

pro·jec'tive

pro·jec'tor

pro'le·tar'i·an

pro'le·tar'i·at

pro·lif'er·ate

pro·lif'er·a'tion

pro·lif'ic

pro·lif'i·ca'tion

pro·lix'

pro·lix'i·ty

pro'logue

pro·long'

pro·lon'gate

pro'lon·ga'tion

pro·longed'

prom'e·nade'

prom'e·nad'ed

prom'i·nence

prom'i·nent

prom'is·cu'i·ty

pro·mis'cu·ous

pro·mis'cu·ous·ly

pro·mis'cu·ous·ness

prom'ise

prom'ised

prom'is·ing·ly

prom'is·so'ry

prom'on·to'ry

pro·mote'

pro·mot'ed

pro·mot'er

pro·mo'tion

pro·mo'tion·al

prompt

prompt'ed

prompt'er

prompt'est

promp'ti·tude

prompt'ly

prompt'ness

pro·mul'gate

pro·mul'gat·ed

pro'mul·ga'tion

pro'nate

pro·na'tion

prone

prong

prong'horn'

pro·nom'i·nal

pro'noun

pro·nounce'

pro·nounce'a·ble

pro·nounced'

pro·nounce'ment

pro·nun'ci·a'tion

proof

proofed

prop

prop'a·gan'da

prop'a·gan'dist

prop'a·gate

prop'a·gat'ed

prop'a·ga'tion

pro·pel'

pro·pel'lant

pro·pelled'

pro·pel'ler

pro·pen'si·ty

prop'er

prop'er·ly

prop'er·ty

proph'e·cy

proph'e·sied

proph'e·sy

proph'et

pro·phet'ic

pro·phet'i·cal·ly

pro'phy·lac'tic

pro'phy·lax'is

pro·pin'qui·ty

pro·pi'ti·ate

pro·pi'ti·at'ed

pro·pi'ti·a'tion

pro·pi'ti·a·to'ry

pro·pi'tious

pro·po'nent

pro·por'tion

pro·por'tion·a·ble

pro·por'tion·al

pro·por'tion·al·ly

pro·por'tion·ate

pro·por'tion·ate·ly

pro·por'tioned

pro·pos'al

pro·pose'

pro·posed'

prop'o·si'tion

pro·pound'

pro·pound'ed

pro·pri'e·tar'y

pro·pri'e·tor

pro·pri'e·to'ri·al

pro·pri'e·to'ri·al·ly

pro·pri'e·tor·ship'

pro·pri'e·to'ry

pro·pri'e·ty

pro·pul'sion

pro·pul'sive

pro'rate'

pro'rat'ed

pro·ra'tion

pro'ro·ga'tion

pro·rogue'

pro·rogued'

pro·sa'ic

pro·sa'i·cal·ly

pro·sce'ni·um

pro·scribe'

pro·scribed'

pro·scrip'tion

prose

pros'e·cute

pros'e·cut·ed

pros'e·cu'tion

pros'e·cu'tor

pros'e·lyte

pros'e·lyt'ed

pros'e·lyt·ize

pros'e·lyt·iz'er

pros'i·er

pros'i·est

pros'i·fy

pros'i·ly

pros'i·ness

pros'o·dy

pros'pect

pros'pect·ed

pro·spec'tive

pros'pec·tor

pro·spec'tus

pros'per

pros'pered

pros·per'i·ty

pros'per·ous

pros'per·ous·ly

pros'the·sis

pros·thet'ic

pros'trate

pros'trat·ed

pros·tra'tion

pros'y

pro·tag'o·nist

pro'te·an

pro·tect'

pro·tect'ed

pro·tect'ing·ly

pro·tec'tion

pro·tec'tion·ism

pro·tec'tion·ist

pro·tec'tive

pro·tec'tive·ly

pro·tec'tive·ness

pro·tec'tor

pro·tec'tor·ate

pro'té·gé

pro'te·in

pro·test'

prot'es·tant

prot'es·ta'tion

pro·test'ed

pro·test'ing·ly

pro·thon'o·tar'y

pro'to·col

pro'ton

pro'to·plasm

pro'to·type

pro·tox'ide

Pro'to·zo'a

pro·tract'

pro·tract'ed

pro·trac'tile

pro·trac'tion

pro·trac'tive

pro·trac'tor

pro·trude'

pro·trud'ed

pro·tru'sion

pro·tru'sive

pro·tu'ber·ance

pro·tu'ber·ant

proud

proud'er

proud'est

proud'ly

prov'a·ble

prove

proved

prov'en

prov'e·nance

Prov'en·çal'

prov'en·der

prov'erb

pro·ver'bi·al

pro·ver'bi·al·ly

pro·vide'

pro·vid'ed

prov'i·dence

prov'i·dent

prov'i·den'tial

prov'i·den'tial·ly

pro·vid'er

prov'ince

pro·vin'cial

pro·vin'cial·ism

pro·vin'ci·al'i·ty

pro·vin'cial·ly

pro·vi'sion

pro·vi'sion·al

pro·vi'sion·al·ly

pro·vi'so

pro·vi'so·ry

prov'o·ca'tion

pro·voc'a·tive

pro·voke'

pro·voked'

pro·vok'ing·ly

prov'ost

prow

prow'ess

prowl

prowled

prowl'er

prox'i·mal

prox'i·mal·ly

prox'i·mate

prox·im'i·ty

prox'i·mo

prox'y

prude

pru'dence

pru'dent

pru·den'tial

pru·den'tial·ly

pru'dent·ly

prud'er·y

prud'ish

prune

pruned

pru'ri·ence

pru'ri·ent

pru·ri'tus

Prus'sian

pry

pry'ing·ly

psalm

psalm'book'

psalm'ist

psal'mo·dist

psal'mo·dy

psal'ter

pseu'do·nym

pso·ri'a·sis

psy'chi·at'ric

psy'chi·at'ri·cal·ly

psy·chi'a·trist

psy·chi'a·try

psy'chic

psy'chi·cal

psy'chi·cal·ly

psy'cho·a·nal'y·sis

psy'cho·bi·ol'o·gy

psy'cho·dy·nam'ics

psy'cho·gen'e·sis

psy'cho·ge·net'ic

psy'cho·log'i·cal

psy·chol'o·gist

psy·chol'o·gy

psy'cho·path'ic

psy'cho·pa·thol'o·gy

psy·chop'a·thy

psy·cho'sis

psy·chot'ic

Ptol'e·ma'ic

pto'maine

pub'lic

pub'li·ca'tion

pub'li·cist

pub·lic'i·ty

pub'lic·ly

pub'lish

pub'lished

pub'lish·er

puce

puck

puck'er

puck'ered

pud'dings

pud'dle

pud'dled

pud'dler

pu'den·cy

pudg'i·ness

pudg'y

pueb'lo

pu'er·ile

pu'er·il'i·ty

puff

puf'fin

puff'i·ness

puff'y

pug

pu'gil·ism

pu'gil·ist

pu'gil·is'tic

pug·na'cious·ly

pug·nac'i·ty

pu'is·sance

pu'is·sant

pul'chri·tude

pul'chri·tu'di·nous

pul'ing

pul'ing·ly

pull

pulled

pul'let

pul'ley

Pull'man

pul'lu·late

pul'mo·nar'y

Pul'mo'tor

pulp

pulp'i·er

pulp'i·est

pulp'i·ness

pul'pit

pul'pit·eer'

pulp'y

pul'sate

pul'sat·ed

pul·sa'tion

pul·sa'tor

pul'sa·to'ry

pulse

pul'ver·i·za'tion

pul'ver·ize

pul'ver·iz'er

pum'ice

pump

pum'per·nick'el

pump'kin

pun

punch

punched

pun'cheon

punch'ings

punc·til'i·o

punc·til'i·ous

punc·til'i·ous·ly

punc·til'i·ous·ness

punc'tu·al

punc'tu·al'i·ty

punc'tu·al·ly

punc'tu·ate

punc'tu·at'ed

punc'tu·a'tion

punc'ture

punc'tured

pun'dit

pung

pun'gen·cy

pun'gent

pu'ni·ness

pun'ish

pun'ish·a·ble

pun'ished

pun'ish·ment

pu'ni·tive

punk

punt

pu'ny

pup

pu'pa

pu'pae

pu'pil

pup'pet

pup'pet·eer'

pup'pet·ry

pup'py

pur'blind'

pur'chase

pur'chased

pur'chas·er

pure

pure'ly

pur'er

pur'est

pur'ga·tive

pur'ga·to'ry

purge

purged

pu'ri·fi·ca'tion

pu'ri·fied

pu'ri·fi'er

pu'ri·fy

pur'ism

pur'ist

Pu'ri·tan

pu'ri·tan'ic

pu'ri·tan'i·cal

Pu'ri·tan·ism

pu'ri·ty

purl

pur'lieu

pur·loin'

pur'ple

pur'plish

pur·port'

pur·port'ed

pur'pose

pur'pose·ful

pur'pose·ful·ly

pur'pose·ful·ness

pur'pose·less

pur'pose·ly

pur'pos·ive

purr

purred

purse

pursed

purs'er

purs'lane

pur·su'ance

pur·su'ant

pur·sue'

pur·sued'

pur·suit'

pur'sui·vant

pur'sy

pu'ru·lence

pu'ru·len·cy

pu'ru·lent

pur·vey'

pur·vey'ance

pur·vey'or

pur'view

pus

push

push'cart'

push'er

pu'sil·la·nim'i·ty

pu'sil·lan'i·mous

puss'y·foot'

pus'tu·lant

pus'tu·lar

pus'tu·late

pus'tu·la'tion

pus'tule

put

pu'ta·tive

pu'tre·fac'tion

pu'tre·fac'tive

pu'tre·fied

pu'tre·fy

pu·tres'cence

pu·tres'cent

pu'trid

putt

put'tee

putt'er

put′ty

puz′zle

puz′zled

puz′zler

puz′zles

py·e′mi·a

pyg′my

py·ja′ma

py′lon

py·lo′rus

py′or·rhe′a

pyr′a·mid

py·ram′i·dal

pyre

py′rex

py·rex′i·a

py·ri′tes

py·rog′ra·phy

py′ro·ma′ni·a

py·rom′e·ter

py·ro·tech′nics

py·rox′y·lin

Pyr′rhic

py′thon

Q

quack

quack'er·y

quad

quad'ran'gle

quad·ran'gu·lar

quad'rant

quad'rat

quad·rat'ic

quad·rat'ics

quad'ra·ture

quad·ren'ni·al

quad·ren'ni·al·ly

quad·ren'ni·um

quad'ri·lat'er·al

qua·drille'

quad'ri·par'tite

quad'ru·ped

quad'ru·ple

quad'ru·plet

quad'ru·plex

quad·ru'pli·cate

quaff

quag'mire'

qua'hog

quail

quailed

quaint

quaint'ly

quaint'ness

quake

quaked

quak'er

quak'ing·ly

qual'i·fi·ca'tion

qual'i·fied

qual'i·fi'er

qual'i·fy

qual'i·ta'tive

qual'i·ties

qual'i·ty

qualm

quan'da·ry

quan'ti·ta'tive

quan'ti·ties

quan'ti·ty

quan'tum

quar'an·tine

quar'an·tined

quar'rel

quar'reled

quar'rel·some

quar'ri·er

quar'ry

quar'ry·man

quart

quar'tan

quar'ter

quar'ter·back'

quar'tered

quar'ter·ings

quar'ter·ly

quar'ter·mas'ter

quar'ter·saw'

quar·tet'

quar'tile

quar'to

235

quartz	queue	quin·tet'
quash	quib'ble	quin'tu·plet
qua'si	quick	quip
qua·ter'na·ry	quick'en	qui'pu
quat'rain	quick'ened	quire
quat're·foil'	quick'er	quirk
qua'ver	quick'est	quirt
qua'vered	quick'lime'	quit
qua'ver·ing·ly	quick'ly	quit'claim'
quay	quick'ness	quite
quay'age	quick'sand'	quit'rent'
quea'sy	quick'sil'ver	quit'tance
queen	quick'step'	quit'ter
queen'ly	quid'di·ty	quiv'er
queer	qui·es'cence	quiv'ered
queer'er	qui'et	quiv'er·ing·ly
queer'est	qui'et·ed	quix·ot'ic
quell	qui'et·ly	quiz
quelled	qui'et·ness	quiz'zi·cal
quench	qui'e·tude	quoin
quenched	qui·e'tus	quoit
quench'less	quill	quon'dam
que'ried	quilled	quo'rum
quer'u·lous	quill'work'	quo'ta
que'ry	quilt	quot'a·ble
quest	quilt'ed	quo·ta'tion
quest'ing·ly	quince	quote
ques'tion	qui'nine	quot'ed
ques'tion·a·ble	quin·quen'ni·al	quoth
ques'tion·er	quin'tal	quo·tid'i·an
ques'tion·ing·ly	quint·es'sence	quo'tient
ques'tion·naire'	quin'tes·sen'tial	quot'ing

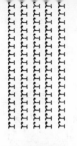

R

rab'bet

rab·bin'i·cal

rab'bit

rab'bit·ry

rab'ble

rab'id

rab'id·ly

ra'bi·es

rac·coon'

race

raced

rac'er

race'way'

ra·chit'ic

ra·chi'tis

ra'cial

ra'cial·ly

rac'i·ly

rac'i·ness

rack

rack'et

rac'on·teur'

rac'y

ra'di·al

ra'di·al·ly

ra'di·ance

ra'di·ant

ra'di·ant·ly

ra'di·ate

ra'di·at'ed

ra'di·a'tion

ra'di·a'tor

rad'i·cal

rad'i·cal·ism

rad'i·cal·ly

ra·dic'u·lar

ra'di·i

ra'di·o

ra'di·o·ac'tive

ra'di·o·ac·tiv'i·ty

ra'di·o·gram'

ra'di·o·graph'

ra'di·om'e·ter

ra'di·o·phone'

ra'di·o·pho'to·graph

ra'di·o·scope'

ra'di·o·sen'si·tive

ra'di·o·tel'e·gram

rad'ish

ra'di·um

ra'di·us

ra'di·us·es

ra'dix

ra'don

raf'fi·a

raf'fle

raf'fled

raft

raft'er

rafts'man

rag

rag'a·muf'fin

rage

raged

rag'ged

rag'lan

ra·gout'	ram	ranked
rag'pick'er	ram'ble	ran'kle
rag'time'	ram'bled	ran'kled
rag'weed'	ram'bler	rank'ling·ly
raid	ram·bunc'tious	ran'sack
rail	ram'e·kin	ran'som
rail'bird'	ram'i·fi·ca'tion	ran'somed
railed	ram'i·fied	rant
rail'head'	ram'i·fy	rant'ed
rail'ing·ly	rammed	rant'ing·ly
rail'ings	ram'mer	ra·pa'cious
rail'ler·y	ramp	ra·pac'i·ty
rail'road'	ram'page	rap'id
rail'road'er	ramp'ant	ra·pid'i·ty
rail'way'	ram'part	rap'id·ly
rai'ment	ram'rod'	ra'pi·er
rain	ram'shack'le	rap'ine
rain'bow'	ranch	rap·port'
rain'coat'	ranch'er	rap·scal'lion
rained	ran·che'ro	rapt
rain'fall'	ranch'man	rap·to'ri·al
rain'spout'	ran'cho	rap'ture
rain'storm'	ran'cid	rap'tur·ous
rain'y	ran·cid'i·ty	rap'tur·ous·ly
raise	ran'cid·ly	rap'tur·ous·ness
raised	ran'cor	rare
rai'sin	ran'cor·ous	rar'e·fac'tion
ra'ja	ran'dom	rar'e·fy
rake	range	rare'ly
rak'ish	ranged	rare'ness
ral'lied	rang'er	rar'er
ral'ly	rank	rar'est

rar'i·ty

ras'cal

ras·cal'i·ty

ras'cal·ly

rash

rash'er

rash'est

rash'ly

rash'ness

rasp

rasp'ber'ry

rasped

rasp'ing·ly

rat

rat'a·ble

ratch'et

rate

rat'ed

rath'er

raths'kel'ler

rat'i·fi·ca'tion

rat'i·fied

rat'i·fy

rat'ings

ra'tio

ra'ti·oc'i·na'tion

ra'ti·oc'i·na'tive

ra'tion

ra'tion·al

ra'tion·al·ism

ra'tion·al·ist

ra'tion·al·is'tic

ra'tion·al·i·za'tion

ra'tion·al·ize

ra'tion·al·ized

ra'tion·al·ly

ra'tioned

rat'line

rat·tan'

rat'ter

rat'tle

rat'tle·brain'

rat'tle·brained'

rat'tled

rat'tle·head'ed

rat'tler

rat'tle·snake'

rat'tlings

rat'tly

rau'cous

rav'age

rav'aged

rave

raved

rav'el

rav'eled

ra'ven

rav'en·ous

rav'en·ous·ly

rav'en·ous·ness

ra'vi'gote'

ra·vine'

rav'ings

ra·vi·o'li

rav'ish

rav'ished

rav'ish·er

rav'ish·ing·ly

rav'ish·ment

raw

raw'boned'

raw'er

raw'est

raw'hide'

raw'ness

ray

ray'less

ray'on

raze

razed

ra'zor

ra'zor·back'

ra'zor·edge'

reach

reached

reach'ings

re·act'

re·act'ance

re·ac'tion

re·ac'tion·ar'y

re·ac'ti·vate

re'ac·ti·va'tion

read

read'a·bil'i·ty

read'a·ble

read'er

read'i·ly

read'i·ness

read'ings

re'ad·just'

re'ad·just'a·ble

re'ad·just'ment

re'ad·mis'sion

re'ad·mit'

read'y

re'af·firm'

re'af·fir·ma'tion

re·a'gent

re'al

re'a·lign'

re'al·ism

re'al·ist

re'al·is'tic

re'al·is'ti·cal·ly

re·al'i·ty

re'al·iz'a·ble

re'al·i·za'tion

re'al·ize

re'al·ized

re'al·ly

realm

re'al·tor

re'al·ty

ream

reamed

ream'er

re·an'i·mate

reap

reap'er

re'ap·pear'

re'ap·pear'ance

re'ap·point'

re'ap·point'ment

rear

reared

re·ar'gue

re·arm'

re·ar'ma·ment

re·armed'

rear'most

re'ar·range'

re'ar·range'ment

rear'ward

rea'son

rea'son·a·ble

rea'son·a·ble·ness

rea'son·a·bly

rea'soned

re'as·sem'ble

re'as·sert'

re'as·sert'ed

re'as·sign'

re'as·sume'

re'as·sur'ance

re'as·sure'

re'as·sured'

re'bate

re'bat·ed

reb'el'

re·belled'

re·bel'lion

re·bel'lious

re·bind'

re·birth'

re·born'

re·bound'

re·buff'

re·buffed'

re·build'

re·built'

re·buke'

re·buked'

re·buk'ing·ly

re'bus

re·but'

re·but'tal

re·but'ted

re·but'ter

re·cal'ci·trance

re·cal'ci·trant

re·call'

re·called'

re·cant'

re'can·ta'tion

re·cant'ed

re·cap'i·tal·ize

re'ca·pit'u·late

re'ca·pit'u·lat'ed

re'ca·pit'u·la'tion

re'ca·pit'u·la·to'ry

re·cap'ture

re·cast'

re·cede'

re·ced'ed

re·ceipt'

re·ceipt'ed

re·ceiv'a·ble

re·ceiv'a·bles

re·ceive'

re·ceived'

re·ceiv'er

re·ceiv'er·ship

re'cent

re'cent·ly

re·cep'ta·cle

re·cep'tion

re·cep'tion·ist

re·cep'tive

re·cep'tive·ly

re·cep'tive·ness

re'cep·tiv'i·ty

re·cep'tor

re·cess'

re·cessed'

re·cess'es

re·ces'sion

re·ces'sion·al

re·ces'sive

re·charge'

re·charged'

re·cher'ché'

re·cid'i·vism

re·cid'i·vist

rec'i·pe

re·cip'i·ent

re·cip'ro·cal

re·cip'ro·cal·ly

re·cip'ro·cate

re·cip'ro·cat'ed

re·cip'ro·ca'tion

re·cip'ro·ca'tive

re·cip'ro·ca'tor

rec'i·proc'i·ty

re·cit'al

re·cit'al·ist

rec'i·ta'tion

rec'i·ta·tive'

re·cite'

re·cit'ed

reck

reck'less

reck'less·ly

reck'less·ness

reck'on

reck'oned

reck'on·er

reck'on·ings

re·claim'

re·claim'a·ble

re·claimed'

rec'la·ma'tion

re·cline'

re·clined'

re·cluse'

rec'og·ni'tion

rec'og·niz'a·ble

re·cog'ni·zance

rec'og·nize

rec'og·nized

re·coil'

re·coiled'

rec'ol·lect'

rec'ol·lect'ed

rec'ol·lec'tion

re'com·mence'

rec'om·mend'

rec'om·men·da'tion

rec'om·mend'a·to'ry

rec'om·mend'ed

re'com·mit'

rec'om·pen'sa·ble

rec'om·pense

rec'om·pensed

rec'on·cil'a·ble

rec'on·cile

rec'on·ciled

rec'on·cile'ment

rec'on·cil'i·a'tion

rec'on·cil'i·a·to'ry

rec'on·dite

re·con'nais·sance

rec'on·noi'ter

rec'on·noi'tered

re·con'quer

re'con·sid'er

re·con'sti·tute

re'con·struct'

re'con·struct'ed

re·con·struc'tion

re·con·struc'tive

re·con'vert

re·con·vey'

re·cord'

re·cord'ed

re·cord'er

re·cord'ings

re·count'

re·count'ed

re·coup'

re·couped'

re·coup'ment

re·course'

re·cov'er

re·cov'er·a·ble

re·cov'er·y

rec're·ant

re'·cre·ate'

rec're·a'tion

rec're·a'tion·al

re·crim'i·nate

re·crim'i·na'tion

re·crim'i·na'tive

re·crim'i·na·to'ry

re'cru·des'cence

re'cru·des'cent

re·cruit'

re·cruit'ed

re·cruit'ment

re·crys·tal·li·za'tion

re·crys'tal·lize

rec'tan'gle

rec·tan'gu·lar

rec·tan'gu·lar'i·ty

rec'ti·fi'a·ble

rec'ti·fi·ca'tion

rec'ti·fied

rec'ti·fi'er

rec'ti·fy

rec'ti·lin'e·ar

rec'ti·tude

rec'tor

rec'tor·ate

rec·to'ri·al

rec'to·ry

re·cum'ben·cy

re·cum'bent

re·cu'per·ate

re·cu'per·at'ed

re·cu'per·a'tion

re·cu'per·a'tive

re·cu'per·a·to'ry

re·cur'

re·curred'

re·cur'rence

re·cur'rent

re·cur'rent·ly

rec'u·sant

red

red'bird'

red'breast'

red'bud'

red'den

red'dened

red'der

red'dest

red'dish

re·deal'

re·deem'

re·deem'a·bil'i·ty

re·deem'a·ble

re·deemed'

re·deem'er

re·demp'tion

Re·demp'tor·ist

re·demp'to·ry

re'de·ter'mine

re'de·vel'op

re'di·rect'

re'di·rect'ed

re·dis'count

re'dis·cov'er

re'dis·trib'ute

re'dis·tri·bu'tion

re·dis'trict

red'ness

red'o·lence

red'o·lent

re·dou'ble

re·doubt'

re·doubt'a·ble

re·dound'

re·draft'

re·dress'

re·dressed'

re·duce'

re·duced'

re·duc'er

re·duc'i·ble

re·duc'tion

re·dun'dance

re·dun'dan·cy

re·dun'dant

re·dun'dant·ly

re·du'pli·cate

re·du'pli·cat'ed

re·du·pli·ca'tion

red'wood'

re-ech'o

re-ech'oed

reed

reed'bird'

reed'i·ness

re-ed'it

re-ed'u·cate

re'-ed·u·ca'tion

reed'y

reef

reef'er

reek

reek'ing·ly

reel

re'-e·lect'

re'-em·bark'

re'-em·bar·ka'tion

re'-em·ploy'

re'-en·act'

re'-en·force'

re'-en·force'ment

re'-en·gage'

re'-en·grave'

re'-en·list'

re-en'ter

re-en'trance

re-en'try

re'-es·tab'lish

re'-ex·am'i·na'tion

re'-ex·am'ine

re'-ex·port'

re'-ex·por·ta'tion

re·fec'to·ry

re·fer'

ref'er·a·ble

ref'er·ee'

ref'er·ence

ref'er·en'dum

re·ferred'

re·fig'ure

re'fill

re'fi·nance'

re·fine'

re·fined'

re·fine'ment

re·fin'er

re·fin'er·y

re·fit'

re·flect'

re·flect'ed

re·flect'ing·ly

re·flec'tion

re·flec'tive

re·flec'tor

re'flex

re·flex'ive

re'flux

re'for·est·a'tion

re·form'

ref'or·ma'tion

re·form'a·tive

re·form'a·to'ry

re·formed'

re·form'er

re·fract'

re·fract'ed

re·frac'tion

re·frac'tion·ist

re·frac'tive

re'frac·tiv'i·ty

re·frac'tor

re·frac'to·ry

re·frain'

re·frained'

re·fresh'

re·freshed'

re·fresh'er

re·fresh'ing·ly

re·fresh'ment

re·frig'er·ant

re·frig'er·ate

re·frig'er·at'ed

re·frig'er·a'tion

re·frig'er·a'tive

re·frig'er·a'tor

ref'uge

ref'u·gee'

re·ful'gence

re·ful'gent

re·fund'

re·fund'ed

re·fur'nish

re·fus'al

re·fuse'

re·fused'

ref'u·ta'tion

re·fute'

re·fut'ed

re·gain'

re·gained'

re'gal

re·gale'

re·galed'

re·gale'ment

re·ga'li·a

re·gal'i·ty

re'gal·ly

re·gard'

re·gard'ed

re·gard'ful

re·gard'less

re·gat'ta

re'ge·la'tion

re'gen·cy

re·gen'er·a·cy

re·gen'er·ate

re·gen'er·at'ed

re·gen'er·a'tion

re·gen'er·a'tive

re·gen'er·a'tor

re'gent

reg'i·cid'al

reg'i·cide

re·gime'

reg'i·men

reg'i·ment

reg'i·men'tal

reg'i·men'tals

reg'i·men·ta'tion

reg'i·ment'ed

re'gion

re'gion·al

re'gion·al·ism

re'gion·al·ize

re'gion·al·ly

reg'is·ter

reg'is·tered

reg'is·trar

reg'is·tra'tion

reg'is·try

re'gress

re·gres'sion

re·gres'sive

re·gret'

re·gret'ful

re·gret'ful·ly

re·gret'ful·ness

re·gret'ta·ble

re·gret'ted

reg'u·lar

reg'u·lar'i·ty

reg'u·lar·i·za'tion

reg'u·lar·ize

reg'u·late

reg'u·lat'ed

reg'u·lates

reg'u·la'tion

reg'u·la'tor

re·gur'gi·tate

re·gur'gi·tat'ed

re·gur'gi·ta'tion

re'ha·bil'i·tate

re'ha·bil'i·tat'ed

re'ha·bil'i·ta'tion

re·hash'

re·hears'al

re·hearse'

re·hearsed'

re·heat'

reign

reigned

re'im·burse'

re'im·bursed'

re'im·port'

re'im·por·ta'tion

rein

re'in·car'nate

re'in·car·na'tion

rein'deer'

reined

re·in·force′

re·in·forced′

re·in·sert′

re·in·stall′

re·in·state′

re·in·stat·ed

re·in·state′ment

re·in·sur′ance

re·in·sure′

re·in·te·grate

re·in·tro·duce′

re·in·vest′

re·in·vig′o·rate

re·is′sue

re·it′er·ate

re·it′er·at′ed

re·it′er·a′tion

re·it′er·a′tive

re·ject′

re·ject′ed

re·jec′tion

re·joice′

re·joiced′

re·joic′es

re·joic′ing·ly

re·join′

re·join′der

re·ju′ve·nate

re·ju′ve·nat′ed

re·ju′ve·na′tion

re·ju′ve·na′tive

re·ju′ve·nes′cence

re·ju′ve·nes′cent

re·kin′dle

re·lapse′

re·lapsed′

re·late′

re·lat′ed

re·la′tion

re·la′tion·al

re·la′tion·ship

rel′a·tive

rel′a·tive·ly

rel′a·tiv·ism

rel′a·tiv′i·ty

re·la′tor

re·lax′

re′lax·a′tion

re·laxed′

re·lax′es

re·lay′

re·layed′

re·lease′

re·leased′

rel′e·gate

rel′e·gat′ed

rel′e·ga′tion

re·lent′

re·lent′ed

re·lent′ing·ly

re·lent′less

rel′e·vance

rel′e·van·cy

rel′e·vant

re·li′a·bil′i·ty

re·li′a·ble

re·li′ant

rel′ic

re·lief′

re·lieve′

re·lieved′

re·li′gion

re·li′gious

re·li′gious·ly

re·lin′quish

re·lin′quished

re·lin′quish·ment

rel′i·quar′y

rel′ish

rel′ished

re·live′

re·load′

re·lo′cate

re·lo′cat·ed

re′lo·ca′tion

re·lo′ca·tor

re·lu′cent

re·luc′tance

re·luc′tant

re·luc′tant·ly

re·ly′

re·main′

re·main′der

re·mained′

re·make′

re·mand'

re·mand'ed

re·mark'

re·mark'a·ble

re·mar'ried

re·mar'ry

re·me'di·a·ble

re·me'di·al

rem'e·died

rem'e·dy

re·mem'ber

re·mem'bered

re·mem'brance

re·mind'

re·mind'ed

re·mind'er

re·mind'ful

re·mind'ing·ly

rem'i·nis'cence

rem'i·nis'cent

re·miss'

re·mis'sion

re·mit'

re·mit'tal

re·mit'tance

re·mit'ted

re·mit'tent

re·mit'ter

rem'nant

re·mod'el

re·mon'e·ti·za'tion

re·mon'e·tize

re·mon'strance

re·mon'strant

re·mon'strate

re·mon'strat·ed

re·mon'strat·ing·ly

re'mon·stra'tion

re'mon'stra·tive

re·morse'

re·morse'ful

re·morse'ful·ly

re·morse'less

re·mote'

re·mote'ness

re·mot'er

re·mot'est

re·mount'

re·mov'a·bil'i·ty

re·mov'a·ble

re·mov'al

re·move'

re·moved'

re·moves'

re·mu'ner·ate

re·mu'ner·at'ed

re·mu'ner·a'tion

re·mu'ner·a'tive

ren'ais·sance'

re'nal

re·nas'cent

rend

ren'der

ren'dered

ren'der·ings

ren'dez·vous

ren·di'tion

ren'e·gade

re·nege'

re·ne·go'ti·ate

re·new'

re·new'a·ble

re·new'al

re·newed'

ren'net

re·nom'i·nate

re·nom'i·na'tion

re·nounce'

re·nounced'

ren'o·vate

ren'o·vat'ed

ren'o·va'tion

re·nown'

re·nowned'

rent

rent'al

rent'ed

re·num'ber

re·nun'ci·a'tion

re·nun'ci·a'tive

re·nun'ci·a·to'ry

re·o'pen

re·or'der

re'or·gan·i·za'tion

re·or'gan·ize

re·o'ri·ent

re·paid'

re·paint'

re·pair'

re·paired'

re·pair'er

rep'a·ra·ble

rep'a·ra'tion

re·par'a·tive

rep'ar·tee'

re·past'

re·pa'tri·ate

re·pay'

re·pay'ment

re·peal'

re·pealed'

re·peal'er

re·peat'

re·peat'ed·ly

re·peat'er

re·pel'

re·pelled'

re·pel'lence

re·pel'len·cy

re·pel'lent

re·pel'ling·ly

re·pent'

re·pent'ance

re·pent'ed

re'per·cus'sion

re'per·cus'sive

rep'er·toire

rep'er·to'ry

rep'e·tend

rep'e·ti'tion

rep'e·ti'tious

re·pet'i·tive

re·phrase'

re·pine'

re·pined'

re·place'

re·placed'

re·place'ment

re·plant'

re·plen'ish

re·plen'ished

re·plen'ish·ment

re·plete'

re·ple'tion

re·plev'in

rep'li·ca

rep'li·ca'tion

re·plied'

re·ply'

re·port'

re·port'ed

re·port'er

re·pose'

re·posed'

re·pose'ful

re·pos'i·to'ry

re'pos·sess'

re'pos·sessed'

rep're·hend'

rep're·hen'si·ble

rep're·hen'sion

rep're·hen'sive

rep're·sent'

rep're·sen·ta'tion

rep're·sent'a·tive

rep're·sent'ed

re·press'

re·pres'sion

re·pres'sive

re·prieve'

re·prieved'

rep'ri·mand

rep'ri·mand'ed

rep'ri·mand'ing·ly

re'print'

re·print'ed

re·pris'al

re·prise'

re·proach'

re·proached'

re·proach'ful

re·proach'ful·ly

re·proach'ful·ness

rep'ro·bate

rep'ro·ba'tion

re'pro·duce'

re'pro·duc'er

re'pro·duc'tion

re'pro·duc'tive

re·proof'

re·prove'

re·proved'

re·prov'ing·ly

rep'tile

rep·til'i·an

re·pub'lic

re·pub'li·can

re·pub'li·can·ism

re·pub'li·can·ize

re·pub'lish

re·pu'di·ate

re·pu'di·a'tion

re·pug'nance

re·pug'nant

re·pulse'

re·pulsed'

re·pul'sion

re·pul'sive

re·pul'sive·ness

re·pur'chase

rep'u·ta·ble

rep'u·ta'tion

re·pute'

re·put'ed

re·put'ed·ly

re·quest'

re'qui·em

re·quire'

re·quired'

re·quire'ment

req'ui·site

req'ui·si'tion

re·quit'al

re·quite'

re·quit'ed

rere'dos

re·run'

re·sale'

re·scind'

re·scind'ed

re·scis'sion

re·score'

res'cue

res'cued

re·search'

re·search'er

re·sec'tion

re·sem'blance

re·sem'ble

re·sem'bled

re·sent'

re·sent'ed

re·sent'ful

re·sent'ful·ness

re·sent'ment

res'er·va'tion

res'er·va'tion·ist

re·serve'

re·served'

re·serv'ist

res'er·voir

re·set'

re·set'tle

re·set'tle·ment

re·ship'

re·ship'ment

re·side'

re·sid'ed

res'i·dence

res'i·den·cy

res'i·dent

res'i·den'tial

re·sid'u·al

re·sid'u·ar'y

res'i·due

re·sid'u·um

re·sign'

res'ig·na'tion

re·signed'

re·sign'ed·ly

re·sil'i·en·cy

re·sil'i·ent

res'in

res'in·ous

re·sist'

re·sist'ance

re·sist'ant

re·sist'i·ble

re·sis'tive

re'sis·tiv'i·ty

re·sist'less

re·sol'u·ble

res'o·lute

res'o·lute·ness

res'o·lu'tion

re·solv'a·ble

re·solve'

re·solved'

re·sol'vent

res'o·nance

res'o·nant

res'o·nate

res'o·na'tor

re·sort'

re·sort'ed

re·sound'

re·sound'ed

re·sound'ing·ly

re·source'

re·source'ful

re·source'ful·ness

re·spect'

re·spect'a·bil'i·ty

re·spect'a·ble

re·spect'ed

re·spect'er

re·spect'ful

re·spec'tive

re·spec'tive·ly

re·spell'

re·spir'a·ble

res'pi·ra'tion

res'pi·ra'tor

re·spir'a·to'ry

re·spire'

re·spired'

res'pite

re·splend'ence

re·splend'en·cy

re·splend'ent

re·spond'

re·spond'ed

re·spond'ent

re·sponse'

re·spon'si·bil'i·ties

re·spon'si·bil'i·ty

re·spon'si·ble

re·spon'sive

re·spon'sive·ness

rest

re·state'

re·state'ment

res'tau·rant

res'tau·ra·teur'

rest'ed

rest'ful

rest'ful·ly

rest'ful·ness

res'ti·tu'tion

res'tive

res'tive·ly

res'tive·ness

rest'less

rest'less·ness

re·stock'

res'to·ra'tion

re·stor'a·tive

re·store'

re·stored'

re·strain'

re·strained'

re·strain'ed·ly

re·strain'ing·ly

re·straint'

re·strict'

re·strict'ed

re·stric'tion

re·stric'tive

re·sult'

re·sult'ant

re·sum'a·ble

re·sume'

re·sumed'

re·sump'tion

re·sur'gence

re·sur'gent

res'ur·rect'

res'ur·rect'ed

res'ur·rec'tion

re·sus'ci·tate

re·sus'ci·tat'ed

re·sus'ci·ta'tion

re·sus'ci·ta'tive

re·sus'ci·ta'tor

re'tail

re'tailed

re'tail·er

re·tain'

re·tained'

re·tain'er

re·take'

re·tal'i·ate

re·tal'i·at'ed

re·tal'i·a'tion

re·tal'i·a'tion·ist
re·tal'i·a'tive
re·tal'i·a·to'ry
re·tard'
re'tar·da'tion
re·tard'ed
re·tard'er
retch
retched
re·tell'
re·tell'ings
re·ten'tion
re·ten'tive
re'ten·tiv'i·ty
ret'i·cence
ret'i·cent
ret'i·cent·ly
ret'i·cle
re·tic'u·lar
re·tic'u·late
re·tic'u·lat'ed
re·tic'u·la'tion
ret'i·cule
ret'i·na
ret'i·nal
ret'i·ni'tis
ret'i·nue
re·tire'
re·tired'
re·tire'ment
re·tir'ing·ly
re·told'

re·tort'
re·tort'ed
re·touch'
re·touch'er
re·trace'
re·trace'a·ble
re·tract'
re·tract'ed
re·trac'tile
re·trac'tion
re·trac'tive
re·trac'tor
re-tread'
re·treat'
re·treat'ed
re·trench'
re·trenched'
re·trench'ment
re·tri'al
ret'ri·bu'tion
re·trib'u·tive
re·triev'al
re·trieve'
re·trieved'
re·triev'er
ret'ro·ac'tive
ret'ro·ac·tiv'i·ty
ret'ro·cede'
ret'ro·ces'sion
ret'ro·ces'sive
ret'ro·flex
ret'ro·flex'ion

ret'ro·grade
ret'ro·grad'ed
ret'ro·gress
ret'ro·gres'sion
ret'ro·gres'sive
ret'ro·spect
ret'ro·spec'tion
ret'ro·spec'tive
ret'ro·ver'sion
re·turn'
re·turn'a·ble
re·turned'
re·un'ion
re·u·nite'
re-use'
re-used'
re·vac'ci·nate
re·val'i·date
re·val'or·ize
re·val·u·a'tion
re·val'ue
re·vamp'
re·veal'
re·vealed'
re·veal'ing·ly
re·veal'ment
rev'eil·le
rev'el
rev'e·la'tion
rev'e·la·to'ry
rev'eled
rev'el·er

rev'el·ry

re·venge'

re·venged'

re·venge'ful

rev'e·nue

re·ver'ber·ant

re·ver'ber·ate

re·ver'ber·at'ed

re·ver'ber·a'tion

re·ver'ber·a'tive

re·ver'ber·a'tor

re·ver'ber·a·to'ry

re·vere'

re·vered'

rev'er·ence

rev'er·end

rev'er·ent

rev'er·en'tial

rev'er·ie

re·ver'sal

re·verse'

re·versed'

re·vers'i·bil'i·ty

re·vers'i·ble

re·ver'sion

re·ver'sion·ar'y

re·vert'

re·vert'ed

re·vert'i·ble

re·vest'

re·vet'

re·vet'ment

re·vict'ual

re·view'

re·viewed'

re·view'er

re·vile'

re·viled'

re·vile'ment

re·vil'ing·ly

re·vin'di·cate

re·vise'

re·vised'

re·vis'er

re·vi'sion

re·vi'sion·ism

re·vi'sion·ist

re·vis'it

re·viv'al

re·viv'al·ism

re·viv'al·ist

re·vive'

re·vived'

re·viv'i·fi·ca'tion

re·viv'i·fi'er

re·viv'i·fy

rev'o·ca'tion

re·vok'a·ble

re·voke'

re·voked'

re·volt'

re·volt'ed

re·volt'ing·ly

rev'o·lu'tion

rev'o·lu'tion·ar'y

rev'o·lu'tion·ist

rev'o·lu'tion·ize

rev'o·lu'tion·ized

re·volve'

re·volved'

re·volv'er

re·vue'

re·vul'sion

re·vul'sive

re·ward'

re·ward'ed

re·ward'ing·ly

re·wind'

re·wire'

re·word'

re·worked'

re·write'

re·writ'ten

rhap·sod'ic

rhap'so·dist

rhap'so·dize

rhap'so·dized

rhap'so·dy

rhe'ni·um

rhe'o·stat

rhe'sus

rhet'o·ric

rhe·tor'i·cal

rhet'o·ri'cian

rheum

rheu·mat'ic

rheu'ma·tism

rheu'ma·toid

rheum'y

rhine'stone'

rhi·ni'tis

rhi·noc'er·os

rhi·nol'o·gy

rhi'no·scope

rhi·nos'co·py

rhi'zome

rho'di·um

rhom'boid

rhom'bus

rhu'barb

rhyme

rhymed

rhythm

rhyth'mic

rhyth'mi·cal

Ri·al'to

ri'ant

rib

rib'ald

rib'ald·ry

ribbed

rib'bon

rice

rich

rich'er

rich'es

rich'est

rich'ly

rich'ness

rich'weed'

rick'ets

ric'o·chet'

rid'dance

rid'den

rid'dle

ride

rid'er

rid'er·less

ridge

ridged

rid'i·cule

rid'i·culed

ri·dic'u·lous

ri·dic'u·lous·ly

ri·dot'to

rife

rif'fle

rif'fled

riff'raff'

ri'fle

ri'fled

ri'fle·man

ri'flings

rift

rig

rig'a·doon'

rigged

rig'ger

right

right'ed

right'eous

right'eous·ly

right'eous·ness

right'ful

right'ful·ly

right'ly

right'ness

rig'id

ri·gid'i·ty

rig'id·ly

rig'id·ness

rig'or

rig'or·ous

rig'or·ous·ly

rile

riled

rill

rim

rime

rind

ring

ring'bolt'

ring'bone'

ringed

ring'er

ring'ing·ly

ring'lead'er

ring'let

ring'let·ed

ring'mas'ter

ring'side'

ring'worm'

rink	rite	roared
rinse	rit'u·al	roar'ings
rinsed	rit'u·al·ism	roast
ri'ot	rit'u·al·ist	roast'ed
ri'ot·ed	rit'u·al·is'tic	roast'er
ri'ot·er	rit'u·al·ly	rob
ri'ot·ous	ri'val	robbed
ri'ot·ous·ly	ri'valed	rob'ber
ri'ot·ous·ness	ri'val·ry	rob'ber·y
rip	rive	robe
ri·par'i·an	riv'er	robed
ripe	riv'er·side'	rob'in
ripe'ly	riv'et	ro'bot
rip'en	riv'et·ed	ro·bust'
rip'ened	riv'et·er	ro·bust'ly
rip'er	riv'u·let	ro·bust'ness
rip'est	roach	rock
ri·poste'	road	rock'er
rip'ple	road'a·bil'i·ty	rock'et
rip'pled	road'bed'	rock'fish'
rip'pling·ly	road'house'	rock'weed'
rip'ply	road'man	rock'work'
rip'rap'	road'side'	rock'y
rise	road'stead	ro·co'co
ris'en	road'ster	rod
ris'er	road'way'	ro'dent
ris'i·bil'i·ty	road'weed'	ro'de·o
ris'i·ble	roam	rod'man
ris'ings	roamed	roe
risk	roam'er	roent'gen
risked	roam'ings	rogue
risk'y	roar	ro'guer·y

ro'guish	room'i·ness	ro'tat·ed
ro'guish·ly	room'mate'	ro·ta'tion
ro'guish·ness	room'y	ro·ta'tion·al
roil	roost	ro'ta·tive
roiled	roost'er	ro'ta·tor
roist'er	root	ro'ta·to'ry
roll	root'ed	rote
rolled	root'er	ro'te·none
roll'er	root'let	ro'to·gra·vure'
roll'mop'	root'worm'	ro'tor
ro·maine'	rope	rot'ten
Ro'man	rope'danc'er	rot'ten·ness
ro·mance'	rope'mak'er	rot'ter
Ro'man·esque'	rope'work'	ro·tund'
ro·man'tic	ro·quet'	ro·tun'da
ro·man'ti·cal·ly	ro·sa'ceous	ro·tun'di·ty
ro·man'ti·cism	ro'sa·ry	rouge
ro·man'ti·cist	rose	rouged
ro·man'ti·cize	ro'se·ate	rough
romp	rose'mar'y	rough'age
romp'ers	ro·sette'	rough'cast'
ron'deau	rose'wood'	rough'dry'
ron'do	ros'i·ly	rough'en
roof	ros'in	rough'ened
roof'er	ros'i·ness	rough'er
roof'less	ros'ter	rough'est
roof'tree'	ros'trum	rough'hew'
rook'er·y	ros'y	rough'hewn'
room	rot	rough'house'
roomed	Ro·tar'i·an	rough'ish
room'er	ro'ta·ry	rough'ly
room'ful	ro'tate	rough'neck'

rough'ness

rough'rid'er

rou·lade'

rou·leau'

rou·lette'

round

round'a·bout'

round'ed

roun'de·lay

round'er

round'est

round'fish'

round'house'

round'ish

round'ly

round'ness

rounds'man

round'worm'

rouse

roused

rous'ing·ly

roust'a·bout'

rout

route

rout'ed

rout'ed

rou·tine'

rou·tin'i·za'tion

rou·tin'ize

rov'er

rov'ing·ly

rov'ings

row

row

row'boat

row'dy

rowed

row'el

row'eled

row'en

row'er

row'lock

roy'al

roy'al·ism

roy'al·ist

roy'al·ly

roy'al·ty

rub

rubbed

rub'ber

rub'ber·ize

rub'ber·ized

rub'ber·y

rub'bings

rub'bish

rub'ble

rub'down'

ru'be·fa'cient

ru'be·fac'tion

ru·be'o·la

ru'bi·cund

ru·bid'i·um

ru'ble

ru'bric

ru'bri·ca'tor

ru'by

ruch'ing

ruck'sack'

ruck'us

rud'der

rud'der·post'

rud'di·er

rud'di·est

rud'di·ly

rud'di·ness

rud'dy

rude

rude'ly

rude'ness

rud'er

rud'est

ru'di·ment

ru'di·men'tal

ru'di·men'ta·ry

rue

rued

rue'ful

ruff

ruf'fi·an

ruf'fi·an·ism

ruf'fle

ruf'fled

Rug'by

rug'ged

rug'ged·ness

ru'gose

ru·gos′i·ty	rum′ple	rus′set
ru′in	rum′pled	Rus′sian
ru′in·a′tion	rum′pus	rust
ru′ined	run	rust′ed
ru′in·ous	run′a·bout′	rus′tic
rule	run′a·gate	rus′ti·cate
ruled	rune	rus′ti·cat′ed
rul′er	rung	rus′ti·ca′tion
rul′ings	ru′nic	rus′ti·cism
rum	run′ner	rus·tic′i·ty
rum′ble	run′off′	rus′tic·ly
rum′bled	runt	rust′i·er
rum′bling·ly	run′way′	rust′i·est
rum′blings	ru·pee′	rus′tle
ru′mi·nant	rup′ture	rus′tled
ru′mi·nate	rup′tured	rus′tler
ru′mi·nat′ed	ru′ral	rus′tling·ly
ru′mi·nat′ing·ly	ru′ral·ism	rus′tlings
ru′mi·na′tion	ru′ral·i·za′tion	rust′proof′
ru′mi·na′tive	ru′ral·ize	rust′y
rum′mage	ru′ral·ly	rut
rum′maged	ruse	ru′ta·ba′ga
rum′my	rush	ruth
ru′mor	rush′ing·ly	ru·the′ni·um
ru′mored	rush′light′	ruth′less
rump	rusk	rye

S

Sab'ba·tar'i·an

Sab'bath

sab·bat'i·cal

sab'ba·tine

sa'ber

sa'ble

sab'o·tage'

sac'cha·rine

sac'er·do'tal

sa'chem

sa·chet'

sack'but

sack'cloth'

sacked

sack'ful

sa'cral

sac'ra·ment

sac'ra·men'tal

sac'ra·men'tal·ism

sac'ra·men'tal·ist

sac'ra·men'tal·ly

sac'ra·men·tar'i·an

sa'cred

sa'cred·ly

sa'cred·ness

sac'ri·fice

sac'ri·ficed

sac'ri·fi'cial

sac'ri·lege

sac'ri·le'gious

sac'ris·tan

sac'ris·ty

sac'ro·sanct

sa'crum

sad

sad'der

sad'dest

sad'dle

sad'dle·back'

sad'dle·bag'

sad'dled

sad'dler

sad'dler·y

sad'i'ron

sad'ly

sad'ness

sa·fa'ri

safe

safe'guard'

safe'keep'ing

safe'ly

safe'ness

saf'er

saf'est

safe'ty

saf'fron

sag

sa'ga

sa·ga'cious

sa·ga'cious·ly

sa·gac'i·ty

sag'a·more

sage

sagged

sag'it·tal

sa'go

257

sa'hib

said

sail

sail'boat'

sailed

sail'fish'

sail'ings

sail'or

saint

saint'ed

saint'hood

saint'li·ness

saint'ly

sake

sa'ker

sa·laam'

sal'a·bil'i·ty

sal'a·ble

sa·la'cious

sa·la'cious·ly

sa·la'cious·ness

sal'ad

sal'a·man'der

sal'a·ried

sal'a·ry

sale

sal'e·ra'tus

sales'man

sales'man·ship

sales'peo'ple

sales'per'son

sales'room'

sales'wom'an

sal'i·cyl'ic

sa'li·ence

sa'li·ent

sa·lif'er·ous

sa'line

sa·li'va

sal'i·vant

sal'i·vate

sal'i·va'tion

sal'low

sal'low·er

sal'low·est

sal'ly

salm'on

sa·loon'

sal'si·fy

salt

sal'ta·to'ry

salt'cel'lar

salt'ed

salt'i·er

salt'i·est

salt'pe'ter

salt'y

sa·lu'bri·ous

sa·lu'bri·ty

sal'u·tar'y

sal'u·ta'tion

sa·lu'ta·to'ri·an

sa·lu'ta·to'ry

sa·lute'

sa·lut'ed

sal'vage

sal'vaged

sal·va'tion

salve

salved

sal'ver

sal'vo

Sa·mar'i·tan

sa·ma'ri·um

same

same'ness

sam'ite

Sa·mo'an

sam'o·var

sam'pan

sam'ple

sam'pled

sam'pler

sam'plings

sam'u·rai

san'a·tive

san'a·to'ri·um

san'a·to'ry

sanc'ti·fi·ca'tion

sanc'ti·fied

sanc'ti·fy

sanc'ti·mo'ni·ous

sanc'ti·mo'ni·ous·ly

sanc'ti·mo'ni·ous·ness

sanc'tion

sanc'tioned

sanc′ti·tude

sanc′ti·ty

sanc′tu·ar′y

sanc′tum

sand

san′dal

san′dal·wood′

sand′bag′

sand′bank′

sand′blast′

sand′box′

sand′bur′

sand′ed

sand′er

sand′fish′

sand′flow′er

sand′i·ness

sand′man′

sand′pa′per

sand′pip′er

sand′stone′

sand′storm′

sand′wich

sand′wiched

sand′worm′

sand′y

sane

sane′ly

san′er

san′est

sang

san′gui·nar′y

san′guine

san′i·tar′i·um

san′i·tar′y

san′i·ta′tion

san′i·ty

sank

San′skrit

sap

sa′pi·ence

sa′pi·ent

sap′lings

sa·pon′i·fi·ca′tion

sa·pon′i·fy

sap′per

sap′phire

sap′pi·er

sap′pi·est

sap′py

sap′wood′

sar′a·band

Sar′a·cen

sar′casm

sar·cas′tic

sar·cas′ti·cal·ly

sar·co′ma

sar·co′ma·ta

sar′co·phag′ic

sar·coph′a·gus

sar·dine′

Sar·din′i·an

sar·don′ic

sar·don′i·cal·ly

sar′do·nyx

sar·gas′so

sa′ri

sa·rong′

sar′sa·pa·ril′la

sar·to′ri·al

sash

sas′sa·fras

sat

Sa′tan

sa·tan′ic

satch′el

sate

sat′ed

sa·teen′

sat′el·lite

sa′ti·ate

sa′ti·at′ed

sa′ti·a′tion

sa·ti′e·ty

sat′in

sat′i·nette′

sat′ire

sa·tir′ic

sa·tir′i·cal

sa·tir′i·cal·ly

sat′i·rist

sat′i·rize

sat′i·rized

sat′is·fac′tion

sat′is·fac′to·ri·ly

sat′is·fac′to·ry

sat'is·fied		sav'a·ble		sca'lar	
sat'is·fy		sav'age		scald	
sat'is·fy'ing·ly		sav'age·ly		scald'ed	
sa'trap		sav'age·ry		scale	
sat'u·rate		sa·van'na		scaled	
sat'u·rat'ed		sa·vant'		sca·lene'	
sat'u·ra'tion		save		scal'er	
Sat'ur·day		saved		scal'lion	
Sat'urn		sav'ings		scal'lop	
sat'ur·nine		sav'ior		scalp	
sat'yr		sa'vor		scalped	
sat'yr·esque'		sa'vor·less		scal'pel	
sauce		sa'vor·y		scalp'er	
sauce'boat'		saw		scal'y	
sauce'dish'		saw'dust'		scamp	
sauce'pan'		sawed		scamped	
sau'cer		saw'fish'		scam'per	
sau'cer·like'		saw'fly'		scam'pered	
sau'ci·er		saw'horse'		scan	
sau'ci·est		saw'mill'		scan'dal	
sau'ci·ly		saw'yer		scan'dal·i·za'tion	
sau'cy		Sax'on		scan'dal·ize	
saun'ter		say		scan'dal·ized	
saun'tered		say'ings		scan'dal·ous	
saun'ter·er		says		scan'dal·ous·ly	
saun'ter·ing·ly		scab		Scan'di·na'vi·a	
saun'ter·ings		scab'bard		scan'di·um	
sau'ri·an		scab'by		scanned	
sau'sage		sca'bi·es		scan'ner	
sau·té'		sca'bi·ous		scan'sion	
sau·téed'		sca'brous		scan·so'ri·al	
sau·terne'		scaf'fold		scant	

scant'ed

scant'i·ly

scant'i·ness

scant'lings

scant'y

scape'goat'

scape'grace'

scap'u·la

scap'u·lar

scar

scar'ab

scarce

scarce'ly

scarc'er

scarc'est

scar'ci·ty

scare

scared

scarf

scar'i·fi·ca'tion

scar'i·fied

scar'i·fi'er

scar'i·fy

scar·la·ti'na

scar'let

scarred

scathed

scathe'less

scath'ing

scath'ing·ly

scat'ter

scat'ter·brain'

scat'tered

scat'ter·ing·ly

scat'ter·ings

scav'en·ger

sce·na'ri·o

scen'er·y

scene'shift'er

sce'nic

sce'ni·cal

scent

scent'ed

scent'less

scent'wood'

scep'ter

scep'tered

sched'ule

sched'uled

sche·mat'ic

sche·mat'i·cal·ly

sche'ma·tize

sche'ma·tized

scheme

schemed

schem'er

schem'ing·ly

scher·zan'do

scher'zo

schism

schis·mat'ic

schis·mat'i·cal

schist

schiz'oid

schiz'o·phre'ni·a

schiz'o·phren'ic

schnapps

schnau'zer

schnit'zel

schol'ar

schol'ar·ly

schol'ar·ship

scho·las'tic

scho·las'ti·cal

scho·las'ti·cal·ly

scho·las'ti·cism

scho'li·ast

scho'li·um

school

school'book'

schooled

school'house'

school'man

school'mas'ter

schoon'er

schot'tische

sci·at'ic

sci·at'i·ca

sci'ence

sci'en·tif'ic

sci'en·tif'i·cal·ly

sci'en·tist

scim'i·tar

scin·til'la

scin'til·lant

scin'til·late

scin'til·lat'ed	score	scrab'blings
scin'til·lat'ing·ly	scored	scrag'gy
scin'til·la'tion	scor'er	scram'ble
sci'on	scor'ings	scram'bled
scis'sors	scorn	scram'blings
scle·ri'tis	scorned	scrap
scle·ro'sis	scorn'er	scrap'book'
scle·rot'ic	scorn'ful	scrape
scle'ro·ti'tis	scorn'ful·ly	scraped
scle·rot'o·my	scor'pi·on	scrap'er
scoff	Scot	scrap'ing·ly
scoffed	Scotch	scrap'ings
scoff'er	Scotch'man	scrap'man
scoff'ing·ly	Scots'man	scrap'pi·er
scoff'law'	Scot'tish	scrap'pi·est
scold	scoun'drel	scrap'ple
scold'ed	scoun'drel·ly	scrap'py
scold'ing·ly	scour	scratch
scold'ings	scoured	scratched
sco'li·o'sis	scour'er	scratch'i·ness
sconce	scourge	scratch'ings
scone	scourged	scratch'y
scoop	scourg'ing·ly	scrawl
scooped	scour'ings	scrawled
scoop'ing·ly	scout	scrawl'ings
scoot	scout'ed	scraw'ni·ly
scoot'er	scow	scraw'ni·ness
scope	scowl	scraw'ny
scorch	scowled	scream
scorched	scowl'ing·ly	screamed
scorch'er	scrab'ble	scream'ing·ly
scorch'ing·ly	scrab'bled	screech

screeched

screech'i·er

screech'i·est

screech'y

screed

screen

screened

screen'ings

screen'play'

screw

screw'driv'er

screwed

scrib'ble

scrib'bled

scrib'bler

scrib'bling·ly

scrib'blings

scribe

scrib'er

scrim

scrim'mage

scrimp

scrimped

scrimp'i·ly

scrimp'i·ness

scrimp'ing·ly

scrim'shaw'

scrip

script

scrip'tur·al

scrip'tur·al·ism

scrip'tur·al·ist

scrip'ture

scrive'ner

scrod

scrof'u·la

scrof'u·lous

scroll

scrolled

scroll'work'

scroug'er

scrounge

scrub

scrub'bed

scrub'bi·er

scrub'bi·est

scrub'bings

scrub'by

scrub'land'

scruff

scrum'mage

scrump'tious

scrunch

scrunched

scru'ple

scru'pled

scru'pu·los'i·ty

scru'pu·lous

scru'pu·lous·ly

scru'pu·lous·ness

scru'ti·ni·za'tion

scru'ti·nize

scru'ti·nized

scru'ti·niz'ing·ly

scru'ti·ny

scud

scud'ded

scuff

scuffed

scuf'fle

scuf'fled

scuf'fling·ly

scuf'flings

scull

sculled

scull'er

scul'ler·y

scul'lion

scul'pin

sculp'tor

sculp'tur·al

sculp'ture

sculp'tur·esque'

scum

scum'my

scup'per

scup'per·nong

scurf

scur·ril'i·ty

scur'ril·ous

scur'ril·ous·ly

scur'ril·ous·ness

scur'ry

scur'vy

scut'tle

scut'tled

scut'tle·ful	sea'sick'ness	sec're·tar'i·al
scu'tum	sea'side'	sec're·tar'i·at
scythe	sea'son	sec're·tar'y
sea	sea'son·a·ble	se·crete'
sea'board'	sea'son·al	se·cret'ed
sea'coast'	sea'son·al·ly	se·cre'tion
sea'far'er	sea'soned	se·cre'tive
sea'fowl'	sea'son·ings	se·cre'tive·ly
sea'go'ing	seat	se·cre'tive·ness
seal	seat'ed	se'cret·ly
sealed	sea'ward	se·cre'to·ry
seal'er	sea'wor'thi·ness	sect
seal'skin'	sea'wor'thy	sec·tar'i·an
seam	se·ba'ceous	sec·tar'i·an·ism
sea'man	se'cant	sec'ta·ry
sea'man·like'	se·cede'	sec'tion
sea'man·ship	se·ced'ed	sec'tion·al
seamed	se·ces'sion	sec'tion·al·ism
seam'stress	se·ces'sion·ism	sec'tion·al·ize
seam'y	se·ces'sion·ist	sec'tion·al·ized
sea'plane'	se·clude'	sec'tion·al·ly
sea'port'	se·clud'ed	sec'tor
sear	se·clu'sion	sec'u·lar
search	sec'ond	sec'u·lar·ism
searched	sec'ond·ar'i·ly	sec'u·lar·ist
search'er	sec'ond·ar'y	sec'u·lar'i·ty
search'ing·ly	sec'ond·ed	sec'u·lar·i·za'tion
search'light'	sec'ond·er	sec'u·lar·ize
seared	sec'ond·hand'	sec'u·lar·ized
sea'scape	sec'ond·ly	sec'u·lar·iz'er
sea'shore'	se'cre·cy	se·cure'
sea'sick'	se'cret	se·cured'

se·cure'ly

se·cu'ri·ty

se·dan'

se·date'

se·date'ly

se·date'ness

se·da'tion

sed'a·tive

sed'en·tar'y

sedge

sed'i·ment

sed'i·men'tal

sed'i·men'ta·ry

sed'i·men·ta'tion

se·di'tion

se·di'tious

se·di'tious·ly

se·di'tious·ness

se·duce'

se·duced'

se·duc'er

se·duc'i·ble

se·duc'tion

se·duc'tive

se·duc'tive·ly

se·duc'tive·ness

sed'u·lous

sed'u·lous·ly

sed'u·lous·ness

se'dum

see

seed

seed'ed

seed'i·er

seed'i·est

seed'i·ness

seed'less

seed'less·ness

seed'lings

seed'y

seek

seek'er

seem

seemed

seem'ing·ly

seem'ly

seen

seep

seep'age

seep'weed'

se'er

seer'ess

seer'suck'er

see'saw'

seethe

seethed

seg'ment

seg·men'tal

seg'men·tar'y

seg'men·ta'tion

seg're·gate

seg're·gat'ed

seg're·ga'tion

seg're·ga'tion·ist

se'gui·dil'la

seine

seis'mic

seis'mo·graph

seis·mol'o·gy

seiz'a·ble

seize

seized

sei'zure

sel'dom

se·lect'

se·lect'ed

se·lec'tion

se·lec'tive

se·lec'tiv'i·ty

se·lect'man

se·lect'men

se·lec'tor

sel'e·nate

se·le'nic

sel'e·nide

sel'e·nite

se·le'ni·um

self

self'-as·ser'tion

self'-as·ser'tive

self'-as·sured'

self'-cen'tered

self'-col'ored

self'-com·mand'

self'-com·pla'cent

self'-com·posed'

self′-con·ceit′

self′-con·cern′

self′-con′fi·dence

self′-con′scious

self′-con′scious·ness

self′-con·tained′

self′-con′tra·dic′tion

self′-con·trol′

self′-cov′ered

self′-de·ceit′

self′-de·fense′

self′-de·ni′al

self′-de·struc′tion

self′-de·ter′mi·na′tion

self′-de·ter′mined

self′-dis′ci·pline

self′-dis·trust′

self′-ed′u·cat′ed

self′-ef·face′ment

self′-ef·fac′ing·ly

self′-es·teem′

self′-ev′i·dent

self′-ex·am′i·na′tion

self′-ex′e·cut′ing

self′-ex·plain′ing

self′-ex·plan′a·to′ry

self′-ex·pres′sion

self′-for·get′ful

self′-gov′erned

self′-gov′ern·ment

self′-help′

self′-im·por′tance

self′-im·prove′ment

self′-in·duced′

self′-in·duc′tance

self′-in·dul′gent

self′-in′ter·est

self′ish

self′ish·ly

self′ish·ness

self′-knowl′edge

self′less

self′-lim′it·ed

self′-liq′ui·dat′ing

self′-love′

self′-made′

self′-mas′ter·y

self′-o·pin′ion·at′ed

self′-pos·sessed′

self′-pos·ses′sion

self′-pres′er·va′tion

self′-pro·pel′ling

self′-rat′ing

self′-read′ing

self′-re′al·i·za′tion

self′-re·gard′

self′-reg′is·ter·ing

self′-re·li′ance

self′-re·li′ant

self′-re·nun′ci·a′tion

self′-re·proach′

self′-re·proach′ful

self′-re·proach′ing·ly

self′-re·spect′

self′-re·straint′

self′-right′eous

self′-right′eous·ness

self′-sac′ri·fice

self′-sac′ri·fic′ing·ly

self′same′

self′-sat′is·fied

self′-seek′er

self′-serv′ice

self′-start′er

self′-stud′y

self′-styled′

self′-suf·fi′cien·cy

self′-suf·fi′cient

self′-sup·port′

self′-sur·ren′der

self′-sus·tain′ing

self′-un′der·stand′ing

self′-will′

self′-willed′

self′-wind′ing

sell

sell′er

sell′out′

Selt′zer

sel′vage

se·man′tic

sem′a·phore

sem′blance

se·mes′ter

sem′i·cir′cle

sem′i·cir′cu·lar

sem'i·civ'i·lized

sem'i·co'lon

sem'i·con'scious

sem'i·de·tached'

sem'i·fi'nal

sem'i·fi'nal·ist

sem'i·fin'ished

sem'i·month'ly

sem'i·nar'

sem'i·nar'i·an

sem'i·nar'y

Sem'i·nole

sem'i·per'me·a·ble

sem'i·pre'cious

sem'i·se'ri·ous

sem'i·skilled'

Sem'ite

Se·mit'ic

Sem'i·tism

sem'i·tone'

sem'i·week'ly

sem'o·li'na

sem·pi·ter'nal

sen'ate

sen'a·tor

sen'a·to'ri·al

sen'a·to'ri·al·ly

sen'a·tor·ship'

send

send'er

Sen'e·ca

se·nes'cence

se·nes'cent

sen'es·chal

se'nile

se·nil'i·ty

sen'ior

sen·ior'i·ty

sen'na

sen'nit

sen'sate

sen·sa'tion

sen·sa'tion·al

sen·sa'tion·al·ism

sen·sa'tion·al·ly

sense

sense'less

sense'less·ly

sense'less·ness

sen'si·bil'i·ty

sen'si·ble

sen'si·tive

sen'si·tive·ly

sen'si·tive·ness

sen'si·tiv'i·ty

sen'si·ti·za'tion

sen'si·tize

sen'si·tized

sen'si·tiz'er

sen'si·tom'e·ter

sen·so'ri·um

sen'so·ry

sen'su·al

sen'su·al·ism

sen'su·al·ist

sen'su·al·is'tic

sen'su·al'i·ty

sen'su·al·i·za'tion

sen'su·al·ize

sen'su·al·ized

sen'su·al·ly

sen'su·ous

sen'su·ous·ly

sen'su·ous·ness

sen'tence

sen'tenced

sen·ten'tious

sen·ten'tious·ly

sen·ten'tious·ness

sen'ti·ence

sen'ti·en·cy

sen'ti·ment

sen'ti·men'tal

sen'ti·men'tal·ism

sen'ti·men'tal·ist

sen'ti·men·tal'i·ty

sen'ti·men'tal·ize

sen'ti·men'tal·ized

sen'ti·nel

sen'try

sep'a·ra·bil'i·ty

sep'a·ra·ble

sep'a·rate

sep'a·rat'ed

sep'a·rate·ly

sep'a·ra'tion

sep'a·ra'tion·ist	Se·quoi'a	se'ri·ous·ness
sep'a·ra·tism	se·ragl'io	ser'mon
sep'a·ra'tist	se·ra'pe	ser'mon·ize
sep'a·ra'tive	ser'aph	ser'mon·ized
sep'a·ra'tor	se·raph'ic	se'rous
sep'a·ra·to'ry	se·raph'i·cal	ser'pent
se'pi·a	ser'a·phim	ser'pen·tine
se'poy	Ser'bi·an	ser·pig'i·nous
sep'sis	sere	ser'rate
Sep·tem'ber	ser'e·nade'	ser·ra'tion
sep·ten'ni·al	ser'e·nad'ed	ser'ried
sep·tet'	ser'e·nad'er	se'rum
sep'tic	ser'e·na'ta	serv'ant
sep'ti·ce'mi·a	ser'en·dip'i·ty	serve
Sep'tu·a·gint	se·rene'	served
sep'tum	se·rene'ly	serv'er
sep'ul·cher	se·rene'ness	serv'ice
se·pul'chral	se·ren'i·ty	serv'ice·a·bil'i·ty
se·pul'tur·al	serf	serv'ice·a·ble
sep'ul·ture	serf'dom	serv'ice·a·bly
se'quel	serge	serv'iced
se·que'la	ser'geant	Serv'i·dor
se·que'lae	se'ri·al	ser'vile
se'quence	se'ri·al·i·za'tion	ser·vil'i·ty
se·quen'tial	se'ri·al·ize	serv'ings
se·quen'tial·ly	se'ri·al·ly	ser'vi·tor
se·ques'ter	se'ri·a'tim	ser'vi·tude
se·ques'tered	ser'i·cul'ture	ser'vo·mech'·a·nism
se·ques'trate	se'ries	ser'vo·mo'tor
se·ques'trat·ed	ser'if	ses'a·me
se·ques·tra'tion	se'ri·ous	ses'qui·sul'phide
se'quin	se'ri·ous·ly	ses'sion

ses'terce	sex·tet'	shak'en
ses·tet'	sex'ton	shak'er
set	sex'tu·ple	Shake·spear'e·an
set'back'	sex·tu'pli·cate	shake'-up'
set'off'	shab'bi·ly	shak'i·er
set·tee'	shab'bi·ness	shak'i·est
set'ter	shab'by	shak'i·ly
set'tings	shack	shak'i·ness
set'tle	shack'le	shak'o
set'tled	shack'led	shak'y
set'tle·ment	shade	shale
set'tler	shad'ed	shall
sev'er	shad'i·er	shal'lop
sev'er·a·ble	shad'i·est	shal·lot'
sev'er·al	shad'i·ly	shal'low
sev'er·al·ly	shad'i·ness	shal'lowed
sev'er·al·ty	shad'ings	shal'low·er
sev'er·ance	shad'ow	shal'low·est
sev'er·a'tion	shad'owed	shal'low·ly
se·vere'	shad'ow·less	shal'low·ness
sev'ered	shad'ow·y	sham
se·vere'ly	shad'y	sha'man
se·ver'er	shaft	sham'ble
se·ver'est	shag	sham'bled
se·ver'i·ty	shag'bark'	sham'bling·ly
sew	shag'gi·er	shame
sew'age	shag'gi·est	shamed
sewed	shag'gi·ly	shame'faced'
sew'er	shag'gy	shame·fac'ed·ly
sew'er·age	sha·green'	shame'ful
sewn	shake	shame'ful·ly
sex'tant	shake'down'	shame'ful·ness

shame'less·ly	sharp'ness	sheep'skin'
shame'less·ness	sharp'shoot'er	sheer
shammed	sharp'-wit'ted	sheer'er
sham'mer	shas'tra	sheer'est
sham·poo'	shat'ter	sheer'ly
sham·pooed'	shat'tered	sheet
sham'rock	shat'ter·ing·ly	sheet'ed
shan'dy·gaff	shat'ter·proof'	sheet'ings
shang·hai'	shave	sheet'ways'
shang·haied'	shaved	sheet'wise'
shank	shav'er	sheet'work'
shan't	shave'tail'	shek'el
shan'ty	shav'ings	shel'drake'
shape	shaw	shelf
shaped	shawl	shell
shape'less	she	shel·lac'
shape'less·ly	sheaf	shell'back'
shape'less·ness	shear	shell'burst'
shape'li·ness	sheared	shelled
shape'ly	shear'ings	shell'fish'
shard	shears	shell'proof'
share	sheathe	shell'work'
shared	sheathed	shel'ter
share'hold'er	sheaves	shel'tered
shark	shed	shel'ter·ing·ly
sharp	sheen	shel'ter·less
sharp'en	sheep	shelve
sharp'ened	sheep'herd'er	shelved
sharp'en·er	sheep'ish	shelves
sharp'er	sheep'ish·ly	shep'herd
sharp'est	sheep'ish·ness	shep'herd·ed
sharp'ly	sheep'man	shep'herd·ess

Sher'a·ton		shin'gled		shirt'ings	
sher'bet		shin'i·ly		shirt'less	
sher'iff		shin'i·ness		shiv'er	
Sher'pa		shin'ing·ly		shiv'ered	
sher'ry		shin'ny		shiv'er·ing·ly	
Shet'land		shin'plas'ter		shiv'er·ings	
shew'bread'		Shin'to'		shoal	
shib'bo·leth		Shin'to·ism		shoal'ness	
shied		Shin'to·ist		shock	
shield		Shin'to·is'tic		shocked	
shield'ed		shin'y		shock'ing·ly	
shift		ship		shod	
shift'ed		ship'board'		shod'di·er	
shift'i·er		ship'build'er		shod'di·est	
shift'i·est		ship'load'		shod'dy	
shift'i·ly		ship'mas'ter		shoe	
shift'i·ness		ship'mate'		shoe'horn'	
shift'less		ship'ment		shoe'lace'	
shift'y		ship'own'er		shoe'less	
shil·le'lagh		ship'per		shoe'mak'er	
shil'lings		ship'shape'		shoe'man	
shim		ship'worm'		shoes	
shimmed		ship'wreck'		shoe'string'	
shim'mer		ship'wright'		sho'gun'	
shim'mered		ship'yard'		shook	
shim'mer·ing·ly		shire		shoot	
shim'mer·y		shirk		shoot'er	
shin		shirked		shoot'ings	
shin'bone'		shirk'er		shop	
shine		shirr		shop'keep'er	
shin'er		shirred		shop'lift'er	
shin'gle		shirt		shop'man	

shop'per		should		shrewd	
shop'work'		shoul'der		shrewd'er	
shop'worn'		shoul'dered		shrewd'est	
shore		shout		shrewd'ly	
shored		shout'ed		shrewd'ness	
shorn		shove		shriek	
short		shoved		shrieked	
short'age		shov'el		shrift	
short'bread'		shov'eled		shrike	
short'cake'		shov'el·head'		shrill	
short'change'		show		shrilled	
short'com'ings		show'boat'		shrill'er	
short'en		show'down'		shrill'est	
short'ened		showed		shrill'ness	
short'en·ing		show'er		shrill'y	
short'er		show'ered		shrimp	
short'est		show'i·er		shrimp'er	
short'fall'		show'i·est		shrine	
short'hand'		show'i·ly		Shrin'er	
short'hand'ed		show'i·ness		shrink	
short'horn'		show'ings		shrink'age	
short'ish		show'man		shrink'er	
short'leaf'		show'man·ship		shrink'ing·ly	
short'-lived'		shown		shrive	
short'ly		show'room'		shriv'el	
short'ness		show'y		shriv'eled	
short'-range'		shrank		shriv'en	
short'sight'ed		shrap'nel		shroud	
short'-time'		shred		shroud'ed	
shot		shred'ded		shrub	
shot'gun'		shred'der		shrub'ber·y	
shot'ted		shrew		shrub'wood'	

shrug	sib'yl	siege
shrugged	sib'yl·line	si·en'na
shrunk	Si·cil'i·an	si·er'ra
shrunk'en	sick	si·es'ta
shuck	sick'bed'	sieve
shucked	sick'en	sift
shud'der	sick'ened	sift'age
shud'dered	sick'en·ing·ly	sift'ed
shud'der·ing·ly	sick'er	sift'ings
shud'der·ings	sick'est	sigh
shuf'fle	sick'le	sighed
shuf'fled	sick'li·er	sigh'ing·ly
shuf'fling·ly	sick'li·est	sigh'ings
shuf'flings	sick'li·ness	sight
shun	sick'ly	sight'ed
shunt	sick'ness	sight'ings
shunt'ed	sick'room'	sight'less
shut	side	sight'li·ness
shut'off'	side'board'	sight'ly
shut'ter	side'car'	sig'ma
shut'tered	sid'ed	sign
shut'tle	side'long'	sig'nal
shut'tled	side'piece'	sig'naled
shy	si·de're·al	sig'nal·ize
shy'ly	sid'er·ite	sig'nal·ized
shy'ness	side'split'ting	sig'nal·ly
shy'ster	side'walk'	sig'na·to'ry
Si'a·mese'	side'ways'	sig'na·ture
sib'i·lance	side'wise'	sign'board'
sib'i·lant	sid'ings	signed
sib'i·late	si'dle	sign'er
sib'ling	si'dled	sig'net

sig·nif′i·cance

sig·nif′i·cant

sig·nif′i·cant·ly

sig′ni·fi·ca′tion

sig′ni·fied

sig′ni·fy

sign′post′

sign′writ′er

si′lage

si′lence

si′lenced

si′lenc·er

si′lent

si′lent·ly

si′lent·ness

si′lex

sil′hou·ette′

sil′i·ca

sil′i·cate

sil′i·con

sil′i·co′sis

silk

silk′en

silk′i·er

silk′i·est

silk′i·ly

silk′i·ness

silk′weed′

silk′worm′

silk′y

sil′la·bub

sil′li·er

sil′li·est

sil′li·ness

sil′ly

si′lo

silt

silt·ta′tion

silt′ed

sil′van

sil′ver

sil′vered

sil′ver·smith′

sil′ver·ware′

sil′ver·y

sim′i·an

sim′i·lar

sim′i·lar′i·ty

sim′i·lar·ly

sim′i·le

si·mil′i·tude

sim′mer

sim′mered

sim′mer·ing·ly

sim′o·ny

si·moon′

sim′per

sim′pered

sim′per·ing·ly

sim′ple

sim′pler

sim′plest

sim′ple·ton

sim′plex

sim·plic′i·ty

sim′pli·fi·ca′tion

sim′pli·fied

sim′pli·fy

sim′ply

sim′u·la′crum

sim′u·late

sim′u·la′tion

si′mul·ta′ne·ous

si·mul·ta′ne·ous·ly

sin

since

sin·cere′

sin·cere′ly

sin·cere′ness

sin·cer′er

sin·cer′est

sin·cer′i·ty

sine

si′ne·cure

sin′ew

sin′ew·y

sin′ful

sin′ful·ly

sin′ful·ness

sing

sing′a·ble

singe

singed

sing′er

sin′gle

sin′gled

sin'gle·ness	sip'per	siz'es
sin'gle·ton	sir	siz'ings
sin'gly	sir·dar'	siz'zle
sin'gu·lar	sire	siz'zled
sin'gu·lar'i·ty	sired	siz'zling·ly
sin'gu·lar·ly	si'ren	skate
sin'is·ter	sir'loin'	skat'ed
sin'is·tral	si·roc'co	skat'er
sink	sir'up	skein
sink'age	sir'up·y	skel'e·tal
sink'er	si'sal	skel'e·ton
sink'hole'	sis'kin	skel'e·ton·ize
sink'ings	sis'si·fied	skel'e·ton·ized
sink'less	sis'sy	skep'tic
sin'less	sis'ter	skep'ti·cal
sin'less·ly	sis'ter·hood	skep'ti·cal·ly
sin'less·ness	sis'ter-in-law'	skep'ti·cism
sinned	sis'ter·ly	sketch
sin'ner	Sis'tine	sketched
Sin'o·log'i·cal	sis'trum	sketch'i·ly
Si·nol'o·gist	sit	sketch'i·ness
Sin'o·logue	site	sketch'y
Sin'o·phile	sit'ter	skew
sin'ter	sit'tings	skewed
sin'u·os'i·ty	sit'u·ate	skew'er
sin'u·ous	sit'u·at'ed	skew'ered
si'nus·i'tis	sit'u·a'tion	skew'ings
Sioux	sixth	ski
sip	siz'a·ble	ski'a·gram
si'phon	size	ski'a·graph
si'phoned	sized	ski·am'e·try
sipped	siz'er	skid

skid'ded	skir'mished	sky'writ'ing
skied	skir'mish·er	slab
skiff	skir'mish·ing·ly	slack
ski·jor'ing	skirt	slacked
skill	skirt'ed	slack'en
skilled	skirt'ings	slack'ened
skil'let	skit	slack'er
skill'ful	skit'ter	slack'est
skill'ful·ly	skit'tish	slack'ness
skill'ful·ness	skit'tish·ly	slag
skim	skit'tish·ness	slain
skimmed	skit'tles	slake
skim'mer	skive	slaked
skim'ming·ly	skived	slam
skimp	skiv'er	slammed
skimped	skiv'ings	slan'der
skimp'i·ness	skoal	slan'dered
skimp'y	skulk	slan'der·er
skin	skulked	slan'der·ing·ly
skin'flint'	skull	slan'der·ous
skink'er	skunk	slan'der·ous·ly
skinned	skunk'weed'	slan'der·ous·ness
skin'ner	sky	slang
skin'ni·er	sky'lark'	slang'y
skin'ni·est	sky'larked'	slank
skin'ny	sky'light'	slant
skin'worm'	sky'rock'et	slant'ed
skip	sky'scape	slant'ing·ly
skipped	sky'scrap'er	slant'ways'
skip'per	sky'shine'	slant'wise'
skip'ping·ly	sky'ward	slap
skir'mish	sky'writ'er	slap'dash'

slap'stick'	sleek'er	slick'est
slash	sleek'est	slid
slashed	sleek'ly	slide
slash'er	sleek'ness	sli'er
slash'ing·ly	sleep	sli'est
slash'ings	sleep'er	slight
slate	sleep'i·er	slight'ed
slat'er	sleep'i·est	slight'er
slat'ted	sleep'i·ly	slight'est
slat'tern	sleep'i·ness	slight'ing·ly
slat'tern·ly	sleep'less	slight'ly
slaugh'ter	sleep'less·ness	slight'ness
slaugh'tered	sleep'y	slim
slaugh'ter·er	sleet	slime
slaugh'ter·house'	sleeve	slim'i·er
slave	sleigh	slim'i·est
slaved	sleight	slim'i·ly
slav'er	slen'der	slim'i·ness
slav'er·y	slen'der·er	slim'mer
slav'ish	slen'der·est	slim'mest
slav'ish·ly	slen'der·ness	slim'ness
slav'ish·ness	slept	slim'y
slaw	sleuth	sling
slay	sleuthed	slink
slay'er	sleuth'hound'	slink'i·er
slay'ings	slew	slink'i·est
sleave	slewed	slink'y
slea'zi·ness	slice	slip
slea'zy	sliced	slip'case'
sled	slic'er	slip'knot'
sledge	slick	slip'page
sleek	slick'er	slipped

slip'per	sloth'ful·ness	sluice
slip'per·i·ness	slot'ted	sluiced
slip'per·y	slouch	sluice'way'
slip'shod'	slouched	sluic'ings
slit	slouch'i·ly	slum
slith'er	slouch'i·ness	slum'ber
slith'ered	slouch'ing·ly	slum'bered
slit'ter	slough	slum'ber·er
sliv'er	slough	slum'ber·ing·ly
sliv'ered	sloughed	slum'ber·land'
sliv'er·y	slov'en	slum'ber·ous
slob	slov'en·li·ness	slump
slob'ber	slov'en·ly	slumped
sloe	slow	slung
sloe'ber'ry	slowed	slur
slog	slow'er	slurred
slo'gan	slow'est	slur'ring·ly
slo'gan·eer'	slow'go'ing	slur'ry
slogged	slow'ly	slush
sloop	slow'poke'	slush'i·ly
slop	sloyd	slush'i·ness
slope	slub	slush'y
sloped	slubbed	slut'tish
slop'ing·ly	sludge	sly
slopped	slug	sly'boots'
slop'py	slug'gard	sly'ly
slosh	slug'gard·ly	sly'ness
sloshed	slugged	smack
slot	slug'ger	smacked
sloth	slug'gish	smack'ing·ly
sloth'ful	slug'gish·ly	small
sloth'ful·ly	slug'gish·ness	small'er

small'est	smil'ing·ly	smooth'ing·ly
small'ness	smirch	smooth'ly
small'pox'	smirched	smooth'ness
smart	smirk	smote
smart'ed	smirked	smoth'er
smart'en	smirk'ing·ly	smoth'ered
smart'ened	smirk'ish	smoth'er·ing·ly
smart'er	smite	smudge
smart'est	smith	smudged
smart'ing·ly	Smith·so'ni·an	smudg'i·ly
smart'ly	smith'y	smudg'i·ness
smart'ness	smit'ten	smudg'y
smash	smock	smug
smash'up'	smoke	smug'gle
smat'ter	smoked	smug'gled
smat'ter·ings	smoke'house'	smug'gler
smear	smoke'less	smug'ly
smeared	smoke'proof'	smug'ness
smear'i·er	smok'er	smut
smear'i·est	smoke'stack'	smut'ted
smear'i·ness	smoke'wood'	smut'ti·er
smear'y	smok'i·er	smut'ti·est
smell	smok'i·est	smut'ti·ly
smelled	smok'i·ness	smut'ti·ness
smelt	smok'y	smut'ty
smelt'ed	smol'der	snack
smelt'er	smol'dered	snaf'fle
smelt'er·y	smooth	sna·fu'
smidg'en	smooth'bore'	snag
smi'lax	smoothed	snag'ged
smile	smooth'er	snag'gled
smiled	smooth'est	snail

snake

snake'bird'

snaked

snake'like'

snake'stone'

snake'weed'

snake'wood'

snak'i·er

snak'i·est

snak'i·ly

snak'i·ness

snak'y

snap

snap'drag'on

snapped

snap'per

snap'pi·er

snap'pi·est

snap'ping·ly

snap'pish

snap'py

snap'shot'

snap'weed'

snare

snared

snarl

snarled

snarl'ing·ly

snarl'y

snatch

snatched

snatch'ing·ly

snatch'y

snath

sneak

sneaked

sneak'er

sneak'i·er

sneak'i·est

sneak'ing·ly

sneak'y

sneer

sneered

sneer'ing·ly

sneeze

sneezed

sneeze'weed'

snick'er

snick'ered

snick'er·ing·ly

snick'er·ings

sniff

sniffed

sniff'i·ly

sniff'i·ness

sniff'ing·ly

sniff'ings

snif'fle

snif'fled

sniff'y

snig'ger·ing·ly

snip

snipe

snipped

snip'pet

snip'pi·er

snip'pi·est

snip'pi·ness

snip'py

sniv'el

sniv'eled

sniv'el·er

sniv'el·ings

snob

snob'ber·y

snob'bish

snob'bish·ly

snob'bish·ness

snood

snook'er

snoop

snoop'er

snoot

snooze

snore

snored

snor'ing·ly

snor'ings

snor'kel

snort

snort'ing·ly

snort'ings

snout

snow

snow'ball'

snow'bell'

snow'ber'ry	snuf'flings	so'ber·ly
snow'bird'	snug	so·ber·sides'
snow'bound'	snug'ger	so·bri'e·ty
snow'bush'	snug'ger·y	so'bri·quet
snow'cap'	snug'gest	soc'age
snow'drift'	snug'gle	soc'cer
snow'drop'	snug'gled	so'cia·bil'i·ty
snowed	snug'ly	so'cia·ble
snow'fall'	snug'ness	so'cia·bly
snow'flake'	so	so'cial
snow'flow'er	soak	so'cial·ism
snow'i·er	soaked	so'cial·ist
snow'i·est	soap	so'cial·is'tic
snow'plow'	soap'box'	so'cial·i·za'tion
snow'shed'	soaped	so'cial·ize
snow'shoe'	soap'i·ness	so'cial·ized
snow'slide	soap'root'	so'cial·iz'er
snow'slip	soap'stone'	so·ci'e·tal
snow'storm	soap'suds'	so·ci'e·tar'i·an
snow'worm'	soap'y	so·ci'e·tar'i·an·ism
snow'y	soar	so·ci'e·ty
snub	soared	so'ci·o·log'i·cal
snubbed	soar'ing·ly	so'ci·o·log'i·cal·ly
snub'ber	sob	so'ci·ol'o·gist
snub'bing·ly	sobbed	so'ci·ol'o·gy
snub'bings	sob'bing·ly	sock
snuff	so·be'it	sock'et
snuffed	so'ber	sock'et·ed
snuff'er	so'bered	So·crat'ic
snuf'fle	so'ber·er	sod
snuf'fled	so'ber·est	so'da
snuf'fling·ly	so'ber·ing·ly	so·dal'i·ty

sod′den	sol′e·cism	sol′i·tude
so′di·um	soled	so′lo
so′fa	sole′ly	so′loed
soft	sol′emn	so′lo·ist
sof′ten	so·lem′ni·ty	sol′stice
sof′tened	sol′em·ni·za′tion	sol′u·bil′i·ty
sof′ten·er	sol′em·nize	sol′u·ble
soft′er	sol′em·nized	sol′ute
soft′est	sol′emn·ly	so·lu′tion
soft′ly	so′le·noid	solv′a·ble
soft′ness	so′le·noi′dal	sol′vate
soft′wood′	sole′print′	sol·va′tion
sog′gi·ly	sol′fe·ri′no	solve
sog′gi·ness	so·lic′it	solved
sog′gy	so·lic′i·ta′tion	sol′ven·cy
soil	so·lic′it·ed	sol′vent
soiled	so·lic′i·tor	so·mat′ic
so·journ′	so·lic′it·ous	so′ma·tol′o·gy
so·journed′	so·lic′i·tude	som′ber
so·journ′er	sol′id	som·bre′ro
sol′ace	sol′i·dar′i·ty	some
sol′aced	so·lid′i·fi′a·ble·ness	some′bod′y
so′lar	so·lid′i·fi·ca′tion	some′how
so·lar′i·um	so·lid′i·fy	some′one′
sold	so·lid′i·ty	som′er·sault
sol′der	sol′id·ly	some′thing
sol′dered	so·lil′o·quize	some′time′
sol′dier	so·lil′o·quized	some′what′
sol′diered	so·lil′o·quy	some′where′
sol′dier·ly	sol′i·taire′	som·nam′bu·lism
sol′dier·y	sol′i·tar′i·ly	som·nam′bu·list
sole	sol′i·tar′y	som′no·lent

son	so·phis'tic	sort
so'nant	so·phis'ti·cal	sort'ed
so·na'ta	so·phis'ti·cate	sort'er
so·na·ti'na	so·phis'ti·cat'ed	sor'tie
song	so·phis'ti·ca'tion	sor'ti·lege
song'bird'	soph'ist·ry	sos'te·nu'to
song'book'	soph'o·more	sot
song'ful	soph'o·mor'ic	sot'tish
song'ful·ness	soph'o·mor'i·cal	sot'tish·ness
song'ster	so'po·rif'ic	sou·brette'
son'ic	so'pra·ni'no	souf'flé'
son'-in-law'	so·pra'no	sought
son'net	sor'cer·er	soul
son'net·eer'	sor'cer·ess	soul'ful
so·nor'i·ty	sor'cer·y	soul'ful·ly
so·no'rous	sor'did	soul'ful·ness
soon	sor'did·ness	soul'less
soon'er	sore	soul'less·ly
soon'est	sore'head'	soul'less·ness
soot	sore'ly	sound
soot'ed	sore'ness	sound'ed
soothe	sor'ghum	sound'er
soothed	so·ror'i·ty	sound'est
sooth'ing·ly	so·ro'sis	sound'ing·ly
sooth'say'er	sor'rel	sound'ings
soot'i·er	sor'ri·er	sound'less
soot'i·est	sor'ri·est	sound'less·ly
soot'i·ly	sor'row	sound'less·ness
soot'y	sor'rowed	sound'ly
sop	sor'row·ful	sound'ness
soph'ism	sor'row·ful·ly	sound'proof'
soph'ist	sor'ry	soup

soup'bone'	sowed	spare'rib'
sour	sow'er	spar'ing·ly
source	sow'ings	spark
soured	soy	spark'ed
sour'er	soy'bean'	spar'kle
sour'est	spa	spar'kled
souse	space	spar'kler
soused	spaced	spar'kling·ly
sou·tane'	spac'ings	sparred
south	spa'cious	spar'ring·ly
south'east'	spa'cious·ly	spar'row
south'east'er	spa'cious·ness	sparse
south'east'er·ly	spade	sparse'ly
south'east'ern	spad'ed	sparse'ness
south'er·ly	spade'fish'	spars'er
south'ern	spade'work'	spars'est
south'ern·er	spa·ghet'ti	spar'si·ty
south'ern·most	spal·peen'	Spar'tan
south'ward	span	spasm
south'west'	span'drel	spas·mod'ic
south'west'er	span'gle	spas·mod'i·cal
south'west'er·ly	span'gled	spas·mod'i·cal·ly
sou've·nir'	Span'iard	spas'tic
sov'er·eign	span'iel	spas'ti·cal·ly
sov'er·eign·ty	Span'ish	spas·tic'i·ty
so'vi·et'	spank	spat
so'vi·et'ism	spanked	spat'ter
so'vi·et'i·za'tion	spank'ing·ly	spat'tered
so'vi·et'ize	spank'ings	spat'ter·ing·ly
so'vi·et·ol'o·gist	span'ner	spat'ter·ings
sow	spare	spat'ter·proof'
sow	spared	spat'ter·work'

spat'u·la	specked	speed'i·ly
spat'u·late	speck'le	speed'i·ness
spav'ined	speck'led	speed'ing·ly
spawn	spec'ta·cle	speed·om'e·ter
spawned	spec'ta·cles	speed'way'
speak	spec·tac'u·lar	speed'y
speak'er	spec·tac'u·lar·ly	spe'le·ol'o·gist
spear	spec·ta'tor	spe'le·ol'o·gy
speared	spec'ter	spell
spear'fish'	spec'tral	spell'bind'er
spear'head'	spec·trom'e·ter	spell'bound'
spear'mint'	spec'tro·scope	spelled
spear'wood'	spec'trum	spell'er
spe'cial	spec'u·late	spell'ings
spe'cial·ist	spec'u·lat'ed	spel'ter
spe'cial·i·za'tion	spec'u·la'tion	Spen·ce'ri·an
spe'cial·ize	spec'u·la'tive	spend
spe'cial·ized	spec'u·la'tive·ly	spend'er
spe'cial·ly	spec'u·la'tive·ness	spend'ings
spe'cial·ty	spec'u·la'tor	spend'thrift'
spe'cie	spec'u·la·to'ry	spent
spe'cies	spec'u·lum	sper'ma·ce'ti
spe·cif'ic	speech	spew
spe·cif'i·cal·ly	speech'less	spewed
spec'i·fi·ca'tion	speech'less·ly	sphag'num
spec'i·fied	speech'less·ness	sphere
spec'i·fy	speed	spher'i·cal
spec'i·men	speed'boat'	spher'i·cal·ly
spe'cious	speed'ed	sphe·ric'i·ty
spe'cious·ly	speed'er	sphe'roid
spe'cious·ness	speed'i·er	sphinx
speck	speed'i·est	spice

spiced		spin'y		splash'ings	
spic'i·ly		spi'ral		splash'y	
spic'i·ness		spi'raled		splat'ter	
spic'y		spi'ral·ly		splat'ter·work'	
spi'der		spire		splayed	
spi'der·y		spired		splay'foot'	
spied		spir'it		spleen	
spig'ot		spir'it·ed		splen'did	
spike		spir'it·ed·ly		splen'did·ly	
spiked		spir'it·u·al		splen'dor	
spik'y		spir'it·u·al·ism		splen'dor·ous	
spile		spir'it·u·al·ist		sple·net'ic	
spiled		spir'it·u·al·is'tic		splen'i·tive	
spill		spir'it·u·al'i·ty		splice	
spilled		spir'it·u·al·ize		spliced	
spill'way'		spir'it·u·al·ized		splic'er	
spin		spir'it·u·al·ly		splic'ings	
spin'ach		spir'it·u·ous		splint	
spi'nal		spi'ro·chete		splint'ed	
spin'dle		spit		splin'ter	
spine		spit'ball'		splin'tered	
spine'less		spite		splin'ter·proof'	
spin'et		spite'ful		split	
spin'i·er		spite'ful·ly		split'tings	
spin'i·est		spite'ful·ness		split'worm'	
spin'na·ker		spit'fire'		splotch	
spin'ner		spit·toon'		splotched	
spin'ner·et		splash		splotch'y	
spin'ney		splashed		splurge	
spin'ning·ly		splash'i·er		splurged	
spin'ster		splash'i·est		splut'ter	
spin'ster·hood		splash'ing·ly		splut'tered	

spoil	spooled	spout'ings
spoil'age	spoon	sprain
spoiled	spoon'bill'	sprained
spoils'man	spooned	sprang
spoil'sport'	spoon'er·ism	sprat
spoke	spoon'ful	sprawl
spo'ken	spoon'fuls	sprawled
spoke'shave'	spoor	sprawl'ing·ly
spokes'man	spo·rad'ic	spray
spo'li·a'tion	spore	sprayed
spo'li·a'tive	sport	spray'er
spo'li·a·to'ry	sport'ed	spread
spon'dee	spor'tive	spread'er
sponge	spor'tive·ly	spread'ing·ly
sponge'cake'	spor'tive·ness	spree
sponged	sports'man	sprig
spong'er	sports'man·ship	spright'li·er
spon'gi·er	sports'wear'	spright'li·est
spon'gi·est	sport'y	spright'li·ness
spong'ings	spot	spright'ly
spon'gy	spot'less	spring
spon'sor	spot'less·ly	spring'board'
spon'sor·ship	spot'less·ness	spring'bok'
spon'ta·ne'i·ty	spot'light'	spring'fish'
spon·ta'ne·ous	spot'ted	spring'i·ly
spon·ta'ne·ous·ly	spot'ter	spring'i·ness
spon·ta'ne·ous·ness	spot'ti·er	spring'ing·ly
spoof	spot'ti·est	spring'time'
spook	spot'ty	spring'wood'
spook'i·ness	spouse	spring'y
spook'y	spout	sprin'kle
spool	spout'ed	sprin'kled

sprin'kler	spurt'ed	squashed
sprin'kling·ly	sput'nik	squat
sprin'klings	sput'ter	squat'ted
sprint	sput'tered	squat'ter
sprint'er	sput'ter·ing·ly	squaw
sprite	sput'ter·ings	squaw'fish'
sprit'sail'	spu'tum	squawk
sprock'et	spy	squeak
sprout	spy'glass'	squeal
sprout'ed	squab	squealed
sprout'ling	squab'ble	squeam'ish
spruce	squab'bled	squee'gee
spruc'er	squab'bling·ly	squeeze
spruc'est	squab'blings	squeezed
sprung	squad	squelch
spry	squad'ron	squelched
spud	squal'id	squelch'ing·ly
spume	squa·lid'i·ty	squib
spumed	squal'id·ly	squid
spu·mo'ne	squall	squig'gle
spun	squalled	squig'gly
spunk	squall'ings	squint
spunk'i·er	squall'y	squint'ed
spunk'i·est	squal'or	squint'ing·ly
spunk'y	squan'der	squire
spur	squan'dered	squirm
spu'ri·ous	square	squirmed
spu'ri·ous·ly	squared	squirm'ing·ly
spurn	square'head'	squirm'ings
spurned	square'ly	squir'rel
spurred	square'ness	squir'rel·fish'
spurt	squash	squir'rel·proof'

squirt

stab

stabbed

stab'bing·ly

stab'bings

sta·bil'i·ty

sta'bi·li·za'tion

sta'bi·lize

sta'bi·lized

sta'bi·liz'er

sta'ble

stac·ca'to

stack

sta'di·a

sta'di·um

staff

stag

stage

stage'coach'

stage'craft'

staged

stage'hand'

stag'er

stage'wor'thy

stag'ger

stag'gered

stag'ger·ing·ly

stag'horn'

stag'hound'

stag'hunt'

stag'nant

stag'nate

stag'nat·ed

stag·na'tion

staid

stain

stained

stain'less

stair

stair'case'

stair'way'

stake

staked

sta·lac'tite

sta·lag'mite

stale

stale'mate'

stal'er

stal'est

stalk

stalked

stalk'er

stalk'ing·ly

stall

stalled

stal'lion

stal'wart

sta'men

stam'i·na

stam'mer

stam'mered

stam'mer·er

stam'mer·ing·ly

stamp

stamped

stam·pede'

stam·ped'ed

stamp'er

stamp'ings

stance

stanch

stan'chion

stand

stand'ard

stand'ard·i·za'-
tion

stand'ard·ize

stand'ings

stand'off'

stand'pipe'

stand'point'

stand'still'

stank

stan'nate

stan'nic

stan'nous

stan'za

sta'ple

sta'pled

sta'pler

star

star'board

starch

starched

starch'y

stare

stared

star'fish'	states'man·like'	steak
star'gaz'er	stat'ic	steal
star'ing·ly	sta'tion	stealth
stark	sta'tion·ar'y	stealth'i·er
star'less	sta'tioned	stealth'i·est
star'let	sta'tion·er	stealth'i·ly
star'light'	sta'tion·er'y	steam
star'like'	stat'ism	steam'boat'
star'lings	stat'ist	steamed
starred	sta·tis'ti·cal	steam'er
star'ri·er	sta·tis'ti·cal·ly	steam'i·er
star'ri·est	stat'is·ti'cian	steam'i·est
star'ry	sta·tis'tics	steam'i·ness
start	stat'u·ar'y	steam'ship'
start'ed	stat'ue	steam'y
start'er	stat'u·esque'	ste'a·tite
star'tle	stat'u·ette'	steel
star'tled	stat'ure	steel'head'
star'tling·ly	sta'tus	steel'work'
star·va'tion	stat'ute	steel'yard
starve	stat'u·to'ry	steep
starved	stave	steep'er
starve'ling	stay	steep'est
state	stayed	stee'ple
stat'ed	stead	stee'ple·chase'
state'hood	stead'fast	steer
State'house'	stead'fast·ly	steer'age
state'li·ness	stead'fast·ness	steered
state'ly	stead'i·er	steer'ing
state'ment	stead'i·est	steers'man
state'room'	stead'i·ly	stein
states'man	stead'y	stel'lar

stem	stern'er	stiff'est
stemmed	stern'est	stiff'ness
stench	stern'ly	sti'fle
sten'cil	stern'ness	sti'fled
sten'ciled	stern'post'	sti'fling·ly
ste·nog'ra·pher	ster'num	stig'ma
sten'o·graph'ic	ster'nu·ta'tion	stig·mat'a
ste·nog'ra·phy	ster'to·rous	stig·mat'ic
ste·no'sis	stet	stig'ma·tism
sten·to'ri·an	steth'o·scope	stig'ma·ti·za'tion
step	ste've·dore'	stig'ma·tize
step'child'	stew	stig'ma·tized
step'daugh'ter	stew'ard	stile
step'lad'der	stew'ard·ess	sti·let'to
step'moth'er	stewed	still
steppe	stick	still'born'
stepped	stick'er	stilled
step'sis'ter	stick'ful	still'er
step'son'	stick'i·er	still'est
ster'e·o	stick'i·est	still'ness
ster'e·o·phon'ic	stick'i·ly	still'room'
ster'e·op'ti·con	stick'i·ness	still'y
ster'e·o·scope'	stick'le·back'	stilt
ster'e·o·scop'ic	stick'ler	stilt'ed
ster'ile	stick'pin'	stim'u·lant
ste·ril'i·ty	stick'weed'	stim'u·late
ster'i·li·za'tion	stick'y	stim'u·lat'ed
ster'i·lize	stiff	stim'u·lat'ing·ly
ster'i·lized	stiff'en	stim'u·la'tion
ster'i·liz'er	stiff'ened	stim'u·lus
ster'ling	stiff'en·er	sting
stern	stiff'er	sting'er

sting'fish'	stir'rings	stodg'i·er
stin'gi·er	stir'rup	stodg'i·est
stin'gi·est	stitch	stodg'y
sting'ing·ly	stitched	sto'gy
stin'gy	stitch'er	sto'ic
stink	stitch'ings	sto'i·cal
stink'bug'	stitch'work'	sto'i·cal·ly
stink'er	sti'ver	sto'i·cism
stink'ing·ly	sto'a	stoke
stink'pot'	stoat	stoked
stink'weed'	stock	stoke'hold'
stink'wood'	stock·ade'	stok'er
stint	stock·ad'ed	stole
stint'ed	stock'breed'er	sto'len
stint'ing·ly	stock'bro'ker	stol'id
stipe	stocked	sto·lid'i·ty
sti'pend	stock'fish'	stol'id·ly
sti·pen'di·ar'y	stock'hold'er	stom'ach
sti·pen'di·um	stock'house'	stom'ach·ful
stip'ple	stock'i·ness	sto·mach'ic
stip'pled	stock'i·net'	stone
stip'plings	stock'ings	stone'boat'
stip'u·late	stock'job'ber	stoned
stip'u·lat'ed	stock'keep'er	stone'fish'
stip'u·lates	stock'mak'er	stone'ma'son
stip'u·la'tion	stock'man	stone'ware'
stip'u·la·to'ry	stock'own'er	stone'weed'
stir	stock'pile'	stone'wood'
stir'pes	stock'pot'	stone'work'
stirps	stock'tak'er	stone'yard'
stirred	stock'y	ston'i·er
stir'ring·ly	stock'yard'	ston'i·est

ston'i·ly

ston'y

stood

stool

stoop

stooped

stoop'ing·ly

stop

stop'cock'

stope

stop'gap'

stop'o'ver

stop'page

stopped

stop'per

stop'pered

stop'ple

stor'age

store

stored

store'house'

store'keep'er

store'room'

sto'ried

stork

storm

storm'bound'

stormed

storm'i·er

storm'i·est

storm'ing·ly

storm'y

sto'ry

sto'ry·tell'er

stoup

stout

stout'er

stout'est

stout'heart'ed

stout'ly

stout'ness

stove

stow

stow'age

stra·bis'mus

strad'dle

strad'dled

strad'dling·ly

strafe

strag'gle

strag'gled

strag'gler

strag'gling·ly

straight

straight'edge'

straight'en

straight'ened

straight'er

straight'est

straight'for'ward

straight'for'ward·ly

straight'for'ward·ness

straight'way'

straight'ways'

strain

strained

strain'er

strain'ing·ly

strain'ings

strait

strait'en

strait'ened

strait'er

strait'est

strake

strand

strand'ed

strange

strange'lings

strange'ly

strange'ness

stran'ger

strang'est

stran'gle

stran'gled

stran'gler

stran'gles

stran'gling·ly

stran'glings

stran'gu·late

stran'gu·lat'ed

stran'gu·la'tion

strap

strap'less

strap·pa'do

strapped

strap'pings

stra'ta

strat'a·gem

stra·te'gic

stra·te'gi·cal

strat'e·gist

strat'e·gy

strat'i·fi·ca'tion

strat'i·fied

strat'i·fy

strat'o·sphere

stra'tum

straw

straw'ber'ry

straw'flow'er

stray

strayed

streak

streaked

streak'i·er

streak'i·est

streak'y

stream

streamed

stream'er

stream'ing·ly

stream'line'

stream'way'

street

strength

strength'en

strength'ened

strength'en·er

stren'u·ous

stren'u·ous·ly

stren'u·ous·ness

stress

stressed

stress'ful

stretch

stretched

stretch'er

stretch'er·man

stretch'-out'

strew

strewed

strewn

stri'ate

stri'at·ed

stri·a'tion

strick'en

strict

strict'ly

strict'ness

stric'ture

stride

stri'dent

stri'dent·ly

strid'ing·ly

strid'u·lous

strife

strig'il

strike

strike'break'er

strik'er

strik'ing·ly

string

stringed

strin'gen·cy

strin'gent

strin'gent·ly

string'er

string'i·er

string'i·est

string'piece'

string'y

strip

stripe

striped

strip'lings

strip'per

strip'pings

strive

striv'en

strob'o·scope

strode

stroke

stroked

strok'ings

stroll

strolled

stroll'er

strong

strong'box'

strong'er

strong'est

strong'hold'

strong'ly

stron'ti·um

strop

stro'phe

stroph'ic

strove

struck

struc'tur·al

struc'tur·al·ly

struc'ture

struc'tured

stru'del

strug'gle

strug'gled

strug'gler

strug'gling·ly

strug'glings

strum

strummed

strung

strut

strut'ted

strut'ter

strut'ting·ly

strut'tings

strych'nine

stub

stubbed

stub'bi·ness

stub'ble

stub'bly

stub'born

stub'by

stuc'co

stuck

stud

stud'book'

stud'ded

stu'dent

stud'fish'

stud'horse'

stud'ied

stu'di·o

stu'di·ous

stu'di·ous·ly

stu'di·ous·ness

stud'work'

stud'y

stuff

stuffed

stuff'er

stuff'ings

stuff'i·er

stuff'i·est

stuff'i·ly

stuff'i·ness

stuff'y

stul'ti·fi·ca'tion

stul'ti·fied

stul'ti·fy

stum'ble

stum'bled

stum'bling·ly

stump

stump'age

stumped

stump'i·er

stump'i·est

stump'y

stun

stung

stunk

stunned

stun'ner

stun'ning·ly

stunt

stunt'ed

stu'pe·fa'cient

stu'pe·fac'tion

stu'pe·fied

stu'pe·fy

stu·pen'dous

stu'pid

stu·pid'i·ty

stu'pid·ly

stu'por

stu'por·ous

stur'di·ly

stur'di·ness

stur'dy

stur'geon

stut'ter

stut'tered

stut'ter·er

stut'ter·ing·ly

sty	sub·arc'tic	sub·ject'ed
Styg'i·an	sub·a·tom'ic	sub·jec'tion
style	sub·cal'i·ber	sub·jec'tive
style'book'	sub·cap'tion	sub·jec'tive·ly
styled	sub·cel'lar	sub·jec'tive·ness
styl'ings	sub'class'	sub·jec'tiv·ism
styl'ish	sub·com·mit'tee	sub'jec·tiv'i·ty
styl'ish·ness	sub·con'scious	sub·join'
styl'ist	sub·con'scious·ly	sub·join'der
sty·lis'tic	sub·con'scious·ness	sub·joined'
sty·lis'ti·cal·ly	sub·con·stel·la'tion	sub'ju·gate
styl'ize	sub·con'ti·nent	sub'ju·gat'ed
styl'ized	sub·con'tract	sub'ju·ga'tion
sty'lo·graph	sub·con·tract'ed	sub·junc'tive
sty'lo·graph'ic	sub·con·trac'tor	sub·king'dom
sty'lus	sub·cu·ta'ne·ous	sub'lap·sar'i·an
sty'mie	sub·dea'con	sub'lease'
styp'tic	sub·di·vide'	sub'les·see'
Styx	sub·di·vid'ed	sub·les'sor
su'a·bil'i·ty	sub·di·vi'sion	sub·let'
su'a·ble	sub·due'	sub'li·mate
sua'sion	sub·dued'	sub'li·mat'ed
suave	sub·du'ing·ly	sub'li·ma'tion
suave'ly	sub·ed'i·tor	sub·lime'
suave'ness	sub·fam'i·ly	sub·limed'
suav'i·ty	sub'foun·da'tion	sub·lim'er
sub'a·cute'	sub'grade'	sub·lim'est
sub'a·dult'	sub'group'	sub·lim'i·nal
sub·a'gent	sub'head'	sub·lim'i·ty
sub·al'tern	sub·head'ings	sub'lu·nar'y
sub·a·quat'ic	sub·hu'man	sub'lux·a'tion
sub·a'que·ous	sub'ject	sub·mar'gin·al

sub'ma·rine'

sub'ma·rin'er

sub·merge'

sub·merged'

sub·mer'gence

sub·mers'i·ble

sub·mer'sion

sub·me'ter·ing

sub·mis'sion

sub·mis'sive

sub·mis'sive·ly

sub·mis'sive·ness

sub·mit'

sub·mit'tal

sub·mit'ted

sub·mit'ting·ly

sub·nor'mal

sub'nor·mal'i·ty

sub'o·ce·an'ic

sub·or'der

sub·or'di·nate

sub·or'di·nat'ed

sub·or'di·nat'ing·ly

sub·or'di·na'tion

sub·or'di·na'tive

sub·orn'

sub'or·na'tion

sub·orned'

sub·orn'er

sub·phy'lum

sub'plinth'

sub'plot'

sub·poe'na

sub·poe'naed

sub·ro·ga'tion

sub·scribe'

sub·scribed'

sub·scrib'er

sub'script

sub·scrip'tion

sub'se·quent

sub'se·quent·ly

sub·serve'

sub·served'

sub·ser'vi·ence

sub·ser'vi·en·cy

sub·ser'vi·ent

sub·side'

sub·sid'ed

sub·sid'ence

sub·sid'i·ar'y

sub'si·dize

sub'si·dized

sub'si·dy

sub·sist'

sub·sist'ed

sub·sist'ence

sub'soil'

sub'spe'cies

sub'stance

sub·stand'ard

sub·stan'tial

sub·stan'tial·ly

sub·stan'ti·ate

sub·stan'ti·at'ed

sub·stan'ti·a'tion

sub'stan·tive

sub'sta'tion

sub'sti·tute

sub'sti·tut'ed

sub'sti·tu'tion

sub·stra'tum

sub·struc'ture

sub·sur'face

sub·tan'gent

sub·ten'ant

sub·tend'

sub·tend'ed

sub'ter·fuge

sub'ter·ra'ne·an

sub'ter·ra'ne·ous

sub'ti'tle

sub'tle

sub'tler

sub'tlest

sub'tle·ty

sub'tly

sub·tract'

sub·tract'ed

sub·trac'tion

sub'tra·hend'

sub·treas'ur·y

sub·trop'i·cal

sub'urb

sub·ur'ban

sub·ur'ban·ite

sub·ven'tion

sub·ver'sion

sub·ver'sive

sub·vert'

sub·vert'ed

sub'way'

suc·ceed'

suc·ceed'ed

suc·ceed'ing·ly

suc·cess'

suc·cess'ful

suc·cess'ful·ly

suc·ces'sion

suc·ces'sive

suc·ces'sor

suc·cinct'

suc·cinct'ly

suc'cor

suc'cored

suc'co·tash

suc'cu·lence

suc'cu·lent

suc'cu·lent·ly

suc·cumb'

suc·cumbed'

such

suck

sucked

suck'er

suck'le

suck'led

suck'lings

suc'tion

sud'den

sud'den·ly

sud'den·ness

su'dor·if'er·ous

su'dor·if'ic

suds

sue

sued

suède

su'et

suf'fer

suf'fer·a·ble

suf'fer·ance

suf'fered

suf'fer·er

suf'fer·ing·ly

suf'fer·ings

suf·fice'

suf·ficed'

suf·fi'cien·cy

suf·fi'cient

suf'fix

suf'fo·cate

suf'fo·cat'ed

suf'fo·cat'ing·ly

suf'fo·ca'tion

suf'fo·ca'tive

suf'fra·gan

suf'frage

suf'fra·gist

suf·fuse'

suf·fused'

suf·fu'sion

sug'ar

sug'ared

sug'ar·plum'

sug'ar·y

sug·gest'

sug·gest'ed

sug·gest'i·bil'i·ty

sug·gest'i·ble

sug·ges'tion

sug·ges'tive

sug·ges'tive·ness

su'i·cid'al

su'i·cid'al·ly

su'i·cide

suit

suit'a·bil'i·ty

suit'a·ble

suit'case'

suite

suit'ed

suit'ing·ly

suit'ings

suit'or

sulk

sulked

sulk'i·er

sulk'i·est

sulk'i·ly

sulk'i·ness

sulk'y

sul'len

sul'len·ly

sul'len·ness

sul'lied

sul'ly

sul'phate

sul'phide

sul'phite

sul'phur

sul·phu'ric

sul'phu·rous

sul'tan

sul·tan'a

sul'tan·ate

sul'tri·er

sul'tri·est

sul'try

sum

su'mac

sum'ma·ri·ly

sum'ma·ri·ness

sum'ma·rize

sum'ma·rized

sum'ma·ry

sum·ma'tion

summed

sum'mer

sum'mered

sum'mer·y

sum'mit

sum'mon

sum'moned

sump

sump'ter

sump'tu·ar'y

sump'tu·ous

sump'tu·ous·ly

sump'tu·ous·ness

sun

sun'beam'

sun'bon'net

sun'burn'

sun'burned

sun'burst'

sun'dae

Sun'day

sun'der

sun'der·ance

sun'dered

sun'di'al

sun'dry

sun'fish'

sun'flow'er

sun'glass'

sun'glow'

sunk

sunk'en

sun'less

sun'light'

sun'lit'

sunned

sun'ni·ness

sun'ny

sun'proof'

sun'rise'

sun'room'

sun'set'

sun'shade'

sun'shine'

sun'shin'y

sun'spot'

sun'stone'

sun'stroke'

sun'ward

sup

su'per·a·ble

su'per·a·bun'dance

su'per·a·bun'dant

su'per·an'nu·ate

su'per·an'nu·at'ed

su'per·an'nu·a'tion

su·perb'

su'per·cal'en·der

su'per·cal'en-dered

su'per·car'go

su'per·charg'er

su'per·cil'i·ous

su'per·cil'i·ous·ly

su'per·cil'i·ous·ness

su'per·con·duc'-tance

su'per·con'duc-tiv'i·ty

su'per·con·duc'-tor

su'per·cool'

su'per·dread'-nought'

su'per·em'i·nence

su'per·em'i·nent

su'per·er'o·ga'tion	su·per'nal·ly	su·pine'ness
su'per·fam'i·ly	su'per·nat'u·ral	sup'per
su'per·fi'cial	su'per·nat'u·ral·ly	sup·plant'
su'per·fi'ci·al'i·ty	su'per·nat'u·ral·ism	sup·plant'ed
su'per·fi'cial·ly	su'per·nat'u·ral·ist	sup'ple
su'per·fine'	su'per·nor'mal	sup'ple·ment
su'per·flu'i·ty	su'per·nu'mer·ar'y	sup'ple·men'tal
su·per'flu·ous	su'per·po·si'tion	sup'ple·men'ta·ry
su·per'flu·ous·ly	su'per·sat'u·rate	sup'ple·men·ta'tion
su·per'flu·ous·ness	su'per·sat'u·rat'ed	sup'ple·ment'ed
su'per·heat'	su'per·sat'u·ra'tion	sup'pli·ant
su'per·heat'ed	su'per·scribe'	sup'pli·cant
su'per·het'er·o·dyne'	su'per·scribed'	sup'pli·cate
su'per·hu'man	su'per·scrip tion	sup'pli·cat'ed
su'per·hu'man·ly	su'per·sede'	sup'pli·cat'ing·ly
su'per·im·pose'	su'per·sed'ed	sup'pli·ca'tion
su'per·im·posed'	su'per·ses'sion	sup'pli·ca·to'ry
su'per·im'po·si'tion	su'per·son'ic	sup·plied'
su'per·im·po'sure	su'per·sti'tion	sup·pli'er
su'per·in·duce'	su'per·sti'tious	sup·ply'
su'per·in·duced'	su'per·sti'tious·ly	sup·port'
su'per·in·tend'	su'per·stra'tum	sup·port'ed
su'per·in·tend'ed	su'per·struc'ture	sup·port'er
su'per·in·tend'ence	su'per·tax'	sup·pose'
su'per·in·tend'en·cy	su'per·vene'	sup·posed'
su'per·in·tend'ent	su'per·vened'	sup·pos'ed·ly
su·pe'ri·or	su'per·vise'	sup'po·si'tion
su·pe'ri·or'i·ty	su'per·vised'	sup·pos'i·ti'tious
su·per'la·tive	su'per·vi'sion	sup·pos'i·ti'tious·ly
su·per'la·tive·ly	su'per·vi'sor	sup·press'
su'per·man'	su'per·vi'so·ry	sup·pressed'
su·per'nal	su·pine'	sup·pres'sion

sup·pres'sive

sup'pu·rate

sup'pu·rat'ed

sup'pu·ra'tion

sup'pu·ra'tive

su·prem'a·cy

su·preme'

su·preme'ly

sur'base'

sur·cease'

sur·charge'

sur·charged'

sur'cin'gle

surd

sure

sure'ly

sure'ness

sure'ty

sure'ty·ship

surf

sur'face

sur'faced

sur'fac·ings

sur'feit

sur'feit·ed

surge

surged

sur'geon

sur'ger·y

sur'gi·cal

sur'li·er

sur'li·est

sur'li·ness

sur'ly

sur·mise'

sur·mised'

sur·mount'

sur·mount'ed

sur'name'

sur'named'

sur·pass'

sur·passed'

sur·pass'ing·ly

sur'plice

sur'pliced

sur'plus

sur'plus·age

sur·prise'

sur·prised'

sur·pris'ed·ly

sur·pris'ing·ly

sur're·but'tal

sur're·but'ter

sur're·join'der

sur·ren'der

sur·ren'dered

sur'rep·ti'tious

sur'rep·ti'tious·ly

sur'rep·ti'tious·ness

sur'rey

sur'ro·gate

sur'ro·ga'tion

sur·round'

sur·round'ed

sur·round'ings

sur'tax'

sur·tout'

sur·veil'lance

sur·vey'

sur·veyed'

sur·vey'or

sur·viv'al

sur·viv'al·ism

sur·vive'

sur·vived'

sur·vi'vor

sur·vi'vor·ship

sus·cep'ti·bil'i·ty

sus·cep'ti·ble

sus·cep'ti·bly

sus·pect'

sus·pect'ed

sus·pend'

sus·pend'ed

sus·pend'ers

sus·pense'

sus·pense'ful

sus·pen'sion

sus·pen'sive

sus·pen'sive·ly

sus·pen'sive·ness

sus·pi'cion

sus·pi'cious

sus·pi'cious·ly

sus·pi'cious·ness

sus·pire'

sus·tain'

sus·tained'

sus·tain'ed·ly

sus·tain'ing·ly

sus'te·nance

sus'ten·tac'u·lar

sus'ten·ta'tion

su'sur·ra'tion

sut'ler

sut·tee'

su'ture

su'tured

su'ze·rain

su'ze·rain·ty

svelte

swab

swabbed

swad'dle

swad'dled

swad'dling

swad'dlings

swag

swage

swaged

swag'ger

swag'gered

swag'ger·ing·ly

Swa·hi'li

swain

swal'low

swal'lowed

swal'low·er

swal'low-tailed'

swa'mi

swamp

swamped

swan

swan'herd'

swank

swank'i·er

swank'i·est

swank'y

swans'down'

swap

swapped

sward

swarm

swarmed

swart

swarth'y

swash

swas'ti·ka

swat

swatch

swath

swathe

swat'ter

sway

swayed

sway'ing·ly

swear

swear'ing·ly

sweat

sweat'band'

sweat'box'

sweat'er

sweat'i·er

sweat'i·est

sweat'i·ly

sweat'i·ness

sweat'shop

sweat'y

Swed'ish

sweep

sweep'er

sweep'ing·ly

sweep'ings

sweep'stake'

sweet

sweet'bread'

sweet'bri'er

sweet'en

sweet'ened

sweet'en·er

sweet'en·ings

sweet'heart'

sweet'ish

sweet'ish·ly

sweet'ly

sweet'meat'

sweet'ness

sweet'root'

sweet'shop'

sweet'wa'ter

sweet'weed'

sweet'wood'

swell	swipe	sworn
swelled	swiped	swung
swell'er	swirl	swum
swell'fish'	swirled	syb'a·rite
swell'ings	swirl'ing·ly	syc'a·more
swel'ter	swish	syc'o·phan·cy
swel'tered	swished	syc'o·phant
swel'ter·ing·ly	Swiss	syc'o·phan'tic
swept	switch	syl'la·bi
swerve	switch'board'	syl·lab'ic
swerved	switched	syl·lab'i·cate
swift	switch'gear'	syl·lab'i·cat'ed
swift'er	switch'keep'er	syl·lab'i·ca'tion
swift'est	switch'man	syl·lab'i·fi·ca'tion
swift'ly	switch'tail'	syl·lab'i·fy
swift'ness	switch'yard'	syl'la·ble
swig	swiv'el	syl'la·bus
swigged	swiv'eled	syl'la·bus·es
swill	swol'len	syl'lo·gism
swilled	swoon	syl'lo·gis'tic
swim	swooned	syl'lo·gize
swim'mer	swoon'ing·ly	sylph
swim'ming·ly	swoop	syl'van
swin'dle	swooped	sym'bi·o'sis
swin'dled	sword	sym'bi·ot'ic
swin'dler	sword'bill'	sym'bol
swine	sword'fish'	sym·bol'ic
swine'herd'	sword'play'	sym·bol'i·cal
swing	swords'man	sym·bol'i·cal·ly
swing'ing·ly	sword'stick'	sym'bol·ism
swin'ish	sword'tail'	sym'bol·ist
swink	swore	sym'bol·i·za'tion

sym'bol·ize	syn'chro·nize	syn·o'vi·al
sym'bol·ized	syn'chro·nized	syn'o·vi'tis
sym·met'ri·cal	syn'chro·nous	syn·tac'ti·cal
sym'me·try	syn'co·pate	syn'tax
sym·pa·thec'to·my	syn'co·pat'ed	syn'the·ses
sym'pa·thet'ic	syn'co·pa'tion	syn'the·sis
sym'pa·thet'i·cal·ly	syn'co·pe	syn'the·size
sym'pa·thize	syn'cre·tism	syn'the·sized
sym'pa·thized	syn'dic	syn·thet'ic
sym'pa·thiz'er	syn'di·cal	syn·thet'i·cal·ly
sym'pa·thiz'ing·ly	syn'di·cal·ism	syr'inge
sym'pa·thy	syn'di·cal·ize	syr'up
sym·phon'ic	syn'di·cate	sys'tem
sym'pho·ny	syn'di·cat'ed	sys'tem·at'ic
sym'phy·sis	syn'di·ca'tion	sys'tem·a·ti·za'tion
sym·po'si·um	syn'drome	sys'tem·a·tize
symp'tom	syn·ec'do·che	sys'tem·a·tized
symp'to·mat'ic	syn'od	sys'tem·a·tiz'er
symp'tom·a·tol'o·gy	syn'od·ist	sys'tem·a·tol'o·gy
syn'a·gogue	syn'o·nym	sys·tem'ic
syn·apse'	syn·on'y·mous	sys·tem'i·cal·ly
syn·ap'sis	syn·op'ses	sys'to·le
syn'chro·nism	syn·op'sis	sys·tol'ic
syn'chro·ni·za'tion	syn·op'tic	syz'y·gy

T

tab

tab'ard

ta·bas'co

tab'er·nac'le

tab'er·nac'led

ta'bes

tab'la·ture

ta'ble

tab'leau

ta'ble·cloth'

ta'bled

ta'ble·maid'

ta'ble·man

ta'ble·spoon'

tab'let

ta'ble·ware'

tab'loid

ta·boo'

ta'bor

tab'o·ret

ta·bu'

tab'u·lar

tab'u·late

tab'u·lat'ed

tab'u·la'tion

tab'u·la'tor

ta·chis'to·scope

ta·chom'e·ter

ta·chyg'ra·pher

ta·chyg'ra·phy

tac'it

tac'it·ly

tac'i·turn

tac'i·tur'ni·ty

tack

tacked

tack'le

tack'led

tack'ler

tack'y

tact

tact'ful

tact'ful·ly

tact'ful·ness

tac'ti·cal

tac·ti'cian

tac'tics

tac'tile

tact'less

tact'less·ly

tact'less·ness

tad'pole'

taf'fe·ta

taff'rail

taf'fy

tag

tag'board'

tagged

Ta·hi'ti·an

tail

tail'board'

tailed

tail'first'

tail'ings

tail'less

tai'lor

tai'lored	tal'lowed	tan'gent
tail'piece'	tal'low·i·ness	tan·gen'tial
tail'race'	tal'low·root'	tan·gen'ti·al'i·ty
tail'stock'	tal'low·wood'	tan'ge·rine'
taint	tal'low·y	tan'gi·ble
taint'ed	tal'ly	tan'gi·bly
take	tal'ly·ho'	tan'gle
take'down'	tal'ly·man	tan'gled
tak'en	Tal'mud	tan'gle·root'
tak'er	Tal·mud'ic	tan'gling·ly
tak'ing·ly	tal'on	tan'go
tak'ing·ness	tal'oned	tang'y
tak'ings	tam'a·rack	tank
talc	tam'a·rind	tank'age
tal'cum	tam'bour	tank'ard
tale	tam'bou·rine'	tanked
tale'bear'er	tame	tank'er
tal'ent	tamed	tan'nage
tal'ent·ed	tame'ness	tanned
tal'i·pes	tam'er	tan'ner
tal'is·man	tam'est	tan'ner·y
tal'is·man'ic	Tam'il	tan'nic
talk	Tam'ma·ny	tan'nin
talk'a·tive	tamp'er	tan'nings
talked	tam'pered	tan'sy
talk'er	tam'per·proof'	tan'ta·li·za'tion
tall	tam'pon	tan'ta·lize
tall'er	tan	tan'ta·lized
tall'est	tan'a·ger	tan'ta·lum
tall'ish	tan'bark'	tan'ta·lus
tall'ness	tan'dem	tan'ta·mount'
tal'low	tang	tan'trum

tan·vat	tar'di·ness	taste
tan'wood'	tar'dy	tast'ed
tap	tare	taste'ful
tape	tar'flow'er	taste'ful·ly
taped	targe	taste'ful·ness
tape'line'	tar'get	taste'less
tape'man	tar'iff	taste'less·ly
ta'per	tar'la·tan	taste'less·ness
ta'pered	tar'nish	tast'er
ta'per·ing·ly	tar'nished	tast'i·er
tap'es·try	tar'ot	tast'i·est
tape'worm'	tar·pau'lin	tast'i·ly
tap'hole'	tar'pon	tast'ing·ly
tap'house'	tar'ra·gon	tast'ings
tap'i·o'ca	tarred	tast'y
ta'pir	tar'ried	Ta'tar
tap'per	tar'ry	tat'ter
tap'pet	tar'ry·ing·ly	tat'tered
tap'pings	tart	tat'ting
tap'room'	tar'tan	tat'tle
tap'root'	tar'tar	tat'tled
tap'ster	tart'let	tat'tler
tar	tart'ness	tat·too'
tar'an·tel'la	tar'trate	tat·tooed'
ta·ran'tu·la	tar'weed'	tat·too'er
tar'board'	task	taught
tar·boosh'	task'mas'ter	taunt
tar'brush'	task'mis'tress	taunt'ed
tar'bush'	task'work'	taunt'ing·ly
tar'di·er	Tas·ma'ni·an	taupe
tar'di·est	tas'sel	tau'rine
tar'di·ly	tas'seled	taut

taut'en

taut'ened

tau'to·log'i·cal

tau·tol'o·gy

tav'ern

taw'dri·er

taw'dri·est

taw'dri·ly

taw'dri·ness

taw'dry

taw'ny

tax

tax'a·ble

tax·a'tion

taxed

tax'es

tax'i

tax'i·cab'

tax'i·der'mist

tax'i·der'my

tax'i·me·ter

tax'ing·ly

tax·on'o·my

tax'paid'

tax'pay'er

tea

tea'ber'ry

tea'cart'

teach

teach'a·bil'i·ty

teach'a·ble

teach'er

teach'er·age

teach'ing·ly

teach'ings

tea'cup'

teak

tea'ket'tle

teal

team

teamed

team'mate'

team'ster

team'work'

tea'pot'

tear

tear

tear'ful

tear'ful·ly

tear'ful·ness

tear'less

tear'less·ly

tea'room'

tear'stain'

tear'y

tease

teased

teas'er

teas'ing·ly

tea'spoon'

tea'spoon·ful

tea'tast'er

tech'ni·cal

tech'ni·cal'i·ty

tech'ni·cal·ly

tech·ni'cian

tech·nique'

tech·noc'ra·cy

tech'no·crat

tech'no·log'i·cal

tech·nol'o·gy

te'di·ous

te'di·ous·ly

te'di·ous·ness

te'di·um

tee

teed

teem

teemed

teem'ing·ly

tee'ter

tee'ter·board'

tee'tered

teeth

tee·to'tal

tee·to'tal·er

tee·to'tal·ly

tel·au'to·graph

tel'e·cast

tel'e·com·mu'ni·ca'tion

tel'e·gram

tel'e·graph

te·leg'ra·pher

tel'e·graph'ic

te·leg'ra·phy

tel'e·ol'o·gy

tel'e·path'ic

te·lep'a·thy

tel'e·phone

tel'e·phon'ic

te·leph'o·ny

tel'e·pho'to

tel'e·scope

tel'e·scop'ic

tel'e·type

tel'e·type'set'ter

tel'e·type'writ'er

tel'e·vise

tel'e·vised

tel'e·vi'sion

tel'ford

tell

tell'er

tell'ing·ly

tell'ings

tell'tale'

tel·lu'ri·um

tel'pher

tel'pher·age

te·mer'i·ty

tem'per

tem'per·a·ment

tem'per·a·men'tal

tem'per·a·men'tal·ly

tem'per·ance

tem'per·ate

tem'per·ate·ly

tem'per·a·ture

tem'pered

tem'pest

tem·pes'tu·ous

tem·pes'tu·ous·ly

tem·pes'tu·ous·ness

tem'plate

tem'ple

tem'pled

tem'po

tem'po·ral

tem'po·ral·ty

tem'po·rar'i·ly

tem'po·rar'y

tem'po·ri·za'tion

tem'po·rize

tem'po·rized

tem'po·riz'er

tem'po·riz'ing·ly

tempt

temp·ta'tion

tempt'ed

tempt'er

tempt'ing·ly

tempt'ing·ness

tempt'ress

ten'a·bil'i·ty

ten'a·ble

te·na'cious

te·na'cious·ly

te·na'cious·ness

te·nac'i·ty

ten'an·cy

ten'ant

ten'ant·a·ble

ten'ant·ed

ten'ant·less

ten'ant·ry

tend

tend'ed

tend'en·cy

tend'er

ten'dered

ten'der·er

ten'der·est

ten'der·foot'

ten'der·loin'

ten'der·ly

ten'der·ness

ten'don

ten'dril

Ten'e·brae

ten'e·brous

ten'e·ment

ten'et

ten'nis

ten'on

ten'or

ten'pins'

tense

tense'ly

tense'ness

tens'er

tens'est

ten'sile

ten'sion

ten'sor

tent

ten·ta·cle

ten'ta·tive

ten'ter·er

ten'ter·hooks'

ten·u'i·ty

ten'u·ous

ten'u·ous·ly

ten'ure

te'pee

tep'id

te·pid'i·ty

tep'id·ly

ter'a·tol'o·gy

ter·cen'te·nar'y

te·re'do

ter'gi·ver·sate'

term

ter'ma·gant

termed

ter'mi·na·ble

ter'mi·nal

ter'mi·nate

ter'mi·nat'ed

ter'mi·na'tion

ter'mi·na'tive

ter'mi·no·log'i·cal

ter'mi·no·log'i·cal·ly

ter'mi·nol'o·gy

ter'mi·nus

ter'mite

term'less

tern

ter'na·ry

ter'race

ter'raced

ter·rain'

ter'ra·pin

ter·raz'zo

ter·res'tri·al

ter'ri·ble

ter'ri·bly

ter'ri·er

ter·rif'ic

ter·rif'i·cal·ly

ter'ri·fied

ter'ri·fy

ter'ri·fy'ing·ly

ter·rine'

ter'ri·to'ri·al

ter'ri·to'ri·al'i·ty

ter'ri·to'ry

ter'ror

ter'ror·ism

ter'ror·ist

ter'ror·is'tic

ter'ror·i·za'tion

ter'ror·ize

ter'ror·ized

terse

terse'ness

ters'er

ters'est

ter'tian

ter'ti·ar'y

tes'sel·late

tes'sel·lat'ed

tes'sel·la'tion

test

tes'ta·ment

tes'ta·men'ta·ry

tes·ta'tor

test'ed

tes'ter

tes'ti·fied

tes'ti·fy

tes'ti·mo'ni·al

tes'ti·mo'ny

test'ing·ly

test'ings

tes'ty

tet'a·nus

teth'er

teth'ered

tet'ra·gon

te·trag'o·nal

te·tral'o·gy

te·tram'e·ter

te'trarch

te·trig'id

Tex'an

tex'as

text

text'book'

tex'tile	the·at'ri·cal·ly	the'o·ry	
tex'tu·al	the·at'ri·cals	the'o·soph'ic	
tex'tu·al·ism	thee	the'o·soph'i·cal	
tex'tu·al·ist	theft	the'o·soph'i·cal·ly	
tex'tu·al·ly	their	the·os'o·phism	
tex'tur·al	theirs	the·os'o·phist	
tex'tur·al·ly	the'ism	the·os'o·phy	
tex'ture	the'ist	ther'a·peu'tic	
tex'tured	the·is'tic	ther'a·peu'ti·cal	
tha·las'sic	them	ther'a·peu'ti·cal·ly	
thal'li·um	the·mat'ic	ther'a·py	
than	the·mat'i·cal	there	
than'a·top'sis	theme	there'a·bouts'	
thane	them·selves'	there'a·bove'	
thank	then	there·aft'er	
thanked	thence	there·at'	
thank'ful	thence'forth'	there·by'	
thank'ful·ly	thence'for'ward	there'fore	
thank'ful·ness	the·oc'ra·cy	there·from'	
thank'less	the·od'o·lite	there·in'	
thank'less·ly	the'o·lo'gi·an	there·in·aft'er	
thanks·giv'ing	the'o·log'i·cal	there·in'be·fore'	
that	the'o·log'i·cal·ly	there·of'	
thatch	the·ol'o·gy	there·on'	
thatched	the'o·rem	there·to'	
thau'ma·tur'gist	the'o·ret'ic	there'to·fore'	
thau'ma·tur'gy	the'o·ret'i·cal	there·un'der	
thaw	the'o·ret'i·cal·ly	there·un·to'	
the'a·ter	the'o·rist	there'up·on'	
the·at'ri·cal	the'o·rize	there·with'	
the·at'ri·cal·ism	the'o·rized	ther'mal	
the·at'ri·cal'i·ty	the'o·riz'er	therm'i'on	

therm'i·on'ic	thigh	thorn
ther'mite	thill	thorn'bush'
ther'mo·e·lec'tric	thim'ble	thorned
ther·mom'e·ter	thim'ble·ful	thorn'i·er
ther'mo·met'ric	thim'ble·rig'ger	thorn'i·est
ther'mo·met'ri·cal	thin	thorn'y
ther'mo·met'ri·cal·ly	thing	thor'ough
ther'mo·stat	things	thor'ough·bred'
the·sau'rus	think	thor'ough·fare'
these	think'a·ble	thor'ough·go'ing
the'ses	think'er	thor'ough·ly
the'sis	think'ing·ly	thor'ough·ness
thew	thinks	those
they	thin'ly	thou
thick	thin'ner	though
thick'en	thin'ness	thought
thick'ened	thin'nest	thought'ful
thick'en·er	third	thought'ful·ly
thick'er	thirst	thought'ful·ness
thick'est	thirst'ed	thought'less
thick'et	thirst'i·ly	thought'less·ly
thick'et·ed	thirst'i·ness	thought'less·ness
thick'head'ed	thirst'ing·ly	thou'sand
thick'ly	thirst'y	thou'sand·fold'
thick'ness	this	thou'sandth
thick'set'	this'tle	thrall
thick'-skinned'	thith'er	thrall'dom
thick'-wit'ted	thole	thrash
thief	thong	thrashed
thiev'er·y	tho·rac'ic	thrash'er
thiev'ing·ly	tho'rax	thrash'ings
thiev'ish	tho'ri·um	thra·son'i·cal

thread

thread'bare'

thread'ed

thread'weed'

thread'worm'

thread'y

threat

threat'en

threat'ened

threat'en·ing·ly

three

three'some

thren'o·dy

thre'nos

thresh

threshed

thresh'er

thresh'old

threw

thrice

thrift

thrift'i·er

thrift'i·est

thrift'i·ly

thrift'i·ness

thrift'less

thrift'less·ly

thrift'less·ness

thrift'y

thrill

thrilled

thrill'ing·ly

thrips

thrive

thriv'ing·ly

throat

throat'ed

throat'i·er

throat'i·est

throat'i·ly

throat'i·ness

throat'root'

throat'wort'

throat'y

throb

throbbed

throb'bing·ly

throes

throm·bo'sis

throm'bus

throne

throne'less

throne'like'

throng

thronged

throng'ing·ly

throt'tle

throt'tled

throt'tling·ly

through

through·out'

throw

throw'back'

throw'er

thrown

throw'off'

thrum

thrummed

thrush

thrust

thud

thud'ded

thud'ding·ly

thug

thug'ger·y

thu'li·um

thumb

thumbed

thumb'mark'

thumb'nail'

thumb'piece'

thumb'print'

thump

thumped

thump'ing·ly

thump'ings

thun'der

thun'der·bird'

thun'der·bolt'

thun'dered

thun'der·fish'

thun'der·head'

thun'der·ing

thun'der·ing·ly

thun'der·ings

thun'der·ous

thun'der·show'er	tick'lish·ness	tight'en·ing
thun'der·struck'	tid'al	tight'er
thun'der·y	tid'bit'	tight'est
thun'drous	tide	tight'fist'ed
thu'ri·ble	tid'ed	tight'ly
Thurs'day	tide'race'	tight'rope'
thus	tide'wa·ter	tight'wad'
thwack	tide'way'	til'bu·ry
thwacked	ti'died	til'de
thwack'ing·ly	ti'di·er	tile
thwart	ti'di·est	tiled
thwart'ed	ti'di·ly	tile'fish'
thwart'ing·ly	ti'di·ness	til'er
thy	ti'dings	tile'root'
thyme	ti'dy	till
thy'mus	tie	till'a·ble
thy'roid	tie'back'	till'age
thy·self'	tied	tilled
ti·ar'a	tier	till'er
tib'i·a	tiered	tilt
tick	tiff	tilt'ed
ticked	tif'fa·ny	tilth
tick'er	tiffed	tilt'yard'
tick'et	tif'fin	tim'bale
tick'et·ed	ti'ger	tim'ber
tick'ings	ti'ger·ish	tim'bered
tick'le	ti'ger·like'	tim'ber·land'
tick'led	ti'ger·wood'	tim'ber·wood'
tick'ler	tight	tim'ber·work'
tick'ling·ly	tight'en	time
tick'lish	tight'ened	timed
tick'lish·ly	tight'en·er	time'keep'er

time'less

time'less·ly

time'less·ness

time'li·ness

time'ly

time'piece'

tim'er

time'serv'ing

time'ta'ble

tim'id

ti·mid'i·ty

tim'id·ly

tim'ings

tim'or·ous

tim'or·ous·ly

tin

tinct

tinct'ed

tinc'ture

tinc'tured

tin'der

tin'der·box'

tine

tined

tine'weed'

tinge

tinged

tin'gle

tin'gled

tin'gling·ly

tin'glings

tin'horn'

tink'er

tink'ered

tin'kle

tin'kled

tin'kling·ly

tin'klings

tinned

tin'ni·er

tin'ni·est

tin'ni·ly

tin'ni·ness

tin·ni'tus

tin'ny

tin'sel

tin'seled

tin'smith'

tint

tint'ed

tin'tin·nab'u·la'tion

tin'type'

tin'ware'

tin'work'

ti'ny

tip

tipped

tip'pet

tip'ple

tip'pled

tip'pler

tip'si·er

tip'si·est

tip'ster

tip'sy

tip'toe'

tip'toed'

tip'toe'ing·ly

tip'top'

ti'rade

tire

tired

tire'less

tire'less·ly

tire'less·ness

tire'some

tire'some·ly

tire'some·ness

tir'ing·ly

tis'sue

tis'sued

tis'sues

Ti'tan

ti·tan'ic

ti'tan·if'er·ous

ti·ta'ni·um

tit'bit'

tith'a·ble

tithe

tithed

tith'ings

ti'tian

tit'il·late

tit'il·lat'ed

tit'il·lat'ing·ly

tit'il·la'tion

tit'il·la'tive

tit'i·vate

tit'i·vat'ed

tit'i·va'tion

ti'tle

ti'tled

ti'tle·hold'er

tit'mouse'

ti'trate

ti'trat·ed

ti·tra'tion

tit'ter

tit'tered

tit'ter·ing·ly

tit'ter·ings

tit'tle

tit'tup

tit'u·lar

tit'u·lar·ly

tit'u·lar'y

to

toad

toad'fish'

toad'root'

toad'stone'

toad'stool'

toad'y

toast

toast'ed

toast'er

to·bac'co

to·bog'gan

to·bog'ganed

toc·ca'ta

toc'sin

to·day'

tod'dle

tod'dled

tod'dler

tod'dy

toe

toe'cap'

toed

toe'nail'

toe'plate'

tof'fee

to'ga

to·geth'er

to·geth'er·ness

tog'gle

tog'gled

toil

toiled

toil'er

toi'let

toi'let·ry

toi'let·ware'

toil'ing·ly

To·kay'

to'ken

to'kened

told

tol'er·a·ble

tol'er·a·bly

tol'er·ance

tol'er·ant

tol'er·ate

tol'er·at'ed

tol'er·a'tion

tol'er·a'tion·ism

tol'er·a'tive

toll

tolled

toll'gate'

toll'house'

tom'a·hawk

to·ma'to

tomb

tombed

tom'bo·la

tom'boy'

tomb'stone'

tom'cat'

tom'cod'

tome

tom'fool'

tom'fool'er·y

tom'fool'ish·ness

to·mor'row

ton

ton'al

ton'al·ist

to·nal'i·ty

tone

toned

tone'less

tongs	tooth'less·ness	top'side'
tongue	tooth'pick'	top'stone'
tongued	tooth'some	toque
ton'ic	too'tle	torch
ton'i·cal·ly	too'tled	torch'light'
to·nic'i·ty	top	torch'weed'
to·night'	to'paz	torch'wood'
ton'ka	top'coat'	tore
ton'nage	top'er	tor'e·a·dor'
ton·neau'	to'pi·a·rist	tor·ment'
ton'sil	to'pi·ar'y	tor·ment'ed
ton'sil·li'tis	top'ic	tor·ment'ing·ly
ton·so'ri·al	top'i·cal	tor·men'tor
ton'sure	top'knot'	tor·na'do
ton'tine	top'less	tor·pe'do
too	top'loft'y	tor·pe'doed
took	top'man	tor'pid
tool	top'mast'	tor·pid'i·ty
tool'box'	top'most	tor'pid·ly
tooled	to·pog'ra·pher	tor'por
tool'ings	top'o·graph'ic	torque
tool'mak'er	top'o·graph'i·cal	tor'rent
tool'room'	top'o·graph'i·cal·ly	tor·ren'tial
tool'smith'	to·pog'ra·phy	tor·ren'tial·ly
toot	topped	tor'rid
toot'ed	top'per	tor·rid'i·ty
tooth	top'piece'	tor'rid·ly
tooth'ache'	top'ping·ly	tor'sion
tooth'brush'	top'pings	tor'sion·al
toothed	top'ple	tor'so
tooth'less	top'pled	tort
tooth'less·ly	top'sail'	tor'toise

tor'tu·os'i·ty		tot'tered		tou'sle	
tor'tu·ous		tot'ter·ing·ly		tou'sled	
tor'tu·ous·ly		tot'ter·ings		tout	
tor'tu·ous·ness		tot'ter·y		tout'ed	
tor'ture		tou·can'		to·va'rish	
tor'tured		touch		tow	
tor'tur·er		touch'a·ble		tow'age	
tor'tur·ing·ly		touch'down'		to'ward	
tor'tur·ous		touched		to'wards	
tor'tur·ous·ly		touch'hole'		tow'boat'	
To'ry		touch'i·er		towed	
toss		touch'i·est		tow'el	
tossed		touch'i·ly		tow'el·ings	
toss'ing·ly		touch'i·ness		tow'er	
toss'ings		touch'ing·ly		tow'ered	
toss'up'		touch'stone'		tow'er·ing·ly	
to'tal		touch'wood'		tow'er·man	
to'taled		touch'y		tow'head'	
to·tal'i·tar'i·an		tough		tow'line'	
to·tal'i·tar'i·an·ism		tough'en		town	
to·tal'i·ty		tough'ened		town'folk'	
to'tal·i·za'tion		tough'er		town'ship	
to'tal·i·za'tor		tough'est		towns'man	
to'tal·ize		tou·pee'		town'wear'	
to'tal·ized		tour		tow'path'	
to'tal·iz'er		toured		tow'rope'	
to'tal·ly		tour'ism		tox·e'mi·a	
tote		tour'ist		tox'ic	
tot'ed		tour'ma·line		tox·ic'i·ty	
to'tem		tour'na·ment		tox'i·co·log'i·cal	
toth'er		tour'ney		tox'i·col'o·gist	
tot'ter		tour'ni·quet		tox'i·col'o·gy	

tox'i·co'sis	trac'tive	trained
tox'oid	trac'tor	train'er
toy	trac'tor·ize	train'ful
toyed	trade	train'load'
toy'ing·ly	trad'ed	train'man
toy'man	trad'er	trait
toy'shop'	trades'man	trai'tor
trace	tra·di'tion	trai'tor·ous
trace'a·ble	tra·di'tion·al	trai'tor·ous·ly
traced	tra·di'tion·al·ism	tra·jec'to·ry
trac'er	tra·di'tion·al·ly	tram
trac'er·y	tra·duce'	tram'car'
tra'che·a	tra·duced'	tram'mel
tra'che·al	tra·duc'er	tram'meled
tra·cho'ma	tra·duc'ing·ly	tram'mel·ing·ly
trac'ings	traf'fic	tra·mon'tane
track	traf'ficked	tramp
track'age	trag'a·canth	tramped
tracked	tra·ge'di·an	tram'ple
track'er	tra·ge'di·enne'	tram'pled
track'lay'er	trag'e·dy	tram'po·lin
track'less	trag'ic	tram'road'
track'man	trag'i·cal	tram'way'
track'mas'ter	trag'i·cal·ly	trance
tract	trag'i·com'e·dy	trance'like'
trac'ta·bil'i·ty	tra'gus	tran'quil
trac'ta·ble	trail	tran'quil·i·za'tion
trac'ta·bly	trailed	tran'quil·ize
trac·tar'i·an	trail'er	tran'quil·ized
trac'tate	trail'ing·ly	tran'quil·iz'er
trac'tile	train	tran'quil·iz'ing·ly
trac'tion	train'band'	tran·quil'li·ty

tran'quil·ly	trans·fig'ured	trans·la'tion
trans·act'	trans·fig'ure·ment	trans·la'tor
trans·act'ed	trans·fix'	trans·la'to·ry
trans·ac'tion	trans·fixed'	trans·lit'er·ate
trans·al'pine	trans·form'	trans·lu'cence
trans'at·lan'tic	trans'for·ma'tion	trans·lu'cen·cy
tran·scend'	trans·formed'	trans·lu'cent
tran·scend'ed	trans·form'er	trans·lu'cent·ly
tran·scend'ence	trans·form'ing·ly	trans'ma·rine'
tran·scend'en·cy	trans·fuse'	trans·mi'grant
tran·scend'ent	trans·fused'	trans'mi·gra'tion
tran'scen·den'tal	trans·fu'sion	trans·mis'si·ble
tran'scen·den'tal·ism	trans·fu'sions	trans·mis'sion
tran'scen·den'tal·ist	trans·gress'	trans·mit'
trans'con·ti·nen'tal	trans·gressed'	trans·mit'tal
tran·scribe'	trans·gress'ing·ly	trans·mit'ted
tran·scribed'	trans·gres'sion	trans·mit'ter
tran·scrib'er	trans·gres'sor	trans·mog'ri·fi·ca·tion
tran'script	tran'sient	trans·mog'ri·fied
tran·scrip'tion	tran·sis'tor	trans·mog'ri·fy
trans·duc'er	tran·sis'tor·ize	trans·mut'a·ble
trans·duc'tion	trans'it	trans'mu·ta'tion
tran'sept	tran·si'tion	trans·mute'
trans·fer'	tran·si'tion·al	trans·mut'ed
trans·fer'a·bil'i·ty	tran·si'tion·al·ly	tran'som
trans·fer'a·ble	tran'si·tive	trans'pa·cif'ic
trans·fer'al	tran'si·tive·ly	trans·par'en·cy
trans·fer'ence	tran'si·tive·ness	trans·par'ent
trans'ferred'	tran'si·to'ry	tran'spi·ra'tion
trans·fer'rer	trans·lat'a·ble	tran·spir'a·to'ry
trans·fig'u·ra'tion	trans·late'	tran·spire'
trans·fig'ure	trans·lat'ed	tran·spired'

trans·plant'

trans'plan·ta'tion

trans·plant'ed

trans·port'

trans'por·ta'tion

trans·port'ed

trans·port'ing·ly

trans·pos'al

trans·pose'

trans·posed'

trans'po·si'tion

trans·ship'

trans·ship'ment

tran'sub·stan'ti·a'tion

trans·ver'sal

trans·verse'

trap

trap door

tra·peze'

tra·pe'zi·um

trap'e·zoid

trapped

trap'per

trap'pings

Trap'pist

trap'rock'

trap'shoot'ing

trash

trash'i·er

trash'i·est

trash'y

trau'ma

trau'ma·ta

trau·mat'ic

trau·mat'i·cal·ly

trau'ma·tism

trau'ma·tize

trav'ail

trav'el

trav'eled

trav'el·er

trav'e·logue

trav'ers·a·ble

trav'ers·al

trav'erse

trav'ersed

trav'er·tine

trav'es·ty

trawl

trawl'er

tray

treach'er·ous

treach'er·ous·ly

treach'er·ous·ness

treach'er·y

trea'cle

tread

trea'dle

tread'mill'

trea'son

trea'son·a·ble

treas'ure

treas'ured

treas'ur·er

treas'ur·y

treat

treat'ed

trea'tise

treat'ment

trea'ty

tre'ble

tre'bled

tree

treed

tree'nail'

trek

trekked

trel'lis

trel'lised

trem'ble

trem'bled

trem'bling·ly

trem'blings

tre·men'dous

tre·men'dous·ly

tre'mo·lan'do

trem'o·lo

trem'or

trem'u·lous

trem'u·lous·ly

trem'u·lous·ness

trench

trench'an·cy

trench'ant

trench'ant·ly

trench'er

trench'er·man	trice	trig
trend	tri'ceps	trig'ger
trend'ed	tri·chi'na	trig'gered
tre·pan'	trich'i·no'sis	trig'ger·fish'
tre·phine'	tri·chot'o·my	tri'glyph
tre·phined'	trick	trig'o·no·met'ric
trep'i·da'tion	tricked	trig'o·no·met'ri·cal
tres'pass	trick'er·y	trig'o·nom'e·try
tres'passed	trick'i·er	tri·lem'ma
tres'pass·er	trick'i·est	tri·lin'gual
tress	trick'i·ly	trill
tres'tle	trick'i·ness	trilled
tres'tle·work'	trick'le	tril'lion
tri'ad	trick'led	Tril'li·um
tri·ad'ic	trick'ling·ly	tri'lo·bite
tri'al	trick'lings	tril'o·gy
tri'an'gle	trick'ster	trim
tri·an'gu·lar	trick'sy	trimmed
tri·an'gu·lar'i·ty	trick'y	trim'mer
tri·an'gu·late	tri'col'or	trim'mings
tri·an'gu·lat'ed	tri'corn	trim'ness
tri·an'gu·la'tion	tri'cot	tri·month'ly
trib'al	tri'cy·cle	trin'i·ty
trib'al·ism	tri'dent	trin'ket
tri·bas'ic	tried	tri·no'mi·al
tribe	tri·en'ni·al	tri'o
tribes'man	tri·en'ni·al·ly	tri'ode
trib'u·la'tion	tri'fle	tri'o·let
tri·bu'nal	tri'fled	trip
trib'une	tri'fler	tri·par'tite
trib'u·tar'y	tri'fling·ly	tripe
trib'ute	tri'flings	triph'thong

tri'ple	tri'umph·ing·ly	troth
tri'pled	tri·um'vir	trot'line'
tri'plet	tri·um'vi·rate	trot'ted
tri'plex	tri'une	trot'ter
trip'li·cate	tri·va'lent	trou'ba·dour
trip'li·cat'ed	triv'et	trou'ble
trip'li·ca'tion	triv'i·a	trou'bled
tri'ply	triv'i·al	trou'ble·some
tri'pod	triv'i·al'i·ty	trou'ble·some·ly
tripped	triv'i·al·ly	trou'ble·some·ness
trip'per	tro·cha'ic	trou'bling·ly
trip'ping·ly	tro'che	trou'blous
trip'tych	troi'ka	trough
tri'reme	troll	trough'like'
tri'sect'	trolled	trounce
tri'sect'ed	trol'ley	trounced
tri·sec'tion	trom'bone	trounc'ings
tri·sec'tor	troop	troupe
tris·kel'i·on	trooped	troup'er
tris'yl·lab'ic	troop'er	trou'sers
trite	troop'ship'	trous'seau'
trite'ly	trope	trout
trite'ness	tro'phy	trout'let
Tri'ton	trop'ic	trout'ling
tri·tone'	trop'i·cal	trow'el
trit'u·rate	trop'i·cal·ly	trow'eled
trit'u·rat'ed	tro'pism	troy
trit'u·ra'tion	trop'ist	tru'an·cy
tri'umph	tro·pol'o·gy	tru'ant
tri·um'phal	trop'o·pause	tru'ant·ism
tri·um'phant	trop'o·sphere	truce
tri'umphed	trot	tru'cial

truck	trun'cat·ed	tub
truck'age	trun·ca'tion	tu'ba
trucked	trun'cheon	tubbed
truck'er	trun'dle	tub'bi·er
truck'le	trun'dled	tub'bi·est
truck'led	trunk	tub'bings
truck'ling·ly	trun'nion	tub'by
truck'man	truss	tube
truc'u·lence	trussed	tu'ber
truc'u·lent	truss'ings	tu'ber·cle
trudge	trust	tu·ber'cu·lar
trudged	trus·tee'	tu·ber'cu·lin
trudg'en	trus·tee'ship	tu·ber'cu·lo'sis
true	trust'ful	tu·ber'cu·lous
trued	trust'ful·ly	tu'ber·os'i·ty
true'love'	trust'ful·ness	tu'ber·ous
true'ness	trust'i·er	tub'ings
truf'fle	trust'i·est	tu'bu·lar
truf'fled	trust'ing·ly	tu'bu·la'tion
tru'ism	trust'wor'thi·ness	tuck
tru'ly	trust'wor'thy	tucked
trump	trust'y	Tu'dor
trumped	truth	Tues'day
trump'er·y	truth'ful	tuft
trum'pet	truth'ful·ly	tuft'ed
trum'pet·ed	truth'ful·ness	tuft'ings
trum'pet·er	try	tug
trum'pet·ings	try'ing·ly	tug'boat'
trum'pet·like'	try'sail'	tugged
trum'pet·weed'	tryst	tug'ging·ly
trum'pet·wood'	tryst'ed	tug'gings
trun'cate	tset'se	tu·i'tion

tu′la·re′mi·a

tu′lip

tu′lip·wood′

tulle

tum′ble

tum′bled

tum′bler

tum′ble·weed′

tum′bling·ly

tum′brel

tu′me·fac′tion

tu′me·fied

tu′me·fy

tu′mid

tu·mid′i·ty

tu′mor

tu′mor·ous

tu′mult

tu·mul′tu·ous

tu·mul′tu·ous·ly

tu·mul′tu·ous·ness

tu′mu·lus

tun

tu′na

tun′dra

tune

tuned

tune′ful

tune′less

tune′less·ly

tune′less·ness

tun′er

tung′sten

tu′nic

tun′ings

Tu·ni′sian

tun′nel

tun′neled

tun′ny

tu′pe·lo

tur′ban

tur′bid

tur·bid′i·ty

tur′bid·ly

tur′bi·nate

tur′bine

tur′bot

tur′bu·lence

tur′bu·lent

tur′bu·lent·ly

tu·reen′

turf

turfed

turf′man

tur′gid

tur·gid′i·ty

tur′gid·ly

Turk

tur′key

Turk′ish

tur′mer·ic

tur′moil

turn

turn′buck′le

turn′coat′

turn′cock′

turned

turn′er

turn′ings

tur′nip

turn′key′

turn′off′

turn′out′

turn′o′ver

turn′pike′

turn′spit′

turn′stile′

tur′pen·tine

tur′pi·tude

tur′quoise

tur′ret

tur′ret·ed

tur′tle

Tus′can

tusk

tusked

tus′sle

tus′sled

tus′sock

tu′te·lage

tu′te·lar′y

tu′tor

tu′tored

tu·to′ri·al

tux·e′do

twad′dle

twad'dled	twin'klings	ty'phoid
twain	twirl	ty·phoi'dal
twang	twirled	ty'phoon'
twanged	twist	ty'phous
tweak	twist'ed	ty'phus
tweaked	twist'er	typ'i·cal
tweed	twist'ings	typ'i·cal·ly
tweez'ers	twit	typ'i·fi·ca'tion
twice	twitch	typ'i·fy
twid'dle	twitched	typ'ings
twid'dled	twit'ted	typ'ist
twig	twit'ter	ty·pog'ra·pher
twi'light'	twit'tered	ty'po·graph'ic
twill	twit'ter·ing·ly	ty·pog'ra·phy
twilled	twit'ter·ings	ty·poth'e·tae
twin	two	ty·ran'ni·cal
twin'born'	two'fold'	ty·ran'ni·cide
twine	two'some	tyr'an·nize
twined	ty·coon'	tyr'an·nized
twinge	type	ty'ran·niz'ing·ly
twinged	typed	tyr'an·nous
twin'kle	type'set'ter	tyr'an·ny
twin'kled	type'writ'er	ty'rant
twin'kling·ly	type'writ·ten	ty'ro

U

u·biq'ui·tous	ul'ti·mate	um·brel'la
u·biq'ui·tous·ly	ul'ti·mate·ly	um'laut
u·biq'ui·ty	ul'ti·ma'tum	um'pire
ud'der	ul'ti·mo	um'pired
ug'li·er	ul'tra·ism	un·a'ble
ug'li·est	ul'tra·le·gal'i·ty	un'a·bridged'
ug'li·ness	ul'tra·ma·rine'	un'ac·cent'ed
ug'ly	ul'tra·mi'cro·scope	un'ac·cept'a·ble
uh'lan	ul'tra·mod'ern	un'ac·com'mo·dat'ing
u·kase'	ul'tra·mon'tane	un'ac·com'pa·nied
u'ku·le'le	ul'tra·na'tion·al·ism	un'ac·count'a·ble
ul'cer	ul'tra·na'tion·al·ist	un'ac·cus'tomed
ul'cer·ate	ul'tra·red'	un'ac·quaint'ed
ul'cer·at'ed	ul'tra·son'ic	un'a·dorned'
ul'cer·a'tion	ul'tra·vi'o·let	un'a·dul'ter·at'ed
ul'cer·a'tive	ul'u·late	un'af·fect'ed
ul'cer·ous	ul'u·lat'ed	un'al·loyed'
ul'cer·ous·ly	ul'u·la'tion	un·al'ter·a·ble
ul'na	um'ber	un·al'tered
ul'nar	um'bra	un'-A·mer'i·can
ul'ster	um'brage	un·a'mi·a·ble
ul·te'ri·or	um·bra'geous	u·nan'i·mous

un·an'swer·a·ble

un'ap·peas'a·ble

un'ap·proach'a·ble

un'ap·pro'pri·at'ed

un'ap·prov'ing·ly

un·armed'

un'a·shamed'

un·asked'

un'as·sail'a·ble

un'as·signed'

un'as·sim'i·lat'ed

un'as·sist'ed

un'as·sum'ing·ly

un'at·tached'

un'at·tain'a·ble

un'at·tempt'ed

un'at·trac'tive·ly

un·au'thor·ized

un'a·vail'a·ble

un'a·vail'ing·ly

un'a·void'a·ble

un'a·ware'

un·bal'anced

un·bal'last·ed

un·bar'

un·barred'

un·bear'a·bly

un·beat'a·ble

un'be·com'ing·ly

un'be·fit'ting·ly

un'be·known'

un'be·knownst'

unbe·lief'

un'be·liev'a·ble

un'be·liev'er

un'be·liev'ing·ly

un'be·liev'ing·ness

un·bend'

un·bend'ing·ly

un·bi'ased

un·bid'den

un·bind'

un·blem'ished

un·blessed'

un·blocked'

un·blush'ing·ly

un·bolt'

un·bolt'ed

un·born'

un·bos'om

un·bos'omed

un·bound'

un·bound'ed

un·bowed'

un·break'a·ble

un·bri'dled

un·bro'ken

un·buck'le

un·bur'den

un·bur'dened

un·burned'

un·busi'ness·like'

un·but'ton

un·but'toned

un·cage'

un·can'ny

un·cap'ti·vat'ed

un·car'pet·ed

un·cat'a·logued

un·ceas'ing·ly

un'cer·e·mo'ni·ous

un·cer'tain

un·cer'tain·ly

un·cer'tain·ness

un·cer'tain·ty

un·chal'lenged

un·change'a·ble

un·change'a·bly

un·chang'ing·ly

un·char'i·ta·ble

un·chid'ing·ly

un·chris'tened

un·chris'tian

un'ci·al

un·civ'il

un·civ'i·lized

un·clad'

un·claimed'

un·clasp'

un'cle

un·clean'

un·clean'ly

un·closed'

un·clothe'

un·coil'

un'col·lect'ed

un·colt'

un·com'fort·a·ble

un·com'fort·a·ble·ness

un·com'mon

un'com·mu'ni·ca'tive

un·com'pa·nied

un·com'pro·mis'ing

un'con·cerned'

un'con·di'tion·al

un'con·di'tion·al'i·ty

un'con·fined'

un'con·firmed'

un'con·form'i·ty

un'con·gen'ial

un·con'quer·a·ble

un·con'quered

un·con'scion·a·ble

un·con'scious

un·con'scious·ly

un·con'scious·ness

un·con'se·crat'ed

un·con'se·quen'tial

un'con·se·quen'tial·ly

un'con·sid'er·ate·ly

un'con·sid'ered

un'con·sti·tu'tion·al

un'con·sti·tu'tion·al·ly

un'con·strained'

un'con·strain'ed·ly

un'con·tam'i·nat·ed

un'con·tra·dic'to·ry

un'con·trol'la·ble

un'con·trolled'

un'con·ven'tion·al

un'con·ven'tion·al·ly

un'con·vert'ed

un'con·vinced'

un'con·vinc'ing·ly

un'co·op'er·a'tive

un·cork'

un·corked'

un'cor·rect'ed

un'cor·rupt'ed

un·count'a·ble

un·count'ed

un·cou'ple

un·cou'pled

un·couth'

un·couth'ness

un·cov'er

un·cov'ered

un·cowed'

un·creased'

un·crit'i·cal

un·crit'i·ciz'ing·ly

un·crowd'ed

un·crowned'

unc'tion

unc'tu·ous

un·cul'ti·vat'ed

un·cul'tured

un·curbed'

un·curl'

un·cut'

un·dam'aged

un·damped'

un·dashed'

un·dat'ed

un·daunt'ed

un'de·ceive'

un'de·ceived'

un'de·cid'ed

un'de·ci'pher·a·ble

un'de·ci'phered

un·dec'o·rous

un'de·feat'ed

un'de·fend'ed

un'de·filed'

un'de·fin'a·ble

un'de·liv'er·a·ble

un'dem·o·crat'ic

un'de·mon'stra·tive

un'de·ni'a·ble

un'de·pend'a·ble

un'de·pos'it·ed

un'der

un'der·age'

un'der·arm'

un'der·bid'

un'der·bod'y

un'der·brush'

un'der·buy'

un'der·cap'i·tal·i·za'tion

un'der·cap'i·tal·ize

un'der·car'riage

un'der·charge'

un'der·charged'	un'der·mined'	un'der·tak'er
un'der·class'man	un'der·neath'	un'der·tak'ings
un'der·clothes'	un'der·nour'ish	un'der·things'
un'der·coat'	un'der·nour'ished	un'der·tone'
un'der·con·sump'tion	un'der·nour'ish·ment	un'der·took'
un'der·cov'er	un'der·pass'	un'der·tow'
un'der·cur'rent	un'der·pin'nings	un'der·turn'
un'der·cut'	un'der·priv'i·leged	un'der·val'ue
un'der·done'	un'der·pro·duc'tion	un'der·wa'ter
un'der·dose'	un'der·quote'	un'der·wear'
un'der·es'ti·mate	un'der·rate'	un'der·weight'
un'der·ex·pose'	un'der·rat'ed	un'der·world'
un'der·feed'	un'der·score'	un'der·write'
un'der·foot'	un'der·scored'	un'der·writ'er
un'der·gar'ment	un'der·sec're·tar'y	un'de·scrib'a·ble
un'der·glaze'	un'der·sell'	un'de·served'
un'der·go'	un'der·shirt'	un'de·sir'a·ble
un'der·grad'u·ate	un'der·shot'	un'de'sired'
un'der·ground'	un'der·signed'	un'de·stroyed'
un'der·growth'	un'der·sized'	un'de·tect'ed
un'der·hand'ed	un'der·skirt'	un'de·ter'mined
un'der·hand'ed·ly	un'der·slung'	un'de·vel'oped
un'der·hand'ed·ness	un'der·sparred'	un'di·ag·nosed'
un'der·hung'	un'der·stand'	un·di'a·pered
un'der·laid'	un'der·stand'ing·ly	un'di·gest'ed
un'der·lay'	un'der·stand'ings	un·dig'ni·fied
un'der·lie'	un'der·state'	un'di·lut'ed
un'der·line'	un'der·state'ment	un'di·min'ished
un'der·lined'	un'der·stood'	un·dimmed'
un'der·lings	un'der·stud'y	un'di·rect'ed
un'der·manned'	un'der·take'	un·dis'ci·plined
un'der·mine'	un'der·tak'en	un'dis·closed'

un·dis·cov'ered

un·dis·crim'i·nat'ing·ly

un·dis·guised'

un·dis·tin'guished

un·dis·trib'ut·ed

un·di·vid'ed

un·do'

un·do·mes'ti·cat·ed

un·done'

un·doubt'ed

un·doubt'ed·ly

un·dra·mat'i·cal·ly

un·draped'

un·drawn'

un·dress'

un·dressed'

un·drink'a·ble

un·due'

un'du·lant

un'du·late

un'du·lat'ed

un'du·la'tion

un·du'ly

un·du'ti·ful

un·dy'ing·ly

un·earned'

un·earth'

un·earthed'

un·earth'ly

un·eas'i·er

un·eas'i·est

un·eas'i·ly

un·eas'i·ness

un·eas'y

un·eat'a·ble

un·ed'u·ca·ble

un·ed'u·cat'ed

un'em·bar'rassed

un'em·bit'tered

un'em·broi'dered

un'e·mo'tion·al

un'em·ploy'a·ble

un'em·ploy'a·ble·ness

un'em·ployed'

un'em·ploy'ment

un'en·cum'bered

un'en·dan'gered

un·end'ing

un'en·dorsed'

un'en·dur'a·ble

un'en·force'a·ble

un'en·gaged'

un'en·graved'

un'en·grossed'

un'en·larged'

un'en·light'ened

un'en·slaved'

un·en'tered

un'en'ter·pris'ing

un'en·ter·tain'ing

un'en·thu'si·as'tic

un'en·thu'si·as'ti·cal·ly

un·en'vi·a·ble

un·en'vi·a·bly

un·en'vied

un·e'qual

un·e'qual·a·ble

un·e'qualed

un·e'qual·ize

un·e'qual·ized

un·e'qual·ly

un'e·quipped'

un·e·quiv'o·cal

un·e·rad'i·cat'ed

un·e·ras'a·ble

un·e·rased'

un·err'ing

un·err'ing·ly

un'es·sen'tial

un·es'ti·mat·ed

un·eth'i·cal

un·eth'i·cal·ly

un·e'ven

un·e'ven·ly

un·e'vent'ful

un·e·vent'ful·ly

un·ex·am'pled

un'ex·celled'

un'ex·cep'tion·a·ble

un'ex·cep'tion·al

un'ex·cit'a·ble

un'ex·cit'ing

un'ex·cused'

un·ex'e·cut'ed

un'ex·haust'ed

un'ex·pect'ed

un·ex·pect'ed·ly
un·ex·pect'ed·ness
un·ex·plain'a·ble
un·ex·plained'
un·ex·ploit'ed
un·ex·posed'
un·ex·pressed'
un·ex·press'i·ble
un·ex'pur·gat'ed
un·ex·tin'guished
un·ex'tri·cat·ed
un·fad'ed
un·fad'ing·ly
un·fail'ing·ly
un·fair'
un·fair'ly
un·fair'ness
un·faith'ful
un·faith'ful·ly
un·faith'ful·ness
un·fal'ter·ing
un·fa·mil'iar
un·farmed'
un·fash'ion·a·ble
un·fash'ion·a·bly
un·fas'ten
un·fas'tened
un·fa'ther·ly
un·fath'om·a·ble
un·fath'omed
un·fa·tigue'a·ble
un·fa·tigued'

un·fa'vor·able
un·fa'vor·a·bly
un·fear'ing·ly
un·fea'si·ble
un·fea'si·bly
un·fed'
un·feel'ing·ly
un·feigned'
un·felt'
un·fem'i·nine
un·fenced'
un·fe·nes'trat·ed
un·fer·ment'ed
un·fer'ti·lized
un·fet'ter
un·fet'tered
un·filed'
un·fil'i·al
un·fil'i·al·ly
un·fill'a·ble
un·fil'tered
un·fin'ished
un·fit'
un·fit'ting·ly
un·flag'ging·ly
un·flat'ter·ing·ly
un·flick'er·ing·ly
un·flinch'ing·ly
un·flinch'ing·ness
un·flood'ed
un·flur'ried
un·flus'tered

un·fo'cused
un·fold'
un·fold'ed
un·forced'
un·fore·see'a·ble
un·fore·seen'
un·fore·tell'a·ble
un·for'feit·ed
un·for·get'ta·ble
un·for·get'ting·ly
un·for·giv'a·ble
un·for·giv'en
un·for·giv'ing·ly
un·for·giv'ing·ness
un·for·got'ten
un·for'mal·ized
un·formed'
un·for'ti·fied
un·for'tu·nate
un·for'tu·nate·ly
un·found'ed
un·frayed'
un·fre·quent'ed
un·friend'ed
un·friend'li·ness
un·friend'ly
un·frock'
un·frocked'
un·fru'gal
un·fruit'ful
un·fu'eled
un·ful·filled'

un·fund'ed

un·fun'ny

un·fur'bished

un·furl'

un·furled'

un·fur'nished

un·gain'li·ness

un·gain'ly

un·gal'lant

un·gar'land·ed

un·gar'nished

un·gen'er·ous

un·gen'tle

un·gen'tle·man·ly

un·ger'mi·nat'ed

un·gift'ed

un·girt'

un·glazed'

un·glo'ri·ous

un·gloved'

un·god'li·ness

un·god'ly

un·gov'ern·a·ble

un·gov'ern·a·bly

un·gra'cious

un·gra'cious·ly

un·grad'ed

un'gram·mat'i·cal

un·grate'ful

un·grate'ful·ly

un·grate'ful·ness

un·ground'ed

un·grudg'ing·ly

un·guard'ed

un·guard'ed·ly

un'guent

un·guid'ed

un·gummed'

un·hack'neyed

un·hal'lowed

un·ham'pered

un·hand'i·ness

un·hand'some

un·hand'y

un·hanged'

un·hap'pi·er

un·hap'pi·est

un·hap'pi·ly

un·hap'pi·ness

un·hap'py

un·hard'ened

un·harmed'

un·har'ness

un·har'nessed

un·har'vest·ed

un·hatched'

un·healed'

un·health'ful

un·health'ful·ness

un·health'y

un·heard'

un·heat'ed

un·heed'ed

un·heed'ful·ly

un·heed'ing·ly

un·help'ful

un·her'ald·ed

un'he·ro'ic

un·hes'i·tat'ing

un·hes'i·tat'ing·ly

un·hin'dered

un·hinge'

un·hinged'

un·hitch'

un·hitched'

un·ho'li·ness

un·ho'ly

un·home'like'

un·hon'ored

un·hook'

un·hooked'

un·hoped'

un·horse'

un·hum'bled

un·hu'mor·ous

un·hurt'

un'hy·gi·en'ic

un·hy'phen·at'ed

u'ni·corn

u'ni·cy'cle

un'i·den'ti·fi'a·ble

un'i·den'ti·fied

u'ni·fi·ca'tion

u'ni·fied

u'ni·form

u'ni·formed

u'ni·form'i·ty

u'ni·fy

u'ni·lat'er·al

u'ni·lat'er·al·ly

un'il·lu'mi·nat'ing

un'im·ag'i·na·ble

un'im·ag'i·na'tive

un'im·paired'

un'im·peach'a·ble

un'im·ped'ed

un'im·por'tant

un'im·por'tant·ly

un'im·pos'ing

un'im·pressed'

un'im·pres'sion·a·ble

un'im·pres'sive

un'im·proved'

un'in·cor'po·rat'ed

un'in·dem'ni·fied

un·in'dexed

un'in·dict'ed

un'in·flu·enced

un'in·formed'

un'in·hab'it·a·ble

un'in·hab'it·ed

un'in·hib'it·ed

un·in'jured

un·inked'

un'in·scribed'

un'in·spired'

un'in·spir'ing·ly

un'in·struct'ed

un'in·struc'tive

un·in'su·lat'ed

un'in·sur'a·ble

un'in·sured'

un'in·te·grat'ed

un'in·tel'li·gent

un'in·tel'li·gi·ble

un'in·tend'ed

un'in·ten'tion·al

un'in·ten'tion·al·ly

un·in'ter·est·ed

un·in'ter·est·ed·ly

un·in'ter·est·ing·ly

un'in·ter·mit'ting·ly

un'in·ter·rupt'ed·ly

un·in'ti·mat'ed

un·in'tim'i·dat'ed

un'in·tox'i·cat'ed

un'in·vad'ed

un'in·ven'tive

un'in·vig'o·rat'ed

un'in·vit'ing·ly

un'ion

un'ion·ism

un'ion·ist

un'ion·i·za'tion

un'ion·ize

un'ion·ized

u·nique'

u·nique'ly

u·nique'ness

un'ir·ra'di·at'ed

u'ni·son

un·is'sued

u'nit

U'ni·tar'i·an

U'ni·tar'i·an·ism

u'ni·tar'y

u·nite'

u·nit'ed

u·nit'ed·ly

u'ni·ty

u'ni·ver'sal

U'ni·ver'sal·ist

u'ni·ver·sal'i·ty

u'ni·ver'sal·ly

u'ni·verse

u'ni·ver'si·ty

un·jok'ing·ly

un·just'

un·jus'ti·fi'a·ble

un·jus'ti·fi'a·bly

un·jus'ti·fied

un·just'ly

un·kempt'

un·killed'

un·kind'

un·kind'li·ness

un·kind'ly

un·know'a·ble

un·know'ing·ly

un·known'

un·la'beled

un·lace'

un·laced′

un·la′dy·like′

un′la·ment′ed

un·lashed′

un·latch′

un·law′ful

un·law′ful·ly

un·law′ful·ness

un·lead′ed

un·learn′

un·leash′

un·leashed′

un·leav′ened

un·less′

un·let′tered

un·lib′er·at′ed

un·li′censed

un·light′ed

un·lik′a·ble

un·like′

un·like′li·hood

un·like′ly

un·lim′ber

un·lim′bered

un·lim′it·ed

un·lined′

un·list′ed

un·load′

un·load′ed

un·lo′cal·ized

un·lock′

un·locked′

un·looked′

un·loos′en

un·loved′

un·lov′ing·ly

un·luck′i·ly

un·luck′y

un·made′

un·mag′ni·fied

un·maid′en·ly

un·mail′a·ble

un·make′

un·man′

un·man′age·a·ble

un·man′li·ness

un·man′ly

un·manned′

un·man′ner·li·ness

un·man′ner·ly

un·marked′

un·mar′riage·a·ble

un·mar′ried

un·mask′

un·masked′

un·matched′

un·meas′ur·a·ble

un·meas′ured

un·men′tion·a·ble

un·men′tioned

un·mer′ci·ful

un·mer′ci·ful·ly

un·mer′it·ed

un·me′tered

un·mind′ful

un′mis·tak′a·ble

un·mit′i·gat′ed

un·mixed′

un′mo·lest′ed

un·moored′

un·mort′gaged

un·mo′ti·vat′ed

un·mount′ed

un·moved′

un·mov′ing·ly

un·named′

un·nat′u·ral

un·nat′u·ral·ly

un·nav′i·ga·ble

un·nec′es·sar′i·ly

un·nec′es·sar′y

un·need′ed

un·neigh′bor·ly

un·nerve′

un·no′tice·a·ble

un·no′ticed

un·num′bered

un′ob·serv′ant

un′ob·served′

un′ob·tain′a·ble

un·oc′cu·pied

un·of·fi′cial

un·o′pened

un·o·pin′ion·at′ed

un′op·posed′

un·or′ches·trat′ed

un·or'gan·ized
un·or'tho·dox
un'os·ten·ta'tious
un·pac'i·fied
un·pack'
un·paged'
un·paid'
un·paint'ed
un·pal'at·a·ble
un·par'al·leled
un·par'don·a·ble
un·par'doned
un·par'lia·men'ta·ry
un·pas'teur·ized
un·pat'ent·a·ble
un·pat'ent·ed
un'pa·tri·ot'ic
un'pa·tri·ot'i·cal·ly
un'pa·trolled'
un·paved'
un'per·ceived'
un·per'fo·rat·ed
un'per·formed'
un'per·turbed'
un·pit'y·ing
un·pit'y·ing·ly
un·planned'
un·plas'tered
un·play'a·ble
un·pleas'a·ble
un·pleas'ant
un·pleas'ant·ly

un·pleas'ant·ness
un·pleas'ing·ly
un·pledged'
un·plowed'
un·plugged'
un·plumbed'
un'po·et'ic
un'po·liced'
un·pol'ished
un'pol·lut'ed
un'pop'u·lar
un·pop'u·lat·ed
un·pop'u·lous
un·prac'ticed
un·prec'e·dent·ed
un·prec'e·dent·ed·ly
un'pre·dict'a·ble
un·prej'u·diced
un'pre·med'i·tat'ed
un'pre·pared'
un'pre·par'ed·ness
un'pre·pos·sess'ing
un'pre·sent'a·ble
un'pre·tend'ing·ly
un'pre·ten'tious
un'pre·ten'tious·ly
un'pre·ten'tious·ness
un·prin'ci·pled
un·print'a·ble
un·print'ed
un'pro·duced'
un'pro·duc'tive

un'pro·fes'sion·al
un·prof'it·a·ble
un'pro·gres'sive
un·prom'is·ing
un·prompt'ed
un'pro·nounce'a·ble
un'pro·pi'tious
un'pro·tect'ed
un·prov'a·ble
un·proved'
un'pro·vid'ed
un'pro·voked'
un·pub'lished
un·punc'tu·al
un'punc·tu·al'i·ty
un·punc'tu·al·ly
un·pun'ished
un·qual'i·fied
un·quelled'
un·quench'a·bly
un·ques'tion·a·ble
un·ques'tion·a·bly
un·ques'tioned
un·ques'tion·ing·ly
un·ran'somed
un·rav'el
un·rav'eled
un·reach'a·ble
un·read'
un·read'a·ble
un·re'al
un're·al·is'tic

un·re·al'i·ty

un·re·al'ized

un·rea'son·a·ble

un·rea'son·a·bly

un·rea'soned

un·rea'son·ing·ly

un·re·buked'

un·re·ceipt'ed

un·re·cep'tive

un·re·claim'a·ble

un·rec'og·niz'a·ble

un·rec'og·nized

un·rec'og·niz'ing·ly

un·rec'on·cil'a·ble

un·re·cord'ed

un·re·deem'a·ble

un·re·deemed'

un·re·fill'a·ble

un·re·fined'

un·re·frig'er·at'ed

un·re·fut'ed

un·re·gen'er·ate

un·reg'u·lat'ed

un·re·hearsed'

un·re·lat'ed

un·re·lent'ing·ly

un·re·li'a·bil'i·ty

un·re·li'a·ble

un·re·mit'ting

un·re·mu'ner·a'tive

un·re·mu'ner·a'tive·ly

un·rent'a·ble

un·rent'ed

un·re·pent'ed

un·re·port'a·ble

un·re·port'ed

un·rep·re·sent'a·tive

un·re·proach'ing·ly

un·re·proved'

un·re·quit'ed

un·re·served'

un·re·serv'ed·ly

un·re·sist'ing·ly

un·re·solved'

un·re·source'ful

un·re·spon'sive

un·rest'

un·rest'ed

un·re·strained'

un·re·strict'ed

un·re·veal'ing·ly

un·re·ward'ed

un·rhymed'

un·right'eous

un·right'eous·ly

un·right'ful·ly

un·ripe'

un·ri'pened

un·ri'valed

un·roll'

un·rolled'

un·ruf'fle

un·ruf'fled

un·ruled'

un·rul'y

un·sad'dened

un·sad'dle

un·sad'dled

un·safe'

un·said'

un·sal'a·ble

un·sal'a·ried

un·sanc'ti·fied

un·sa'ti·at·ed

un·sat·is·fac'to·ri·ly

un·sat·is·fac'to·ry

un·sat'is·fied

un·sat'is·fy'ing·ly

un·sat'u·rat'ed

un·sa'vor·i·ly

un·sa'vor·y

un·scathed'

un·scent'ed

un·schooled'

un·sci·en·tif'ic

un·scram'ble

un·screw'

un·screwed'

un·scru'pu·lous

un·scru'pu·lous·ly

un·seal'

un·sealed'

un·sea'son·a·ble

un·sea'soned

un·seat'ed

un·sea'wor'thy

un·sec′ond·ed

un′se·cured′

un·see′ing·ly

un·seem′ing·ly

un·seem′ly

un·seen′

un′se·lect′ed

un·self′ish

un·self′ish·ly

un·sen′si·tized

un′sen·ti·men′tal

un·sep′a·rat′ed

un·serv′ice·a·ble

un·set′tle

un·set′tled

un·shack′le

un·shack′led

un·shad′ed

un·shak′a·ble

un·shak′en

un·sharp′ened

un·shav′en

un·sheathe′

un·shed′

un·shel′tered

un·shield′ed

un·ship′

un·shipped′

un·shrink′a·ble

un·shuf′fled

un·sight′ed

un·sight′ly

un·signed′

un·sing′a·ble

un·sink′a·ble

un·sis′ter·ly

un·sized′

un·skilled′

un·skill′ful

un·skimmed′

un·smil′ing·ly

un·smirched′

un·smoked′

un·smudged′

un·snarl′

un·so′cia·ble

un·soft′ened

un·soil′

un·soiled′

un·sold′

un·sol′dier·ly

un′so·lic′it·ed

un′so·phis′ti·cat′ed

un·sought′

un·sound′

un·sound′ly

un·speak′a·ble

un·spe′cial·ized

un·spec′i·fied

un·spoiled′

un·spo′ken

un·sports′man·like′

un·spot′ted

un·sprin′kled

un·sta′ble

un·stained′

un·stamped′

un·stead′i·ly

un·stead′y

un·ster′i·lized

un·stint′ed

un·stint′ing·ly

un·strained′

un·stressed′

un·strung′

un′sub·stan′tial

un′sub·stan′ti·at′ed

un′suc·cess′ful

un·suf′fer·a·ble

un·suit′a·ble

un·sul′lied

un·sum′moned

un·sung′

un′su·per·vised′

un·sure′

un′sur·pass′a·ble

un′sur·passed′

un′sus·pect′ed

un′sus·pect′ing

un′sus·pect′ing·ly

un·swayed′

un·sweet′ened

un·swerv′ing·ly

un·sworn′

un′sym·pa·thet′ic

un·sym′pa·thiz′ing·ly

un'sys·tem·at'ic

un·sys'tem·a·tized

un·taint'ed

un·tal'ent·ed

un·tamed'

un·tan'gle

un·tanned'

un·tast'ed

un·taught'

un·tax'a·ble

un·taxed'

un·teach'a·ble

un·tech'ni·cal

un·tempt'ed

un·ten'ant·a·ble

un·ten'ant·ed

un·tend'ed

un·ter'ri·fied

un·thick'ened

un·think'a·ble

un·think'ing

un·think'ing·ly

un·ti'di·ly

un·ti'dy

un·tie'

un·tied'

un·til'

un·time'ly

un·tint'ed

un·tir'ing·ly

un·ti'tled

un'to

un·told'

un·touch'a·ble

un·touched'

un·to'ward

un·trace'a·ble

un·trad'ed

un·trained'

un·tram'meled

un'trans·lat'a·ble

un·trav'eled

un·tried'

un·trimmed'

un·trod'den

un·trou'bled

un·true'

un·trussed'

un·trust'wor'thy

un·truth'

un·truth'ful

un·tuned'

un·turned'

un·tu'tored

un·twine'

un·twist'

un'un·der·stand'a·ble

un'up·braid'ing·ly

un·us'a·ble

un·used'

un·u'su·al

un·u'su·al·ly

un·ut'ter·a·ble

un·ut'ter·a·bly

un·ut'tered

un·val'i·dat'ed

un·val'ued

un·van'quished

un·var'ied

un·var'nished

un·var'y·ing·ly

un·vaunt'ing·ly

un·veil'

un·veiled'

un·ver'bal·ized

un·ver'i·fied

un·versed'

un·vis'it·ed

un·voiced'

un·walled'

un·war'i·ly

un·warned'

un·war'rant·a·ble

un·war'rant·ed

un·war'y

un·washed'

un·wa'tered

un·wa'ver·ing·ly

un·wea'ried

un·wea'ry·ing·ly

un·wed'

un·wed'ded

un·wel'come

un·well'

un·wept'

un·whole'some

un·whole'some·ly   un·yoked'   up·raised'

un·wield'i·ness   up   up'right'

un·wield'y   u'pas   up'right'ly

un·will'ing   up'beat'   up'right'ness

un·will'ing·ly   up·braid'   up·ris'ings

un·will'ing·ness   up·braid'ed   up'roar'

un·winc'ing·ly   up·braid'ing·ly   up·roar'i·ous

un·wind'   up·bring'ing   up·roar'i·ous·ness

un·wind'ing·ly   up'coun'try   up·root'

un·wink'ing·ly   up'draft'   up·root'ed

un·wise'   up'grade'   up·set'

un·wit'nessed   up'growth'   up·set'ting·ly

un·wit'ting·ly   up·heav'al   up'shot'

un·wom'an·ly   up·held'   up'side'

un·wont'ed   up'hill'   up'stairs'

un·work'a·ble   up·hold'   up'start'

un·work'man·like'   up·hold'er   up'state'

un·world'li·ness   up·hol'ster   up'stream'

un·world'ly   up·hol'stered   up'stroke'

un·worn'   up·hol'ster·er   up'take'

un·wor'ried   up·hol'ster·y   up'-to-date'

un·wor'thi·ly   up'keep'   up'town'

un·wor'thi·ness   up'land'   up·turn'

un·wor'thy   up·lift'   up·turned'

un·wound'   up·lift'ed   up'ward

un·wound'ed   up·lift'ing·ly   up'wind'

un·wrap'   up'most   u·ra'ni·um

un·wrapped'   up·on'   ur'ban

un·wreathe'   up'per   ur·bane'

un·wrin'kled   up'per·most   ur·bane'ly

un·writ'ten   up'pers   ur'ban·ite

un·yield'ing·ly   up·raise'   ur·ban'i·ty

ur'ban·i·za'tion

ur'ban·ize

ur'ban·ized

ur'chin

urge

urged

ur'gen·cy

ur'gent

ur'gent·ly

urg'ings

urn

us

us'a·bil'i·ty

us'a·ble

us'age

use

used

use'ful

use'ful·ly

use'ful·ness

use'less

use'less·ly

use'less·ness

us'er

us'es

ush'er

ush'ered

u'su·al

u'su·al·ly

u'su·fruct

u'su·rer

u·su'ri·ous

u·surp'

u'sur·pa'tion

u·surp'er

u'su·ry

u·ten'sil

u·til'i·tar'i·an

u·til'i·tar'i·an·ism

u·til'i·ties

u·til'i·ty

u'ti·liz'a·ble

u'ti·li·za'tion

u'ti·lize

u'ti·lized

ut'most

u·to'pi·a

u·to'pi·an

u·to'pi·an·ism

ut'ter

ut'ter·ance

ut'tered

ut'ter·ly

ut'ter·most

u'vu·la

u'vu·lar

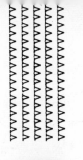

va'can·cy	vag'a·bon'di·a	va·le'ri·an
va'cant	vag'a·bond·ism	val'et
va'cate	vag'a·bond·ize	val'e·tu'di·nar'·i·an
va'cat·ed	va·gar'y	Val·hal'la
va·ca'tion	va'gran·cy	val'iant
va·ca'tioned	va'grant	val'id
va·ca'tion·ist	vague	val'i·date
vac'ci·nate	va'guer	val'i·dat'ed
vac'ci·nat'ed	va'guest	val'i·da'tion
vac'ci·na'tion	va'gus	va·lid'i·ty
vac'ci·na'tor	vain	val'id·ly
vac'cine	vain'glo'ri·ous	va·lise'
vac'il·late	vain'glo'ry	val'ley
vac'il·lat'ed	vain'ly	val'or
vac'il·la'tion	vain'ness	val'or·i·za'tion
vac'il·lat'ing·ly	val'ance	val'or·ize
vac'il·la·to'ry	vale	val'or·ous
va·cu'i·ty	val'e·dic'tion	val'u·a·ble
vac'u·ous	val'e·dic·to'ri·an	val'u·a'tion
vac'u·um	val'e·dic'to·ry	val'ue
vag'a·bond	va'lence	val'ued
vag'a·bond'age	val'en·tine	val'ue·less

valve

val'vu·lar

vamp

vam'pire

va·na'di·um

van'dal

van'dal·ism

van'dal·ize

vane

van'guard'

va·nil'la

van'il·lin

van'ish

van'ished

van'ish·ing·ly

van'i·ty

van'quish

van'quished

van'tage

vap'id

vap'id·ly

va'por

va'por·ings

va'por·i·za'tion

va'por·ize

va'por·ized

va'por·iz'er

va'por·ous

var'i·a·bil'i·ty

var'i·a·ble

var'i·ance

var'i·ant

var'i·a'tion

var'i·col'ored

var'i·cose

var'i·cos'i·ty

var'ied

var'i·e·gate

var'i·e·gat'ed

var'i·e·ga'tion

va·ri'e·tal

va·ri'e·ty

va·ri'o·la

var'i·o'rum

var'i·ous

var'i·ous·ly

var'let

var'nish

var'nished

var'nish·ings

var'y

var'y·ing·ly

vas'cu·lar

vase

Vas'e·line

vas'sal

vas'sal·age

vast

vast'er

vast'est

vast'ly

vat

Vat'i·can

vaude'ville

vault

vault'ed

vaunt

vaunt'ed

vaunt'ing·ly

veal

vec'tor

ve·dette'

veer

veered

veg'e·ta·ble

veg'e·tar'i·an

veg'e·tar'i·an·ism

veg'e·tate

veg'e·tat'ed

veg'e·ta'tion

veg'e·ta'tive

ve'he·mence

ve'he·ment

ve'he·ment·ly

ve'hi·cle

ve'hi·cles

ve·hic'u·lar

veil

veiled

vein

veined

vein'ings

vein'let

vel'lum

ve·loc'i·pede

ve·loc'i·ty

ve'lo·drome	ven'om·ous	ver·bose'
ve·lours'	ven'om·ous·ly	ver·bos'i·ty
vel'vet	vent	ver'dant
vel'vet·een'	vent'ed	ver'dict
vel'vet·y	vent'hole'	ver'di·gris
ve'nal	ven'ti·late	ver'dure
ve·nal'i·ty	ven'ti·lat'ed	verge
ve'nal·i·za'tion	ven'ti·la'tion	verged
ve'nal·ize	ven'ti·la'tor	ver'ger
ve·na'tion	ven'tral	ver'i·est
vend	ven'tri·cle	ver'i·fi'a·ble
vend'ed	ven·tric'u·lar	ver'i·fi·ca'tion
vend·ee'	ven·tril'o·quism	ver'i·fied
ven·det'ta	ven·tril'o·quist	ver'i·fy
vend'i·ble	ven'ture	ver'i·ly
ven'dor	ven'tured	ver'i·si·mil'i-
ve·neer'	ven'ture·some	tude
ve·neered'	ven'ue	ver'ism
ven'er·a·ble	ve·ra'cious	ver'i·ta·ble
ven'er·ate	ve·ra'cious·ly	ver'i·ta·bly
ven'er·at'ed	ve·rac'i·ty	ver'i·ties
ven'er·a'tion	ve·ran'da	ver'i·ty
ven'er·a'tive	ver'bal	ver'meil
Ve·ne'tian	ver'bal·ism	ver'mi·cel'li
venge'ance	ver'bal·ist	ver'mi·cide
venge'ful	ver'bal·i·za'tion	ver·mic'u·late
venge'ful·ness	ver'bal·ize	ver·mic'u·la'tion
ve'ni·al	ver'bal·ized	ver·mic'u·lite
ve'ni·al'i·ty	ver'bal·ly	ver'mi·form
ve'ni·al·ly	ver·ba'tim	ver'mi·fuge
ven'i·son	ver·be'na	ver·mil'ion
ven'om	ver'bi·age	ver'min
		ver'min·ous

ver·nac'u·lar

ver'nal

ver'ni·er

ver'sa·tile

ver'sa·til'i·ty

verse

ver'si·cle

ver'si·fi·ca'tion

ver'si·fied

ver'si·fi'er

ver'si·fy

ver'sion

ver'so

ver'sus

ver'te·bra

ver'te·brae

ver'te·brate

ver'tex

ver'ti·cal

ver'ti·cal·ly

ver·tig'i·nous

ver'ti·go

ver'vain

verve

ver'y

ves'i·cle

ves'per

ves'sel

vest

ves'tal

vest'ed

ves·tib'u·lar

ves'ti·bule

ves'tige

ves·tig'i·al

vest'ment

ves'try

ves'ture

vetch

vet'er·an

vet'er·i·nar'i·an

vet'er·i·nar'y

ve'to

ve'toed

vex

vex·a'tion

vex·a'tious

vexed

vi'a

vi·a·bil'i·ty

vi'a·ble

vi'a·duct

vi'al

vi'and

vi·at'i·cum

vi'bran·cy

vi'brant

vi'brate

vi'brat·ed

vi'brat·ing·ly

vi·bra'tion

vi·bra'tion·less

vi·bra'to

vi'bra·tor

vi'bra·to'ry

vic'ar

vic'ar·age

vi·car'i·ate

vi·car'i·ous

vi·car'i·ous·ly

vice

vice'ge'ral

vice'ge'rent

vice'reine

vice'roy

vic'i·nage

vi·cin'i·ties

vi·cin'i·ty

vi'cious

vi'cious·ly

vi'cious·ness

vi·cis'si·tude

vic'tim

vic'tim·ize

vic'tim·ized

vic'tor

Vic·to'ri·an

vic·to'ri·ous

vic·to'ri·ous·ly

vic'to·ry

Vic·tro'la

vict'ual

vi·cu'ña

vid'e·o

vie

vied

view

viewed

vig'il

vig'i·lance

vig'i·lant

vig'i·lan'te

vig'i·lant·ly

vi·gnette'

vi·gnett'ed

vig'or

vig'or·ous

vig'or·ous·ly

vi'kings

vile

vil'er

vil'est

vil'i·fi·ca'tion

vil'i·fi'er

vil'i·fy

vil'la

vil'lage

vil'lag·er

vil'lain

vil'lain·ous

vil'lain·ous·ly

vil'lain·y

vil'la·nelle'

vin'ai·grette'

vin'cu·lum

vin'di·ca·ble

vin'di·cate

vin'di·cat'ed

vin'di·ca'tion

vin·dic'tive

vine

vin'e·gar

vine'yard

vin'i·fi·ca'tion

vi'nous

vin'tage

vint'ner

vi'ol

vi·o'la

vi'o·late

vi'o·lat'ed

vi'o·la'tion

vi'o·la'tive

vi'o·la'tor

vi'o·lence

vi'o·lent

vi'o·lent·ly

vi'o·let

vi'o·lin'

vi'o·lin'ist

vi'o·lon·cel'list

vi'o·lon·cel'lo

vi'per

vi'per·ous

vi·ra'go

vir'e·o

vir'gin

vir'gin·al

vir·gin'i·ty

vir'ile

vi·ril'i·ty

vir'tu·al

vir'tu·al·ly

vir'tue

vir'tu·os'i·ty

vir'tu·o'so

vir'tu·ous

vir'tu·ous·ly

vir'tu·ous·ness

vir'u·lence

vir'u·len·cy

vir'u·lent

vi'rus

vi'sa

vis'age

vis'-à-vis'

vis'cer·a

vis'cer·al

vis'cid

vis·cid'i·ty

vis'cid·ly

vis'cose

vis·cos'i·ty

vis'count'

vis'cous

vise

vis'i·bil'i·ty

vis'i·ble

vis'i·bly

vi'sion

vi'sion·ar'y

vis'it

vis′it·a′tion	vi·vac′i·ty	voice
vis′it·ed	vi·var′i·um	voiced
vis′i·tor	viv′id	voice′less
vis′ta	viv′id·ly	voice′less·ly
vis′u·al	viv′i·fy	voice′less·ness
vis′u·al·i·za′tion	vi·vip′a·rous	void
vis′u·al·ize	viv′i·sect	void′a·ble
vis′u·al·ized	viv′i·sec′tion	void′ed
vis′u·al·ly	viv′i·sec′tion·ist	vol′a·tile
vi′tal	vix′en	vol′a·til′i·ty
vi·tal′i·ty	vix′en·ish	vol′a·til·i·za′tion
vi′tal·ize	viz′ard	vol′a·til·ize
vi′tal·ized	vi·zier′	vol′a·til·ized
vi′tal·ly	vo′ca·ble	vol·can′ic
vi′ta·min	vo·cab′u·lar′y	vol·ca′no
vi′ti·ate	vo′cal	vol′can·ol′o·gy
vi′ti·at′ed	vo′cal·ism	vo·li′tion
vi′ti·a′tion	vo′cal·ist	vo·li′tion·al
vit′re·ous	vo′cal·i·za′tion	vo·li′tion·al·ly
vit′ri·fac′tion	vo′cal·ize	vol′ley
vit′ri·fi·ca′tion	vo′cal·ized	vol′ley·ball′
vit′ri·fied	vo′cal·ly	vol′leyed
vit′ri·fy	vo·ca′tion	volt
vit′ri·ol	vo·ca′tion·al	volt′age
vit′ri·ol′ic	vo·ca′tion·al·ly	vol·ta′ic
vi·tu′per·ate	voc′a·tive	volt·am′e·ter
vi·tu′per·at′ed	vo·cif′er·ate	volt·am′me·ter
vi·tu′per·a′tion	vo·cif′er·at′ed	volt′me′ter
vi·tu′per·a′tive	vo·cif′er·a′tion	vol′u·bil′i·ty
vi·tu′per·a′tive·ly	vo·cif′er·ous	vol′u·ble
vi·va′cious	vod′ka	vol′u·bly
vi·va′cious·ly	vogue	vol′ume

vol'u·met'ric	vo·rac'i·ty	voy'aged
vo·lu'mi·nous	vor'tex	voy'ag·er
vo·lu'mi·nous·ly	vor'ti·cal	vul'can·i·za'tion
vo·lu'mi·nous·ness	vor'ti·cal·ly	vul'can·ize
vol'un·tar'i·ly	vo'ta·ry	vul'can·ized
vol'un·tar'y	vote	vul'can·iz'er
vol'un·teer'	vot'ed	vul'gar
vol'un·teered'	vot'er	vul·gar'i·an
vo·lup'tu·ar'y	vo'tive	vul'gar·ism
vo·lup'tu·ous	vouch	vul·gar'i·ty
vo·lup'tu·ous·ly	vouched	vul'gar·i·za'tion
vo·lup'tu·ous·ness	vouch'er	vul'gar·ize
vo·lute'	vouch·safe'	vul'gar·ized
vol'vu·lus	vouch·safed'	vul'gar·iz'er
vom'it	vow	vul'gar·ly
vom'it·ed	vowed	vul'gate
vom'i·to'ry	vow'el	vul'ner·a·bil'i·ty
voo'doo	vow'el·i·za'tion	vul'ner·a·ble
voo'doo·ism	vow'el·ize	vul'ner·a·bly
vo·ra'cious	voy'age	vul'ture

W

wad	wag'gling·ly	wake
wad'ded	Wag·ne'ri·an	waked
wad'dings	wag'on	wake'ful
wad'dle	wag'tail'	wake'ful·ly
wad'dling·ly	waif	wake'ful·ness
wade	wail	wak'en
wad'ed	wailed	wak'ened
wad'er	wail'ing·ly	wak'ing·ly
wa'fer	wail'ings	wale
waf'fle	wain	waled
waft	wain'scot	walk
wag	waist	walked
wage	waist'band'	walk'er
waged	waist'coat'	walk'o'ver
wa'ger	waist'line'	walk'-up'
wa'gered	wait	walk'way'
wa'ger·ings	wait'ed	wall
wag'es	wait'er	wall'board'
wagged	wait'ress	walled
wag'gish	waive	wal'let
wag'gle	waived	wall'eyed'
wag'gled	waiv'er	wall'flow'er

349

Wal·loon'	ward'ed	war'rant
wal'lop	ward'en	war'rant·a·ble
wal'low	ward'er	war'rant·ed
wal'lowed	ward'robe'	war'ran·tor
wall'pa'per	ward'room'	war'ran·ty
wal'nut	ware'house'	warred
wal'rus	ware'house'man	war'ren
waltz	ware'room'	war'ship'
waltzed	wares	wart
wam'pum	war'fare'	war'time'
wan	war'i·ly	wart'less
wand	war'i·ness	war'y
wan'der	war'like'	was
wan'dered	war'lock	wash
wan'der·er	warm	wash'a·ble
wan'der·ing·ly	warmed	wash'board'
wan'der·ings	warm'er	wash'bowl'
wane	warm'est	wash'cloth'
waned	warm'heart'ed	washed
wan'gle	warm'ly	wash'er
wan'gled	warm'ness	wash'house'
want	war'mon'ger	wash'ings
want'ed	warmth	wash'out'
want'ing·ly	warn	wash'room'
wan'ton	warned	wash'stand'
war	warn'ing·ly	wash'-up'
war'ble	warn'ings	wash'wom'an
war'bled	warp	wasp
war'bler	warp'age	wasp'ish
war'bling·ly	war'path'	was'sail
war'blings	warped	wast'age
ward	war'plane'	waste

waste'bas'ket	wa'ter·log'	wax'i·ness
wast'ed	wa'ter·logged'	wax'ing·ly
waste'ful	Wa'ter·loo'	wax'wing'
waste'ful·ly	wa'ter·man	wax'work'
waste'ful·ness	wa'ter·mark'	wax'y
waste'land'	wa'ter·mel'on	way
waste'pa'per	wa'ter·proof'	way'bill'
wast'er	wa'ter·proofed'	way'far'er
wast'ing·ly	wa'ter·shed'	way'fel'low
wast'rel	wa'ter·side'	way'laid'
watch	wa'ter·spout'	way'lay'
watch'case'	wa'ter·way'	way'side'
watch'dog'	wa'ter·weed'	way'ward
watched	wa'ter·works'	we
watch'er	wa'ter·y	weak
watch'ful	watt	weak'en
watch'ful·ly	watt'age	weak'ened
watch'ful·ness	wat'tle	weak'er
watch'house'	wat'tled	weak'est
watch'keep'er	watt'me'ter	weak'ling
watch'mak'er	wave	weak'ly
watch'man	waved	weak'ness
watch'tow'er	wave'me'ter	weal
watch'word'	wa'ver	wealth
wa'ter	wa'vered	wealth'i·er
wa'tered	wa'ver·ing·ly	wealth'i·est
wa'ter·fall'	wa'ver·ings	wealth'y
wa'ter·find'er	wav'i·ness	wean
wa'ter·fowl'	wav'y	weaned
wa'ter·i·ness	wax	weap'on
wa'ter·ings	waxed	weap'on·less
wa'ter·line'	wax'en	wear

wear'a·bil'i·ty	weed'ed	wel'fare'
wear'a·ble	weed'i·er	wel'kin
wear'er	weed'i·est	well
wea'ried	weed'y	well'born'
wea'ri·er	week	welled
wea'ri·est	week'day'	well'head'
wea'ri·ly	week'end'	well'hole'
wea'ri·ness	week'lies	well'spring'
wear'ings	week'ly	welt
wea'ri·some	weep	welt'ed
wea'ri·some·ness	weep'ing·ly	wel'ter
wea'ry	wee'vil	wel'tered
wea'sel	weft	wen
weath'er	weigh	wench
weath'er·board'	weighed	wend
weath'er·cock'	weigh'ings	wend'ed
weath'ered	weigh'mas'ter	went
weath'er·proof'	weight	wept
weath'er·proofed'	weight'ed	were
weave	weight'i·er	were'wolf'
weav'er	weight'i·est	west
web	weight'ings	west'er·ly
webbed	weight'y	west'ern
web'bings	weir	west'ern·er
wed	weird	west'ward
wed'ded	weird'ly	wet
wed'dings	weird'ness	wet'ness
wedge	wel'come	wet'ta·bil'i·ty
wedged	wel'comed	wet'ta·ble
wed'lock	wel'com·ing·ly	wet'ted
Wednes'day	weld	wet'ter
weed	weld'ed	wet'test

wet'tings

we've

whack

whacked

whale

whale'back'

whale'bone'

whale'man

whal'er

wharf

wharf'age

wharf'in·ger

what

what·ev'er

what'not'

what'so·ev'er

wheat

wheat'en

wheat'worm'

whee'dle

whee'dled

whee'dling·ly

wheel

wheel'bar'row

wheeled

wheel'house'

wheel'wright'

wheeze

wheezed

wheez'i·er

wheez'i·est

wheez'i·ly

wheez'ing·ly

wheez'y

whelk

whelp

whelped

when

whence

whence'forth'

when·ev'er

when'so·ev'er

where

where'a·bouts'

where·aft'er

where·as'

where·at'

where·by'

where'fore

where·from'

where·in'

where·of'

where·on'

where'so·ev'er

where'up·on'

wher·ev'er

where·with'

where'with·al'

wher'ry

whet

wheth'er

whet'ted

whet'stone'

whey

which

which·ev'er

which'so·ev'er

whiff

whiffed

whif'fle

whif'fled

Whig

while

whiled

whi'lom

whim

whim'per

whim'pered

whim'per·ing·ly

whim'per·ings

whim'sey

whim'si·cal

whine

whined

whin'ing·ly

whin'ings

whin'nied

whin'ny

whip

whip'cord'

whipped

whip'per·snap'per

whip'pet

whip'ping·ly

whip'pings

whip'poor·will'

whip'saw'	whit'en	why
whip'stitch'	whit'ened	wick
whip'stock'	white'ness	wick'ed
whip'worm'	white'wash'	wick'ed·ly
whir	white'washed'	wick'ed·ness
whirl	white'wing'	wick'er
whirled	white'wood'	wick'er·work'
whirl'i·gig'	whith'er	wick'et
whirl'ing·ly	whit'ings	wide
whirl'pool'	whit'ish	wide'ly
whirl'wind'	whit'low	wid'en
whirred	whit'tle	wid'ened
whisk	whit'tled	wide'ness
whisked	whit'tlings	wid'er
whisk'er	who	wide'spread'
whisk'ered	who·ev'er	wid'est
whis'ky	whole	wid'ow
whis'per	whole'heart'ed	wid'owed
whis'pered	whole'heart'ed·ly	wid'ow·er
whis'per·er	whole'sale'	wid'ow·hood
whis'per·ing·ly	whole'sal'er	width
whis'per·ings	whole'some	wield
whist	whole'some·ly	wield'ed
whis'tle	whol'ly	wife
whis'tled	whom	wife'hood
whis'tling·ly	whom·ev'er	wife'less
whis'tlings	whom'so·ev'er	wife'ly
whit	whoop	wig
white	whooped	wig'gle
white'cap'	whoop'ing·ly	wig'gled
whit'ed	whose	wig'gler
white'fish'	who'so·ev'er	wig'glings

wight	wind'break'	wing'spread'
wig'mak'er	wind'ed	wink
wig'wag'	wind'er	winked
wig'wam'	wind'fall'	wink'ing·ly
wild	wind'i·ly	win'kle
wild'er	wind'i·ness	win'ner
wil'der·ness	wind'ing·ly	win'ning·ly
wild'est	wind'ings	win'nings
wild'fire'	wind'jam'mer	win'now
wild'ness	wind'lass	win'nowed
wile	wind'mill'	win'some
wil'i·er	win'dow	win'ter
wil'i·est	win'dowed	win'tered
will	win'dow·pane'	win'ter·ize
willed	wind'pipe'	wipe
will'ful	wind'row'	wiped
will'ful·ly	wind'rowed'	wip'er
will'ful·ness	wind'shield'	wire
will'ing·ly	wind'storm'	wired
will'ing·ness	wind'ward	wire'less
wil'low	wind'ward ly	wire'pull'er
wilt	wind'way'	wire'pull'ing
wilt'ed	wind'y	wire'way'
wil'y	wine	wire'work'
win	wine'ber'ry	wire'work'er
wince	wined	wire'worm'
winced	wine'glass'	wir'y
winc'ing·ly	wine'skin'	wis'dom
wind	wing	wise
wind	winged	wise'a'cre
wind'age	wing'fish'	wise'crack'
wind'bag'	wing'less	wise'crack'er

wise'ly	with'ered	woe'be·gone'
wise'ness	with'er·ing·ly	woe'ful
wis'er	with·held'	woe'ful·ly
wis'est	with·hold'	woe'ful·ness
wish	with·hold'ings	wolf
wish'bone'	with·in'	wolfed
wished	with·out'	wolf'hound'
wish'ful	with·stand'	wolf'ish
wish'ful·ly	with·stood'	wol'ver·ine'
wish'ful·ness	wit'less	wolves
wish'ing·ly	wit'less·ly	wom'an
wisp	wit'less·ness	wom'an·hood
wisp'i·er	wit'ness	wom'an·ish
wisp'i·est	wit'nessed	wom'an·kind'
wisp'y	wit'ti·cism	wom'an·like'
wis·te'ri·a	wit'ti·er	wom'an·li·ness
wist'ful	wit'ti·est	wom'an·ly
wist'ful·ly	wit'ting·ly	wom'en
wist'ful·ness	wit'ty	won
wit	wived	won'der
witch	wives	won'dered
witch'craft'	wiz'ard	won'der·ful
witch'er·y	wiz'ard·ly	won'der·ful·ly
witch'ing·ly	wiz'ard·ry	won'der·ing·ly
witch'weed'	wiz'ened	won'der·land'
with	woad	won'der·ment
with·al'	wob'ble	won'der·work'
with·draw'	wob'bled	won'drous
with·draw'al	wob'bli·ness	won'drous·ly
with·drawn'	wob'bling·ly	won't
with·drew'	wob'bly	wont
with'er	woe	woo

wood	word'age	work'peo'ple
wood'bin'	word'build'ing	work'place'
wood'bine'	word'ed	work'room'
wood'chuck'	word'i·er	work'shop'
wood'craft'	word'i·est	work'ta'ble
wood'cut'	word'i·ly	work'wom'an
wood'ed	word'i·ness	work'wom'en
wood'en	word'less	world
wood'en·head'	word'play'	world'li·ness
wood'fish'	word'y	world'ly
wood'land	wore	worm
wood'man	work	wormed
wood'peck'er	work'a·bil'i·ty	worm'hole'
wood'pile'	work'a·ble	worm'i·er
wood'shop'	work'bag'	worm'i·est
woods'man	work'bas'ket	worm'like'
wood'work'	work'bench'	worm'proof'
wood'work'er	work'book'	worm'wood'
wood'worm'	work'box'	worm'y
wooed	work'day'	worn
woo'er	worked	wor'ried
woof	work'er	wor'ried·ly
wool	work'house'	wor'ri·er
wool'en	work'ing·man'	wor'ri·ment
wool'li·er	work'ings	wor'ri·some
wool'li·est	work'less	wor'ri·some·ness
wool'li·ness	work'man	wor'ry
wool'ly	work'man·like'	worse
wool'work'	work'man·ship	wors'en
wool'work'er	work'men	wors'ened
wooz'y	work'out'	wor'ship
word	work'pan'	wor'shiped

wor'ship·er	wrath'ful	wrin'kli·er
wor'ship·ful	wrath'ful·ly	wrin'kli·est
wor'ship·ful·ly	wrath'ful·ness	wrin'kly
worst	wreak	wrist
worst'ed	wreaked	wrist'band'
wor'sted	wreath	wrist'bone'
worth	wreathed	wrist'let
wor'thi·er	wreck	wrist'lock'
wor'thi·est	wreck'age	writ
wor'thi·ly	wrecked	writ'a·ble
wor'thi·ness	wreck'er	write
worth'less	wren	writ'er
wor'thy	wrench	writhe
would	wrenched	writhed
wound	wrest	writh'ing·ly
wound	wrest'ed	writ'ings
wound'ed	wres'tle	writ'ten
wound'ing·ly	wres'tled	wrong
wound'less	wres'tler	wrong'do·er
wove	wretch	wronged
wo'ven	wretch'ed	wrong'ful
wrack	wretch'ed·ly	wrong'ful·ly
wraith	wretch'ed·ness	wrong'head·ed
wraith'like'	wrig'gle	wrong'ly
wran'gle	wrig'gled	wrong'ness
wran'gled	wrig'gling·ly	wrote
wrap	wrig'gly	wroth
wrapped	wring	wrought
wrap'per	wring'er	wrung
wrap'pings	wrin'kle	wry
wrath	wrin'kled	wry'neck'

xe'non	yard'mas'ter	yell
xen'o·phile	yard'stick'	yelled
xen'o·pho'bi·a	yarn	yel'low
xe'ro·der'ma	yar'row	yel'lowed
xe·rog'ra·phy	yat'a·ghan	yel'low·er
xe·ro'sis	yaw	yel'low·est
X ray	yawl	yel'low·ish
xy'lo·phone	yawn	yel'low·ish·ness
xy·loph'o·nist	yawned	yelp
	yawn'ing·ly	yelped
yacht	ye	yeo'man
yachts'man	yea	yeo'man·ry
yak	year	yes
Yale	year'book'	yes'ter·day
yam	year'ling	yet
yam'mer	year'ly	yew
yank	yearn	Yid'dish
Yan'kee	yearned	yield
yard	yearn'ing·ly	yield'ed
yard'age	yearn'ings	yield'ing·ly
yard'arm'	yeast	yield'ing·ness
yard'man	yeast'y	yo'del

yo'deled	youth'ful	ze'ro
yo'del·er	youth'ful·ly	zest
yo'ga	youth'ful·ness	zest'ful
yo'ghurt	youths	zig'zag'
yoke	yt·ter'bi·um	zinc
yoked	yt'tri·um	Zi'on
yoke'fel'low	Yuc'ca	Zi'on·ism
yo'kel	yule	Zi'on·ist
yo'kel·ry	yule'tide'	zip'per
yolk		zir'con
yon	za'ny	zir·co'ni·um
yon'der	zeal	zith'er
yore	zeal'ot	zo'di·ac
you	zeal'ot·ry	zone
young	zeal'ous	zoned
young'er	zeal'ous·ly	zoo
young'est	zeal'ous·ness	zo'o·log'i·cal
young'ish	ze'bra	zo·ol'o·gist
young'ster	ze'broid	zo·ol'o·gy
your	ze'bu	zoom
yours	ze'nith	zoomed
your·self'	ze'o·lite	Zu'lu
your·selves'	zeph'yr	zy'mase
youth	Zep'pe·lin	zy·mol'o·gy

PART TWO

Part Two consists of 1,314 entries of personal and geographical names divided approximately as follows:

835 Geographical Names. The largest group of names consists of the names of American cities and towns that are likely to be encountered in business dictation. The names of the American states are given. A relatively small group of foreign geographical names is given—the foreign countries and cities that are most likely to occur in American business dictation. The lists are not intended to be complete or exhaustive. The attempt has been made, however, to include the geographical names that occur most frequently in ordinary business dictation.

243 Surnames. This small group of names represents the commonest American surnames that are likely to be used in business dictation. There are tens of thousands of surnames in this country, and no attempt can be made to present a complete list.

113 First Names of Women. This list contains the more frequently used feminine first names.

123 First Names of Men. This list contains the more frequently used masculine first names.

The four groups of names listed above are combined in one alphabetical list in Part Two.

With the exception of the states and of a few of the largest cities, the geographical names are written very fully. This is done with the understanding that the writer will use these full outlines for the names that occur only occasionally in the dictation. When some name occurs more frequently in the dictation, an abbreviated form would be used.

The shorthand writer in Oregon would ordinarily have little occasion to use the outline for *Corpus Christi.* The shorthand writer in Texas might use it so frequently that he would abbreviate it to *kk.*

In order to keep the list in Part Two as short and at the same time as useful as possible, the names of many cities and towns are omitted. This is possible because many American city and town names are composed of nouns and adjectives that appear in Part One—for example, such names as *White River Junction* or *Egg Harbor City.*

Many city and town names are formed by adding to the name of another town a word like *Beach, Grove, Hill, City, Park,* or *Spring.* In most cases such

361

names have been omitted, for they would cause no shorthand writing difficulty.

The writing and transcribing of proper names can present many traps for the shorthand writer. When you write in shorthand the name *Pittsburgh,* you will not know whether to transcribe it *Pittsburg* or *Pittsburgh* until you know whether the dictator had in mind *Pittsburg,* Kansas, or *Pittsburgh,* Pennsylvania. You can be tricked similarly by such pairs as *Worcester,* Massachusetts, and *Wooster,* Ohio.

You may confidently write *b-r-ow-n* in your shorthand notes without realizing that the dictator may not be referring to his familiar correspondent, Mr. *Brown,* but to some strange *Browne* or *Braun.*

Martin J. Dupraw, world's champion shorthand writer, tells of an error he made, but caught in time, because of an unusual proper name. He understood the witness to have said: "We gave it the hour test." Mr. Dupraw transcribed it like that, only to find out, just in time, that the witness had really said: "We gave it the Auer test."

Unless the writer is absolutely sure of the identity of the proper names used by the dictator, he should always check them with the greatest possible care. Almost everyone is annoyed when his name or the name of his city or town is spelled incorrectly.

PERSONAL AND GEOGRAPHICAL NAMES

Aaron	Algernon	Anniston
Aberdeen	Allentown	Anthony
Abilene	Allison	Antioch
Abington	Alphonsine	Antoinette
Abraham	Alphonso	Antwerp
Adams	Alton	Appleton
Adelbert	Altoona	Arabia
Adolph	Alvin	Archibald
Agatha	Amanda	Argentina
Aiken	Amarillo	Arizona
Aileen	Amelia	Arkansas
Ainsworth	Amesbury	Arlington
Akron	Amherst	Arnold
Alabama	Amityville	Arthur
Alameda	Amsterdam	Asheboro
Alaska	Anderson	Asheville
Albany	Andover	Ashley
Albert	Angela	Astoria
Albuquerque	Angelica	Atchison
Alexander	Angora	Atkinson
Alfred	Annabel	Atlanta
Algeria	Annapolis	Atlantic

Augusta	Bedford	Blairsville
Augustin	Belfast	Blakely
Aurelia	Belgium	Blanchard
Aurora	Belinda	Bloomington
Austin	Bellefontaine	Bloomsburg
Australia	Belleville	Bluffton
Austria	Bellevue	Bogota
Avery	Bellingham	Boise
Baird	Belmont	Bolivia
Bakersfield	Beloit	Bonham
Baldwin	Belvedere	Boniface
Ballard	Bemidji	Boonville
Baltimore	Benedict	Bordeaux
Bangkok	Benjamin	Boston
Bangor	Bennett	Bosworth
Barberton	Bennington	Boulder
Barcelona	Bentley	Bowen
Barlow	Bergenfield	Bowman
Barnard	Berkeley	Boyd
Barnesville	Bernard	Boyle
Barrington	Bernstein	Braddock
Bartholomew	Bertha	Bradenton
Bartlett	Berwick	Bradford
Bartow	Bethlehem	Bradley
Basil	Beulah	Brattleboro
Batavia	Beverly	Brazil
Batesville	Biloxi	Bremen
Baton Rouge	Binghamton	Bremerton
Bauer	Birmingham	Brenham
Bayonne	Bismarck	Brentwood
Beatrice	Blackstone	Brian
Beckley	Blackwell	Bridgeport

Bridgeton	Camden	Centralia
Brigham	Camilla	Chalmers
Brisbane	Campbell	Chambersburg
Bristow	Canada	Chandler
Brockton	Canfield	Chanute
Bronxville	Cannon	Chapman
Brookfield	Canonsburg	Charleston
Brownsville	Canton	Charlottesville
Brunswick	Caracas	Chattanooga
Bryan	Carbondale	Cheboygan
Bryant	Carlisle	Chelsea
Bucharest	Carlotta	Cherbourg
Budapest	Carlsbad	Cherokee
Buenos Aires	Carlson	Cheyenne
Buffalo	Carlstadt	Chicago
Bulgaria	Carlton	Chicopee
Burbank	Carmel	Childress
Burke	Carnegie	Chillicothe
Burlington	Carol	Chippewa Falls
Burma	Carpenter	Chisholm
Burns	Carrollton	Christabel
Burroughs	Carson	Christchurch
Burton	Carter	Christina
Butte	Cartersville	Christine
Byron	Carthage	Christopher
Cadillac	Casper	Cicely
Caesar	Catharine	Cicero
Calcutta	Catskill	Cincinnati
Calhoun	Cecelia	Claremont
California	Cedarhurst	Clarinda
Callahan	Cedartown	Clarksburg
Calumet City	Celia	Clarksville

Claudia	Connor	Curtis
Clearfield	Conrad	Cuthbert
Clearwater	Constance	Cynthia
Cleburne	Conway	Dagmar
Clement	Cooley	Dalton
Cleveland	Coolidge	Daly
Clifford	Copenhagen	Daniel
Coaldale	Corbin	Danville
Coatesville	Cork	Daphne
Coeur d'Alene	Cornelia	Darby
Coffeyville	Corning	Davenport
Cohen	Corona	Davidson
Coldwater	Corpus Christi	Dawson
Coleman	Cortland	Dearborn
Collier	Corvallis	Deborah
Collingdale	Corwin	Dedham
Collingswood	Costa Rica	Deerfield
Collinsville	Covington	Defiance
Cologne	Crafton	Delaware
Colorado	Crandall	Delhi
Colton	Cranford	Delia
Columbia	Crawford	Denise
Columbus	Creston	Denison
Comstock	Cromwell	Denmark
Concord	Crowley	Denver
Concordia	Cuba	Des Moines
Condon	Cudahy	Detroit
Conklin	Culbertson	Dewey
Conley	Cullman	Dexter
Connecticut	Cumberland	Diana
Connersville	Cummings	Dickinson
Connolly	Cummins	Dillon

District of Columbia

Dolores

Dominic

Donald

Donora

Donovan

Dormont

Dorothy

Dougherty

Doyle

Dresden

Dublin

Dubuque

Dudley

Duluth

Dunbar

Duncan

Dunkirk

Dunmore

Dunn

Duquesne

Durham

Dwight

Easthampton

Eastman

Easton

Eau Claire

Ecuador

Edgar

Edinburgh

Edmonton

Edward

Edwardsville

Edwin

Effingham

Egan

Egbert

Egypt

Eileen

Elbert

Eleanor

Electra

Elgin

Elizabeth

Elizabethton

Elkhart

Elkins

Ellensburg

Elliott

Ellsworth

Elmhurst

Elmira

El Paso

Elvira

Elwood

Ely

Elyria

Emil

Emily

Emmanuel

Emporia

Endicott

England

Englewood

Enrico

Enright

Ernest

Ernestine

Erwin

Esther

Esthonia

Ethel

Ethiopia

Euclid

Europe

Evangeline

Evanston

Evansville

Evelina

Everard

Everett

Exeter

Fairbanks

Fairbury

Fairfield

Fairmont

Fargo

Farrell

Fayetteville

Feldman

Ferdinand

Ferguson

Ferndale

Findlay

Finley

Fisher

Fitchburg	Galion	Greeley
Fitzgerald	Gallagher	Greensboro
Flagstaff	Gallup	Greensburg
Fleming	Galveston	Greenville
Florence	Gardner	Greenwood
Florida	Garfield	Gregory
Floyd	Gasper	Gretchen
Fond du Lac	Gastonia	Griffiths
Ford	Geneva	Grinnell
Fort Atkinson	Genevieve	Guam
Fort Lauderdale	Genoa	Guatemala
Fort Madison	George	Gutenberg
Fort Myers	Georgia	Guthrie
Fort Wayne	Gerald	Hackensack
Fort Worth	Germany	Haggerty
Foster	Gertrude	Halifax
Fostoria	Gettysburg	Hamburg
Framingham	Gibson	Hamilton
Frances	Gifford	Hammond
Francis	Gilbert	Hampton
Frankfort	Girard	Hancock
Franklin	Glasgow	Hanford
Frederic	Gleason	Hannibal
Fredonia	Gloria	Hanover
Freehold	Gloversville	Hanson
Freeport	Goddard	Harding
Fullerton	Godfrey	Harold
Fulton	Goodwin	Harriet
Gabriel	Gordon	Harriman
Gaffney	Gould	Harrington
Gainesville	Grafton	Harrisburg
Galesburg	Great Britain	Harrison

Hartford	Honolulu	Isolde
Hartman	Hopewell	Israel
Hattiesburg	Hopkinsville	Istanbul
Haverford	Horatio	Ithaca
Haverstraw	Hornel	Ivan
Hawaii	Hortense	Jacksonville
Hawthorne	Houston	Jacobs
Hayward	Howard	Jacqueline
Healy	Howell	Jamaica
Hedwig	Hubert	Jamestown
Heloise	Hudson	Janesville
Hempstead	Humboldt	Janet
Henderson	Humphrey	Japan
Henrietta	Hungary	Jason
Herbert	Huntington	Jasper
Herkimer	Huron	Jeannette
Herman	Hutchinson	Jeffersonville
Higgins	Hyattsville	Jeffrey
Hilda	Iceland	Jemima
Hillsboro	Idaho	Jennifer
Hinsdale	Illinois	Jeremiah
Hinton	India	Jersey City
Hobart	Indiana	Jerusalem
Hoboken	Indianapolis	Jessamine
Hoffman	Inglewood	Jessica
Holdenville	Iowa	Jocelin
Hollywood	Ironton	Johnson
Holt	Ironwood	Johnston
Holyoke	Irvington	Johnstown
Homewood	Irwin	Jonathan
Honduras	Isaac	Jonesboro
Hong Kong	Isidore	Joplin

Joseph		La Crosse		Leipsig	
Judith		Lafayette		Leningrad	
Julian		Lakeland		Lenoir	
Juliet		Lakewood		Leominster	
Julius		Lambert		Leon	
Justin		Lancaster		Leonard	
Kalamazoo		Lancelot		Leonia	
Kalispell		Lansdale		Leopold	
Kankakee		Lansford		Leroy	
Kansas		Lansing		Leslie	
Kansas City		La Paz		Lettice	
Karl		La Porte		Lewiston	
Katharine		Larchmont		Lexington	
Kathleen		Laredo		Lillian	
Kearny		Larksville		Lima	
Keith		Larson		Lincoln	
Kennedy		La Salle		Lindstrom	
Kenneth		Las Vegas		Lionel	
Kenosha		Latrobe		Lisbon	
Kenton		Laughlin		Litchfield	
Kentucky		Laura		Lithuania	
Kerrville		Laurel		Liverpool	
Keyser		Laurens		Livingston	
Kilgore		Lavinia		Llewellyn	
Kingsford		Lawrence		Lloyd	
Kingston		Lawrenceville		Lockhart	
Kirkwood		Lazarus		Lockport	
Knoxville		Leah		Lodi	
Kokomo		Leavenworth		Logansport	
Korea		Lebanon		Lois	
Lackawanna		Lehighton		Lombard	
Laconia		Lehman		London	

Longview	Manila	McCarthy
Lorain	Manistique	McCook
Lorenzo	Manitoba	McCormack
Los Angeles	Mannheim	McDonald
Louis	Manuel	McGregor
Louise	Maplewood	McKenzie
Louisiana	Marblehead	McKinney
Louisville	Marcella	McMillan
Lowell	Marcia	Meadville
Lubbock	Marcus	Medford
Lucretia	Margaret	Melbourne
Ludington	Marian	Melissa
Luella	Marianna	Menasha
Lufkin	Marion	Mercedes
Lumberton	Marlboro	Meriden
Luther	Marquette	Merrill
Luxembourg	Marseilles	Methuen
Lydia	Marshall	Mexico
Lynbrook	Martin	Meyer
Lynchburg	Martinsburg	Miami
Lyndhurst	Martinsville	Michigan
Lynwood	Mason	Middleboro
Lyons	Massachusetts	Midland
Madisonville	Massillon	Mildred
Magdalene	Mathilda	Milford
Maguire	Matthew	Millburn
Mahanoy City	Maxwell	Millbury
Mahoney	Maynard	Milledgeville
Malden	Maysville	Milton
Malvern	Mayville	Milwaukee
Manchester	Maywood	Minersville
Manhattan	McAdoo	Minneapolis

Minnesota	Naomi	New Zealand
Mississippi	Naperville	Niagara Falls
Missouri	Napoleon	Nicaragua
Mitchell	Nashua	Norfolk
Mobile	Nashville	Norma
Monica	Natalie	Norman
Monmouth	Natchez	Northampton
Monroe	Natchitoches	North Carolina
Montana	Nathaniel	North Dakota
Montebello	Natick	Norwalk
Montevideo	Naugatuck	Norway
Montpelier	Nazareth	Norwich
Montreal	Nebraska	Norwood
Mooresville	Needham	Nova Scotia
Moorhead	Nelson	Nyack
Morocco	Neptune	Oakwood
Morris	Netherlands	O'Brien
Morse	Nevada	Ocala
Mortimer	Newark	O'Connor
Moscow	Newberry	Odessa
Moultrie	New Britain	O'Donnell
Moundsville	New Brunswick	Oelwein
Muncie	Newburgh	Ogdensburg
Munhall	New Hampshire	Ohio
Munich	New Haven	Oklahoma
Murdock	New Jersey	Olean
Muriel	New London	Olney
Murray	New Mexico	Olson
Muscatine	New Orleans	Olympia
Muskegon	New Rochelle	Omaha
Myers	Newton	Oneida
Myrtle	New York	O'Neil

Ontario	Pelham	Portsmouth
Ophelia	Pendleton	Portugal
Oregon	Pennsylvania	Potter
Orlando	Pensacola	Pottsville
Oscar	Peoria	Poughkeepsie
Oshkosh	Percival	Powell
Oslo	Perth Amboy	Presque Isle
Ossining	Petaluma	Prichard
Oswald	Petersburg	Princeton
Oswego	Petersen	Priscilla
Ottawa	Peterson	Providence
Owego	Philadelphia	Provo
Owensboro	Philander	Pueblo
Packard	Philippine Islands	Puerto Rico
Paducah	Phillipsburg	Putnam
Painesville	Phoenixville	Quebec
Palestine	Piedmont	Quinn
Pamela	Pittsburgh	Rachel
Panama	Pittsfield	Racine
Paraguay	Pius	Radford
Parkersburg	Plainfield	Rahway
Parsons	Plattsburg	Randall
Pasadena	Pleasantville	Randolph
Passaic	Plymouth	Rankin
Patchogue	Ponca City	Raton
Paterson	Pontiac	Ravenna
Patrick	Portage	Raymond
Pawtucket	Port Arthur	Rebecca
Peabody	Port Chester	Redwood City
Pearson	Porterville	Regina
Peekskill	Port Huron	Reginald
Pekin	Portland	Reinhardt

Rensselaer	Rudolph	Sault Ste. Marie
Reuben	Rupert	Savannah
Revere	Rushville	Sawyer
Reynolds	Russia	Sayreville
Rhea	Rutherford	Schenectady
Rhinelander	Ryan	Schneider
Rhode Island	Ryerson	Schroeder
Richard	Sacramento	Schultz
Richfield	Saginaw	Schuyler
Richmond	St. Albans	Schwartz
Richwood	St. Augustine	Scotland
Ridgeway	St. Joseph	Seattle
Rio de Janeiro	St. Louis	Sedalia
Roanoke	St. Petersburg	Seminole
Robbinsdale	Salisbury	Serena
Robert	Salt Lake City	Seville
Robinson	Sampson	Seward
Rochester	Samuel	Sewickley
Rockford	San Angelo	Sexton
Rockland	San Antonio	Seymour
Rockville	San Diego	Shanghai
Roderick	Sandusky	Sharon
Romania	San Fernando	Sharpsburg
Roosevelt	Sanford	Sheboygan
Rosalind	San Francisco	Sheffield
Rosemary	San Jose	Shelbyville
Roseville	San Luis Obispo	Sheldon
Rossville	San Mateo	Shenandoah
Roswell	San Rafael	Sheridan
Rotterdam	Santa Barbara	Sherman
Rowena	Santiago	Sherwood
Ruby	Sarasota	Shippensburg

Shirley	Steubenville	Teaneck
Shorewood	Stewart	Tenafly
Shreveport	Stillwater	Tennessee
Siam	Stockholm	Terre Haute
Sicily	Stoneham	Texas
Silvester	Stoughton	Thaddeus
Silvia	Stratford	The Hague
Simmons	Straus	Theodore
Simpson	Stroudsburg	Thomasville
Sinclair	Struthers	Tifton
Singapore	Stuart	Timothy
Sioux Falls	Sturgis	Tipton
Solomon	Stuttgart	Titusville
Somerset	Suffolk	Tokyo
Somerville	Sullivan	Toledo
Sorensen	Sumner	Topeka
South America	Sumter	Toronto
Southampton	Sunbury	Torrington
South Carolina	Susan	Trenton
South Dakota	Sweetwater	Trinidad
Southington	Switzerland	Truman
Sparks	Sybil	Tucson
Spartanburg	Sydney	Tulsa
Spokane	Sylvester	Turkey
Springfield	Syracuse	Tuscaloosa
Stafford	Tacoma	Tyrone
Stamford	Tallahassee	Ukraine
Stanford	Tampa	Underhill
Stanley	Tampico	Union
Statesboro	Tarrytown	United Kingdom
Staunton	Taunton	United States
Sterling	Taylorville	Upton

Uruguay	Warsaw	Willmar
Utah	Washington	Wilmette
Utica	Waterbury	Wilmington
Valentine	Waterville	Wilson
Valeria	Watsonville	Winfield
Vanderlip	Waverly	Winifred
Van Horn	Waynesboro	Winnipeg
Venezuela	Weatherford	Winona
Vera Cruz	Webster	Winslow
Vermont	Welch	Winston-Salem
Vernon	Wellesley	Winthrop
Vicksburg	Wellington	Wisconsin
Victoria	Wellsburg	Woburn
Vienna	Westbrook	Woodbury
Vincennes	West Chester	Woodward
Vincent	Westfield	Woonsocket
Viola	Weston	Wooster
Virgil	West Virginia	Worcester
Virginia	Westwood	Worthington
Vivian	Weymouth	Wyoming
Wabash	Wheaton	Xenia
Waddington	Wheeling	Yakima
Wadsworth	Whitman	Yates
Wakefield	Whittier	Yokohama
Walker	Wichita	Yonkers
Wallace	Wilbur	York
Wallington	Wilfred	Youngstown
Walpole	Wilkes-Barre	Ypsilanti
Walsh	Wilkinsburg	Yugoslavia
Walter	Willard	Yuma
Waltham	Williamsport	Zanesville
Warrensburg	Williston	Zion